A Reader's Guide to

Shakespeare and his Contemporaries

by Marguerite Alexander

Heinemann – London
Barnes & Noble – New York

Heinemann Educational Books Ltd

LONDON EDINBURGH MELBOURNE AUCKLAND HONG KONG
SINGAPORE KUALA LUMPUR NEW DELHI IBADAN NAIROBI
JOHANNESBURG KINGSTON PORT OF SPAIN

First published 1979 by Pan Books as
An Introduction to Shakespeare and his Contemporaries
in the Pan Literature Guides Series
First published in this casebound edition 1979

ISBN (UK) 0 435 18040 1
ISBN (USA) 0-06-490149-1

Library of Congress Number 79-53435

Published in Great Britain by
Heinemann Educational Books Ltd
22 Bedford Square, London WC1B 3HH
Published in the U.S.A. 1979 by
Harper & Row Publishers, Inc.
Barnes & Noble Import Division

Printed and bound in Great Britain by
Richard Clay (The Chaucer Press) Ltd,
Bungay, Suffolk

A Reader's Guide to
Shakespeare and his Contemporaries

Reader's Guide Series

General Editor: Andrew Mylett

Shakespeare and His Contemporaries
Marguerite Alexander

Fifty British Novels 1600–1900
Gilbert Phelps

Fifty American Novels
Ian Ousby

Fifty Modern British Poets
Michael Schmidt

Forthcoming

Fifty British Plays 1660–1900
John Cargill Thompson

Fifty European Novels
Martin Seymour-Smith

Fifty American Poets
Peter Jones

Fifty Modern British Novels
Andrew Mylett

Fifty British Poets 1300–1900
Michael Schmidt

Fifty Modern British Plays
Benedict Nightingale

Contents

1 **The Elizabethan and Jacobean Scene** 9

2 **William Shakespeare** 18

3 **Shakespeare: Comedy** 28
The Comedy of Errors 31
The Two Gentlemen of Verona 36
The Taming of the Shrew 40   Love's Labour's Lost 45
A Midsummer Night's Dream 50
The Merchant of Venice 57
Much Ado about Nothing 64
As You Like It 70   Twelfth Night 75

4 **Shakespeare: Dark Comedy** 82
Measure for Measure 83   All's Well that Ends Well 91
Troilus and Cressida 97

5 **Shakespeare: Poetry** 103
Venus and Adonis 104   The Rape of Lucrece 107
The Sonnets 110

6 **Shakespeare: English History** 122
Richard III 125   Richard II 132
Henry IV, Part One 138   Henry IV, Part Two 145
Henry V 150

7 **Shakespeare: Roman History** 157
Julius Caesar 158   Antony and Cleopatra 164
Coriolanus 171

8 Shakespeare: Tragedy 177
Titus Andronicus 181   Romeo and Juliet 185
Hamlet 191   Othello 198   King Lear 204
Macbeth 214   Timon of Athens 221

9 Shakespeare: Romance 227
Cymbeline 229   The Winter's Tale 237
The Tempest 243

10 Shakespeare and the Critics 252

11 Elizabethan Tragedy 258
Gorboduc, by Thomas Norton and
Thomas Sackville 260
The Spanish Tragedy, by Thomas Kyd 265
Christopher Marlowe 272
Tamburlaine the Great, Part One 273
Tamburlaine the Great, Part Two 279
The Jew of Malta 284   Doctor Faustus 290

12 Elizabethan and Jacobean Comedy 297
Ben Jonson 298   Volpone 301   The Alchemist 309
Bartholomew Fair 316   Beaumont and Fletcher 323
The Knight of the Burning Pestle 323   Philaster 330

13 Jacobean Tragedy 337
The Revenger's Tragedy, by Cyril Tourneur 338
John Webster 345   The White Devil 345
The Duchess of Malfi 352   Middleton and Rowley 358
Women Beware Women 359   The Changeling 365
'Tis Pity She's a Whore, by John Ford 371

Further Reading 377

Index 380

1 The Elizabethan and Jacobean Scene

In 1574, the first ever commercial, professional acting companies in London were given official recognition. From then until 1642, when the Puritan Parliament imposed a total ban on playing, the English theatre enjoyed a period of vigour and energy that has never been matched since. Both the excellence of the theatre over this period and the degree of public support that it enjoyed were a peculiarly English phenomenon, as Fynes Moryson, a much travelled Englishman, noted in his *Itinerary* in 1617; 'as there be, in my opinion, more Playes in London than in all the partes of the worlde I have seen, so doe these players, or comedians, excell all other in the worlde.'

The Puritan ban on playing was in itself a recognition of the theatre's importance in English life. Dramatists throughout the period, before the Puritans' uneasiness was given legal backing, may have attributed their opponents' attitude to a straightforward unwillingness to see other people enjoying themselves, but for the Puritans, the denial of the pleasure principle was reinforced by a genuine belief that the theatre had an unholy power to influence people's lives.

Indeed, the English theatre as it first blossomed under Elizabeth I (1558-1603) had its roots in the religious drama of the Middle Ages – the pageant-like miracle plays and the allegorical moralities which encouraged their audiences to renounce the sinfulness of their lives and to see the hereafter as the only certain reality. By the sixteenth century the religious element in these plays was becoming decadent and incidental, and the audiences were drawn more by the spectacle and diversion than by the uplift. Nonetheless, from our twentieth-century standpoint, the gap between even decadent religious drama in the early sixteenth century, and the plays being produced by Shakespeare and Marlowe towards the end of that century, celebrating as they did the primacy of man and his attempts to achieve mastery over his own destiny, seems almost insurmountable. Clearly, other factors were at work.

By the time Elizabeth came to the throne, the Renaissance was bringing a revival of interest in classical drama – based on Latin rather than Greek models and with comedy just preceding tragedy into respectability. The comedies of Terence and Plautus were not only being performed for their own sakes (though privately, mainly in academic institutions), but they provided models for comedy that could be imitated: a five-act structure, dramatic rules to be observed, types of plot and character which would become increasingly anglicized. The earliest examples of English classical comedy – William Stephenson's *Gammer Gurton's Needle* (c.1551) and *Ralph Roister Doister* (c.1553), writtten by Nicholas Udall, the then headmaster of Eton – were of mainly academic interest when they were written, but they did lay the foundations for at least certain elements in the English comic tradition. Shakespeare's first comedy, *The Comedy of Errors*, is Plautine; and Ben Jonson, next to Shakespeare the major comedy writer of the period, never lost his reverence for classical and academic first principles.

The classical model for Elizabethan tragedy was Seneca. With its emphasis on the stoic dignity of the hero faced with the acts of gods who were powerful but not necessarily just, Senecan tragedy represented more of a break from the religious origins of English drama than comedy. It is fair to say, however, that it was the commercial potential of the new tragedy, rather than its philosophic content, which recommended it to the first theatre managers. Seneca's own plays had been somewhat dry, intended for recitation rather than performance, and the earliest English example, *Gorboduc*, in 1561, written for the academic atmosphere of the Inns of Court, followed the master by confining the horrors to the description. Senecan tragedy in Italy, however, had developed along more lurid lines: stages littered, not just with dead, but with dismembered corpses were found to have considerable audience appeal. It was to the Italian Senecan tradition that Thomas Kyd was indebted in his *The Spanish Tragedy* of about 1589 – a play in which the hero bites out his tongue on stage, and which proved so popular that it still featured in the repertory of one of the London playing companies when the theatres were closed down. Shakespeare's first tragedy, *Titus Andronicus*, written c. 1590, was written in this mode: rape, mutilation and cannibalism ensured the play an immediate success but subsequent Shakespeareans have found *Titus* something of an embarrassment, and it has become fashionable to dismiss the play as a youthful folly. The irony is that Shakespeare may well have written *Titus* to prove that he was as capable as University men of writing classical tragedy.

This brings us to one of the conditions crucial to the extraordinarily concentrated dramatic activity throughout the period – the number of men of talent, even genius, who were attempting to make their living from the theatre. England under Elizabeth was characterized by a degree of restlessness and social mobility undreamt of in mediaeval times. Many of the old certainties in people's thinking, and the old inevitabilities about what they did with their lives, had been undermined. The authority of the church, at any rate in its influence on people's thinking, had been weakened. In the Middle Ages, a degree from one of the universities had been followed almost inevitably by a career in the church. This was no longer so under Elizabeth.

Christopher Marlowe (1564-1593) came down from Cambridge to London where he embarked on a career as a dramatist and a subsidiary one as a government agent. He was branded as an atheist; whatever his precise theological views, writing plays certainly gave him the opportunity to express highly unorthodox views about man's destiny and aspirations. His notoriety, down to our own day, has been secured by his unconventional life and his outstanding literary achievements. But there is no reason to suppose that there were not many like him who came to London to seek their fortunes and whose work has not survived the passage of time.

The numbers of University wits seeking fame and fortune from the London theatres were swollen by the products of the newly mushrooming grammar schools – men whose learning made the humbler trades of their fathers seem unattractive. The career of Shakespeare, the son of a Stratford-on-Avon glover, is the supreme example of this pattern.

London under Elizabeth held all the charms of a growing metropolis. England, a small and relatively poor country, consolidated her position as head of Protestant Europe with the victory over Spain in 1588. The world generally was opening up, and some of the plays of the period, notably Marlowe's *Tamburlaine the Great* and Shakespeare's *Antony and Cleopatra*, assume a much greater scale for events than would have been imaginatively possible a century before. One of Shakespeare's last plays, *The Tempest*, written under James I, was inspired by the extraordinary escape from shipwreck of a party of English colonists travelling to Virginia.

There was something about the temper of the age which was particularly adapted to the drama – much as the dominant form under Victoria was the painstakingly lengthy and detailed novel. Elizabeth's was, if one can use the term, a theatrical age. The Queen's speeches and letters are distinguished by a self-dramatizing rhetoric worthy of Shakespeare's own kings; as she grew older, she had herself painted in a stylized manner which denied the years but heightened her symbolic function. Mary Queen of Scots at her execution displayed as great a sense of style and presence as any Jacobean heroine. In plays, art imitates life, but for the Elizabethans this was a two-way process and life unashamedly imitated art.

Elizabeth was an intellectual, a lover of the arts. The

leading playing companies were brought in to provide court entertainment, and many of Shakespeare's plays had their first appearance at court. *The Merry Wives of Windsor* was written at the Queen's insistence – like many of her subjects, she lamented that Shakespeare had killed off Falstaff in *Henry V*, and so demanded his resurrection. The Queen's patronage was not financially especially remunerative – she was notoriously niggardly about payment – but it was of considerable practical assistance in helping the playing companies to function freely in London.

In some ways independent of the Queen were the Puritan City Fathers. They objected to the theatres, not only on moral grounds, but also because, as employers of apprentices, they resented the disruption to their business activities caused by the apprentices' theatregoing. The court did not share the City Fathers' objections and after 1574, by the practice of issuing licences to the playing companies, was openly taking the players under its wing. In the latter part of Elizabeth's reign, the theatrical scene was dominated by two major companies: the Admiral's, led by the actor-manager Alleyn; and the Chamberlain's Men, in which Shakespeare was a shareholder. In 1603, when James I came to the throne, the king took over the patronage of the Chamberlain's (thereafter known as the King's Men), and gave the patronage of two others to his wife and son – so the link between court and theatre was even closer.

Under Elizabeth, there was no real division between court taste and public taste, so that the theatre was a genuinely popular entertainment. The playing companies, which had begun on an *ad hoc* basis performing in inn-yards, in the 1570s started building the public amphitheatres which we now regard as so characteristic of the Elizabethan theatre. They were open to the skies, with a projecting apron stage flanked by seats. Inevitably, this arrangement brought actors and audience into a more intimate relationship than the type of theatre which has survived from the revival of the theatre at the Restoration to our own day: the proscenium arch stage faced by a self-contained auditorium.

The admission prices were within most people's reach; the entertainment the audiences were offered no different from that enjoyed at court. The variety of tastes to be catered for – the plays had, after all, to be commercially viable – goes some way towards explaining the tremendous richness of Shakespeare's work. He can in one play (the later comedies are good examples of this) bring together the disparate elements of slapstick, sophisticated verbal fencing, full-blown lyric verse and bawdy, without any sense of strain.

Drama is the most practical of all literary forms, and theatrical conditions throughout the period are responsible for many of these dramatic conventions which are most alien to twentieth-century audiences. The soliloquy – that eminently useful kind of speech which involves a character speaking directly to the audience without being heard by other characters – evolved in a theatre where the audience actually impinged on the playing space (a few seats were available on the stage for those prepared to pay the higher price). All female parts were played by men. Audiences who found in this no affront to their credibility were prepared to accept the dramatic device of the young heroine (who was anyway played by a man) disguising herself as a boy without exciting a whisper of suspicion as to her sex among the other characters. A high degree of practical realism was not considered essential for the enjoyment of a play: a battle scene could be suggested by a few men running on with swords, a scene could be set in a speech of descriptive verse. The audience's readiness to supply deficiencies by co-operating imaginatively was relied on by the playwrights. Shakespeare in particular was aware of the life-enhancing power of the imagination; more practically, he reminds his audiences from time to time of their duty to place their imaginations at the players' disposal. In *A Midsummer Night's Dream*, Theseus is indulgent towards the laughably inept play-within-a-play:

> The best in this kind are but shadows, and the worst are no
> worse, if imagination amend them.

Nonetheless, staging did become more elaborate, and the watershed for this, as for so many of the changes in the theatre during the period, was the accession of James I in 1603. A discernible rift occurred (though like all generalizations this is subject to exceptions) between the taste of the court and the taste of the general public. James's Queen Anne was a great lover of masques – pretty theatrical pieces incorporating dance and mime, requiring sumptuous costumes and increasingly lavish sets: under James and then Charles I (1625 – 1649), sets for court masques were being designed by Inigo Jones. Ben Jonson, who is best known today for his sharp urban comedies, found the many court masques he was writing well into Charles I's reign a better outlet for his lyric powers.

The masque was never a popular entertainment: it owed much of its popularity at court to the opportunities it offered the courtiers for picturesque posing. Masques were expensive to stage, and their public performance was limited to the growing number of small indoor theatres whose high admission prices ensured their exclusiveness. The two categories of theatre reflected the widening rift between citizens and gentry which developed into active hostility with the Civil War.

A taste for more sophistication in theatrical presentation was not confined to the masque. During the latter part of the period (from about 1605 onwards) a kind of mechanical trickiness finds its way into the drama; the use of trap chairs and phials with the power to test virginity indicate that the playwrights were discovering the sensational possibilities of science. In the tragedies of the later period – the work of Tourneur, Ford and Middleton – the deaths of the characters are more remarkable for the subtlety of the means than the passion of the verse. Middleton's *Women Beware Women* ends with a masque in which a row of cupids step out of line and fire arrows at the unsuspecting villain: 'Plague of these cupids' is the victim's, Hippolyto's, reaction.

The tragedies of the later Jacobean and Caroline periods have more than a whiff of decadence about them. Their atmosphere is summarized by Andrew Gurr, in *The Shakespearean Stage*:

> The world frequently appears as pervasively corrupt and corrupting, where all motives are expedient and evil brings about the downfall of everyone.

And of particular interest to these playwrights as breeding grounds of corruption and depravity were enclosed, self-regarding courts, with almost Byzantine networks of evil linking the characters. It is difficult to escape the assumption that the example of the English royal court after Elizabeth must have had some influence here. Under James and Charles there was a widening gap between court and country in terms both of manners and morals. James in particular felt considerable distaste for the common people and sought to keep himself separate; he was a poor judge of character and deeply susceptible to flattery.

With the exception of the escapist pastoral comedies that were popular at court (royalty was acquiring a 'merry shepherdess' fixation that in the following century, in France, would play its part in Marie Antoinette's downfall), the plays written in the Jacobean and Caroline periods were more jaundiced than they had been under Elizabeth. Satire became sharper and influenced tragedy as well as comedy (the plays of Middleton and Tourneur show the satiric mode in tragedy at its best and Jonson's are some of the finest satiric comedies in the language). While the tragedies of the period have their own emotional truth, they confine themselves, with the exception of Shakespeare's tragedies, which belong to the early part of the period, to a limited range of emotions: innocence is virtually unknown, lust has forced out any kind of political interest and curiosity in phenomena like incest has reached a peak. A new mode in horrific tragedy emerged with the plays of Webster, who was prepared to sacrifice overall design in the interest of individually chilling effects.

Seeking to identify the change throughout the period as a whole, we are confronted with a gradually shrinking canvas; Shakespeare and Marlowe (Shakespeare ceased writing tragedies in 1608, Marlowe died in 1593), who attempted to give their themes a universal significance, were followed by a generation of playwrights who had more interest in the individual emotional or psychological state. At its best, the work of the Jacobean writers of tragedy, geared as it was to the discriminating audiences of the indoor theatres, was capable of a subtlety and complexity that Marlowe and Kyd (who formed the first Elizabethan generation of tragic writers) never aspired to. Nonetheless, much of the energy and dynamism of the Elizabethan stage seems to have evaporated. As the country at large lost its confidence in ever-widening possibilities, so did the dramatists.

2 William Shakespeare

Dominating the Elizabethan and Jacobean theatre like a colossus is Shakespeare – not only because of his position in the English theatre generally, which hardly needs re-stating, but also because of his remarkable output as a writer. Between around 1590 (we are not absolutely clear about the dating of his earliest plays) and 1613 he wrote thirty-seven plays, all but seven of which (*King John*, the three parts of *Henry VI*, *The Merry Wives of Windsor*, *Pericles* and *Henry VIII*) are included in this selection; besides a handful of long narrative poems and the finest and most complete sonnet sequence in the English language.

Shakespeare's life, however, is disappointingly badly documented. Paradoxically, this lack of documentation has added fuel to the fire of Shakespearean scholarship, and biographers have discovered almost as many ways of inter-preting his life as critics have of interpreting his plays. The few details and brushstrokes that have been scraped to-gether from contemporary accounts and records have left the way clear for fantasy: small wonder that so many biographers and commentators have found the temptation irresistible. J. Dover Wilson, in his book *The Essential Shakespeare* finds the commemorative bust of Shakespeare in Stratford parish church (which, as it happens, is the only portrait of Shakespeare that can claim any real authority) too unpoetic, incongruously suggestive of 'an affluent and retired butcher'. So he commends our attention to a rather romantic painting of a young man who happened to be twenty-four in the same year as the poet. R. J. C. Wait, a recent commentator on the *Sonnets*, has found in Shakespeare's metaphorical use of autumn leaves veiled references to his balding head.

Behind the romancing, however, there lies a genuine regret that we know so little with certainty about Shakespeare. He was born in April 1564 in Stratford-on-Avon, the son of John Shakespeare, a glover, and Mary Arden, the daughter of a Warwickshire farmer who had distant aristocratic connections. He was almost certainly educated at Stratford grammar school: the fact that he was not entered at either of the universities has led to the claim that he lacked sufficient learning to have written his own plays, Francis Bacon being the chief contender for the honour. There is nothing in the plays, however, to suggest a remarkable degree of academic learning; and since the Baconian heresy is of fairly recent origin, with no root in contemporary hearsay, it can be dismissed.

There is a tradition, of which Shakespeare's first biographer, Nicholas Rowe, writing in 1709 was aware, that he had been for a time a country schoolmaster. This has some plausibility, and would explain Shakespeare's nodding acquaintance with the work of Plautus and Seneca, to whom he first turned as models for comedy and tragedy, and his veneration for the work of Ovid, to whose stories and ideas he was indebted throughout his career.

In November 1582, at the tender age of eighteen, Shakespeare married Anne Hathaway, and six months later his first daughter, Susanna, was born. A curious feature of Shakespearean commentary is that, since the early eighteenth century, when Shakespeare was dismissed as a hack writer who by some freak of nature happened to be a genius, each succeeding age has been anxious to stamp its own moral character on him. During the Victorian period, the hasty birth of his first daughter was felt as a severe blow. So a theory was formed, which still has some currency, that Shakespeare's marriage must have been preceded by a binding betrothal ceremony which rendered the marriage a mere formality. Anthony Burgess, one of Shakespeare's more recent biographers, has brought his subject firmly into the permissive age by arguing strenuously against the betrothal idea; and moreover, has seemed to find in the suggestion an affront to his hero's virility.

In 1585 a twin son and daughter, Hamnet and Judith were born; and from then until 1592, when we know with certainty that he was already working for Lord Strange's Company in London, his life is obscure, except for the schoolmaster tradition. We cannot categorically state that he was an immediate success in London, for we have no way of knowing how long he had been there before 1592, possibly re-furbishing plays that other people had written, but success certainly came to him early. His first attempts at comedy, tragedy and history – *The Comedy of Errors*, *Titus Andronicus* and *Henry VI* – were great popular successes, and his first narrative poem, *Venus and Adonis*, went into seven editions between 1593 and 1602.

Shakespeare probably entered Lord Strange's Company as an actor. In 1595, when they became the Chamberlain's Men, the Company was reorganized on a shareholding basis, with Shakespeare one of the eight shareholders. This placed him in a more fortunate position than most other dramatists of the day for making money out of his plays. At that time the copyright of a play – in as far as copyright laws existed – was bought by the playing company with the play; so Shakespeare, as a shareholder in the Chamberlain's, was assured a steady return from his writings. Shakespeare's financial success rankled, producing sour comments from Robert Greene among others, and the first hints of injustice that a man of so little formal education should become so prosperous by his writing. The fact that he was also an actor would further contribute to hostility. Dramatists regarded actors as inferior beings who mangled the writer's work, and were more fortunately placed than the writer to make money from it.

One of the few things that we know about Shakespeare with any certainty is that he was an excellent businessman.

As the money came in, he bought up property in and around Stratford: presumably throughout his career in London he continued to regard his birth town as his home. His father had for a time been prominent in local Stratford politics, and there may well have been an element of the respectable burgher in Shakespeare's character. He also inherited gentlemanly pretensions. His father had considered establishing his right to bear arms with the Herald's Office; Shakespeare did actually establish that right himself in 1598, taking as his motto 'Non sans Droict' (Not without right). Shakespeare's aspirations were a source of some mirth to at least one fellow dramatist for they were satirized by Ben Jonson in *Every Man in His Humour*, where a character decked out in a boar's head bears the legend, 'Not without mustard'. Since Shakespeare himself may well have taken this part in the play's first production, we can conclude that he bore Jonson no malice.

Indeed, while Jonson's opinion of Shakespeare's work was mixed – he praised him for his truth to nature but took him to task for not observing classical rules more strictly in his work – his feelings for Shakespeare personally were warm: 'I loved the man . . . on this side idolatry as much as any.' Contemporary accounts stress Shakespeare's civility, his conciliatory, easy manner, – 'sweet Will Shakespeare'. His charm must have helped him win the patronage of the Earl of Southampton, to whom he dedicated his narrative poems *Venus and Adonis* and *The Rape of Lucrece* (1593 and 1594), and who may well have supplied Shakespeare with the cash to buy his holding in the Chamberlain's Men. If, as many critics believe, Southampton was also the source of inspiration and dedicatee of the *Sonnets*, then the practical help he gave Shakespeare was to some extent embittered by considerable personal anguish on the poet's side – a matter which will be discussed in more detail in the section on the *Sonnets*.

Shakespeare lived and worked in London for about twenty years, producing just under two plays a year. His last play was *Henry VIII*, first performed in June 1613. It may well have been written in Stratford, almost certainly by special request of his Company, now the King's Men. The play immediately preceding *Henry VIII* was *The Tempest* in which, quite uncharacteristically for Shakespeare, there seems to be an unmistakable personal note. Prospero, the play's central figure, who has long been a practitioner in magic arts, a creator of visions, and for the course of the play's action, a manipulator of men through his spells, formally renounces his magic in a direct address to the audience. He will be a man as other men, with no greater powers than his fellows. The association of magic arts with poetic arts had some currency, and it is hard not to see in this Shakespeare's farewell to the theatre.

Shakespeare was a most practical man, anxious to make money from his plays, treating his skills on one level as a job like any other, as a means of advancing himself socially. But there is a sense in which such skills separate the practitioner from other men. Ann Righter, in her stimulating book, *Shakespeare and the Idea of the Play*, argues that the change in tone and subject matter perceptible in Shakespeare's plays after about 1600 was due in part to a disillusionment with the stage:

> It is the whole conception of the play, of something imitated, reproduced at second-hand, which seems to disgust him. The actor is a man who cheapens life by the act of dramatising it; the shadows represented on the stage are either corrupt or totally without value, 'signifying nothing'.

In one of his sonnets Shakespeare speaks directly about his work, and the effects he feels it has had on his personality:

> Thence comes it that my name receives a brand,
> And almost thence my nature is subdu'd
> To what it works in, like the dyer's hand. (Sonnet 111)

Whatever his reasons, Shakespeare returned to Stratford in 1613. His retirement was brief: he died in April 1616 at the age of fifty-two. Apart from a legend started by an unfriendly Stratford clergyman that shortly before his death he indulged in prolonged drinking bouts with Ben Jonson, from which he never recovered, we have no information on the cause of his death.

More than with most great writers, his death was the cue for a prolonged debate on his work. Chapter Ten will examine in more detail the changes and fluctuations in the critical approach to Shakespeare, but a few points are worth making now. Shakespeare, with the exception of what we like to read of him into Prospero, is the least intrusive of writers. Critics have found what they have claimed to be irrefutable evidence in his work that he was a Catholic, a Puritan, an atheist; an anti-Semitic and a lover of Jews; a homosexual and an abandoned womanizer. The fact is that he found it possible to be all these things at once in as far as his characters represent any of these attitudes. Writers who have taken a strong line themselves – like Dr Johnson or George Bernard Shaw – have found Shakespeare lacking in fibre because he so irritatingly declines to lay his cards on the table. Yet this personal reticence was possibly his greatest strength. Keats, who was sympathetic to Shakespeare's methods, called him 'the chameleon poet' – an epithet so apt that it is still the best description of certain aspects of Shakespeare's artistry. Shakespeare was the least egocentric of writers – a gift which enabled him to take his colour from the subject matter rather than impose his own colour on it. In the best of his work, his characters speak with absolute authenticity and individuality. While the audience will inevitably, indeed is meant to judge those characters, Shakespeare nonetheless manages to create the illusion that judgments are achieved independently, not imposed by the writer.

It was his truth to life, or to nature, that earned Shakespeare most praise in the seventeenth and eighteenth centuries. Related to this was the belief that Shakespeare was an instinctive writer, not guided by consciously applied artistic principles. What has done most to dispel this myth has been the work done in the last century and this on the dating of Shakespeare's plays. This has revealed, not only a predictable development in skills, but also a tendency to work through certain ideas to the limit imposed by any particular genre; and then to pass on to another genre, which would allow him to develop new ideas and provide him with new ways of working through continuing preoccupations.

In terms of skills, Shakespeare was throughout his career spectacularly gifted in his handling of language. Indeed, some of his earlier plays (*A Midsummer Night's Dream* is a notable example) are more 'poetic' in the sense of being full of startling images and lyrical description than his later work. But as his career progressed, his pleasure in the sheer use of words became less obtrusive. His blank verse and his prose became more flexible, denser in their range of meaning, capable of great emotional subtlety and of heightening the dramatic rather than lyrical quality of events. A line like Hamlet's 'A little more than kin, and less than kind', has a concentrated allusiveness that the earlier work lacks.

The gift which has perhaps recommended Shakespeare most to the popular imagination is his handling of character. In this, too, there are discernible shifts in emphasis throughout his career. In the early 1590s his characters tend, with the exception of Richard III – a superb piece of theatrical bravura – to be subordinate to the story. It was in the later 1590s that he seems really to have discovered his gift for character creation – a gift which in one or two plays got the better of his wider dramatic intentions. Shylock in *The Merchant of Venice* and Falstaff in *Henry IV* are so stunningly three-dimensional that they have acquired a place in English culture which is almost independent of the plays themselves. As his skill matured, however, he learned to control his genius for creating character. Characters like Hamlet and Cleopatra (the early 1600s) and Caliban in *The Tempest* (1613) have a kind of resonance which time has done nothing to diminish, but their impact advances rather than hinders the audience's grasp of the plays' themes.

The changes in Shakespeare's approach to character

suggest the main area in which he reveals his conscious artistic intentions: his increasing preoccupation with theme and search for genres which would best express his themes. Until around 1600 he confined himself, apart from his poetry, almost exclusively to comedies and histories (the tragedies *Titus Andronicus* and *Romeo and Juliet* are the only exceptions and, as we shall see, rather special cases). Of comedy and history one generalization can be usefully made here: both tend towards the establishment of harmony. Underlying Shakespeare's comedy is the assumption that, if the villains are exposed and banished and the lovers' misunderstandings unravelled in time, then the world can be made to seem a benign place. In the histories he is deeply cynical about people's motives, yet there is a fundamental belief that the right monarch – aware of his responsibilities, his path to the throne untainted by bloodshed – is capable of establishing peace and order.

After about 1600 the mood of his work changes in a way that suggests that he found his earlier solutions too simple. Only one indisputable comedy, *Twelfth Night*, was written after that date, and *Henry VIII*, his only other history, was an encore by special request. It is tempting to look for answers in his own life that might account for this shift: the story behind the *Sonnets* does, as we shall see, provide some clues. Historically, there are discernible changes in the English theatre generally, reflecting the country's reaction to the Essex rebellion in 1601 and the death of Elizabeth and accession of James I in 1603.

Between 1601 and 1608 he wrote three plays – *Measure for Measure, All's Well that Ends Well,* and *Troilus and Cressida* – which are technically comedies in as far as the principal characters do not die and in two of them marriage is offered as a kind of solution. But as we shall see later in more detail, Shakespeare seems to be questioning the comic conventions even in the act of using them. These plays were written in a period dominated by Shakespeare's great tragedies: lust, envy, greed, ingratitude and overweening ambition erupt and destroy; and while the tragedies end on a note of harmony, the moral order re-established, it is the tranquillity of complete exhaustion.

In his last plays (1609 – 1613) Shakespeare, exhausted himself, perhaps by writing eight tragedies in as many years, turned to a new form, the romance. In many ways these plays (*Pericles*, *The Winter's Tale*, *Cymbeline*, and *The Tempest*) with their young heroines, young love and resolved misunderstandings, represent a return to the comic world; they have, in addition, more fantastic, fairy-tale elements than any other of Shakespeare's plays. It is possible to see in this new taste for the fantastic a withdrawal into personal fantasy by the writer. Lytton Strachey argued that the last plays tell of a complete capitulation on Shakespeare's part; his arguments are summarized by Peter Alexander in *Shakespeare's Life and Art* (James Nisbet and Co):

> the poet, no longer able to contemplate the world with the composure necessary for sanity, abandoned reality for good and turned to fairy tales, creating by the magic of his style an artistic world remote from reality and its disgusting sights.

It would be sad if these plays were indeed the unrealizable fantasies of an old man (it is clear that Shakespeare regarded himself as old at an age that seems ludicrous to us now). However, we would have to read them very superficially not to notice that the greed, jealousy, ambition et cetera that are allowed to run their destructive course in the tragedies, are central to the romances, even though presented differently. Wickedness is shown, not as burning itself out in a devastating orgy, but as something mankind has to learn to live with; misunderstandings are resolved, but only after considerable and lengthy suffering; young love is offered, not as a final solution, but as the hope each generation gives to its life-battered or corrupted parents. All the evidence is that these plays represent Shakespeare's attempt, towards the end of his life, to reconcile himself to reality rather than retreat from it.

The following thirty-three entries for Shakespeare's work are arranged according to genre – Comedy, Dark Comedy, Poetry, English History, Roman History, Tragedy, and Romance. This arrangement does follow chronology reasonably closely. It should be remembered, however, that the comedies, histories and the poetry were written contemporaneously; similarly the dark comedies, the tragedies and the Roman plays.

3 Shakespeare: Comedy

What is love? 'tis not hereafter;
Present mirth hath present laughter;
What's to come is still unsure:
In delay there lies no plenty;
Then come kiss me, sweet and twenty
Youth's a stuff will not endure.
Twelfth Night (II.iii)

The kind of comedy written by Shakespeare, which inevitably colours many of our assumptions about Elizabethan
and Jacobean comedy generally, was in fact developed by
him from a tradition that many of the more literate of his
contemporaries would have considered subordinate, and
even inferior, to classical comedy. A full discussion of classical comedy will be more appropriate in relation to Ben
Jonson's works, for Jonson was the chief Elizabethan critical
exponent of classical comedy, and his work provides the
finest examples of that tradition throughout the period. It is
enough to say here that the classical tradition, developed by
the Elizabethans from the work of Plautus and Terence, was
primarily satirical. A certain norm of social behaviour is
implied in the plays, characters are judged and satirized to
the degree that they deviate from that norm. Classical
comedy engages the audience's judgment more than its
sympathies and emotions. Technically, the comedy of
Jonson and his predecessors is tightly structured; dramatic
probability is maintained, despite the inevitable improb-

abilities of plot, by a careful exclusion of the magical, the strange and the exotic.

Shakespeare's comic genius is not essentially satirical, although *Love's Labour's Lost* is a sustained satire on an idea, and in *Twelfth Night* he uses methods to expose a character (Malvolio) which are reminiscent of Jonson's approach. In all his comedies except the first, *The Comedy of Errors*, he ignores the classical unities of time and place (involving the limitation of the action to a single place and a single day); and in that alone of his comedies the audience's sympathies are suspended in favour of an enjoyment of plot and narrative pace. Unlike Jonson, Shakespeare deploys the exotic and the strange: while his humour remains recognizably English, his settings are romantically remote (Illyria, the Forest of Arden, Belmont, Athens) and he makes free use of such improbabilities as salvation from shipwreck.

In short, his comedies are romantic, a development of a tradition established by Peele, Lyly and Greene. His comic world, with its echoes of folk lore and country practices, is less rational than Jonson's, and has its roots in something much older than classical comedy – in the country revels honouring the wine and vegetable god Dionysius, who suffers, dies and returns to life. Where Jonson's emphasis is on the social norm, Shakespeare's comedies uphold the pleasure principle and the cyclical nature of human life: all his comedies end in marriage and the possibility of another generation. Like Jonson's characters, Shakespeare's are required to 'adjust' in the course of the play, but not so much to society (although this is implicit) as to themselves. Self-deceptions are overcome, a new world of feeling is entered, through romantic love – depicted in all these plays as a fruitful and life-enhancing experience.

Characteristic of Shakespeare's method in bringing his characters to this 'enhanced' state is his use of nature – what Northrop Frye in *The Argument of Comedy** calls a

*The essays by Northrop Frye and Helen Gardner are both included in *Shakespeare's Comedies* (Penguin), a critical anthology edited by Laurence Lerner.

'green world'. *The Two Gentlemen of Verona, A Midsummer Night's Dream, The Merchant of Venice* and *As You Like It* all have an alternative world, outside the rational social boundaries, while *Twelfth Night* and *Love's Labour's Lost*, seem anyway to be set in a world apart.

Shakespeare's comedies are all concerned to some extent with the imagination: he sees the origin of love in the imagination rather than the reason (a source of considerable humour in some of his plays), and in some of the comedies explicitly demands the imaginative co-operation of the audience, going out of his way to remind them that the theatre is an experience of the imagination, but a real experience nonetheless, which holds out possibilities of enhanced awareness for the real audience as well as for the imaginary characters. In Shakespeare's comedies, the audience's sympathies are actively engaged – sometimes too much so: critics continue to argue about whether Shylock in *The Merchant of Venice* is really a villain, or whether the malevolent and ungenerous Malvolio in *Twelfth Night* deserves the fate meted out to him – questions which would never arise in Jonson's world of clear-cut values and unambiguous characters.

In terms of character, one of Shakespeare's great contributions to romantic comedy, and indeed subsequently to the English novel, is his heroine. His heroines are as important to some of his comedies as his heroes are to his tragedies. More attractive, stronger, more dynamic than their men, his great comic heroines – Viola, Rosalind and Beatrice, and their more embryonic but attractive predecessors, Julia, Helena and Portia – are at the centre of the plays' entanglements, and a focal point for the sympathy of the audience, who respond to their dilemmas and share their hopes for a happy outcome. Resourceful, loving, generous and witty, internally at ease with themselves, although the world may from time to time be out of sorts with them, Shakespeare's heroines established an ideal for the heroine in fiction which has never been completely superseded.

They know what they want out of life (usually, it must

be admitted, a particular man). Where means are open to further their ends they take them; otherwise, they hang on patiently until circumstances move their way. In their final victory lies much of the hope that comedy has to offer. Helen Gardner, in an illuminating essay on *As You Like It**, summarizes this aspect of Shakespearean comedy, attributing her views to Suzanne Langer (author of *Form and Feeling*) who, according to Professor Gardner,

> has called comedy an image of life triumphing over chance. She declares that the essence of comedy is that it embodies in symbolic form our sense of happiness in feeling that we can meet and master the changes and chances of life as it confronts us.

Shakespearean comedy is hopeful, a celebration of the human right to happiness. Some characters are necessarily excluded from the final atmosphere of harmony and reconciliation, and the distinction between the blessed and the excluded is not necessarily a moral one, though hardened villains are inevitably banished. Lack of generosity, an inability to share in the pleasure of others – these are the cardinal sins. Fools and parasites are tolerated, for their own sake and to highlight the quality of generosity, of mind and purse, that distinguishes the principals.

The Comedy of Errors

DATE Certainly by the early 1590s, possibly earlier
PRINCIPAL CHARACTERS
Aegeon: A merchant of Syracuse
Aemelia: Lady Abbess of Ephesus, Aegeon's lost wife
Antipholus of Ephesus ⎱ Twin brothers, sons
Antipholus of Syracuse ⎰ of Aemelia and Aegeon
Dromio of Ephesus ⎱ Twin brothers, slaves
Dromio of Syracuse ⎰ to the Antipholus twins
Adriana: Wife of Antipholus of Ephesus
Luciana: Her sister

The Duke of Ephesus
Balthazar: A merchant
Angelo: A goldsmith
Pinch: A schoolmaster
Luce: Servant to Adriana
SCENE Ephesus

Plot

ACT ONE Aegeon, a merchant of Syracuse, is apprehended
and sentenced to death by the Duke of Ephesus for trans-
gressing a law which forbids traffic between Syracuse and
Ephesus. The merchant explains how he came to hazard his
life. On a sea-voyage to Syracuse some twenty-five years
before, he lost his wife, one of his identical twin sons and one
of a pair of identical twins whom he had bought at birth as
slaves for his sons. He brought up his surviving son and the
surviving slave in Syracuse but lost them too when they
went off in search of their brothers. His own five-year
search for the children he reared himself will end that day in
Ephesus 'with the evening sun' unless, in the course of the
day, he can find in the city a thousand marks ransom.
Unknown to the grieving father, however, their search has
brought his son Antipholus and his slave Dromio to Ephesus
where their lost brothers are living. The first confusion
arising from the absolute identity of the two sets of twins is
the urgent summons to dinner that is issued by Dromio of
Ephesus to Antipholus of Syracuse.

ACT TWO Adriana, the wife of the Ephesian Antipholus,
describes herself to her sister Luciana as 'A wretched soul,
bruis'd with adversity' (II.i) – a state to which her husband's neglect and adulterous behaviour have reduced her.
She confronts the bewildered Antipholus of Syracuse with
her anxieties; he, speculating on whether he might not have
been 'married to her in my dream' (II.ii), decides to submit
to her 'offer'd fallacy' and to dine with her.

ACT THREE Antipholus of Ephesus is turned away from his
home when he returns with some companions for dinner,

on the grounds that the master is already dining within; he makes do instead with the company of a cheerful courtesan. His brother, meanwhile, is tackled by Luciana on the way he should be treating Adriana. In the course of the lecture he shocks his 'sister-in-law' by declaring his love for her – 'Teach me, dear creature, how to think and speak' (III.ii). Dromio of Syracuse too appears to have quite different taste in women from his twin brother as he flees the attentions of Luce, an amorous kitchen maid who claims his love. Antipholus and Dromio of Syracuse decide to vacate this disturbing household into which they have chanced. Passing through the streets of the city, Antipholus of Syracuse is given a gold necklace that was commissioned by his brother; the goldsmith refuses payment.

ACT FOUR Antipholus of Ephesus is arrested for refusing to pay for the necklace which he never received; and the bail that he sends Dromio of Syracuse to his wife to obtain finds its way to Antipholus of Syracuse instead. Adriana's tolerance of her husband snaps as she learns of his declaration of love to Luciana, and then receives the complaints of the courtesan who demanded of Antipholus of Syracuse, and was refused, the necklace 'he' had promised her in exchange for a ring. As Antipholus and Dromio of Syracuse decide to leave this bewitched city, their twin brothers are exorcised and then bound as madmen at Adriana's insistence.

ACT FIVE Antipholus and Dromio of Syracuse take refuge from the accusations of disgruntled tradesmen in a priory. The Abbess of the priory emerges to lecture Adriana, who is outside demanding her husband, on her duties as a wife: 'thy jealous fits/Have scar'd thy husband from the use of wits.' (V.i) News is then brought of the escape from confinement of Antipholus and Dromio of Ephesus, who are assumed to be within the priory. Their actions no longer have the power to surprise: 'Witness you,' says Adriana, 'That he is borne about invisible.' (V.i) Finally, of course, the two sets of twins are brought together on stage and are claimed by Aegeon, who has arrived to keep his appointment with death, as his sons and bondsmen. Aegeon is pardoned by the Duke, but there is a further surprise in store for the characters and the audience – the revelation that the Abbess is Aemelia, Aegeon's lost wife. All depart for the inevitable reunion feast.

Critical commentary

The Comedy of Errors was probably Shakespeare's first comedy. Like *Titus Andronicus*, which was certainly his first tragedy, it is closer than his later work to the standard theatrical fare of the time. He took for his sources two plays by Plautus, the *Menaechmi* and the *Amphitruo*, adapting from his Latin models not only his story, but a classical farce approach that he was never to employ with the same thoroughness again. Farce humour derives from the way normal people behave in abnormal situations. Density of characterization (one of the marks of Shakespeare's mature comedy) is not required; more important are the pace of the action and the deftness with which it is handled, so that the audience is never allowed time to ponder the improbability of events. In *The Comedy of Errors*, alone of his plays except his last, *The Tempest*, Shakespeare conforms to the classical unities of time and space – a discipline which, in this early comedy, concentrates the possibilities for confused identity and contributes to the play's highly polished surface and to the audience's awareness of it as a self-contained artefact.

Farce is a mode which operates on the surface: the central device of *The Comedy of Errors*, after all, is the total *physical* identity of two sets of twins. The personalities of the two sets of brothers are differentiated enough for the comedy, but differentiated without subtlety and along broadly obvious lines. Antipholus of Syracuse is grave and melancholy, his brother a cheerful philanderer. Their differences in taste are radical: 'She that doth call me husband, even my soul/Doth for a wife abhor' (III.ii) says Antipholus of Syracuse of Adriana. His reactions to Adriana are paralleled by Dromio of Syracuse to his brother's beloved Luce, given in a speech which is one of the play's comic highlights: 'she's the kitchen-wench, and all grease; and I know not what use to put her to but to make a lamp of her and run from her by her own light.' (III.ii)

The problems of farce for the dramatist are largely technical. Shakespeare mastered them so completely in this, his first comedy, that it is not surprising that he did not pursue the form except in the more idiosyncratic *The Merry Wives of Windsor*, Falstaff's return to the stage by popular request. Farce works by directing the audience's response towards the enjoyment of plot rather than by engaging the audience's sympathies on behalf of the characters. Shakespeare's supreme achievements as a writer of comedy were to be romantic, with plot confusions evoking not only laughter, but sympathy for the victim, and with the loss of everyday logic that accompanies those confusions seen as the entry to a life of fresh possibilities. Glimpses of Shakespeare's later approach can indeed be caught in *The Comedy of Errors*. The play opens with the sorrowful tale of Aegeon, who expects to die with his quest for his sons unfulfilled; and closes on a note of harmony and reunion (in the Abbess's words: 'After so long grief, such festivity!' (V.i)) as Aegeon is united not only with those he sought, but with the wife and son that he never expected to see again. Thus the opening and closing scenes, with their clear appeals to the audience's sympathies, provide a naturalistic frame within which the farce is contained. Antipholus of Syracuse, on arrival in Ephesus, states his intention of 'losing' himself (in other words, his melancholy) in the city. In the event, he loses not only his melancholy but his identity and his bearings – he and his Dromio speculate on whether the city is bewitched. For them indeed the prosaic port has a kind of magic, for they find their brothers and Antipholus his mother and a wife in Luciana. In *The Comedy of Errors*, however, the romantic elements are not stressed; they are not, as they will be in the later comedies, the play's substance, but the mechanics necessary to resolve the farce – the play's real business.

The Two Gentlemen of Verona

DATE Early 1590s

PRINCIPAL CHARACTERS

Valentine   } The two
Proteus   } gentlemen
Silvia: Beloved of Valentine
Julia: Beloved of Proteus
Duke of Milan: Silvia's father
Thurio: Valentine's rival for Silvia
Speed: Valentine's page
Launce: Proteus' page
Lucetta: Julia's serving woman
Antonio: Proteus' father
Panthino: Antonio's servant
Eglamour: An agent in Silvia's escape
Host where Julia lodges
SCENE Verona, Milan and a forest outside Milan

Plot

ACT ONE Valentine and Proteus, two young gentlemen of Verona who are attached by an unusually strong friendship, make their farewells: Valentine is going to Milan, in the hope of gaining friends and privileges at the Duke's court; Proteus is kept in Verona by his, as yet unpublicized, love for Julia. Proteus' father Antonio, however, anxious for his son's worldly success, despatches him to Milan to join his friend. Vows of fidelity are exchanged between Julia and Proteus.

ACT TWO By the time of Proteus' arrival in Milan Valentine has himself fallen in love with Silvia, the Duke's daughter. After an appropriate period of fencing and testing, Silvia admits her love for Valentine, but the way is complicated by Thurio, a suitor preferred by the Duke. The young couple have planned an elopement, the details of which Valentine reveals to Proteus, who has now joined him. Proteus, however, reveals to the audience that he is himself smitten by love for Silvia. Back in Verona, Julia decides to follow Proteus to Milan.

ACT THREE Aware that he is outraging all the laws of friendship and love, Proteus betrays Valentine's elopement plans to the Duke. Valentine is outlawed from Milan. When Proteus is employed by the Duke to recommend Thurio's suit to Silvia he breaks faith again by using the opportunity to press his own love on Silvia.

ACT FOUR Valentine is waylaid by gentlemen outlaws on his journey from Milan and is adopted as their leader. Julia meanwhile has arrived in Milan disguised as a boy. There she is confronted with her lover's treachery. Using the name 'Sebastian' she gets herself taken on as Proteus' page, in which role she has the painful task of pleading her lover's cause with Silvia.

ACT FIVE Silvia is unmoved by Proteus' love and demonstrates her continuing fidelity for Valentine by running away to find him, under the chivalrous protection of a reliably chaste knight, Sir Eglamour. Sir Eglamour's valour, however, is inferior to his chastity, and he disappears when they are attacked by outlaws – Valentine's men, but not in Valentine's presence. Silvia is rescued by Proteus and Julia/Sebastian, who have followed her. Unknowingly overlooked by Valentine, Proteus tries to rape Silvia out of pique at her continued unresponsiveness. Valentine comes to the rescue and in words which hardly seem strong enough for the occasion accuses Proteus of perfidy. Proteus offers his apologies, Valentine accepts them and, loyal to the last to the friendship he has sworn Proteus, offers him to Silvia. Julia/Sebastian, a witness to the offer that could crush all her hopes of Proteus, has recourse to a timely swoon. Her identity is revealed and Proteus decides that he loves her after all. The Duke arrives with Sir Thurio who renounces all claim on Silvia at the suggestion that he fight Valentine to win her. The Duke, aware now of Thurio's cowardice, acknowledges Valentine to be the better man. The characters withdraw to Milan for the inevitable double wedding.

The play is enlivened in the earlier scenes by the presence

of Launce and Speed, the two gentlemen's pages. Their contribution to the plot is minimal but they provide welcome humour.

Critical commentary

The Two Gentlemen of Verona is Shakespeare's first and least successful attempt at romantic comedy. Indeed, much of the play's interest is in his rudimentary use of motifs and conventions which he was to handle with more skill in later work. The play's theme is the conflicting demands of love and friendship. In mediaeval courtly literature, whose values were still current in the literature of Shakespeare's day, love and friendship were seen as absolute states, with laws of their own which made exaggerated demands on the individual. Proteus says magniloquently of his love for Julia: 'I leave myself, my friends and all, for love.' (I.i); while Valentine regards the overwhelming nature of his love for Silvia as a punishment by the god of love for his previous mockery of love's excesses: 'I have done penance for contemning love;/Whose high imperious thoughts have punish'd me.' (II.iv) Friendship requires a similar degree of selflessness from its practitioners: when Valentine offers Silvia to Proteus in the final scene, he shows himself prepared to make the ultimate sacrifice for a friend.

The system breaks down, of course, when the value of stifling one's impulses is questioned, as it is by Proteus when he falls in love with Silvia, 'I to myself am dearer than a friend'. (II.vi) It is interesting that Proteus' love for Julia has been inflamed by Valentine's exaggerated praise of her – the laws of love demanding that his mistress should be a paragon among women. Proteus at this point finds himself unable to play the game; he cannot accept with equanimity that his best friend might have something better than he has himself.

Proteus' attitude is unquestionably more realistic than Valentine's. Indeed, while the actual mechanics of the story depict a conflict between love and friendship, Shakespeare's treatment of character has shifted the emphasis to the clash between real emotions and the emotions demanded by convention. Not that Proteus is shown sympathetically: his efforts to win Silvia involve too much double-dealing, and a petulance that becomes violent when he finds that he cannot shift her affections.

The character who most engages the audience's sympathies is Julia. Her love for Proteus involves her in no clash of loyalties except one that she quickly and rightly dismisses: in disguise, as Proteus' servant Sebastian, she ought to do her best to win Silvia round:

> I am my master's true – confirmed love,
>
> But cannot be true servant to my master,
>
> Unless I prove false traitor to myself. (IV.iv)

Shakespeare entirely respects Julia's sense of self. She anticipates the later comic heroines in her resourcefulness, in her readiness to assume disguise and take to the road to preserve what is most precious to herself – Proteus. But for her swoon in the final scene, Valentine's ridiculous offer of Silvia to Proteus might have been taken up.

Shakespeare does not, in fact, directly ridicule the conventions of love and friendship in this play, but a degree of irony makes itself felt in the way he deploys subsidiary characters, especially Launce and Speed, the two pages. Valentine's conventional prattlings about love are placed in a refreshingly unromantic context by Speed when he tells his master that his follies in love 'shine through you like the water in an urinal.' (II.i) When Launce is thinking of taking a wife, he enumerates the practical reasons for his choice: '"*She can fetch and carry*", Why, a horse can do no more: nay, a horse cannot fetch but only carry; therefore is she better than a jade.' (III.i)

It is in Launce's relationship with his dog, Crab, however, that Shakespeare makes his most ingenious implied comments on friendship rather than love. With Launce and Crab, the normal relationship between master and dog is as near as possible reversed: 'I have sat in the stocks for puddings he hath stolen, otherwise he had been executed;

I have stood on the pillory for geese he hath killed, otherwise he had suffered for't'. (IV.iv) The selflessness which would be universally acknowledged as absurd in Launce could so easily be shown to be absurd in Valentine. Shakespeare refrains from undermining Valentine's courtly aspirations directly, making instead a kind of scapegoat of Launce. It is a weakness of the play, however, that the burlesque elements should make such an impact, for Shakespeare is not bent on undermining the ideals of love and friendship so much as on ridiculing the extremes to which they might drive people.

The Taming of the Shrew

DATE 1592-4

PRINCIPAL CHARACTERS IN THE INDUCTION

A Lord
Christopher Sly
Hostess
Page

PRINCIPAL CHARACTERS IN THE PLAY PROPER

Baptista Minola: A gentleman of Padua
Katharina } Baptista's
Bianca   } two daughters
Petruchio: Katharina's suitor, and then husband
Lucentio: In love with Bianca
Vincentio: His father
Hortensio } Further suitors
Gremio   } to Bianca
Curtis } Servants
Grumio } to Petruchio
Tranio   } Lucentio's
Biondello } servants
SCENE Padua and Petruchio's country house

Plot

INDUCTION Christopher Sly, a tinker, emerges drunk from an inn and falls asleep by the side of the road. A hunting party chances upon him. A Lord, the leader of the hunting party, for his own amusement has the inert Sly carried off to the Lord's own house, dressed in finery, presented with a wife (one of the Lord's pages, disguised) and told that his memories of himself as Sly are a lunatic delusion. After a little argument Sly submits to the situation and celebrates the return of his wits (on which all around are congratulating him) by watching a play that is performed in the Lord's home by travelling players. Apart from one brief interruption by Sly, the play itself is completely self-contained, and distinguished initially from Sly's English world by some emphasis on the Italian setting.

ACT ONE Lucentio, a young man from Pisa, has come to Padua to study, accompanied by his servant Tranio. Unobserved themselves, they witness a family wrangle involving Baptista and his daughters Katharina and Bianca: Bianca is immediately characterized by her submissive studiousness, Katharina by her shrewish disposition. Gremio and Hortensio, both in love with Bianca, are pressing their suits on Baptista, who tells them that there is no hope of a marriage with Bianca until Katharina is disposed of. The party moves off and Lucentio reveals that he too has been bewitched by Bianca; abandoning his studies and identity together, he tells Thranio to impersonate him while he gains admission into Baptista's house as a schoolmaster for Bianca. The ranks of adventuring young men are further swollen by the arrival of Petruchio, who has 'come to wive it wealthily in Padua'. (I.ii) Told about Katharina by his friend Hortensio, he declares himself ready to take her on – at a price.

ACT TWO Petruchio, on meeting Kate, studiously ignores her shrewishness and sets an early date for the wedding.

ACT THREE When the wedding day arrives, Petruchio keeps Katharina waiting for the ceremony, and when he appears, his manner of dress is a calculated insult. He whisks her off to his country home before the wedding feast. Lucentio, meanwhile, using the name Cambio, has been pressing his love on Bianca under cover of Latin construction. His chief rival,

Hortensio, disguised as Licio, a music teacher, has less success with their pupil.

ACT FOUR At home in the country, Petruchio subjects his bride to a week of harrassment, depriving her of food and sleep in order to bring her to heel like a dog: he manages to present his actions as motivated by love and concern. In Padua the apparent Lucentio (Tranio disguised) is winning Baptista over with the size of his patrimony. To substantiate his case, a wandering Pedant is pressed into service to play the part of Lucentio's father, Vincentio, in the marriage negotiations. Just as these are being finalized, the real Lucentio elopes with Bianca. Hortensio, meanwhile, has quitted the field in a huff to marry a rich widow.

ACT FIVE The arrival of Lucentio's actual father, the real Vincentio, produces further plot complications. All are reconciled by Lucentio and Bianca's wedding feast, to which Petruchio brings Kate, now a changed woman. The three newly married husbands (Petruchio, Lucentio and Hortensio) put their wives to an obedience test, which Kate wins. Petruchio's victory is complete when he hears Kate lecture Bianca and the Widow on wifely submission.

Critical commentary

Although the apparent central interest of *The Taming of the Shrew* is love, it in fact belongs more to the farce world of *The Comedy of Errors* than to the string of romantic comedies which begins with *The Two Gentlemen of Verona*. A characteristic of farce is that the devices and the workings of plot are of more importance than individual characters and the play's emotional content. The farce interest in plot device for its own sake explains elements in *The Shrew* which are most tedious today – the proliferation of disguises serving no purpose but to stir up a kind of artificial interest in their unravelling. In the central story of Petruchio and Kate, the audience's attention is engaged by his methods of taming her: if our sympathies were too closely enlisted in Kate's interest, we would be outraged rather than amused by Petruchio's treatment of her. Kate is first and foremost a shrew, and as such exists to be tamed.

Modern critics have been more squeamish and equivocal in their assessment of the play than audiences. Peter Alexander, in *Shakespeare's Life and Art* finds in it 'evidence of the brutality of Elizabethan taste' (there are a number of unnecessary beatings on stage, although Petruchio's methods of bringing Kate to heel are largely psychological), but he does acknowledge in the play an abiding human interest. He sees it as 'a comic treatment of the perilous maiden theme, where the lady is death to any suitor who woos her except the hero, in whose hands her apparent vices turn to virtues.' *The Shrew* belongs to that body of literature whose theme (Shakespeare was to use it again in *Much Ado about Nothing*) is unwilling love: the central parties are finally brought to admit a love that at first their will revolted against.

The story of Petruchio and Kate has a vigour that makes the sub-plot of Bianca and her suitors look vapid, which is possibly why Shakespeare found it necessary to enliven the Bianca story with the disguises. On first meeting Kate, Petruchio's conversation turns to bedding her; far from placing her on a conventional romantic pedestal, he declares his intention to make her 'Conformable as other household Kates' (II.i); an ambition which he fulfils magnificently. In his later comedies, Shakespeare was to show considerable intuitive sympathy for women, but *The Shrew* is an almost aggressively male-oriented play. Women are only seen briefly alone together (Act Three, Scene One, Katharina and Bianca, for the space of twenty lines), while there is a pervading feeling of male solidarity. Women are talked of as 'rotten apples' (I.i); tactics are freely discussed; Petruchio is first regarded as a saviour by Bianca's wooers, who are anxious to see the field clear of Kate, and at the end is adopted by them as a hero for his success in taming her. Money is dear to the hearts of all the men, and terms are discussed with some relish, both in relation to the girls' dowries, and in Baptista's inquiries into the suitability of the suitors. Katharina he is anxious to get off his hands, but Bianca, who is more sought after, is given to the highest bidder. Only Lucentio seems to want to keep financial arrangements in the background of his wooing: Tranio, disguised as his master, looks after the practical side, while Lucentio, as Cambio, concentrates his attention on Bianca. If this was an attempt by Shakespeare to show the disinterestedness of romantic love – an article of faith in his later comedies – then it fails, largely because Lucentio and Bianca do not compel our attention.

Of more interest to the critics is the relationship between the Christopher Sly Induction and the play itself – chiefly for what we can infer from it of Shakespeare's views on comedy. Christopher Sly is brought by the Lord and his minions to submit to an illusion – the illusion that he himself is a wealthy lord. At first he resists: 'What! would you make me mad? Am I not Christopher Sly?' (Induction, ii). Like other characters in Shakespeare's comedies, however, Sly is brought to submit to the illusion as a means of grasping an offered pleasure, the unaccustomed comfort of being treated like a lord. The idea of illusion as potentially life-enhancing applies to the theatre itself – the audience must suspend its credibility and submit to the illusion to achieve the maximum offered pleasure. The link between theatrical illusion and illusion in life is specifically made by the Sly Induction, where the Lord imposes on Sly by deliberately theatrical means – interestingly, the wife Sly is offered is a disguised boy, as are all the ladies in Shakespeare's plays. And when Sly has settled into the illusion of himself as a lord, the further illusion of the play can begin. Shakespeare is deliberately exploiting here the 'unreal' nature of what he as a dramatist has to offer. In playing with different levels of illusion, he is baffling the audience's sense of what is real and unreal; perhaps he regarded this as the ideal frame of mind to which to have subdued his audience.

Love's Labour's Lost

DATE Sometime after 1593

PRINCIPAL CHARACTERS

Ferdinand, King of Navarre

Berowne ⎫
Longaville ⎬ His lords
Dumaine ⎭

Princess of France

Boyet ⎫ Her
Marcade ⎭ lords

Rosaline ⎫
Maria ⎬ Her ladies
Katharine ⎭

Don Adriano de Armado: A Spaniard at Navarre's Court

Moth: His page

Jaquenetta: A country wench with whom Armado falls in love

Sir Nathaniel: A curate

Holofernes: A schoolmaster

Dull: A constable

Costard: A country clown

SCENE Navarre – Ferdinand's court and surrounding park.

Plot

ACT ONE The King of Navarre and his companions, the lords Berowne, Longaville and Dumaine, have sworn an oath to spend three years in study and fasting, away from the society of women. To remove temptation from their path a law has been passed outlawing women from within a mile of the court. Only Berowne is sceptical, but consents in a spirit of camaraderie. No sooner has the oath been sworn than diplomatic necessity demands its relaxation: the Princess of France is due on a mission from her father; she can be lodged in the park, away from the court, but must nonetheless be seen. The ascetic atmosphere of Navarre's court is further undermined by Armado, a guest of the king, who has fallen in love with Jaquenetta, a simple country wench.

ACT TWO When Navarre and his lords visit the Princess and her ladies, each predictably singles out a lady (Navarre, the Princess; Berowne, Rosaline; Longaville, Maria; Dumaine, Katherine) but they nonetheless conceal their treachery to their vow out of shame.

ACT THREE The affair between Armado and Jaquenetta proceeds apace. Berowne speculates on why he has fallen in love with the least attractive of the three ladies.

ACT FOUR When Navarre and his companions discover each other's treachery – they unwittingly choose the same part of the park to polish up the verses they have written to their respective ladies – their confederacy is given a new basis: now comrades in love, they first declare their feelings for their ladies by letter, each sending a token of affection, and then lay plans to visit the ladies to press their suits further – disguised, for reasons which are not made clear, as Muscovites.

ACT FIVE The Princess is primed about the Muscovite scheme by her lord, Boyet. The ladies, who have anyway taken an ironic view of the lords' original oath (to chastity and study), trick them into forswearing themselves a second time. When the 'Muscovites' arrive the ladies are disguised, distinguished only by their lovers' gifts – which in each case the wrong lady is wearing. Fresh protestations of love are sworn, each lord singling out his lady by the love token. The lords make no headway as Muscovites, and when they return as themselves are confronted by their fresh perjury. Good humour has been restored when a messenger arrives with news of the King of France's death. They are all jolted into seriousness. The lords plead their earnestness, the ladies insist that the year's statutory mourning shall serve as a testing time for their lovers. The Princess and Rosaline impose further tasks: Navarre must subject himself to a year's genuine asceticism in a hermitage, Berowne to a year tending the sick, before their love will be accepted. News is brought also in the final scene of Jaquenetta's pregnancy by Armado.

In addition to the court and love interest, *Love's Labour's*

Lost has not so much a sub-plot as a series of comic interludes. The comedy is mainly linguistic: the fantastic language of Armado and the pedantic language of the schoolmaster Holofernes and the curate, Sir Nathaniel, are satirized for the audience by Armado's page, Moth, and by Costard, a clown. The main point of overlap between this group of characters and the principals is the inept entertainment that Holofernes and Sir Nathaniel organize for the lords and ladies in the final act, just before the news of the King of France's death.

Critical commentary

Written at the time of his patronage by the Earl of Southampton, *Love's Labour's Lost* is the most consciously aristocratic of Shakespeare's plays. This shows itself partly in his observation of 'elegant' behaviour, much of the dialogue between the nobility taking the form of sophisticated wordplay. The characters at the centre of the stage can, up to a point, treat life as a game; the action of the play establishes where that point, between game and earnest, lies. The play is also aristocratic in the narrower sense of including characters who were based on originals known at court. Navarre and his companions are possibly meant to suggest Southampton's own group of friends; we can with more assurance find parallels between Armado and Sir Walter Raleigh and Holofernes and John Florio, the translator of Montaigne.

Love's Labour's Lost is the most satirical of Shakespeare's comedies. At the end of a dialogue in which Moth has been mocking Armado for his love for Jaquenetta, the master asks the page: 'How hast thou purchased this experience?' Moth's reply is: 'By my penny of observation' (III.i). Shakespeare is here satirizing those who base their lives too closely on ideas taken second-hand from books, and not closely enough on first-hand experience and observation of the real world.

Navarre sees love as antithetical to fame and glory: the regime which he imposes on himself and his lords will 'make us heirs of all eternity'. (I.i) Berowne disgraces himself by his initial objections, 'O! these are barren tasks, too hard to keep,/Not to see ladies, study, fast, not sleep.' (I.i) but he does draw attention to two serious flaws in the demands the young men are making on themselves: not only that they are unrealistic, beyond what they should sensibly expect of themselves, but more important, that they are fundamentally pointless ('barren tasks'). An abiding concern of comedy has always been the infirmity of human purpose; the gap between intention and the reality of performance. With Navarre and his bookmen, their aspirations are satirized as much as their failure to fulfil them. The point is underlined when, immediately after they all put their signatures to the oath, Costard is brought before them for talking with Jaquenetta within the proscribed boundaries. His defence cuts no ice with Navarre, but it does with the audience: 'it is the manner of a man to speak to a woman.' (I.i)

When the young men have experienced love themselves, they use the same argument as Costard, albeit expressed in a more sophisticated way by Berowne: 'We cannot cross the cause why we were born.' (IV. iii)

The acknowledgement of their own nature does not in itself let them off the hook, either of the playwright's mockery or of the ladies': Shakespeare shows them going on to justify the breaking of their oath with the same perverted logic that they used in underwriting it:

> It is religion to be thus forsworn;
> For charity itself fulfils the law,
> And who can sever love from charity? (IV.iii).

Women in this play are felt to be closer to natural realities than men. This is illustrated most crudely in the burlesqued love-affair of Armado and Jaquenetta, the would-be poet and the creature of instinct. 'I will tell thee wonders,' Armado promises. 'With that face?' retorts Jacquenetta. (I. ii). Berowne sees female beauty as central to the argument between first-hand and second-hand experience: 'For where is any author in the world/Teaches such beauty as a woman's eye?' (IV.iii) In the event, the Princess and her ladies have a harsher reality in store for their lovers than their beauty, contemplated at first hand. The ladies see the young men as profoundly lacking in seriousness. The Princess and her retinue themselves play games with words – fashion demands a high level of verbal proficiency of them – but they recognize those games for what they are; Navarre and his men, however, are taken in by their own games. It is because Navarre and his lords failed to recognize their original asceticism for what it was – play-acting within a benign and controlled environment – that the Princess and Rosaline demand a real asceticism of their lords: 'frosts and fasts, hard lodging and thin weeds' are in store for Navarre; 'the speechless sick' and 'groaning wretches' for Berowne who, according to Rosaline, has been too inclined to treat life satirically. This regime will teach them the reality of what they lightly undertook, and their willingness to take on this reality will test their love – which, as far as the ladies are concerned, could prove to be just as shallow as their earlier oaths.

It is often said of *Love's Labour's Lost* that it is the most artificial of all Shakespeare's comedies. Artificiality is a concept that applies to a number of different aspects of this play. In as far as Shakespeare's intentions are satirical, it is artificiality in one form or another that he is satirizing: Navarre and his companions mistake play-acting for reality; Armado, Sir Nathaniel and Holofernes are being mocked for using language – fantastic in Armado's case, pedantic in Holofernes' and Sir Nathaniel's – in ways that totally fail to communicate. They illustrate the follies of learning at a more specific and superficial level than do Navarre and his lords.

Artificiality is not only satirized in this play, however; it is a feature of Shakespeare's own style. Writing this play as a young man, newly adopted into aristocratic circles, he, as much as his characters, is displaying his own verbal trickiness. Moreover, the scheme of the play allows very little room for individual characterization: it is essential that all the young men meet identical fates and their characters, and those of the women with whom they fall in love, are barely differentiated, with the exception of Berowne, and possibly Rosaline. Shakespeare likes to end his comedies with multiple weddings, but in no other of the comedies are the characters and love-histories of the couples so similar as they are in this play.

A problem with comedy – by its nature more artificial than history and tragedy – is to ease the audience at the end from the self-contained comic world onto a level of naturalism more appropriate to the reality the audience will confront on leaving the theatre. In *Love's Labour's Lost* Shakespeare successfully handles the transition from artificiality to naturalism – surprisingly so, given the pervading artificiality of the play. The news of the King of France's death jolts the play sharply into reality and the characters into seriousness. The tests then imposed by the women – reasonable enough, given the young men's initial oaths to asceticism – come more naturally after the intimations of mortality which even a death off-stage provides. The play closes with Odes to Spring and Winter from Armado, Sir Nathaniel and Holofernes – beautiful in themselves, even if quite out of character with those gentlemen's earlier verbal excesses. After the enclosed courtly atmosphere, the suggestion of a natural world that is harsh as well as lovely is welcome.

A Midsummer Night's Dream

DATE 1595

PRINCIPAL CHARACTERS

Theseus:	Duke of Athens
Hippolyta:	Conquered Queen of the Amazons and Theseus' betrothed
Lysander	} Young men in love
Demetrius	} with Hermia

Hermia: Who loves Lysander
Helena: Who loves Demetrius
Egeus: Hermia's father
Philostrate: Master of the Revels to Theseus
THE FAIRIES
Oberon: The fairy king
Titania: The fairy queen
Puck, or Robin Goodfellow
Assorted fairy attendants (Moth, Cobweb, Peaseblossom,
Mustard-seed)
THE MECHANICALS WHO STAGE A PLAY FOR THESEUS' WEDDING
Peter Quince: Prologue in the play
Bottom: Pyramus in the play
Francis Flute: Thisbe in the play
Snug: Lion in the play
Tom Snout: Wall in the play
Robin Starveling: Moonshine in the play
SCENE Athens and a wood outside Athens

Plot

ACT ONE opens as Theseus and Hippolyta set their wedding
date at four days hence. Theseus is appealed to by Egeus, an
Athenian nobleman, about his recalcitrant daughter
Hermia: Egeus wants her to marry Demetrius, she favours
Lysander. According to an Athenian law invoked by the
Duke, Hermia must either die or enter a convent if she fails
to comply with her father. She is given until the Duke's
wedding day to make her choice. Not relishing the offered
alternatives, Hermia and Lysander decide to elope. They
tell their plans to Helena, who is herself in love with
Demetrius and was supplanted in Demetrius' affections by
Hermia. Helena, eager even for Demetrius' gratitude,
decides to betray Hermia's and Lysander's secret to him.
Still in Athens, plans are going ahead for an entertainment
on the royal wedding day. The performers are a group of
mechanicals led by Nick Bottom; their choice of play, the
tragical love-story of Pyramus and Thisbe. They decide to
withdraw to the wood outside the city for rehearsals.

ACT TWO The action is confined to the wood outside Athens, the dominion of Oberon, the fairy king. He and his wife, Titania, are quarrelling over the possession of a changeling boy whom Titania has reared; their dispute has upset nature, blighted the crops. Unable to acquire the boy by direct means, Oberon decides to make a fool of his queen by magic. He dispatches Puck, a malevolent sprite, in search of a flower, love-in-idleness, which has the power to produce violent and immediate love. While Puck is gone, Oberon, who is invisible to mortals, witnesses a rejection scene between Demetrius, who is pursuing the eloping Hermia and Lysander, and Helena, who is pursuing Demetrius. When Puck returns, after Helena's and Demetrius' departure, he is told to use the same love-in-idleness to win back Demetrius' love for Helena. In another part of the woods, Titania retires to sleep in her fairy bower. Lysander and Hermia arrive and, weary themselves, bed down in the wood. Puck anoints the eyes of the sleeping Titania, and of Lysander (Oberon had specified a couple in Athenian dress and Puck has come upon the wrong couple). Helena, having lost Demetrius, comes upon her sleeping friends. Lysander wakes up, falls instantly in love with Helena and abandons the still sleeping Hermia in pursuit of his new love.

ACT THREE In yet another part of the wood (which conveniently offers scope for much independent activity) Puck finds the mechanicals rehearsing their play. He spirits Bottom away, transforms him with an ass's head, at the sight of which his companions flee in fright, and puts him in the way of Titania. When the fairy queen awakes, she is at once smitten with a wholly inappropriate passion for Bottom. Bewildered but confident of his power to cope with the situation, Bottom allows himself to be carried off to her fairy bower. Meanwhile Hermia, in search of Lysander, is being pursued by Demetrius. They are observed by Oberon and Puck. Oberon, realizing that further confusion has been caused, sends Puck off in search of Helena. Demetrius, now abandoned by Hermia, lies down and sleeps, thus providing Oberon with the opportunity to anoint him with love-in-idleness. When Helena arrives, hotly pursued by Lysander, Demetrius stirs and at once falls in love with her. Helena thinks the men are mocking her. Hermia, again on the scene, assumes that her friend has poisoned Lysander's mind towards her. The women quarrel and the men fight. Since Puck is manipulating the fighters and confounding them with fogs, they come to no harm. Weary at last, the four lovers fall into the final sleep of the night and are then subjected to the final piece of magic of the night: Oberon ensures that Lysander, on waking, will return to his first love, Hermia.

ACT FOUR Oberon has acquired the changeling boy while Titania has been besotted with Bottom. The task accomplished, he frees his queen from the spell. She abandons the sleeping Bottom with mortified disgust. The sleeping bodies of the four lovers have been on stage throughout. Disturbed by the arrival of Theseus, Hippolyta and Egeus on a hunting party, the lovers assume that the night's adventures have been a dream. Demetrius' renewed love for Helena survives the night, however, and the changed situation is accepted by the Duke and Egeus, who give Hermia leave to marry Lysander. The lovers will celebrate their marriage with Theseus and Hippolyta. Bottom, too, awakes from what he, too, assumes to have been a dream; he rejoins his companions in Athens, and preparations for the play are completed.

ACT FIVE Theseus and Hippolyta, Helena and Demetrius, Hermia and Lysander, now married, while away the hours before bed with the mechanicals' play: the crude rendering of the tragic tale is a source of some humour to the sophisticated audience. When the lovers have departed for bed, the fairies come to bless the bridal beds. In an Epilogue, Puck admits the whole play to have been a 'vision' and a 'dream' and the actors 'shadows'.

Critical commentary

A Midsummer Night's Dream was almost certainly written to celebrate an important court wedding. While it was not

Shakespeare's practice to write plays exclusively for private performance, *The Dream* displays features of the kind of drama popular in court circles. It owes more than any other of his plays, except *The Tempest*, to the masque, lending itself easily to spectacular presentation (elegant court and pretty fairies) and to stylized movement; there are songs for the fairies and a burlesque provided by the mechanicals, reminiscent of the antimasque element of the masque. Indeed, the relationship between *The Dream* and the masque is closer than the few superficial borrowings that might recommend the play to a court audience. As Enid Welsford has pointed out in her book, *The Court Masque**, the shifts in the lovers' relationships form a pattern which resembles a dance formation: at some point before the action of the play begins there were two couples, Hermia and Lysander and Helena and Demetrius; when the play opens the two men are playing court to one woman, Hermia; they both move on to the other woman, Helena; by the end of the play they have returned to their original pairs. The lovers (the men particularly) are scarcely differentiated in character, like masquers: what matters more than their individual personalities are the structures they form.

The Dream is one of the most structurally symmetrical of Shakespeare's plays. The action begins in Athens where all the mortals, as opposed to the fairies, are introduced. The lovers and the mechanicals withdraw to the wood, where they are 'worked upon' by the fairies. When the night's adventures are over and, with morning, the power of the fairies wanes, Theseus and Hippolyta bring their hunting party to the wood. Their departure to Athens for the wedding celebrations brings home the lovers and the mechanicals; and with midnight ('fairy time'), the visit of the fairies to court. The play is framed by the court nuptials of Theseus and Hippolyta which we know from the first act

*The material in Enid Welsford's *The Court Masque* which is relevant to *A Midsummer Night's Dream* can be found in *Shakespeare's Comedies*, edited by Laurence Lerner (Penguin) and in the Signet edition of the play.

must conclude the action: Hermia's choice must be made by then, the mechanicals' play must be ready. Within this frame are three sub-plots, all overseen by Oberon: the lovers' adventures, the quarrel and reconciliation of Oberon and Titania, the theatrical efforts of the mechanicals. *The Dream* is the first of Shakespeare's plays to demonstrate his skill in drawing a number of threads into a coherent whole.

The multiple marriages that conclude the play, and the reconciliation of a further couple, Oberon and Titania, have an obvious appropriateness for the wedding celebrations to which *The Dream* contributed. The play celebrates, not only marriage as a state, but the harmony that can be achieved through marriage, and of which marriage is a symbol. Theseus and Hippolyta are introduced at a point where they have worked through an earlier discord to an amity that will be sealed by marriage. Theseus says:

> Hippolyta, I woo'd thee with my sword,
> And won thy love doing thee injuries;
> But I will wed thee in another key. (I.i)

The Duke and his bride are excluded from the main body of the action because their harmony is achieved: they have only to wait for the formalities.

They are excluded for another reason. Theseus is a ruler, a man of action. He weds Hippolyta 'With pomp, with triumph, and with revelling.' (I.i), but there are obvious political advantages to their union. The only way he knows to deal with Hermia's predicament (one of the discords to be resolved by the play) is to apply the law to her. He has his limitations. His comment of the lovers' tale of their night's adventures is: 'The lunatic, the lover, and the poet,/ Are of imagination all compact.' (V.i)

These lines are revealing enough about Theseus, but they also suggest the symbolic values of Athens and the wood outside: the one is a place of reason, the other of imagination. Oberon, whose domain is the wood, manipulates the imagination as the Duke is a manipulator in the practical world.

Oberon is an image of the poet, the spinner of dreams. At

the height of the quarrel betwen Helena and Hermia, Helena calls the other 'a counterfeit' and 'a puppet'. This unthinking abuse has broader connotations than Helena herself is aware of: all four of the lovers are indeed puppets in Oberon's hands. We feel in this play that Shakespeare is viewing his own art with some detachment. Oberon's manipulation of the lovers demonstrates in microcosm what Shakespeare does in all his comedies: organize his characters through their discords until the final comic harmony is achieved. In comedy, lovers' distress is handled in a way that exploits the humour rather than the pain. Puck, witnessing the distress of these particular lovers, expresses the audience's reaction: 'Lord, what fools these mortals be!' (III.ii)

Theseus sees a link between the poet and the lover in the quality of imagination. In *The Dream*, the investigation of love which is proper to romantic comedy is linked with Shakespeare's preoccupation with his own art by the play's emphasis on the place of the imagination in both. Helena, bewildered by Demetrius' transfer of his love to Hermia, rightly concludes that love has no rational basis. The young men are not so sensible: worked upon by Oberon, they try to justify their change of heart with logic, and in doing so demonstrate their folly, exploited for its humour in Lysander's plea to Helena: 'The will of man is by his reason sway'd,/ And reason says you are the worthier maid' (II.ii). Love in Shakespearean comedy is shown as sudden, consuming, and having little to do with the personality of the beloved. While the lovers are still operating at this highly suggestive level, they come within Oberon's domain of the imagination. He resolves their discords on the level that they can respond to; when harmony is achieved among them, they are fit to return to Athens, the play's symbol for sense and responsibility.

The transforming power of the imagination is demonstrated in Titania's brief erotic obsession with Bottom. The anomaly is apparent to Bottom himself – 'reason and love keep little company together now-a-days' (III.i) – but he is willing to go along with Titania. Bottom is the first of Shakespeare's great comic creations, and the only one of the characters manipulated by Oberon who is worthy of individual attention. Comedy derived so plainly from the exploitation of Bottom's assishness (the ass's head works because it is appropriate) could be merciless, but Shakespeare throughout endows Bottom with absolute faith in himself: because he never sees himself as a laughable object, there is no cruelty in the laughter.

Bottom's self-confidence is evident, not only in his brush with Titania, but in his attitude towards the Pyramus and Thisbe play. He feels no trepidation about performing before a sophisticated court audience: his only fear is that his acting skills will prove too realistic for the timid ladies. In his handling of the play within a play, Shakespeare's preoccupation with the power of the imagination is given a new twist. The mechanicals' efforts, so fine in their own eyes, are greeted with scorn by their audience (a scorn of which the performers are mercifully unaware), with the exception of Theseus. He reprimands one of Hippolyta's witty sallies at the actors' expense with 'The best in this kind are but shadows, and the worst are no worse, if imagination amend them' (V.i). The comedy of the play within a play is in the failure of the actors to capture their audience's imagination. Shakespeare felt sufficiently secure in his own powers in *The Dream*, a play about imagination, to risk a demonstration of theatrical failure on stage; and to confess at the end, in Puck's Epilogue, the unreal or 'imagined' quality of the whole entertainment.

The Merchant of Venice

DATE 1596
PRINCIPAL CHARACTERS
Antonio: A merchant of Venice
Bassanio: Antonio's friend, Portia's suitor

Lorenzo ⎱ Friends of Antonio
Gratiano ⎰ and Bassanio
Shylock: A Jewish money-lender
Tubal: Shylock's friend
Jessica: Shylock's daughter
Launcelot Gobbo: A clown, Shylock's servant
Old Gobbo: Launcelot's father
Salarino ⎱ Friends of Antonio, useful in the
Salanio ⎰ play as imparters of information
Portia: A wealthy heiress, lady of Belmont
Nerissa: Her serving woman
Prince of Arragon ⎱ Unsuccessful suitors
Prince of Morocco ⎰ to Portia
Balthasar: Portia's servant whose name she adopts on disguise
Stephano: Another servant to Portia
The Duke of Venice
SCENE: Venice and Belmont

Plot

ACT ONE Antonio, a wealthy merchant, is approached by his friend Bassanio for a loan of 3,000 ducats with which to equip himself for a journey to Belmont: there he hopes to win the lady Portia in marriage. All Antonio's funds are ventured at sea, but he offers himself as security for the sum to Shylock, a Jewish money-lender. Shylock and Antonio are enemies of long-standing: in what the money-lender describes as a 'merry bond', Antonio will be required, if the debt is not repaid in three months, to surrender a pound of his flesh in lieu of the sum. Meanwhile, the audience has been introduced to Belmont and Portia. With her serving woman Nerissa, she discusses the terms of her father's will. Any suitor for herself and her fortune must submit to a test: faced with three caskets (of gold, silver and lead) he must decide which contains Portia's picture, and hence her father's posthumous permission to marry her.

ACT TWO In three Belmont scenes (i, vii and ix), two of Portia's noble suitors, the Princes of Morocco and Arragon, fail the casket test: choosing gold and silver respectively, they are mocked by scrolls within the caskets for being easily deluded by appearances. In Venice, Shylock's servant Launcelot Gobbo leaves the Jew's service for Bassanio's, at the same time acting as go-between for Shylock's daughter Jessica and Lorenzo, a Christian and a friend of Bassanio's. Jessica, disguised as a boy, elopes with Lorenzo, taking money and jewels with her from Shylock's house. Bassanio leaves for Belmont.

ACT THREE In Venice, the news is that Antonio's ships have miscarried. Shylock informs Antonio, by now under guard, that he intends exacting the terms of his bond. In Belmont Bassanio gains Portia's love and, to her joy, chooses the right casket (lead). News is brought by Lorenzo of Antonio's plight. An immediate double marriage is proposed (Nerissa and Gratiano are following their betters into wedlock), so that Bassanio can journey to Venice and Antonio. After Bassanio's departure, Portia leaves Belmont in the charge of Lorenzo and Jessica, claiming that she and Nerissa intend withdrawing to a convent until their husbands' return.

ACT FOUR In Venice, Antonio is brought to trial. Shylock refuses all pleas for clemency by the Duke of Venice, and Bassanio's offer to pay three times the original debt. A young lawyer (Portia, using the name Balthasar) is introduced by the Duke. Shylock is deaf to Portia's eloquent plea for mercy and, led on by Portia, insists on the justice and legality of his bond. Shylock is routed when Portia declares that no provision has been made in the bond for the spilling of blood as the flesh is removed. When Shylock demands repayment in money, Portia retaliates with an old Venetian law that demands for the state the goods of any alien who has conspired against the life of a Venetian citizen. Shylock is allowed to keep half his goods on the condition (which he complies with) that he turn Christian; Antonio, who is given the other half, states his intentions of keeping the property in trust for Jessica and Lorenzo.

ACT FIVE The three married pairs (Portia and Bassanio,

Lorenzo and Jessica, Nerissa and Gratiano), together with Antonio, are reunited at Belmont. Portia's presence at the trial is revealed and Antonio learns, through Portia, that some of his ships have been saved.

Critical commentary

The Merchant of Venice has probably attracted more twentieth-century critical comment than any other of Shakespeare's comedies. Much of this has hinged on the characterization of Shylock. Even in the nineteenth century actors were tempted by Shylock's tragic potential, the ease with which he could be made to dominate the play. For the twentieth century, Shylock's Jewishness has posed special problems: if, as can be argued, Shakespeare intended Shylock as a stock Jewish villain, can we respond to him as such? There are anyway ambiguities in the play, not all of which can be dismissed as the fantasies of an anachronistic twentieth-century liberalism.

It is as well to start with those aspects of the play about which there is a reasonable degree of agreement. *The Merchant* is the only one of Shakespeare's comedies where the actual geographical situation (as opposed to the ideas with which Shakespeare himself might invest a place) is of material importance. Venice for the Elizabethans was a by-word for splendour and cosmopolitanism: ten years after *The Merchant*, in *Othello*, Shakespeare was to demonstrate how another alien (Othello is black, Shylock Jewish) would find himself out of his depth among the super-subtle Venetians. In *The Merchant*, it is Venice's financial power that Shakespeare finds most intriguing. In his book *The Dyer's Hand** W. H. Auden sees as a critical difference between English and Venetian society the fact that in Venice:

*The relevant extracts from the books by W. H. Auden and John Palmer are included in *Shakespeare's Comedies* edited by Laurence Lerner (Penguin), which has a particularly full section on *The Merchant of Venice*.

Money has ceased to be simply a convenient medium of exchange and has become a form of social power which can be gained or lost.

The Merchant is a play about money. Two narrative devices of a fairy-tale logic and improbability (the casket test and the 'merry bond') are linked to each other and linked to the real world by their common concern with money. We take it on trust that Bassanio falls in love with Portia, but her personal, aesthetic appeal is inseparable from the lure of her money, as his description of her to Antonio makes clear:

> – her sunny locks
> Hang on her temples like a golden fleece;
> Which makes her seat of Belmont Colchos' strond,
> And many Jasons come in quest of her. (I.i)

Intended more comically, but with a similar underlying logic, is Shylock's reaction to Jessica's defection: 'My daughter! O my ducats! O my daughter!' (II.viii, as described by Salanio to Salarino). For Shylock, his sense of Jessica's loss is indistinguishable from his sense of financial loss.

The implacable hatred between Antonio and Shylock has its roots in their antithetical attitudes to money. Antonio has an orthodox Christian's distaste for usury and when Shylock produces Biblical justification for making money 'breed', Antonio retorts, 'a breed of barren metal'. (I.iii) Shylock finds Antonio's liberality threatening:

> I hate him for he is a Christian;
> But more for that in low simplicity
> He lends out money gratis, and brings down
> The rate of usance here with us in Venice. (I.iii)

The connection between religion and money attitudes is not arbitrary. John Palmer, in his book, *Comic Characters in Shakespeare** argues that Antonio's Christian carelessness

*The relevant extracts from the books by W. H. Auden and John Palmer are included in *Shakespeare's Comedies* edited by Laurence Lerner (Penguin), which has a particularly full section on *The Merchant of Venice*.

makes his submission to Shylock's bond plausible; that Shakespeare's intention was 'to contrast the narrow, alert and suspicious character of the Jew, member of a persecuted race, with the free, careless and confident disposition of the Christian sure of his place in the sun.'

As in a number of other comedies, Shakespeare shows us, in Venice and Belmont, two different worlds reacting on one another. Belmont is an enchanted place, an Elysium for the chosen, presided over by Portia, who is dispenser of money, justice and harmony. Venice is the harsh, mercantile world from which all the chief characters except Shylock finally retreat, in preference for Belmont. The obvious differences between the two worlds are underlined by the way time appears to operate differently in each. Bassanio sets out for Belmont from Venice as soon as he has the money and the bond is sealed. He elects to do the casket test immediately rather than linger in uncertainty. (III.ii) In Venice, meanwhile, the bond, set for three months, has expired. In Belmont time stands still; Venice's time is marked by bills, bonds, completion dates.

This brings us to one of *The Merchant*'s central ambiguities. Can we accept that Bassanio, and hence Gratiano and Lorenzo, deserve the permanent freedom from anxiety offered by Belmont? In an isolated fairy-tale world, Bassanio's victory with the caskets would be sufficient justification: he has shown himself able to distinguish real worth from deceptively tempting appearances. But Belmont is not isolated. The real world of Venice makes frequent encroachments, and in Venice Bassanio is a young man who has spent more than he has and needs a rich wife: Portia's gold is important to him, though he has the wit to realize what the caskets require of him and to choose lead. And with him in Belmont are included Lorenzo and Gratiano, careless young men who are dependent on other people's money. The question of desert and justice would not concern us – harmony in Shakespearean comedy commonly includes the weak as well as the strong – were it not that so much of the play, culminating in the court scene, is about justice.

Any ambivalent feelings we have about Shylock, and about the treatment meted out to him in the play, are of a different order. The sentimentality that a twentieth-century audience might be expected to feel about Jews ought not to be allowed to cloud the fact that Shylock, by demanding a pound of Antonio's flesh, puts himself beyond the human pale. Moreover, his shrill insistence on justice untempered by mercy for Antonio influences the Duke's and Portia's judgment of him. Shylock is rightly excluded from Belmont, and from the possibility of reconciliation: he has no place there, not only because of his inhumanity, but because of his austerity – a quality alien to the spirit of comedy, and for Shylock part of the sacramental dignity of his religion. He replies to an invitation of Bassanio's to dinner:

> I will buy with you, sell with you, talk with you, walk with you,
> and so following; but I will not eat with you, drink with you,
> nor pray with you. (I.iii)

The problem with Shylock is not, as it is with Bassanio, of reaching a conclusion about his ethical merit in relation to his fate in the play. It is that, as a character, he easily over-powers all the other characters in depth and authenticity. His very language is different – clipped, intense, passionate, remarkable for the absence of metaphor – to the extent that he has his own idiom:

> Fair sir, you spet on me on Wednesday last;
> You spurn'd me such a day; another time
> You call'd me dog; and for these courtesies
> I'll lend you this much moneys? (I.iii)

Shakespeare may well have intended Shylock to be a stock Jewish villain, but he clearly acquired in the writing of the play an imaginative grasp of the Jew's predicament: 'Hath not a Jew eyes? hath not a Jew hands, organs, dimensions, senses, affections, passions?' (III.i) It is unlikely that Shakespeare conceived Shylock as an archetype of a perse-cuted race, given the climate of his own times; but he provided temptation enough for critics to read him and actors to play him in that way.

The Merchant of Venice has become so much Shylock's play that one is apt to overlook that the merchant of the title is Antonio. He is a melancholic, withdrawn figure, no fit hero for romantic comedy. Indeed, his fate illustrates the inherent cruelty of Shakespearean comic harmony. In the final scene, tagging along behind the newly married into the lighted Belmont is the wifeless Antonio. Salanio has said of Antonio's feelings for Bassanio earlier in the play: 'I think he only loves the world for him.' (II.viii) In the trial scene, when Bassanio offers his own life in place of his benefactor's, Antonio replies: 'I am a tainted wether of the flock,/ Meetest for death' (IV.i).

We know from the *Sonnets* that Shakespeare too, loved a man. In *The Merchant of Venice* and later, as we shall see, in *Twelfth Night*, he shows himself aware that the harmony expressed in marriage, with which he closes his comedies, could exclude; and the hint of melancholy which he allows himself preserves the endings of these plays from glossy artificiality.

Much Ado about Nothing

DATE 1598

PRINCIPAL CHARACTERS

Don Pedro: Prince of Arragon

Claudio ⎱ fellow soldiers and
Benedick ⎰ friends of Pedro

Don John: Pedro's villainous bastard brother

Borachio ⎱ Don John's followers
Conrade ⎰ and accomplices

Leonato: Governor of Messina

Hero: His daughter

Antonio: His brother

Beatrice: His niece

Margaret and Ursula: Their gentlewomen

Friar Francis
Balthazar: Don Pedro's servant
Dogberry and Verges: Constable and Headborough
SCENE Messina

Plot

ACT ONE Don Pedro and his retinue, newly returned from
the wars, are being entertained by Leonato, the Governor of
Messina. Claudio falls in love with Hero, the Governor's
daughter, and Don Pedro undertakes to woo her on his
friend's behalf at a masked ball that evening. When Don
John hears of Claudio's hopes he determines to make mischief for him. Recently, and only formally reconciled to his
brother Don Pedro, he bears Claudio a grudge: 'That
young start-up hath all the glory of my overthrow.' (I.iii)
Meanwhile, a witty antagonism has been established
between Benedick, a professed misogynist, and Beatrice,
who affects to scorn men.

ACT TWO Don Pedro gains Hero for Claudio at the masked
ball but not before Claudio has shown his gullibility in
believing, on the strength of Don John's insinuations, that
Pedro has wooed Hero for himself. Friendship is restored
and a scheme is hatched by Pedro to while away the week
until the wedding: Beatrice and Benedick are to be made to
believe that each loves the other and is concealing that love
through pride. Benedick, the first victim, overhears Pedro,
Claudio and Leonato discuss Beatrice's agonizing love for
him; he at once capitulates on his misogyny and resolves to
return her love. A more sinister scheme has meanwhile been
planned by Don John and Borachio: Borachio will talk with
Margaret, Hero's gentlewoman, at Hero's bedroom window, dressed as her mistress, in full view of Pedro and
Claudio. The prospective bridegroom will mistake Margaret
for Hero; Hero will be dishonoured and the marriage
balked.

ACT THREE Beatrice is tricked by Hero and Ursula into a
belief in Benedick's love. Don Pedro and Claudio prove to

be equally malleable victims when Don John tells them he has proof of Hero's dishonesty – proof which will be staged the night before the wedding. Help is on hand for Hero from an unexpected quarter, however. When Borachio boasts to Conrade that the scene at the window has been staged and has successfully poisoned Claudio's mind against his bride, he is overheard by the Watch and he and Conrade are arrested. Dogberry and Verges, bumbling and incompetent custodians of law and order, are informed of the villainy by their prisoners, Borachio and Conrade, and visit Leonato just before the wedding with the news; Leonato is too busy to listen and dismisses them.

ACT FOUR At the church, Claudio publicly rejects Hero, who falls into a swoon and is left for dead by her bridegroom and Don Pedro. Friar Francis, who was to have officiated at the wedding, is convinced of Hero's innocence and tells Leonato to secrete his daughter and give out news of her death; this pretence will, it is hoped, 'change slander to remorse' in Claudio and allow proof to emerge of Hero's innocence. Beatrice and Benedick confess their love to each other; as proof of love Beatrice demands that Benedick kill his friend Claudio to avenge the innocent Hero. Dogberry and Verges, hearing of Hero's 'death' decide to confront Leonato with Borachio and Conrade.

ACT FIVE Hero's name is cleared when the villains are produced and Benedick's challenge to Claudio is cancelled by the latter's remorse. Leonato is responsible for the play's final scheme: Claudio, as proof of his penitence, must agree to marry a hitherto unmentioned niece of Leonato's. Presented with his new bride, Claudio discovers Hero, freed now from her death-in-life. Beatrice and Benedick announce their own impending marriage. The celebrations are complete when word is brought of Don John's capture.

Critical commentary

Much Ado has always been justly praised for its verbal brilliance. More than any of the other comedies, this play depicts people who are self-consciously at leisure: soldiers enjoying a respite from the wars, with pretty girls on hand to entertain them. They pass their time in devising schemes and in sharpening their wits on each other. An elegant and courtly example is set by Don Pedro, the play's highest ranking character, while Beatrice is easily the wittiest of Shakespeare's heroines. Although in terms of the play's structure Hero is nominally the first lady, audiences have always awarded the accolade to her more articulate cousin.

Yet beneath the brilliant surface, *Much Ado* is an uneasy blend of the romantic and the more detached and satiric comic traditions. In Elizabethan satirical comedy, as we shall see in more detail in relation to Ben Jonson's plays, the fundamental relationship within a play is between the per-petrator of a trick and his gull: since Jonson maintains total detachment throughout, the audience feels free to enjoy the trickery of the knaves and to revel in its own superior aware-ness of events. The plot of *Much Ado* is an elaborate network of schemes and tricks: Don John tricks Claudio into believ-ing first, that Don Pedro has stolen a march on him with Hero, and later in Hero's impurity; Claudio himself, along with Leonato and Don Pedro, tricks Benedick into believing in Beatrice's love for him; Beatrice is similarly duped by her intimates, Hero and Ursula; Claudio is deceived by the Friar into thinking Hero dead, and by Leonato into a belief in a 'second Hero'. There is scarcely a character in the play who is not either a perpetrator or a victim of a scheme. Yet Shakespeare does not attempt a Jonsonian detachment: with it all, the romantic interest is maintained, the audi-ence's sympathies are engaged at certain points. Hence the uneasiness.

The situation that develops between Claudio and Hero is one of potential tragedy: indeed, the theme of the jealous husband was to be handled tragically in *Othello* and with more serious regard to pernicious consequences in *The Winter's Tale*. Here the theme is treated comically – comic-ally in the sense that in romantic comedy marriage is felt to heal all wounds – but the comic solution seems artificial and inappropriate in *Much Ado*. This is entirely due to the characterization of Claudio. Hero it is easy to accept as a victim but not Claudio, although he is technically Don John's dupe. The orthodox line on Claudio is lucidly expounded in *Shakespeare and Elizabethan Poetry* (Chatto and Windus) by M. C. Bradbrook,* who urges us to see Claudio as an Elizabethan audience would have done. Claudio falls in love with Hero on sight – 'In mine eye she is the sweetest lady that ever I looked on' (I.i), without the exploration of character that precedes Beatrice and Benedick's lovemaking. When he receives what he takes to be adverse evidence about her character, his visual image of her is unchallenged, but he thinks that for the first time he is learning what lies behind it:

> You seem to me as Dian in her orb,
> As chaste as is the bud ere it be blown;
> But you are more intemperate in your blood ... (IV.i)

Yet one feels that the 'orthodox' interpretation accounts only partially for Claudio's behaviour: Shakespeare was not content to leave him there, a romantic and rather superficial young man who is easily duped. What the audience finds offensive about Claudio is his flippancy after Hero's apparent death: cracking feeble jokes with Benedick about the changes Beatrice's love has wrought in him (V.i), and with Don Pedro just as he is about to take on the 'second' Hero: 'I'll hold my mind, were she an Ethiop' (V.iv); remaining quite unmoved by Leonato's grief. This contrasts badly with those areas where Shakespeare has deliberately enlisted the audience's sympathies – with Beatrice's unswerving loyalty to her cousin, and with the poignancy of Leonato's grief at the moment when he feels his child to be guilty:

> But mine, and mine I lov'd, and mine I prais'd,
> And mine that I was proud on, mine so much
> That I myself was to myself not mine. (IV. i)

---

*M. C. Bradbrook's views on *Much Ado* can be conveniently found in *Shakespeare – Modern Essays in Criticism* edited by Leonard F. Dean (OUP).

Claudio's gulling by Don John, although the subject-matter is dangerously close to the tragic, comes within the province of romantic comedy; Claudio's levity suggests a different kind of play – the dark comedies on which Shakespeare was to embark a few years after *Much Ado*, in which the whole basis of love and honour are treated with more cynicism than in the romantic comedies.

Audiences have no reservations about the Beatrice and Benedick sub-plot. Linked to the main plot by the common themes of credulity and self-deceit, Shakespeare explores through Beatrice and Benedick the perennially enjoyable theme of lovers too proud to admit their love. The humour lies, not so much in the tricks played on them, but in the eagerness with which they seize the excuse to abandon their former antagonism. In a number of comedies Shakespeare demonstrates that love has its roots in the imagination rather than the reason, and exploits for its humour the way that young men particularly will seek to find a rational basis for their love. This source of humour finds its supreme moment in Benedick's justification to himself for his change of heart: 'the world must be peopled. When I said I would die a bachelor, I did not think I should live till I were married.' (II.iii) Beatrice is a heroine who is as distinguished in her passion as in her wit, as when she demands of Benedick as proof of his love, 'Kill Claudio.' (IV.i) Her loyalty in the face of adverse appearances provides an important point of emotional gravity in a play where characters are so easily gulled. The plain-spokenness of these lovers – Benedick abandons his attempts at love poetry with: 'no, I was not born under a riming planet, nor I cannot woo in festival terms.' (V.ii) – supplies a welcome foil to the more formally correct wooing of Claudio and Hero.

The interludes in the play which a modern reader is likely to find most tedious, although they stage well, are the Dogberry and Verges scenes. These two do, however, contribute crucially both to the plot and the theme. The fact that it is given to them, incompetent as they are, to unmask the villains, deprives the story of much of its tragic potential.

They share with their betters a respect for words, although they lack the courtiers' skill: the verbal humour that they contribute is in the form of malapropisms. Dogberry's belief in his own cleverness parallels the pride and self-importance of the major characters; self-importance is burlesqued in him, while his superiors learn in the course of the play that they have trusted their own brains or judgment too far.

As You Like It

DATE Between 1598 and 1600
PRINCIPAL CHARACTERS
Duke Senior: Living in exile in the forest of Arden
Duke Frederick: His usurping brother
Rosalind: Duke Senior's daughter
Celia: Duke Frederick's daughter
Oliver: Son and heir of the late Sir Rowland de Boys
Orlando: His ill-treated younger brother
Jaques: Another son of Sir Rowland, in attendance on the banished duke
Amiens: Another lord attending on Duke Senior
Le Beau: A courtier attending Frederick
Sir Oliver Martext: A vicar
Touchstone: A court jester
Charles: A wrestler
Audrey: The country-wench who marries Touchstone
Adam: Oliver's servant, loyal to Orlando
Dennis: Another servant to Oliver
Silvius and Phebe: A pair of pastoral lovers
Corin: Another shepherd
SCENE France: Frederick's court, Oliver's house, the Forest of Arden

Plot

ACT ONE brings discord to a head in two families. Orlando upbraids his elder brother Oliver with the ill-treatment he receives from him, claiming that he is treated more as a servant than as a brother. To prove his nobility, Orlando undertakes a wrestling match against Charles, a professional wrestler, at Duke Frederick's court. Orlando routs Charles, to the admiration of Celia, Duke Frederick's daughter, and Rosalind, his niece, who lives as her cousin's companion while her father is in exile. Rosalind and Orlando fall in love but before they have opportunity to make their feelings known to each other they are both dismissed from Frederick's court: Orlando because his father was greatly beloved by the exiled Duke; Rosalind because the Duke is now nervous about her presence at his court. Celia follows Rosalind into exile, Rosalind disguised as Ganymede, a shepherd, Celia as Aliena, a shepherdess and his sister. Their intention is to seek Rosalind's father in the Forest of Arden. With them goes Touchstone, the court jester.

ACT TWO Rosalind and Celia buy themselves a cottage in Arden with Corin, a real shepherd, as sitting tenant. In another part of the forest Duke Senior has set up court, with the melancholic Jaques among his courtiers. The exodus to Arden gathers force when Orlando learns from Adam, the servant, that Oliver's mind is further poisoned against him: the pair set off to join Duke Senior, eventually introducing themselves to his court at sword point, Orlando demanding food for the famished Adam. They are made welcome.

ACT THREE Rosalind finds pinned to a tree verses to herself from Orlando. As Ganymede she offers herself to Orlando as a surrogate Rosalind: by wooing him, 'Ganymede' claims that Orlando will be cured of his love for Rosalind. Touchstone, meanwhile, has found Audrey, a sluttish country wench whom he intends marrying. The ranks of lovers are further augmented by the introduction of Silvius, an ardent shepherd, and Phebe, his scornful beloved. Matters are complicated when it becomes clear that Phebe has fallen in love with Ganymede/Rosalind.

ACT FOUR The 'feigned' wooing of Ganymede/Rosalind by Orlando proceeds apace. Orlando's brother Oliver joins the forest community: sent by Duke Frederick to speed Orlando to his death on some trumped-up charge, he describes to Rosalind and Celia (who are still disguised) how Orlando rescued him from a lion. Oliver is now a thoroughly reformed man.

ACT FIVE Celia and Oliver have fallen in love – a circumstance which makes both Rosalind and Orlando impatient for the reality behind the pretend courtship. Rosalind/ Ganymede, setting herself up as *dea ex machina*, promises to bring Orlando his beloved, Duke Senior his daughter, and to impress on Phebe the futility of her love for Ganymede. All is duly accomplished in the final scene. News is brought of Duke Frederick's conversion: he will hand power to his brother and become a hermit. Jaques decides to join him.

Critical commentary

In *As You Like It*, and in *Twelfth Night*, which followed it, Shakespeare is generally felt to have reached the height of his comic powers. *Twelfth Night*'s alternative title, *What You Will*, is a close analogue for *As You Like It* and in these plays particularly Shakespeare seems bent on creating that sense of radiant happiness which is the finest potential of romantic comedy.

As in a number of Shakespeare's other comedies, *As You Like It* juxtaposes two worlds, each with its own significance. Institutionalized self-seeking characterizes Frederick's court and Oliver's house, while Arden is the place of refuge from the evils of civilization – the latter so evocative that it has become a prototype of the pastoral idyll. Closely adapted from Lodge's tale *Rosalynde*, *As You Like It* is the closest Shakespeare ever came to writing a pastoral romance. The play owes much of its success, however, to the degree of detachment he managed to preserve from the pastoral conventions, which has the effect of making the final happiness more convincing, less artificial, than in conventional pastoral. Villainy, on the other hand, is treated with studied conventionality. The villains are characterized by a generalized, psychologically underplayed malice. This leaves the audience prepared to accept their final conversion; but more important, those elements in human nature which threaten the comic spirit and are perhaps too apparent in *The Merchant of Venice* and *Much Ado*, the two immediately preceding comedies, are never allowed to impinge on the world Shakespeare creates in *As You Like It*.

The pastoral, popular in Shakespeare's time, has its roots in classical literature: as long as there were cities, men were dreaming of a place of escape. What makes Arden special, however, is that it is something more than a fantasy of escape; it carries its own perils. It is a place where the wind blows and chills, and Orlando and Adam are nearly famished for want of food; but the inclemency of the elements is one of the benefits that Arden offers. Duke Senior says of his exposure to harsh conditions: 'This is no flattery; these are counsellors/ That feelingly persuade me what I am.' (II.i) *As You Like It* gives expression to an idea to which Shakespeare was to return in *King Lear*: that men can only discover their true nature in relation to created nature; that towns and the props of civilization 'flatter' us into a distorted view of ourselves. Clearly, the idea of Arden as a place of refuge is present, but the refuge it offers is from the destructive side of human nature; it is not a refuge from life. When Duke Senior and his court are entertained by a song, this is the aspect of Arden that the song celebrates:

Blow, blow, thou winter wind,
Thou art not so unkind
As man's ingratitude . . . (II.vii)

The exiles in Arden exhibit, by their behaviour, a rejection of the self-seeking values of conventional society. Orlando carries the exhausted Adam (II.vi); he demands food for his servant at sword point, but the violence is unnecessary because the food is freely given. Celia follows her cousin into exile rather than see her banished alone.

The proper subject of pastoral writing has always been love, and Shakespeare explores the subject in *As You Like It* through four very different couples. Here too, the pastoral conception of love, while not ridiculed, is 'placed', viewed with some detachment. Silvius, the adoring shepherd sighing out his love under the trees, and Phebe, the contemptuous shepherdess, secure in her own powers, are the pair who conform most closely to the pastoral norm. Shakespeare could have used them as a charming pictorial vignette, but the dénouement of their relationship is realistic enough: Silvius, used by Phebe to deliver a love-letter (which she claims is a letter of abuse) to Ganymede, discovers his mistress's potential for deceit; Phebe, cheated of Ganymede when 'he' reappears as Rosalind, settles for the man in Silvius if not for the individual.

In romantic comedy the recognition of underlying sexual need is rarely explicit: the emphasis is on the overwhelming attractiveness of the individual rather than on the instinctive need for a mate. In none of the relationships in *As You Like It* however, is the sexual basis ignored — Rosalind tells Orlando that Celia and Oliver are 'in the very wrath of love, and they will together' (V.ii) – but its most bald expression is given to Touchstone. He has no illusions about Audrey as a person (her 'foulness' is made much of throughout) but he knows exactly what he wants of her: 'man hath his desires; and as pigeons bill, so wedlock would be nibbling' (III.iii).

Rosalind and Orlando represent the play's ideal of love – completely taken with each other as individuals, loyal and tested. The image could cloy with its sweetness and seem unapproachably unreal. Shakespeare's success with the play's central romantic relationship is in the characterization of Rosalind (Orlando, like most of his young comic heroes, is not in himself particularly impressive). Like Viola, her successor in *Twelfth Night*, Rosalind displays wit and a sense of exhilaration in a crisis – qualities which have ensured her popularity through many changes of fashion in heroines. Rosalind's disguise as Ganymede is crucial. There is a sense in Shakespeare's work in which characters learn through 'feigning' as children learn through play: through their 'mock' wooing, Rosalind and Orlando deepen their experience of each other and test out the ground; this is more important than the standard test of Orlando's love that is Rosalind's justification for the game. Moreover, Rosalind, as Ganymede, is allowed a measure of cynicism: 'men have died from time to time, and worms have eaten them, but not for love.' (IV.i) At the remove of disguise she can express ideas which, as a woman, may disturb her, without endangering the ideal love that Rosalind is meant to suggest. Psychological realism and romance – irreconcilable in some of the other comedies – are both preserved.

So Rosalind 'places' her love, distances it for herself and for the audience, as Ganymede. Jaques, Duke Senior's melancholy attendant lord, serves the same function in relation to the play as a whole. Convinced of man's folly, and of the folly of love in particular, he stands outside the play's network of relationships. His sourness is to some extent rooted in the conviction that hope of happiness and of a better life are a snare and a delusion. In his most famous speech, beginning: 'All the world's a stage/And all the men and women merely players . . .' (II.vii) he claims that man has no control over his own life; that he is a 'player' in a pre-ordained drama, not the author of his own fate. It is Jaques's cynicism, rather than the wickedness of the villains, that is the irreconcilable element in *As You Like It*. But, because there is more than a hint of the poseur about Jaques, his cynicism, while touching the brightness with shadow, never finally undermines the play's values.

Twelfth Night; or What You Will

DATE 1601

PRINCIPAL CHARACTERS

Orsino: Duke of Illyria

Olivia: A countess, beloved of the Duke

Viola: Survivor of a shipwreck, known for most of the play as 'Cesario', the Duke's page

Sebastian: Her brother

Sir Toby Belch: Olivia's uncle
Sir Andrew Aguecheek: Sir Toby's friend, Olivia's suitor
Valentine ⎫ The Duke's
Curio ⎭ attendant gentlemen
Maria: Olivia's serving woman
Malvolio: Olivia's steward
Feste: Olivia's clown
Fabian: A gentleman in Olivia's service
Antonio: A sea captain, friend of Sebastian
Another sea captain, friend of Viola
SCENE Illyria

Plot

ACT ONE Orsino, Duke of Illyria, is completely possessed by his love for the countess Olivia: she has sworn to mourn her dead brother for seven years, a vow which excludes the possibility of marriage. A young girl, Viola, is shipwrecked off the Illyrian coast. Thinking that she has lost her brother in the shipwreck she assumes a boy's disguise, aided by a friendly sea captain. Using the name 'Cesario' she is taken on as the Duke's page, quickly finds favour with him and is made his emissary to Olivia. The play's first emotional complication is Viola's love for Orsino. Matters are further complicated when Olivia falls in love with 'Cesario'. The audience has meanwhile been introduced to Sir Toby Belch, Olivia's drunken kinsman, Sir Andrew Aguecheek, his foolish sidekick, who is being encouraged by Sir Toby to seek Olivia in marriage, Maria, Olivia's gentlewoman, who endeavours to moderate their excesses, and Malvolio, Olivia's steward, who is hostile to the debauchery of Sir Toby and his friends.

ACT TWO Viola's brother Sebastian, himself preserved from the wreck, has likewise found his way to Illyria. He is accompanied by Antonio, the captain who saved his life and an old enemy of Orsino's. Antonio decides nonetheless to risk his life in Illyria on account of his love for Sebastian. Olivia makes her love known to 'Cesario'. Hostilities reach crisis point between Sir Toby and his retinue and Malvolio, Olivia's austere and upright steward, when Malvolio attempts to quell Sir Toby's nocturnal revellings. Maria promises to devise a means of revenge on Malvolio. Her trick is a complete success: Malvolio, observed by Sir Toby, Sir Andrew and Fabian, finds a letter, apparently in Olivia's hand, but in fact written by Maria. The letter hints at the mistress's love for her steward and incites him to behaviour that Maria knows will be repugnant to Olivia.

ACT THREE It has become apparent in Olivia's household that Olivia favours Cesario. Sir Toby and Fabian encourage Sir Andrew to challenge Cesario to a duel. The fighters are timid and incompetent. Antonio, passing by at the time, intervenes on Cesario's behalf, mistaking 'him' for Sebastian. Antonio is arrested by Orsino's officers, and when he begs Cesario to return a purse that he had in fact given to Sebastian, he is appalled by what he takes to be Sebastian's 'feigned' ignorance. Malvolio, meanwhile, has appeared before Olivia in the manner recommended by the letter – over-familiar, smiling frequently, wearing yellow stockings, cross-gartered. Olivia, thinking her steward mad, has him placed under Sir Toby's surveillance.

ACT FOUR Sebastian, mistaken on all sides for Cesario, is urged by Olivia to go through a formal betrothal ceremony. Readily embracing his luck (Olivia is rich and beautiful), Sebastian agrees. Malvolio, meanwhile, incarcerated by Sir Toby as a madman, is visited by Olivia's Fool Feste, disguised as Sir Topas, a curate. After much teasing, Feste finally gives Malvolio paper with which to reveal his sorry plight to Olivia.

ACT FIVE Viola bears the brunt of all the confusions of identity – accused by Antonio of ingratitude, Orsino and Olivia of treachery (for denying all knowledge of the betrothal), by Sir Andrew and Toby of offering them violence – until Sebastian appears and all is revealed. Orsino immediately transfers his affections to Viola, Olivia is prepared to settle for Sebastian, and a third couple is provided by Sir Toby and Maria, brought together by the jest on Malvolio. Only Malvolio, offered justice by Olivia when the trick is exposed, retains his grudges beyond the final curtain.

Critical commentary

Presumably written for a Christmas entertainment, *Twelfth Night* is the last, and arguably the finest, of Shakespeare's romantic comedies. It is in many ways a perfect synthesis of elements from the earlier comedies: shipwreck and identical twins are both found in *The Comedy of Errors;* Viola, like earlier heroines, disguises herself as a boy; more specifically, like Julia in *The Two Gentlemen of Verona* she acts as page and emissary for her beloved; like Rosalind she inspires love in another woman. Malvolio is gulled and observed as he swallows the bait, as Beatrice and Benedick had been in *Much Ado*. The melancholic man who loves and suffers for a younger man is not only paralleled in *The Merchant* but in both plays is called Antonio. If *Twelfth Night*'s derivativeness suggests that Shakespeare was aware of coming to the end of the comic road, then it must be stressed that the play bears no marks of weariness.

The twin themes of *Twelfth Night* are deceit and self-deception. In his article 'The Masks of Twelfth Night'* Joseph H. Summers has pointed out that as the feast of the Epiphany (the twelfth day of Christmas) was an occasion for dressing-up and for trickery, so all the more prominent characters in the play are either deliberately assuming a mask against the world (Viola, who poses as a boy and Feste, the professional fool) or wearing masks by which they are themselves deceived. The second group of characters (the self-deceivers) are disabused in the course of the play. Within this group is Orsino, who is not so much in love with Olivia as in love with the idea of love. It is not without relevance that we do not see him face to face with his 'beloved' until the final scene. Instead of actually seeing

*Joseph L. Summers' essay is included in *Shakespeare: Modern Essays in Criticism*, edited by Leonard F. Dean (OUP).

her, he prefers to languish in the hothouse atmosphere of his court, nourishing his emotions. His first words are 'If music be the food of love, play on' (I.i). When he has had a surfeit of music he retires to 'sweet beds of flowers'; his reason – 'Love-thoughts lie rich when canopied with bowers.' The transfer of his affections to Viola represents a kind of maturity; he has at least known her as an individual, if not as a woman.

Olivia too is acting out an idea – the idea of the mourning sister. When we first learn of her vow through one of Orsino's messengers, there is a hint in the description that her grief is not alive and active so much as pickled:

And water once a day her chamber round
With eye-offending brine; all this, to season
A brother's dead love. (I.i)

By falling in love she comes to terms with her real rather than assumed nature, her mask having been adopted to protect herself from her own potential for passion. If she is afraid of men then it is apt that her transition from mourning sister to Sebastian's wife should be effected through her love for the boy/girl Cesario/Viola, who is incapable of threatening masculinity. The ready acquiescence of Sebastian should not disturb a modern audience. There is undoubtedly something of the adventurer about him, but in the world of Shakespearean comedy he would be a fool indeed to allow any scruple to stand in the way of the good fortune he is offered. Shakespeare has rightly underplayed Sebastian psychologically: if we were given more insight into his thinking, he might become offensive.

It is Viola who is responsible for both Orsino and Olivia dropping their masks and who provides the play with a centre of emotional realism. There is a striking parallel between her circumstances and Olivia's: Viola too has lost a beloved brother, or so she thinks, but she is more resilient in her grief than Olivia and has a sturdier instinct for self-preservation. When she falls in love with Orsino, her situation is inevitably painful and she cannot resist the odd oblique reference to her state:

My father had a daughter lov'd a man,
As it might be, perhaps, were I a woman,
I should your lordship. (II.iv)

– but in general she is buoyant, humourous and as optimistic as circumstances permit.

The themes of deceit and self-delusion are combined in the superb sub-plot – the gulling of Malvolio by Maria and Sir Toby. The mechanical deceit practised on Malvolio is in fact of secondary importance to the revelation of the steward's cherished image of himself. Indeed, Maria's scheme works so well because she knows her victim so thoroughly and the audience is prepared to accept Malvolio's undoing by earlier indications of his character: he lacks generosity – something that the other self-deceived characters, Orsino and Olivia, pre-eminently exhibit. The 'justice' of Maria's trick lies in the extent to which he reveals his own fantasies about himself before he picks up the deceiving letter. He pictures himself 'in a branch'd velvet gown' – 'having come from a day-bed, – where I have left Olivia sleeping', enjoying the spectacle of 'Toby . . . curtseying' before him. The trick itself is almost superfluous.

There is evidence that for Shakespeare's first readers and audiences Malvolio was the star attraction. Some twentieth-century critics have been more ambivalent in their enthusiasm, claiming that the trick played on Malvolio is of a cruelty in excess of the offence – despite the fact that Ben Jonson, for example, was more merciless towards his gulls. Within the terms of Elizabethan comedy Malvolio represents the enemy. Maria calls him a 'kind of Puritan' because he uses his office as steward to frustrate the spirit of pleasure in others: 'Dost thou think, because thou art virtuous, there shall be no more cakes and ale?' (II.iii) Toby asks him. One of the functions of comedy is to provide a suspended moment of pleasure in an uncertain world – an idea expressed in one of Feste's songs:

Present mirth hath present laughter;
What's to come is still unsure . . . (II.iii)

This is the principle that ensures Toby's inclusion in the happy ending, for all that, as his relationship with Sir Andrew illustrates, he is a parasite and an exploiter of the weak and foolish. The unease we feel about Malvolio is similar to the unease we feel about Shylock: within the terms of the play justice is done, but given the limitations of the trick, Shakespeare has made us too aware of Malvolio's inner life. The steward has his fantasies – exploited to the full for their humour, but the fact that he has them at all is human, even touching.

There is another parallel with *The Merchant* in *Twelfth Night*, a similar shadow cast on the matrimonial triumph. Each play has its Antonio who is prepared to risk everything for his love for a younger man and who is finally excluded from the pairing. In *Twelfth Night* however, a note of bitter passion enters with Antonio's horror of 'Sebastian's' perfidy: 'But o! how vile an idol proves this god . . . None can be call'd deform'd but the unkind' (III.iv). In *Twelfth Night* the bitterness can fade as the confusions of plot are unravelled: the deceit is not, as it were, germane to mankind, but of the playwright's own manufacturing, so that by the end of the play we can feel sad for Antonio rather than cynical about human nature. But the possibility of ingratitude and deceit has made itself felt, perhaps for Shakespeare more than for his audiences; and after this play he wrote no others where the possibility of human deceit could be dismissed so lightly, either explained away or banished from the stage.

There is other evidence in the play that Shakespeare was aware of mining the end of his comic seam. The chief reveller, Sir Toby, is elderly and his marriage to Maria does to some extent mark the end of his carousing. And Feste, who even more than Antonio is an outsider, a commentator rather than a participant in human affairs, is aware both of the transience of the happiness that the lovers are reaching after – 'Then come kiss me, sweet and twenty,/Youth's a stuff will not endure' (II.iii) – and of the world beyond the comic pool of light: 'For the rain it raineth every day.' (V.i) is the refrain of the song with which he closes the play.

4 Shakespeare: Dark Comedy

Roses have thorns, and silver fountains mud . . . (Sonnet 35)

During the years 1600 to 1608 Shakespeare was mainly employed in the writing of his great tragic masterpieces. There are, however, a few exceptions: *Twelfth Night,* the last of the comedies, belonging to the early part of the period; and three plays which in many ways defy the normal classifications of genre – *Measure for Measure, All's Well that Ends Well* and *Troilus and Cressida.* These three have either been dismissed or welcomed by critics as 'problem plays'. 'Problem' in this context has a variety of connotations, from suggestions that Shakespeare was not absolutely sure what he wanted to say or achieve in these plays, or that if he was sure in his intentions he failed in the execution, to speculations that he might well have had problems in his own life at the time when they were written.

The three plays in this section have generally, for want of a term that suits them better, been included with the comedies. Technically, they are: none of them ends in the death of the principals, though death is closer to hand than in the true comedies; two of them, *Measure for Measure* and *All's Well*, close with marriage and on a note of reconciliation and forgiveness. The sense of achieved harmony, however, that characterizes the best of Shakespeare's romantic comedies is missing; we cannot in these plays accept the artificiality of the comic form. Aspects of human nature which in the earlier comedies are contained by the form – deceit, treachery, opportunism, lack of generosity and lust –

are brought to the centre of the stage. Some of these are the irreconcilable elements of the comedies – the nastiness that had to be overcome before happiness is achieved – whereas in these plays they are reconciled, but by violence.

The grafting of a comic form on such unpromising material – unpromising, that is, for comedy – produces ambiguities within the plays. Some ambiguity there is always in Shakespeare's work – the recognition of another viewpoint that is implicit in all irony – but the central problem here is how far we can assume that the ambiguity is intentional, and how far it reflected an unsureness on Shakespeare's part about his own intention.

The kind of ambiguity and the degree of assurance that we feel about the writer's intentions differ from play to play. In *Measure for Measure* Shakespeare is ostensibly holding up for admiration characters whom we cannot feel to be admirable. The audience's response could be due to a failure of execution on Shakespeare's part; but there is evidence in his undermining of his characters that he intended to leave his audience baffled. Our response to certain characters in *All's Well* is more straightforward, and certain ideals survive untarnished throughout the play: our difficulty here is with the unworthy hero who is offered a redemption that the audience would deny him. *Troilus and Cressida* demonstrates the vulnerability of ideals – in this case of love and of honour – in a world where people will shrink at nothing to achieve their ends; it is the closest to tragedy of the three plays. Differing more from each other than any other collection of plays grouped within a genre, they nonetheless stand together in their apartness from the rest of Shakespeare's work.

Measure for Measure

DATE 1603-4
PRINCIPAL CHARACTERS
Duke of Vienna.

Angelo: His deputy
Escalus: A respected lord and statesman
Claudio: Sentenced to execution by Angelo
Isabella: His sister
Lucio: Claudio's friend
Juliet: Claudio's beloved
Mariana: Once the betrothed of Angelo
Friars Thomas and Peter
Francisca: A nun
VIENNESE SUB-CULTURE:
Elbow: A constable
Froth: A victim of bawds
Mistress Overdone: Keeper of a brothel
Pompey: Overdone's servant
Abhorson: An executioner
Barnardine: A dissolute prisoner
SCENE Vienna

Plot

ACT ONE The Duke announces his departure from Vienna
for reasons kept deliberately obscure. Angelo, a man of
noted sanctity, is made his deputy. The Duke reveals the
purpose of his abdication to Friar Thomas: having allowed
Viennese laws to fall into abuse by his own permissiveness,
he looks to Angelo to reinforce them. The shift of power is
also intended as a test of Angelo: disguised as a Friar the
Duke will remain in Vienna and observe whether his
deputy's sanctity survives the exercising of power. Angelo's
first acts are to order the plucking down of the Viennese
brothels (to the consternation of Mistress Overdone, a noted
bawd), and the sentencing to death of Claudio, whose
beloved, Juliet, is pregnant by him. At Claudio's request
Lucio, a babbler and frequenter of brothels, persuades
Claudio's sister, Isabella, who has recently entered a convent as a novice, to plead with Angelo on her brother's
behalf.

ACT TWO Angelo is deaf to Isabella's pleas for mercy but

moved by her person; sexually tempted for the first time in his life he offers to release Claudio if Isabella surrenders her virginity to him. Isabella is appalled: 'More than our brother is our chastity.' (II.iv) The audience, meanwhile, has been introduced further to Viennese low life. The law, in the person of the incompetent Elbow, is demonstrably weak in its dealings with the wily pimp, Pompey. The Duke is presented in his ecclesiastical role, confessing Juliet.

ACT THREE The Friar/Duke visits Claudio in prison to prepare him for death; there he overhears Isabella telling Claudio of Angelo's scheme. Claudio is anxious for his sister's compliance and Isabella renounces him as a brother. The Duke takes Isabella aside with a plan of his own: if she agrees to Angelo's proposals, arrangements will be made for Mariana, once betrothed but now rejected by Angelo, to take Isabella's place in the deputy's bed. The Duke suffers the inconvenience of disguise when Lucio claims to be an intimate of the Duke, regaling the 'Friar' with stories of the Duke's womanizing.

ACT FOUR Mariana agrees to the bed-trick. The law catches up with Pompey, but he is allowed a remission of sentence if he agrees to assist Abhorson, the executioner. The Duke waits in the prison with the provost for Claudio's expected pardon but instead a letter arrives confirming the execution order and requiring Claudio's head to be sent to the deputy. The Duke prevails on the provost to spare Claudio and send the head of a prisoner who has recently died of fever. The Duke now prepares for his 'return'; Mariana and Isabella are instructed to plead their cause (Angelo's perfidy) at the city gates.

ACT FIVE The Duke 'returns' with great pomp. At first he dismisses as madness the accusations made against Angelo (both Mariana and Isabella, under instructions from the 'Friar' are claiming to have been deflowered by the deputy); the Duke then absents himself, confirms their accusations when he returns as 'Friar', and then reveals himself to have been Duke all along. Angelo is made to marry Mariana and is then sentenced to death. He is saved by the pleas for mercy by Mariana and, more importantly, by Isabella, who is moved to practise the mercy that she preached. Claudio is produced and allowed to marry Juliet. Lucio suffers for his slander: he is made to marry the whore whom he confided to the Friar Duke that he got with child. The Duke proposes marriage to Isabella who gives no answer.

Critical commentary

The relationship between *Measure for Measure* and the earlier comedies is obvious, but the links tend to emphasize the differences. In the romantic comedies the play's harmony is achieved, the characters come to terms with themselves, through the enlightening experience of love. In *Measure for Measure* the relationship between the sexes is central but the ideal of romantic love is heavily compromised throughout. The under-plot concerns the frequenters and keepers of the brothels, the exploitation implicit in the trade being encapsulated in the relationship between Pompey and Froth, his foolish and gullible customer; much of the verbal humour in these scenes derives from puns on venereal disease. Angelo's attempts to clean up the city are undermined by the confidence of the bawds that society will always find a place for them.

In romantic comedy the ideal of love may be burlesqued in an under-plot, though never as coarsely as it is in this play, but the attitude to love of the noble-born is still essentially noble. The most sympathetic pair of lovers in this play are Claudio and Juliet, but their reasons for delaying a ceremony that should have taken place are mercenary: 'Only for propagation of a dower/Remaining in the coffer of her friends' (I.ii). Much more interesting is Angelo's downfall. He has been able to preserve the unblemished austerity of his life because sexual temptation has never touched him: 'Ever till now, When men were fond, I smil'd and wonder'd how.' (II.ii) What he feels for Isabella is almost an inversion of the reverence that romantic lovers feel for the beloved; recognizing that no strumpet could have captured his imagination, he wonders whether Isabella's attraction is not the excitement of ravaging the citadel:

> Having waste ground enough,
> Shall we desire to raze the sanctuary,
> And pitch our evils there? (II.ii)

Most important, his experience of loving, or rather lusting after Isabella, fails to enhance his personality or to extend his vision of himself and others. The substitute in his bed passes unnoticed, the severity of his attitude towards Claudio is unsoftened. Once 'Isabella' is deflowered he wants to put the experience past him. He does, in fact, give us a reason for allowing Claudio's execution to go ahead: 'his riotous youth, with dangerous sense,/Might in the times to come have ta'en revenge' (IV.iv). Angelo relies on Isabella's modesty silencing her, but Claudio might have exposed him and Angelo's good name is of primary importance to him.

This brings us to another link with the romantic comedies. They all of them to some extent investigate the boundaries between illusion and reality: the nature of theatrical illusion is implicit; when a character assumes a disguise, the difference between what she is and what she seems is exploited; the plot of comedy is designed to 'cure' certain characters of their illusions about themselves. The idea of 'seeming' is central to Shakespeare's treatment of Angelo. The Duke distrusts his deputy from the beginning because he:

> scarce confesses
> That his blood flows, or that his appetite
> Is more to bread than stone: hence shall we see,
> If power change purpose, what our seemers be. (I.iii)

Angelo's 'seeming' differs from the seeming of the early comedies however in being both real and sinister: it is not the pretend 'seeming' of disguise. And when he can no longer retain his own illusions about himself he will go to

any lengths to preserve those illusions in the eyes of others –
to the extent of abusing the power invested in him.

Indeed, the nature of justice, like the nature of love,
comes under question in *Measure for Measure*. To take the
burlesque offered by Viennese low life first: when Elbow
tries to bring Pompey to justice, the foolish constable is
completely outwitted by the wily pimp, to the extent that
Escalus wonders 'Which is the wiser here? Justice, or
Iniquity?' (II.i) Elbow may have right on his side, but right
proves ineffectual where the criminal classes have a mon-
opoly of brains. When Pompey is finally brought to justice
he is made the executioner's assistant. The irony of this
scarcely needs elaborating, except to say how far it reflects
a view of justice present in other plays that Shakespeare
wrote over this period, especially *King Lear*: 'see how yond
justice rails upon yon simple thief . . . change places; and,
handy-dandy, which is the justice, which is the thief?'
(*King Lear*, IV.vi)

In Vienna, justice is powerless against the reality of sex;
and the dividing line in virtue between the judges and the
judged is impossible to determine. Angelo, of course, is
worse than Claudio, who suffers directly as a result of the
deputy's conception of the law: they both succumb to lust,
but Angelo is prepared to use his position to blackmail his
victim. Even before his downfall, however, when his sincerity is unquestioned, Angelo stands for a narrow conception of the law – legality rather than true justice. Isabella
contrasts divine justice and human justice, as represented
by Angelo, with some bitterness:

> but man, proud man,
> Drest in a little brief authority,
> Most ignorant of what he's most assur'd,
> His glassy essence, like an angry ape,
> Plays such fantastic tricks before high heaven
> As makes the angels weep . . . (II.ii)

The references to divine justice and the scriptural connotations implicit in the play's theme ('Judge not that ye be not

judged.' Matthew, vii.1) have encouraged a number of critics into a fully Christian interpretation of *Measure for Measure*. G. Wilson Knight in his essay 'Measure for Measure and the Gospels', included in his book *The Wheel of Fire*, argues that the play is a kind of Christian parable. This view hinges on the function of the Duke in the play. By any standards, he interprets his duties as leader somewhat eccentrically: having given Angelo power he works behind the scenes to ensure that the worst consequences of the deputy's authority are avoided. Certain of his actions suggest a more than human interpretation of his role. Disguised as a friar he freely confesses his subjects whom he sees it as his duty to bring to an improved spiritual state: Angelo must be brought to know himself and to learn to live with other people's knowledge of him; Isabella, having recommended mercy to Angelo, must bend her own austerity sufficiently to plead for Angelo's life. Angelo specifically compares the Duke's watchfulness with God's: 'When I perceive your Grace, like power divine,/Hath look'd upon my passes.' (V.i)

For these reasons, Wilson Knight sees the Duke as a kind of allegorical figure representing divine providence. There are a number of objections to this view. It was not Shakespeare's habit at any point to write straightforward allegory; and, if he intended it in *Measure for Measure*, the play is too psychologically realized to work on a simple allegorical basis. Moreover, such an interpretation leaves too many unexplained ambiguities in the Duke's own character. His decision to give Angelo the task of clearing up the flesh pots of Vienna suggests too great a dependence on his own popularity. He says early in the play: 'I love the people,/But do not like to stage me to their eyes' (I.i), but his return to the city is elaborately staged to set him off in the best light. The character to whom he is most unforgiving is Lucio, the only one whose crime (slanders about the absent Duke with which he regales the 'Friar') reflects adversely on the Duke himself. Finally, if the Duke is Providence, what is he doing marrying Isabella?

The Duke has too many human qualities, indeed failings, to allow us to accept him in a divine capacity. If he is not God, he is a man playing at God – a puppeteer who enjoys manipulating people for his own glory. If we cannot accept the Duke as an allegorical figure, then he too is coming under scrutiny; the cynicism with which Shakespeare is viewing authority includes the Duke's authority.

The unease that we feel about this play, and especially about the ending, is I think, entirely deliberate. Shakespeare is demonstrating that human nature, as he apparently viewed it over this period, is unamenable to the light hearted treatment of comedy. The final scene of *Measure for Measure* is almost a burlesque of the conventional comic ending. There is much talk of forgiveness and reconciliation, but when Claudio is brought in alive not one word passes between him and Isabella. Isabella's plea for Angelo's life is apparently meant to suggest spiritual growth; but what impresses the audience about her plea is the stirring in her of sexual vanity:

> I partly think
> A due sincerity govern'd his deeds,
> Till he did look on me . . . (V.i)

The four 'happy' couples are Lucio and the whore he got with child; Angelo and Mariana, the woman he was tricked into deflowering; Claudio and Juliet, the most human of the four, but nonetheless well beyond the point where nuptial rejoicing is relevant – and the Duke and Isabella.

The Duke's proposal to Isabella is the most absurd – though not, it must be said, the most sinister – abuse of power in the play. It cannot be unintentional that Isabella, for whom the preservation of her virginity has been of paramount importance, never actually replies to the Duke's proposal. Isabella is, in fact, the most curious and the most disturbing of all Shakespeare's comic heroines. It is not so much her refusal to fall in with Angelo's scheme which distresses us – as a prospective nun it is about the worst thing he could have asked of her – as her fundamental lack of warmth. When she pleads with Angelo it is the abstract issues rather than her brother's plight which stir her to eloquence. When she visits Claudio to tell him of Angelo's scheme, she offers him not a shred of Christian comfort. It is not only her personality that repels, however, but the ambivalence in her ethical code: what would be a mortal sin for her – the surrender of her virginity – she connives at for Mariana. In the Vienna of *Measure for Measure* Isabella is the one figure of purity; because of the way she is presented, she compromises the very values she represents.

All's Well that Ends Well

DATE Sometime between 1601 and 1606
PRINCIPAL CHARACTERS
Countess of Roussillon
Bertram: Her son, ward of the King of France
Helena: A young girl brought up by the Countess
Parolles: Bertram's friend
The King of France
Lafeu: An elderly lord in the French court
The brothers Dumaine, French lords, later captains serving the Duke of Florence
The Duke of Florence
Widow Capilet of Florence
Diana: Her daughter
Violenta ⎱ The widow's
Mariana ⎰ friends
SCENE France – the Countess of Roussillon's household and the royal court in Paris; Florence

Plot

ACT ONE opens on a note of mourning and foreboding. The recently widowed Countess of Roussillon dispatches her son Bertram to the King's court in Paris; the King, an old friend of Bertram's father, is waiting for death, having been given up as incurably ill by his physicians. Living with the Countess is Helena, whose own father, a doctor of remarkable powers, died some six months before. Helena is in love with Bertram, whom she acknowledges to be outside her social orbit. When the Countess hears of this love, she expresses modified approval. Helena is given leave to journey to Paris to try one of her father's remedies on the ailing King; Helena appears to think that the King's cure would further her suit with Bertram. Meanwhile, the audience has been introduced to Bertram's friend Parolles, a swaggering braggart whom nobody but Bertram takes seriously.

ACT TWO Helena, now in Paris, strikes a bargain with the King: if she fails to cure him she is prepared to be executed; if her remedy works, the King will bestow her in marriage on a lord of her own choosing. The King makes a miraculous recovery and Helena chooses Bertram from the assembled court. Bertram tries to refuse her but is compelled into marriage by the King. He sends Helena home to the Countess saying that the consummation of their marriage must be briefly delayed; meanwhile, he makes secret preparations to journey to Florence to fight for the Duke of Florence. He turns a deaf ear to the warnings he is given by Lafeu, a distinguished French lord, about Parolles.

ACT THREE At Roussillon, letters arrive from Bertram announcing his flight: he will only recognize Helena as a wife if she manages to conceive a child by him. The Countess stands by Helena and renounces her son but Helena, stricken with remorse at dividing mother from son, disappears, leaving word that she is making a pilgrimage. As a pilgrim, Helena arrives in Florence and makes contact with the Widow Capilet, whose daughter, Diana, is being pursued by Bertram, now the Duke of Florence's General of Horse. The Widow and Diana agree to co-operate in a scheme which could reconcile Helena to Bertram.

ACT FOUR Two schemes reach fruition. The two lords Dumaine, anxious to open Bertram's eyes to his friend's character, ambush and blindfold Parolles; Parolles, thinking himself in enemy hands, slanders the valour of the Dumaine brothers and of Bertram in the hope of saving his life. Once the blindfold is released Parolles realizes that he has lost Bertram's friendship. Meanwhile, Bertram has given Diana an ancestral ring in exchange, as he thinks, for her virginity. News is brought him of Helena's death and he prepares to return to France now that Helena is removed and he has distinguished himself as a soldier. The Widow, Diana and Helena, who supplied Diana's place in Bertram's bed and who has given out word of her own death, set out for France also. At Roussillon, the Countess and Lafeu plan the marriage of Bertram to Maudlin, Lafeu's daughter; the marriage will seal Bertram's forgiveness and reconciliation to his family.

ACT FIVE Lafeu, who has no illusions about Parolles, nonetheless takes him into his service. Bertram, returning as he thinks to triumph, is enmeshed by incriminating circumstances: having formally declared his regrets for the dead Helena, he produces a wedding ring for Maudlin given him, as he thinks, by Diana, which is recognized by the King as one he gave Helena. He is accused of murdering the wife that he found so inconvenient. Diana appears and confronts Bertram with a promise he made to marry her on his wife's death, producing his ring as proof. When Bertram has further disgraced himself by insulting her, Diana brings in the now visibly pregnant Helena. For the first time Bertram acknowledges her as his wife.

Critical commentary

In the absence of any firm evidence for dating, *All's Well* is now widely felt, because of certain similarities of theme, tone and narrative device, to belong with Shakespeare's other 'problem' comedies. The ideals of honour and romantic love, heavily compromised in both *Measure for Measure* and *Troilus and Cressida* are undermined in *All's Well*; the bed-trick, used to bring Angelo and Mariana together in *Measure for Measure*, is used for the same purpose on Helena and Bertram; *All's Well* shares with the other problem comedies a predominantly sombre tone which would be felt as intrusive in romantic comedy. Nonetheless, there are important differences between the plays. There is in *All's Well* a hopefulness, even given the unpromising elements in human nature, which seems to look forward to Shakespeare's last plays, the romances.

These unpromising elements – the links between *All's Well* and the other plays in the group – can be tackled first. The negative spirit of the play is closely identified with Parolles whose presence undermines the ideals of honour and chivalry. Lafeu says of him: 'the soul of this man is his clothes.' (II.v) Parolles is a 'seemer' and his claims to valour are as hollow as the drum that he bangs. His primary consideration is the preservation of his skin but when he has been tricked by the Dumaine brothers into a display of honest cowardice, he is almost relieved at no longer having to keep up the pretence of manly virtue:

> Yet am I thankful: if my heart were great
> 'Twould burst at this. Captain I'll be no more;
> But I will eat and drink, and sleep as soft
> As captain shall: simply the thing I am
> Shall make me live . . . (IV.iii)

The essential Parolles is his will to survive, the play not only recognizes his baseness, but his right to live. Lafeu accepts his proffered service on these terms: 'Though you are a fool and a knave, you shall eat' (V.ii). There is a sense in which *All's Well* is about survival, though not necessarily survival on terms as base as Parolles': his presence supplies a single thread in a larger fabric, but more of this later.

In as far as *All's Well* has a hero, it is Bertram. His quality is revealed partly through his relationship with Parolles, in whom Bertram alone in the play cannot distinguish the false from the true. In his assessment of Helena, Bertram again is alone in failing to recognize true worth in a social inferior. He is within his rights not to want to marry her, but he treats her throughout with calculated offensiveness.

When he is in a tight situation – as he is in Paris after his marriage to Helena, and in Florence after what he assumes to be his seduction of Diana, his instinct is to flee. He is not even moved by Helena's death, though he could be safely moved since she has, he thinks, lost all power to threaten him. Bertram, like Parolles, is dishonourable, though in a different way, for he does not lack physical courage. Indeed, he is a 'seemer' of another order in that in him physical courage is a front for moral cowardice, as his mother recognizes: 'his sword can never win/The honour that he loses' (III.ii).

The unease we feel about Bertram is similar to the unease that survives the happy ending of *Measure for Measure*. In the latter play, intractable human material which has been almost too well realized psychologically is forced with some grotesqueness into a happy ending. The story of *All's Well* – of a young girl who by her magically curative powers achieves the husband of her choice – has its roots in folk lore, but the folk lore elements sit uneasily on characters who are depicted with some degree of modern scepticism. For this reason there is a school of thought that maintains that *All's Well* was written, and should be taken, in a spirit of irony: according to this view, Helena is as much a self-seeking survivor as Parolles and the audience is expected to laugh up its sleeve at the vision of conjugal happiness offered by the play's conclusion.

An assessment on how far the irony in the play reaches depends largely on how we respond to Helena. She certainly has points of contact with Parolles. Both of lower social standing than the people with whom they move, they use such means as they have at their disposal to take what they want out of life. There is a parallel of a kind between Helena's 'Our remedies oft in ourselves do lie' (I.i) when she makes her decision to win Bertram if she can, and Parolles' – 'simply the thing I am/Shall make me live' (IV.iii) – but Helena does, as it were, represent the positive side of Parolles' self-preservation. Lavishly and warmly praised for her virtue by the older generation in the play, she was thought by Coleridge to be Shakespeare's 'loveliest character'. She is in a direct line of descent from Shakespeare's heroines of romantic comedy: like them she is warm and direct; unlike them she is not content to take a largely passive role until events move her way. Shakespeare's other comic heroines are resourceful, but their resourcefulness expresses itself mainly in the adopting of disguise and in hinting at their love under cover. The romantic heroines are playful but there is nothing playful about Helena. Her resourcefulness is disturbing: she chooses Bertram before the assembled court and uses underhand means to conceive a child to him. As with many of the links between the romantic comedies and the dark comedies (like the development of disguise into 'seeming'), what was fun in the comic heroines is real in Helena. Her vitality is sexual as well as emotional – but her sexuality is positive and contributes to the play's hopefulness. At the end of the play she is expecting Bertram's child and the house of Roussillon, about which there has been much talk in the course of the play, will continue. Helena recognizes that life is by no means benign but she maintains a tough optimism:

> . . . the time will bring on summer,
> When briers shall have leaves as well as thorns,
> And be as sweet as sharp. (IV. iv)

In *Measure for Measure* a question-mark hangs finally over all the characters; in *Troilus and Cressida* the good and the wise are largely ineffectual. In *All's Well* the older generation are wise and good and by no means ineffectual, in contrast to romance, where the older generation are crabbed, their wishes thwarted by the passions of the young. *All's Well* is not a romance, and the old, depicted with warmth and without irony, are on the side of right: the relationship between the Countess and her daughter-in-law is both just and affectionate, one of the pleasures of the play. Much of the sombreness of *All's Well* is elegiac rather than ironic: the old have almost had their day but they recognize it. Before the King is cured by Helena he wishes:

> Since I nor wax nor honey can bring home,
> I quickly were dissolved from my hive,
> To give some labourers room. (I.ii)

The old feel that the ideals of their generation have been betrayed by Bertram, who is unworthy of his noble father; but they forgive and look to the future. The play is about survival and the necessity for life to go on, but in a much broader sense than Parolles' philosophy recognizes.

Troilus and Cressida

DATE 1602-6

PRINCIPAL CHARACTERS IN TROY

Priam: King of Troy

Hector
Troilus
Paris } Priam's sons
Deiphobus
Helenus

Margarelon: Priam's bastard son

Helen: Wife of the Greek Menelaus, mistress of Paris

Cressida: Daughter of Calchas, defector to the Greeks

Andromache: Hector's wife

Cassandra: Priam's daughter

Aeneas } Trojan
Antenor } commanders

Pandarus: Cressida's uncle

PRINCIPAL CHARACTERS IN THE GREEK CAMP

Agamemnon: The Greek General

Menelaus: His brother, Helen's husband

Achilles
Ajax
Ulysses } Greek
Nestor   } commanders
Diomedes
Patroclus

Thersites: A deformed non-combatant
Calchas: Treacherous Trojan priest
SCENE Troy and the Greek camp outside the city

Plot

A PROLOGUE sketches in some of the historical background to the Trojan war.

ACT ONE Troilus, next to his brother Hector, the 'white hope' of the Trojan army, seeks the interest and manipulative powers of Pandarus, uncle of his beloved Cressida. Approached by Pandarus, Cressida refuses to admit her love for Troilus, though she does later in soliloquy. *In the Greek camp* the Greek leaders are bewailing their lack of success. Ulysses, the elder statesman, attributes their failure to a laxity in observing the natural order: Achilles, their strongest fighter, scorns intellect in favour of brawn and mocks his superiors. Aeneas brings a challenge from Hector to any Greek prepared to engage in single combat. The challenge is meant for Achilles but Ulysses plots with Nestor to have the challenge answered by Ajax in the hope that hurt pride will spur Achilles to action.

ACT TWO *In Troy*, Priam and his sons debate on whether to hand Helen over to the Greeks in order to put an end to the war. Paris, her lover, argues for her retention; Hector that she has not been worth the bloodshed. Troilus defends the romantic and chivalric ideal, and hence the keeping of Helen; his views win the day. *In the Greek camp*, Thersites acts as a kind of chorus in commenting on the brainlessness of the best fighters (Achilles and Ajax); and on the sordid cause for which they are fighting – 'All the argument is a cuckold and a whore.' (II.iii) Achilles continues to show insolence to his superior, Agamemnon, preferring to stay in bed with Patroclus, his 'male whore' (Thersites' description).

ACT THREE *In Troy*, Troilus is taken by Pandarus to Cressida's home. After swearing their undying love, the lovers are ushered to bed by Pandarus. *In the Greek camp*,

Cressida's father, Calchas, a defector to the Greeks, asks that his daughter be sought in exchange for Antenor, the newly captured Trojan hero; the Greek leaders agree.

ACT FOUR *In Troy* Diomedes arrives as ambassador from the Greeks with Antenor. The exchange of Antenor and Cressida is completed. Troilus, after swearing and urging fidelity, hands Cressida over to Diomedes, giving her his sleeve as a memento. Cressida is welcomed *in the Greek camp*. When Hector comes among the Greeks to make good his challenge he fights with Ajax (who is half Trojan) but refuses to draw blood because they are cousins.

ACT FIVE Still *in the Greek camp*, Hector is entertained in Achilles' tent after the contest, while Troilus (who has accompanied his brother) is taken by Ulysses to Calchas' tent. There Troilus observes Diomedes' wooing of Cressida and her capitulation: she gives him Troilus' sleeve in token of her promised sexual submission. Disillusioned by love, Troilus channels his energies into fighting as, after the civilities, battle commences in earnest. With Hector, who has been urged not to fight that day (Andromache, Cassandra and Priam have all had premonitions of his death), he is responsible for large numbers of Greek dead. Among the dead is Patroclus, Achilles' paramour. Stirred at last into action Achilles, accompanied by his Myrmidons, ambushes Hector, who is unarmed, and kills him. Hector had earlier delayed fighting with Achilles when the latter was unarmed. The Trojans see the loss of Hector as prefiguring the fall of Troy.

Critical commentary

Belonging to the same period as the great tragedies *Troilus and Cressida* shares with *Hamlet* particularly considerable intellectual distinction. G. Wilson Knight claims in his book *The Wheel of Fire* that *Troilus* is the most philosophical of all Shakespeare's plays; and indeed, Shakespeare shows himself in this play to be capable of long, sustained and closely argued dialectic. Ulysses' speech – 'The specialty of rule hath been neglected' (I.iii) – in which he claims that the Greeks will only function properly when they have achieved in their ranks the order that governs nature, has become something of a set piece. The Trojans' debate on whether to hand Helen back to the Greeks is a lengthy discussion on objective and subjective value; Troilus asking, with the rhetoric of romance – 'What is aught but as 'tis valu'd?' (II.ii); and Hector retorting that 'value dwells not in particular will' and that Helen in herself is valueless.

Troilus is a play about ideals and how they function in a sordid world. The ideals examined are the romantic and chivalric ideals of love and war: indeed, in this particular play the one closely affects the other since the war is being fought over a love affair. Both armies want to win, but few on either side can find any nobility left in the cause. Menelaus, the injured husband, is kept very much in the background and otherwise the attitude of the Greeks towards Helen is insulting. Thersites comments sourly to himself: 'all the argument is a cuckold and a whore; a good quarrel to draw emulous factions and bleed to death upon.' (II.iii) On his embassy to Troy, Diomedes does not spare Paris his opinion of Helen, speaking of her 'bawdy veins' and 'contaminated carrion weight' and wishing him joy of 'The lees and dregs of a flat tamed piece.' (IV.i)

Among the Trojans, Paris, of course, has a personal interest in keeping Helen, but his family can see nothing elevated about his loyalty, except Troilus, the young romantic lover, who has managed to preserve the ideal of Helen intact and separate from the real Helen:

Is she worth keeping? why, she is a pearl,
Whose price hath launch'd above a thousand ships
And turn'd crown'd kings to merchants. (II.ii)

Troilus' argument is a false one – that because Helen has caused so much bloodshed she must be worth the bloodshed she has caused – but it nonetheless wins the day by swaying Hector.

Where Troilus stands firm on the ideal of romantic love, Hector is the play's foremost exponent of chivalry and honour. Hector decides that they must continue fighting for Helen, not because of her intrinsic worth, but because – ''tis a cause that hath no mean dependance/ Upon our joint and several dignities.' (II.ii) If Helen is indeed worthless, then recognition of her worthlessness not only renders meaningless all that they have been fighting for, but seriously undermines the ideals on which the principal Trojans base their lives.

Idealism is noticeably lacking in the Greek camp, yet the Greeks win the day: they slay Hector and corrupt Cressida – and achieve both because they are not handicapped by notions of honour. The ideals of Hector and Troilus are defeated by a world which is too squalid to contain them. Hector is not only a strong and valiant fighter, he fights like a gentleman: he spares the weak, his kin (Ajax) and the unarmed (Achilles). His counterpart in strength in the Greek camp is Achilles, but Achilles is no hero. Confined to his tent by Patroclus, who entertains him by mimicking the Greek generals, he is deaf to the arguments of honour with which his leaders hope to rouse him. Thersites wanders the Greek camp exclaiming, 'Lechery, lechery, still wars and lechery': it is a comment both on the cause of the war (Helen) and on Achilles' behaviour. It is Patroclus' death that finally rouses Achilles, his loyalty to his paramour providing in microcosm the 'argument' of the whole war. He kills Hector unarmed and outnumbered. In a fair world, Hector might have been the victor, but such as Hector are vulnerable in an unfair world, as Ajax' tribute to the dead hero makes clear:

> If it be so, yet bragless let it be;
> Great Hector was a man as good as he. (V.ix)

Against this background the love story of Troilus and Cressida is played out. Troilus is the archetypal courtly lover – sighing and impatient before the consummation of his love, anxious to place that love on the level of the infinite, outside the ravages of 'injurious time' (IV.iv). Love for him is as glorious as war is for Hector, and Shakespeare gives him an awareness of the 'legend in the making' aspect of his own love: all true lovers, he declares, will swear by him, 'as true as Troilus' (III.ii): 'I am as true as truth's simplicity,/And simpler than the infancy of truth.' (III.ii) Some commentators have stretched Shakespeare's un-doubted cynicism in this play to the depiction of Troilus: according to this argument, the ideal of love is treated satirically and Troilus himself is a fool. When he observes Cressida's capitulation to Diomedes, his first reaction is to separate his ideal Cressida from the real Cressida, as he had earlier done with Helen – 'rather think this not Cressid . . . no; this is Diomed's Cressida.' (V.ii)

There is something foolish in this, but it is also pathetic and Shakespeare exploits the pathos; it is not so much that the ideal of love is undermined in Troilus as that its fragile nature is demonstrated in an imperfect world.

It is possible to make a figure of pathos of 'false Cressid': well worth reading is Jan Kott's analysis of her in *Shakespeare Our Contemporary*, where he argues that her fate is in itself a comment on a world in the throes of war. Left behind in Troy by her treacherous father, in the hands of her pro-curing uncle Pandarus, she has no faith or confidence. She loves Troilus, but when he asks what she sees in 'the fountain of our love' she replies: 'More dregs than water, if my fears have eyes.' (III.ii) Used by both Trojans and Greeks as a bargaining point, she lacks a centre of orienta-tion. She succumbs to Diomedes, despising herself for her perfidy and with no hope in the outcome. Ulysses dismisses her as 'one of the daughters of the game': such she may well become, but Ulysses' prophecy fulfilled would be at least as much the fault of circumstances as of herself. The character-ization of Cressida is partly responsible for *Troilus*' curiously modern tone. After being virtually neglected in the eigh-teenth and nineteenth centuries, *Troilus and Cressida* is beginning to attract the kind of attention that it deserves.

5 Shakespeare: Poetry

Not marble, nor the gilded monuments
Of princes, shall outlive this powerful rime . . . (Sonnet 55)

For part of the period 1592-4 the London theatres were
closed because of plague; Shakespeare, newly making his
mark as a dramatist, turned his attention to narrative
poetry. The publication of *Venus and Adonis* in 1593 and *The
Rape of Lucrece* in 1594 established him as a literary figure in
a way that his earlier theatrical efforts (*Henry VI*, *The
Comedy of Errors*, *Titus Andronicus*), popular successes though
they were, did not. One of the earliest references we have to
Shakespeare's early career from contemporary account is
an attack on him by Robert Greene, a man of letters who
died in penury. The precise terms of the attack have been
the subject of much critical debate since: was Shakespeare
being accused of plagiarism, ignorance, confounding the
division between actor and playwright? The tone of the
attack is, however, unmistakable. As Anthony Burgess said
in his recent biography of Shakespeare:

> The true bitterness . . . lies in a realisation that the literary men
> have failed to capture the popular theatrical market, and that
> its future seems to lie with grammar-school upstarts.

Greene's unkind comments about Shakespeare were published in 1592. The publication of *Venus and Adonis* in the
following year may well have been Shakespeare's proof

that he, a 'grammar-school upstart', could compete with literary men on their own terms: *Venus and Adonis*, like *The Rape of Lucrece*, retells a story from Ovid in a form which was fashionable rather than popular. The success, or at any rate the acceptance of both poems, would have been secured by the fact that both are dedicated to the Earl of Southampton.

Of undoubted value to Shakespeare's reputation in his own day, Shakespeare's narrative poems have now become the least accessible of all his work. They are cast in forms, the mythological romance (*Venus and Adonis*) and the tragical morality (*The Rape of Lucrece*), which have long been out of fashion; they were, moreover, forms to which Shakespeare never returned, which perhaps implies his own realization that his talents were best displayed through other outlets. Their chief interest now lies in the suggestion of ideas that were developed more fully as his dramatic powers matured.

Venus and Adonis

The story of *Venus and Adonis* is adapted from Ovid's version of the myth in the *Metamorphoses*. Ovid tells of the pastoral idyll enjoyed by Venus, the goddess of love, and the human Adonis, an idyll which came to a violent end when Adonis was killed by a boar during a hunting expedition. Shakespeare made two important alterations: events which in Ovid occur over a period of time are compressed into a single day and night; Ovid's Adonis is a willing partner in the affair, Shakespeare's a reluctant boy who is not only unwilling but probably incapable of responding to Venus' sexual advances. An additional attraction in Shakespeare's poem is his sensuous evocation of the lushly intimate landscape against which the lovers' drama is played.

Venus and Adonis opens at dawn with the 'sick-thoughted' Venus detaining the 'rose-cheek'd' Adonis from a purposed hunting party: detailed characterization is not a feature of myth, and it is enough for Venus to be all pulsating love and

Adonis the declared epitome of male beauty. Nonetheless, Shakespeare's principal innovation – Adonis' reluctance – has in itself injected humour into the situation. Venus, having tied her lover's horse to a tree to prevent an untimely getaway, turns her attention to the man.

> Backward she push'd him, as she would be thrust,
> And govern'd him in strength, though not in lust.

Adonis is told that he can buy his release with a kiss, which he attempts, but baulks, so Venus turns to subtler methods of persuasion, arguing that celibacy is a waste of nature's gifts:

> Fair flowers that are not gather'd in their prime
> Rot and consume themselves in little time.

This argument was to be used by Shakespeare again in the *Sonnets*, but with rather more urgency. Another dialectic link between *Venus and Adonis* and the *Sonnets* is the idea of beauty imposing a duty on the possessor to reproduce: 'Thou wast begot; to get it is thy duty.' Adonis' reply to Venus' entreaties is that the sun, now at its midday height, is burning his face.

He turns back to his horse who is described as displaying every attribute of horsely beauty: as the depiction of Venus and Adonis also illustrates, myth deals in archetypes rather than individuals. The horse, more loyal to nature than to his master, obligingly chooses that moment to provide Venus, in equine terms, with a telling example for her argument. His attention caught by a sportive young mare, it is the work of a moment to break through his cords and gallop after her. As Venus points out, the horse is wiser than his master in taking 'advantage on presented joy'. The technique of reinforcing and modifying a theme through parallels was to be a marked feature of Shakespeare's more mature work, used with great subtlety through different pairs of lovers in the later comedies and reaching its supreme application in the double plot of *King Lear*. In *Venus and Adonis*, Shakespeare finds it necessary for the 'point' of the horse to be elaborately presented by Venus. Faced by his horse's defection, Adonis for the first time tries arguing rather than wriggling himself out of the situation: his un-ripeness for love is cited and illustrated by natural examples – 'Who plucks the bud before one leaf put forth?' – His arguments fail to move Venus, as hers have had no effect on him.

The day, meanwhile, has been drawing to its close and as the sun begins to set, Adonis' resolve to leave hardens – even to the point of offering to kiss Venus goodnight to secure her co-operation – an unwise move, which throws the god-dess into a frenzy of passion – 'Her face doth reek and smoke, her blood doth boil.' Fear sharpens her passion as he declares his intention of going hunting the following day. Falling upon him with abandon,

> The warm effects which she in him finds missing,
> She seeks to kindle with continual kissing.

When Adonis' only response is to complain that she is crushing him she directs her energies elsewhere, begging him, if he must hunt, to avoid the boar. From Venus' des-cription of the boar he too, like the horse, emerges as no ordinary beast but as an instrument of total destruction: 'His snout digs sepulchres where'er he goes.' She advises more manageable animals like hares and foxes. After some further argument Venus tries to impress on her beloved the urgency of reproducing himself in a world where the young and beautiful are so vulnerable to death and disease. Adonis tells her sharply that the lust she feels for him she is trying to dress up as love. Adonis departs at nightfall re-affirming his intention to hunt in the morning.

During the night, Venus is wracked by fears for Adonis' safety:

> 'For he being dead, with him is beauty slain,
> And, beauty dead, black chaos comes again.'

Shakespeare was to return to this idea, as the legitimate fear of the lover, in the *Sonnets*; while in the tragedies he was to demonstrate the fragility of innocence and beauty in a world where chaos reigns. Venus' premonitions of Adonis' death are justified: stirred by the sound of the hunt in the morning she rushes off to locate it and finds Adonis pierced by a boar. In this archetypal world of myth, she can prophesy that – 'Sorrow on love hereafter shall attend'. With Adonis' death the age of innocence passes. 'Weary of the world' Venus departs for Paphos.

The Rape of Lucrece

The Rape of Lucrece, published in 1594, fulfilled the promise made in the dedication of *Venus and Adonis* to honour the Earl of Southampton, dedicatee of both poems, with 'some graver labour'. The pastoral setting, mythological figures and innocently impulsive sexuality of the earlier poem are replaced in *Lucrece* by historical figures living in an authoritarian society. The poet himself, whose celebration of the sensuous verges on the excessive in *Venus and Adonis*, adopts a stance of unambivalent moral judgment in *Lucrece*.

The story of Lucrece – regarded as an exemplar of feminine virtue in classical and mediaeval literature – had been told with some brevity by Ovid, Livy and Chaucer, versions which we take it Shakespeare had consulted. Lucrece, a beautiful and chaste Roman matron, attracts the jealous lust of Lucius Tarquinius, King of the Tarquins. During the absence of her husband, Collatine, Tarquin visits Lucrece; after being entertained by her as her husband's friend he rapes her. The next morning Lucrece sends for her husband and father and, after making them promise vengeance on her ravisher, stabs herself. When the crime has been revealed to the citizens of Rome they agree to Tarquin's banishment.

Shakespeare tells Lucrece's story at greater length than any of his sources, but begins it at a more advanced stage: previous meetings between Tarquin and Lucrece are omitted from the narrative, which opens with Tarquin's ride to Collatium, his designs on Lucrece already fully formed. Beginning the poem *in medias res* gives the narrative an urgency which in itself suggests the quality of Tarquin's lust:

> Borne by the trustless wings of false desire,
> Lust-breathed Tarquin leaves the Roman host . . .

This urgency is sustained in a variety of ways until the rape is accomplished. Tarquin's acceptance of Lucrece's unsuspecting hospitality is fraught with menace:

> But she, that never cop'd with stranger eyes,
> Could pick no meaning from their parling looks,
> Nor read the subtle-shining secrecies
> Writ in the glassy margents of such books . . .

Night, conventionally described as 'mother of dread and fear', is also a 'vaulty prison'. Indeed, much of the poem's imagery specifically impresses Lucrece's vulnerability on the reader. She is compared to a trapped bird, a deer, a mouse to Tarquin's cat. More effective is the imagery arising from Tarquin's actions and reflecting his intentions:

> His falchion on a flint he softly smiteth,
> That from the cold stone sparks of fire do fly;
> Whereat a waxen torch forthwith he lighteth,
> Which must be lode-star to his lustful eye;
> And to the flame thus speaks advisedly:
> 'As from this cold flint I enforc'd this fire,
> So Lucrece must I force to my desire.'

Tarquin is not without scruple, however, and his attempts to contain the immediacy of his desire by placing it against the universal – 'Who buys a minute's mirth to wail a week?/ Or sells eternity to get a toy' – have been compared to Macbeth's. His lust wins the day, however, lust depicted by Shakespeare as an active force, propelling Tarquin through the darkened house, forcing locks until Lucrece's chamber is reached. The sleeping Lucrece is conventionally described as virginally pale – her 'perfect white' hand resembling an April daisy, her breasts 'ivory globes', her skin 'alabaster' and her chin 'snow-white'; even her sweat is 'pearly' – but Shakespeare achieves a real sense of desecration nonetheless. Tarquin's reactions after the rape is accomplished are predictable: reason and self-disgust return and he departs from Lucrece's house, and from the poem, bearing 'the burden of a guilty mind'.

At this point, the poem has more than half its course still to run. Not only the pace but the nature of the work changes, and the attention of all but the most devoted reader is in jeopardy. The problem is primarily one of genre. The part of the poem leading up to and including the rape takes its form from the historical morality, in which tales from history were told with a strong moral bias. Shakespeare makes this form work for him by the vigour of his narrative and by his imaginative grasp of Tarquin's predicament. Most of the remainder of the poem after the rape is cast as a lament – a form popular with the Elizabethans, in which an injured lady tells over her wrongs, inviting the reader's sympathy.

Rhetorical and static, the lament was not a form to which Shakespeare's talents were best adapted. He had anyway failed to prepare the ground adequately for the total shift in focus from Tarquin to Lucrece. In the early part of the poem Lucrece is suggested emblematically: through lilies and roses, helpless animals, the paleness of her skin and the cleanliness of her bed-linen, so that she has no substance as a person. To her transparent purity she adds in the longer second half of the poem a droning, measured voice as she calls rhetorically on abstractions like Night, Time, Opportunity and Honour. Change in literary fashion can take part of the blame for the failure of Lucrece's lament, but even allowing for that, her personal idiom seems to block the reader's response. Before the rape, when she is addressing Tarquin rather than the reader – in itself a more dramatic situation – her accusations of hypocrisy fail to carry passionate conviction:

Thou art not what thou seem'st; and if the same,
Thou seem'st not what thou art, a god, a king.

She emerges as pallid as her alabaster skin. What is baffling
is that elsewhere in his work Shakespeare showed considerable imaginative sympathy with women who were the
victims of male treachery.

The only interlude in the latter part of the poem with any
real vitality is a description of a picture of Troy. Lucrece,
grown breathless perhaps by lamenting, having despatched
a letter to her husband, beguiles the interval of waiting for
her husband's arrival by looking at a picture of Troy. For
the Elizabethans Troy was a familiar analogue, traditionally an allegory of the body, whose fall would suggest
Lucrece's own rape, the Trojan war the type of all human
enmity and violence, the lengthy digression on Troy would
for the Elizabethan reader add a universal dimension to the
victory of violence over virtue depicted in *Lucrece*. Lucrece
finds in the picture a close parallel for her own suffering in
Hecuba, Queen of Troy:

> Her cheeks with chaps and wrinkles were disguis'd;
> Of what she was no semblance did remain;
> Her blue blood chang'd to black in every vein,
> Wanting the spring that those shrunk pipes had fed,
> Show'd life imprisoned in a body dead.

In Shakespeare's description of Hecuba the individual is
not, as it is with Lucrece, subordinate to the symbol, but
it is Hecuba whose suffering carries more universal resonance. Lucrece, having praised the painter's skill with
Hecuba, nonetheless thinks – 'he did her wrong/To give her
so much grief and not a tongue.' Shakespeare might have
done well to follow the painter's example: if his heroine had
been more individualized, and her tongue not quite so
active, some of the ideas she was intended to carry might
have made more impact on the poem.

The Sonnets

Shakespeare's *Sonnets* have over the last century been given
a degree of critical attention which is more than justified by

their artistic merit, but which has been sadly weighted towards the trivial and the irrelevant. Published in 1609 by Thomas Thorpe, the *Sonnets* are dedicated to their 'onlie begetter', 'Mr. W. H.'; the dedication is initialled 'T.T.' Considerable scholarly energy has been directed to proving that 'Mr W. H.' is Shakespeare's, not Thorpe's dedicatee, and to identifying him with the young man to whom the first one hundred and twenty-six sonnets are addressed. The field of speculation as to the historical identity of the young man has by now narrowed to Henry Wriothesley, Earl of Southampton, the dedicatee of *The Rape of Lucrece* and *Venus and Adonis*, and to William Herbert, Earl of Pembroke; the evidence for neither is sufficiently convincing to eliminate the other.

The last twenty-eight sonnets are written to a woman whose 'darkness' is total: of dark hair and swarthy complexion, 'blacke' and treacherous in her deeds, the nature of her attraction for Shakespeare seems to have been an enigma even to him. Her identity has remained stubbornly obscure, despite the fascination she has exercised over scholars like A. L. Rowse.

The relationship that we glimpse through the first one hundred and twenty-six sonnets is the more extraordinary. They tell of Shakespeare's love for a younger man who finally emerges as unworthy of the love that he has inspired, and of Shakespeare's efforts to reconcile through the sonnet form his personal and artistic need for an ideal love with his increasingly dispiriting awareness of the situation's truth. The Friend must, one feels, have had an influence on Shakespeare's writing generally, and some would hold him indirectly responsible for the most dramatic of the dramatist's shifts in direction. Although published in 1609, the *Sonnets* were probably written in the late 1590s; they may therefore reflect the determining watershed in personal experience between the mature romantic comedies with their confident assertions of the regenerative power of love, and the plays written after 1600, in which treachery, deceit and corruption dominate. Of the Friend himself, apart from what we can deduce about his personality from the *Sonnets*, all that we can say with certainty is that he was clearly younger than Shakespeare and of a higher social rank.

One approach to the *Sonnets* is through the 'story' that they tell, but regarded as a narrative they are thin in incident. The most startling 'event' is the affair on which the Friend and the Dark Lady embark (40-42 to the Friend, 133-4 and 144 to the Dark Lady), a piece of duplicity that wounded the poet deeply:

> That thou hast her, it is not all my grief,
> And yet it must be said I lov'd her dearly,
> That she hath thee, is of my wailing chief (42)

It is made clear in Sonnets 78-86 that the Friend, who has presumably accepted Shakespeare's poetic offerings with complacency if not gratitude, is finding the attention of another poet, whose style it seems is more expansively rhetorical than Shakespeare's ('Was it the proud full sail of his great verse' (86)), more to his liking:

> You to your beauteous blessings add a curse,
> Being fond on praise, which makes your praises worse. (84)

Otherwise, the *Sonnets* tell of routine periods of separation, and of a longer period of separation and silence broken by Sonnet 100, which as we shall see seems to mark the beginning of a new phase in the friendship.

The rest of the 'story' is speculation, much of it centring on whether Shakespeare did or did not have a homosexual relationship with the Friend. Certainly 33-6 refer to something specific that has happened, unconnected with the Dark Lady, which has moral as well as emotional implications:

> 'Tis not enough that through the cloud thou break,
> To dry the rain on my storm-beaten face,
> For no man well of such a salve can speak,
> That heals the wound, and cures not the disgrace ... (34)

Some kind of homosexual experience would seem to fit both

the emotional intensity and the self-disgust, but if so, the sense of disgrace and of 'bewailed guilt' (36) would suggest something rather different from habitual homosexuality. One of the best commentaries on the nature of Shakespeare's feelings for the Friend is Martin Seymour-Smith's in his edition of the *Sonnets*. He sees the Sonnets as providing a poetic insight into what may be described, paradoxically, as 'a heterosexual's homosexual experience. Shakespeare wanted to love the Friend without sex; the narcissistic element introduced into the situation' (by physical love of one's own sex) 'was, to him, a wasting enemy, like Death or Time.'

Seymour-Smith writes elsewhere in his Introduction:

> The 'story' that is unfolded in the *Sonnets* . . . is mainly a psychological one. They are more appropriately described as the record of a developing psychological situation than the history of two love-affairs.

The situation which occasioned them was complex and dynamic; editors (like Dover-Wilson in his New Cambridge edition) who suggest adjustments to the *Sonnets*' original order which would give the sequence more logical consistency overlook the fact that a man's feelings can shift and return in obedience to impulses other than logic and chronological fitness. Shakespeare strove, personally and artistically, to grapple with the truth of an ever-changing situation; their integrity is one of the most dazzling qualities of the *Sonnets*.

Critical commentary

The *Sonnets* open on a note of kindly formality which reflects the disparity in age and social position between the poet and the Friend. The first seventeen sonnets form a complete, almost separable group; in them Shakespeare, possibly at the request of the young man's family, is encouraging his Friend to marry and beget an heir. He does this, not by urging dynastic considerations but by appeals to the imagination. Now 'the world's fresh ornament' (1), the young man cannot expect to enjoy what Shakespeare clearly considers to be a unique beauty forever. He must consider the time 'When forty winters shall besiege thy brow' (2) and when 'winter's wragged hand' will 'deface' his 'summer' (6).

Shakespeare does not concentrate all his resources, however, on the fact of human transience – surely a more urgent consideration for himself than for a young man barely emerged from adolescence. Beauty, he argues, imposes a duty on the possessor to reproduce; it is not an outright gift but something held in trust for the next generation – an idea with which the scion of a noble house would be familiar in a more material context:

> Unthrifty loveliness, why dost thou spend
> Upon thyself thy beauty's legacy ? (4)

The picture of the Friend already emerging is of a rather self-absorbed, self-regarding young man who is reminded that self-love is a species of self-hate:

> No love toward others in that bosom sits
> That on himself such murderous shame commits. (9)

We gather that Shakespeare's efforts to make marriage seem attractive have no effect, and towards the end of the Marriage group the immortalizing power of his own verse is being put forward as a potent, if inferior weapon against time:

> And, all in war with Time for love of you,
> As he takes from you, I engraft you new. (15)

After 17, no further mention is made of the Friend marrying and Shakespeare's verse as a hedge against mortality and decay is a major theme of the remaining sonnets addressed to the Friend.

With Sonnet 18 ('Shall I compare thee to a summer's day?') the tone is at once more intimate as the 'specialness' of the Friend for Shakespeare is beginning to emerge. While his beauty can aptly be compared to a summer's day, he bears qualities of the spirit which are superior in the poet's eyes to mere physical beauty. Praised here at the expense of nature, he is later shown to compare favourably with any woman (20). His beauty resembles a woman's ('thou the master-mistress of my passion') but he is free from the guile associated with feminine beauty – 'shifting change', eyes that are 'false in rolling'. That Shakespeare has in fact fallen in love with the young man is made clear in a poetic conceit which at the same time rejects the idea of a physical conclusion to that love:

> And for a woman wert thou first created,
> Till Nature as she wrought thee fell a-doting,
> And by addition me of thee defeated,
> By adding one thing to my purpose nothing. (20)

Women, the sonnet concludes, can have the 'use' of that addition, while the Friend's love is reserved for the poet.

While Shakespeare is confident that the Friend returns his love, his chief consideration is expression — how to convey adequately in words both the uniqueness of the Friend and the quality of his own feelings for him. The humility that characterizes those feelings – he sees himself as 'an unperfect actor on the stage' (23), his 'wit' as 'poor' and his 'loving' rendered 'tatter'd' (26) through the inadequate medium of his verse – is made additionally interesting by the poet's concern for the truth of his art. He writes with contempt of those poets 'who heaven itself for ornament doth use' (21); who in effect debase both the subject of their verse and the heavenly objects (sun, moon and stars) which they employ for exaggerated comparison. Shakespeare is himself content to recognize that 'my love is as fair/As any mother's child' (21) – what more can one say of any human being? – as he states his own poetic ideal: 'O! let me, true in love, but truly write' (21). That ideal remains constant through all the shifts in the relationship. When a Rival Poet is offering the Friend headier blandishments, he defends the comparative austerity of his own approach with:

Who is it that says most? which can say more
Than this rich praise,—that you alone are you? (84)

Shakespeare's sense of the uniqueness of the individual and the duty imposed on poets to respect that uniqueness, informs all the *Sonnets*, even an apparently abusive parody addressed to the Dark Lady: 'My mistress' eyes are nothing like the sun' *but* she has her own distinctive quality:

And yet, by heaven, I think my love as rare
As any she belied with false compare. (130)

We first become aware that the poet's ideal of truth is in conflict with the more complex ideal represented by the Friend in sonnets 33-6. We learn of the Friend's 'sins' and 'sensual fault' (35) and of the Poet's 'grief', 'disgrace' and 'sorrow'. How does he reconcile his need for the Friend to be perfect with his own sense of truth? There is a sense in which the poetry itself is the reconciliation; and the poetic pattern which emerges from his handling of this crisis (33-6) is, with variations, repeated as further blows are dealt (40-42, 48-9).

Shakespeare begins by dramatizing what has been revealed about the Friend in such a way that the Friend's essential goodness (as the poet sees it) is distanced from the badness. The Friend is like the sun who, having promised 'a glorious morning' is masked by 'region cloud': in other words, the sun/Friend is independent of, has no control over, the clouds/baseness that are sullying his splendour. (In other sonnets Shakespeare is more specific, less metaphorical in his excuses for the Friend – youth and beauty are subject to flattery and often irresistible temptations.) In the following sonnet (34), the same metaphor is used to suggest that perhaps the Friend might be held responsible: the Friend/sun *made* me 'travel forth without my cloak', and when he breaks through the cloud 'To dry the rain on my storm-beaten face', ''Tis not enough' – the damage has been done. In 35 the imagery, far from separating the Friend from his own baseness, suggests that his corruption is an integral part of his beauty: 'Roses have thorns, and silver fountains mud' (35). Shakespeare cannot, however, long sustain an image of his Friend besmirched with mud – 'Such civil war is in my love and hate' – that it is finally less painful to take all the blame on himself:

> I may not evermore acknowledge thee,
> Lest my bewailed guilt should do thee shame. (36)

One of the most painful aspects of the *Sonnets* is Shakespeare's occasional abject humility, until a more independent sequence begins with 100. He *wants* the Friend to be 'all the better part of me' (39), so when the Friend humiliates – 'thou, to whom my jewels trifles are' (48) – and disappoints him, he looks for the cause in himself:

> To leave poor me, thou hast the strength of laws,
> Since why to love, I can allege no cause. (49)

Sometimes a sarcastic tone salvages his self-respect:

> Being your slave, what should I do but tend
> Upon the hours and times of your desire? (57)

but the sarcasm is superficial: Shakespeare is a slave and they both know it. There are few readers who will not from time to time find themselves wishing that Shakespeare's readiness to connive at the Friend's ill-treatment of him were not sometimes ironically intended: 'Speak of my lameness, and I straight will halt' (89).

Elsewhere, however, irony is used to suggest both his original expectations of the young man and the reality of his disappointment. The Friend is free if he wishes to take such assertions as ' – you like none, none you, for constant heart' (53) at face value. Towards the end of the Sonnets to the Friend, the poet comes to realize what the reader has long suspected – that the young man is in possession of the kind of beauty that promises everything but proves to be a facade:

> – heaven in thy creation did decree,
> That in thy face sweet love should ever dwell;
> Whate'er thy thoughts or thy heart's workings be . . . (93)

His final separation of the Friend's beauty from his character is an honest acknowledgement of both the corruption and of the irresistible spell of the beauty:

> O! what a mansion have those vices got
> Which for their habitation chose out thee . . . (95)

Not all the sonnets addressed to the Friend have the Friend as their primary theme. Transience and decay are themes in their own right, and certainly Time in the *Sonnets* is no mere static abstraction, conventionally held responsible for the passing of beauty and love, but an actively malevolent force. Time is a 'bloody tyrant' (16) whose 'fell hand' (64) wields a 'sithe' with which he hacks indiscriminately at mankind. Many of the *Sonnets* are concerned with ways of defeating Time – progeny and the establishment of a family line in the earliest appeals to the Friend (1-17), and then 'my verse' in which 'my love' will live 'ever young' (19).

Shakespeare seems to have had a particularly pressing sense of the passage of time – something he shared with Ovid, his favourite Latin poet, and the handful of sonnets where the influence of Ovid is most keenly felt have an intensity which owes little to the conventional and passing tributes to the Friend (55, 59, 60, 64 and 65). The urgent sense of mutability in these sonnets is achieved by concentrating, not on those natural objects which are most vulnerable to time, like flowers, but on the most durable works of men and nature: marble; brass; stone; the earth itself, which is finally subject to erosion, and the sea, which can be claimed as land:

> When I have seen the hungry ocean gain
> Advantage on the kingdom of the shore,
> And the firm soil win of the watery main,
> Increasing store with loss, and loss with store . . . (64)

The work of centuries is concentrated against a cosmic time-scale to seem the work of moments. Shakespeare's response is resigned:

> Ruin hath taught me thus to ruminate—
> That Time will come and take my love away. (64)

apart from the superbly assertive –

> Not marble, nor the gilded monuments
> Of princes shall outlive this powerful rime. (55)

That kind of assertiveness is rare in the *Sonnets*. Shakespeare believes that his work will survive but chiefly because he is celebrating such a uniquely special subject; his own feelings are important only in relation to the Friend, his moods of despondency ungrudgingly attributed to his own unworthiness. Nonetheless with Sonnet 100, when he resumes his theme after a considerable period of silence, a change is discernible. Whatever his feelings for his Friend now – and he claims that they are unchanged, 'strengthen'd though more weak in seeming' (102) – the tone suggests that they have moved this side idolatry, and that the poet is writing from a more independent position. Not only the Friend but 'I'll live in this poor rime' (107); 'worse essays prov'd thee my best of love' (110), but the poet's right to experiment with different kinds of love is implied. He still stresses his inferiority, but places the blame for it on fortune,

> That did not better for my life provide
> Than public means which public manners breeds. (111)

– fortune that has been kinder to the young man than to himself.

The picture that we have of Shakespeare towards the close of the sonnets to the Friend is of a man who has come to terms with himself: 'I am that I am' (121). He admits to having violated his own highest standards but still has confidence in a fundamental sense of truth that sets him apart from more conventional sinners: 'on my frailties why are frailer spies?' (121). The most startling change in these concluding sonnets to the Friend is Shakespeare's realization that he must find his sense of truth and beauty in himself, not in another person. That ideal that he hoped to achieve with the Friend is given a final salute in the beautiful 'Let me not to the marriage of true minds admit impediments' (116) but his new detachment has rendered the young man redundant in Shakespeare's life. It is arguable that, in human terms, the poet demanded too much of him.

It is tempting to look for parallels in Shakespeare's plays to the situation depicted in the *Sonnets*. My own view is that his interpretation of the Trojan position in *Troilus and Cressida* reflects the dilemma that he had himself grappled with in relation to the young man. The Trojans had invested so much idealism in Helen, had shed so much blood over her that to hand her back to the Greeks would nullify the values by which they had been living; Shakespeare had invested so much in the idea of the Friend that he tried for a time through the *Sonnets* to separate the ideal from the real person that was emerging: his confidence in his own judgment – for he had in some sense identified the Friend with truth – is at stake. As his sense of truth became more assertive, so the sonnets are underscored by an often tortuous irony which still leaves him the loophole of an ideal Friend, until that too is abandoned.

The relationship with the Dark Lady is nothing like so unequal as the relationship with the Friend, in terms of how much each partner is investing in it; and the humour and drop in intensity that characterize the twenty-eight sonnets (127-54) addressed to his mistress come as something of a relief after the earlier ones. The satisfaction he derives from her is not aesthetic,

> In faith, I do not love thee with mine eyes,
> For they in thee a thousand errors note . . . (141)

–nor does he believe it to be based on judgment and reason. Indeed, the concentration on the Dark Lady's 'foulness' of face is as much metaphorical as literal, and the perversion of his sight is probably intended to suggest the perversion of his judgment:

Thou blind fool, Love, what dost thou to mine eyes,
That they behold, and see not what they see ... (137)

Their love is based on duplicity, but Shakespeare is honest about the satisfactions arising from it: he treats his mistress as a 'true' woman so that she in return 'might think me some untutor'd youth' (138). Shakespeare's awareness of his age runs through the *Sonnets*; the Dark Lady has the heart-warming power to make him feel young again as his apparent devotion makes her forget the treacheries and infidelities of which she is guilty. And this mutually agreeable deception is achieved through sex:

Therefore I lie with her, and she with me,
And in our faults by lies we flatter'd be. (138)

The responsibility for the affair between the Friend and the Dark Lady is placed firmly on the lady; in one of the sonnets addressed to her, Shakespeare is quite explicit about the place of each in his life:

Two loves I have of comfort and despair,
Which like two spirits do suggest me still:
The better angel is a man right fair:
The worser spirit a woman, colour'd ill. (144)

This undoubtedly expresses the roles to which he originally assigned them: the Dark Lady would provide for the lower, more sensuous side of his nature, while the Friend would act as a lodestar for the finer, nobler parts of his being. Certainly the 'comfort' that his mistress offered was of a fairly modest kind compared with what had been expected of the Friend; but it is questionable which finally, as far as we can tell from the *Sonnets*, brought Shakespeare more 'despair'.

6 Shakespeare: English History

And bid the merry bells ring to thine ear
That thou art crowned, not that I am dead.
Henry IV Part Two (IV.v)

The history play was the one Elizabethan dramatic genre which had claims to being a native English development. Interest in comedy and tragedy had been stirred by classical models, but the closest parallel to the history in classical literature is the epic: the sense of a nation is at least as important as the impact of individual characters.

If we exclude *Henry VIII* (1613), which departs somewhat from the pattern established in the earlier histories and in which he had anyway only a shared claim to authorship, Shakespeare wrote nine English history plays: *Henry VI* Parts One, Two and Three, *King John, Richard III, Richard II, Henry IV*, Parts One and Two, and *Henry V*. Of these *Henry VI*, an early and shambolic work which, because of its loose, episodic structure rarely invites performance, and *King John*, which is removed in historical period from Shakespeare's other histories, are not included in the present study.

The histories were written over a period of about ten years, beginning with *Henry VI* in the late 1580s and ending with *Henry V*, in 1599, contemporaneously with the comedies – indicating that Shakespeare, or his company, thought fit to present a serious and a lighter play each season. With the exception of *King John*, they cover events in English history of the late fourteenth and fifteenth centuries. In terms of historical chronology they end with *Richard III*, which closes on a note of triumphant piety towards the Tudors as Richard is overthrown by the Earl of Richmond who, as Henry VII, was founder of the Tudor dynasty and grandfather of Elizabeth I. The chief source for all of them is Holinshed's *Chronicles* of English history, available to Shakespeare in the edition of 1587. Shakespeare wrote the plays in two cycles (though there is inevitably some debate among critics about how far we can assume that they were intended as cycles). *Henry VI* and *Richard III* which deal with the War of the Roses, the more immediate historical context for the Elizabethans, belong to the early part of his career. With *Richard II* in 1595 he began his second and artistically superior cycle which traces events from the deposition of Richard by Henry IV, through the rebellion which disturbed the latter's reign, to the military victories of Henry V in France; at the end of *Henry V*, the troubled reign of his young son Henry VI is anticipated. The development of the second cycle will be examined in detail; *Richard III* is included as an isolated example of Shakespeare's earlier historical writing.

To the lay reader or theatre-goer, Shakespeare's histories form a remarkable homogeneous group, scarcely needing explanation as a genre. Because of the innovatory nature of the English history play however, its purpose and generic characteristics have been the subject of some academic critical debate. One area of general agreement is the point of departure of history from comedy and tragedy, both of which deal with individuals: the individual's search for happiness; the effect on the individual soul of suffering or moral decline. In the history plays, increasingly as his craft matured, Shakespeare examined the problems of subordinating private aspirations to national goals: the histories deal with public and political rather than personal ethics.

Within that general structure, what were Shakespeare's aims in the histories? One view relates the emergence of the history play to the tide of nationalistic fervour that swept England at the time of the Spanish threat: Shakespeare was celebrating England. However, while a case for overridingly patriotic intention can be made for *Henry V*, generally agreed to be Shakespeare's attempt at a national epic, in no other of the history plays is England shown to have such power to unite, though the idea of England is always treated with affection.

Another view is that Shakespeare's purpose in the histories was didactic. Lily B. Campbell, in her scholarly book *Shakespeare's Histories* (Methuen), argues that Shakespeare, along with other Elizabethans, regarded history as a 'mirror' in which patterns in contemporary events could be recognized; history supplied lessons and warnings to be heeded. Ms Campbell has assembled a remarkable body of evidence to support her thesis, of which one example must suffice. Richard II is depicted in Shakespeare's play as extravagant, over-susceptible to flattery, cold towards his own family – all accusations that had been made against Elizabeth I. Elizabeth herself, in a self-consciously dramatic moment that in itself recalls Shakespeare's Richard, is reputed to have said, 'I am Richard II, know ye not that?' The deposition scene in *Richard II* was considered ideologically inflammatory and was censored under Elizabeth. It was included, however, when Essex and his followers commissioned a performance of the play as a curtain raiser to their rebellion. All of which undoubtedly suggests that the political lessons to be drawn from Shakespeare's histories were taken seriously. But many of Ms Campbell's other parallels seem strained – indicative more of her own scholarly work than of what we can deduce of Shakespeare's methods from his work as a whole.

Opinion is likewise divided on the political philosophy reflected in the histories. E. M. W. Tillyard argues in *Shakespeare's History Plays* (Chatto) that it follows the orthodox Tudor view of harmony: the political body, in obedience to a universal law governing the planets and working its way through most aspects of human life, has its own internal harmony which is from time to time disrupted but which is nonetheless its natural state. The king's duty was to maintain and protect that state of harmony and order. It is true that the plays tend to close on a note of achieved harmony, but with the exception of *Henry V*, which celebrates the shedding of foreign blood, only after considerable civil bloodshed. Other critics see the reality of the history plays there, in the bloodshed, the personal ambitions and the political manoeuvrings – in man's destructive compulsion to acquire power. Certainly, in the tragedies Shakespeare seems to see man's natural state as one of chaos rather than order. However, it requires some forcing of the evidence to see the histories as tending towards the same kind of chaos.

The history plays work more through balance. In them Shakespeare is measuring his public figures, intractible human material as they are, against an ideal – the subordination of personal impulses to the public good. Only twice is the ideal achieved – in John of Gaunt, uncle of the king and father of the rebel Bolingbroke in *Richard II*, and in Henry V. John of Gaunt, however, is depicted as survivor of a passing breed, a man whose views are no longer respected; Henry V as becoming a model king at the expense of private humanity. Yet despite the inevitable ironies – all Shakespeare's public figures will utter the appropriate sentiments in public, no matter what their private ambitions – the ideal remains to be attempted if seldom realized. National stability demands it – and nobody has yet proved that Shakespeare did not have as much respect for national stability as the next Elizabethan.

Richard III

DATE 1593-4
PRINCIPAL CHARACTERS
King Edward IV
The Princes Edward, Prince of Wales (afterwards King Edward V) and Richard, Duke of York, his sons

Richard, Duke of Gloucester ⎫
(later Richard III)   ⎬ Brothers of King Edward
George, Duke of Clarence   ⎭
Queen Elizabeth: Wife of King Edward
Earl Rivers, Marquess of Dorset, Lord Grey and Sir Thomas
Vaughan: Brother, sons and friend of Queen Elizabeth
Duchess of York: Mother of King Edward and his brothers
Lady Anne: Widow of Edward Prince of Wales (son of the late
King Henry VI), later wife of Richard III
Queen Margaret: Widow of Henry VI
Archbishops of Canterbury and York
Duke of Buckingham ⎫ Friends and then
Lord Hastings   ⎬ victims of Richard III
Sir James Tyrrell: Hired by Richard to murder the princes
Henry, Earl of Richmond, afterwards King Henry VII
SCENE England

Plot

ACT ONE The War of the Roses has ended in victory for the
House of York and the accession of Edward IV. Edward is
sick, however, and his brother Richard, consumed with
ambition, is preparing his own way to the throne. He has
poisoned the King's mind against their brother Clarence,
at the same time persuading Clarence that the slanders
against him proceed from Queen Elizabeth's kin. He seeks
to divert any residual sympathy for the Lancastrian cause
by marrying Anne, widow of the Lancastrian Prince of
Wales – a remarkable achievement in persuasion since
Richard admits to having killed her husband and father-in-
law. A further survivor of Lancastrian rule is Queen
Margaret: the sense of trepidation at court occasioned by
the King's illness is heightened by Margaret's gloating, and
by her curses. The entire house of York and Queen Elizabeth's kin come under her curse of unnatural death or, for
the ladies, of mourning and lamentation – curses which the
action of the play proves prophecies. Act One closes
dramatically with the death at the hands of hired murderers

of Clarence, the first victim of Richard's scheming: he dies repenting his treachery in the recent wars.

ACT TWO Edward IV, aware of his approaching death, makes peace between his kinsmen and friends and the Queen. Oaths are sworn which are later broken. The feeling of harmony is shattered by news of Clarence's death, which hastens the King to his own: Edward had countermanded the execution order, Richard had confirmed it and tells the King that word of his fraternal change of heart came too late. The women, always custodians of personal grief in the histories, are prominent in this act. The Duchess of York assumes care of her grandchildren, Clarence's orphans, and tells over earlier troubles she has sustained. Edward IV dies and his widow's grief is heightened by fear – justified when she hears that Rivers, Grey and Vaughan, her own protectors, have been seized on Richard's orders. Richard and Buckingham depart to collect the young King Edward V; Elizabeth hastens to sanctuary with her other son, Prince Richard.

ACT THREE Richard prevails on the Archbishop of Canterbury to break sanctuary so that Prince Richard can be united with his brother, the young king: both children are sent by Richard to the Tower, ostensibly for safety. The next victim of Richard's ambition is Hastings: discovering through private soundings that Hastings would oppose any moves made by Richard to have himself crowned king, Richard accuses Hastings at a council meeting of conspiring against his person by witchcraft. Hastings follows Rivers, Grey and Vaughan to death. Meanwhile Buckingham has been trying, unsuccessfully, to work up support for Richard among the citizens of London. Lack of popular support notwithstanding, in a scene that has been elaborately contrived by Buckingham and Richard, Buckingham, with the Lord Mayor and other citizens, interrupts Richard at his religious devotions: flanked by two priests, with a prayer book in his hand, he is 'prevailed upon' to accept the crown.

ACT FOUR Richard, now king, is full of fears about the

security of his tenure. He has the young princes murdered by Sir James Tyrrell and his wife Anne put to death so that he can marry Elizabeth, the princes' sister – a match for which he appears to win the support of her mother, the Queen, in a scene which is almost a parody of his earlier wooing of Anne. Ominous news is brought to Richard from all sides: armies are massing throughout the country; the Earl of Richmond, who has a Lancastrian claim on the throne, has taken ship from France; Buckingham, who found Richard cold once the throne was achieved, is preparing to fight for Richmond's cause.

ACT FIVE Buckingham has been captured and executed. Otherwise there is no comfort for Richard. While his tent and Richmond's are pitched on Bosworth field the night before the decisive battle, the ghosts of Richard's victims (Edward IV and his son, Clarence, Rivers, Grey and Vaughan, Hastings, the young princes, Anne and Buckingham) appear to wish Richmond success and Richard 'despair and die'. Richard is slain by Richmond, who sees his cause as God's cause. Richmond's proposed marriage to the young Elizabeth, sister of the murdered princes, will unite the houses of York and Lancaster.

Critical commentary

Richard III was one of the most popular of Shakespeare's plays with his first audiences. Richard himself, a stereotype of villainy for the Elizabethans, his character already outlined in unusually close detail in Holinshed's *Chronicles*, Shakespeare's chief source, dominates the play with remarkable energy and dramatic force. *Richard III* had the additional advantage for the Elizabethans of presenting the Tudor cause, in the person of Richmond, as God's cause. Modern critical interest is still concentrated on the characterization of Richard, and on the way Shakespeare has worked the scheme of God's vengeance into the plot.

Despite attempts by historians to sift fact from fear and fantasy in determining what the historical Richard was like,

Shakespeare's portrait still has an unchallenged hold on the popular imagination. Similarly, although scholars are still arguing about whether Shakespeare had read Machiavelli, Richard's mischievous political methods remain for many laymen the essence of Machiavelli's political approach. Yet Richard, a product of Shakespeare's early career, is very much a stage villain – gloating, untouched by finer impulses, delighting in mischief for its own sake, his corrupt moral nature physically suggested in his misshapen body. Richard's success, however, lies in the awareness that Shakespeare has given him of his own staginess – in his self-conscious theatricality.

Until he gains the throne, each goal is attained by his ability to surprise the other characters and to choose the theatrically right moment for his effects. His affrontery in wooing Anne over the coffin of the father-in-law that he murdered surprises her into believing in his love. In the council chamber, when the coronation of the young prince is to be determined, he lulls Hastings by his geniality into a belief in his open disposition; Hastings is convinced that

> – there's never a man in Christendom
> Can lesser hide his hate or love than he;
> For by his face straight shall you know his heart. (III.iv)

Richard returns to the room, his face transformed, to level his ludicrous accusation of witchcraft against Hastings. The citizens of London are disarmed by his piety into 'persuading' him to accept the crown (III.vii), when earlier the suggestion had caused them to look 'deadly pale'. (III.v)

He has already explained to the audience the usefulness of a sanctimonious manner –

> And thus I clothe my naked villany
> With odd old ends stol'n forth of holy writ
> And seem a saint when most I play the devil . . . – (I.iii)

and it is indeed his contempt of religion and his total lack of moral scruple which enable him to achieve the throne. Built into the play's structure, however, is the certainty that those who ignore God's ways are finally the victims of God's vengeance. Early in the play (I.iii) the Lancastrian Queen Margaret curses all those who were responsible for the deaths in her own family. All her curses are realized, and the victims die acknowledging the just vengeance of God. Even the young princes, innocent in themselves, balance the death of the innocent Lancastrian Edward: 'Edward for Edward pays a dying debt' (IV.iv), chants Margaret. England pays for her collective crimes with the blood of princes.

Within this context, we know from the beginning that Richard, God's scourge on England in one sense, must nonetheless bring about his own destruction: he overreaches himself by mistaking earthly power for the ultimate reality. The unseen force in this play about kings is the King of Kings. Edward IV, aware before his own death of the ultimate authority that he may not always have recognized, warns his survivors:

> Take heed you dally not before your king;
> Lest he that is the supreme King of kings
> Confound your hidden falsehood, and award
> Either of you to be the other's end. (II.i)

While Richard is clearing his way to the throne, scorning all other authority, the only comfort for the bystanders is to pray for God's ultimate vengeance.

Vengeance comes when, as Queen Margaret has prophesied, Richard's sins are 'ripe' upon him. Before it comes, however, the atmosphere of the play is one of deep foreboding – and Shakespeare's success in creating this atmosphere greatly enhances Richard's sinister value. Queen Elizabeth's grief at her husband's death is sharpened by a fear that is entirely justified by events; the citizens in the streets cry 'woe to that land that's govern'd by a child' (II.iii); the Earl of Derby dreams menacingly of Richard as a boar; Queen Margaret, a neglected symbol of royal ruin, wanders the court cursing, and then gloating as she witnesses the decline of the house of York. Beyond these somewhat mechanical atmospheric aids, however, is the almost sick feeling of fear achieved by Shakespeare's use of women and children in the play. The women, prominent on the stage, take an entirely passive role in events – fearing for their young and telling over past sorrows. In Act Four, Scene Four, Queen Margaret, her prophecies fulfilled, joins the Duchess of York and Queen Elizabeth in a choric keening. Mostly each woman is isolated by her own burden of grief, so contrast heightens the effectiveness of the meeting of Elizabeth, the Duchess of York and Anne at the Tower (IV.i): forbidden to visit the young princes, they unite in their fears for the children's welfare.

Children appear on stage more in *Richard III* than in any other of Shakespeare's plays: indeed, the murder of the young princes has the same hold over the public imagination as the malevolent characterization of Richard. Not only the young princes but Clarence's children are brought into the action – all of them pawns in a wider political game. It is in fact after the murder of his nephews, the play's climactic horror, that Richard, his goal achieved, begins to lose his control over events: from then on his contempt for God's justice rebounds on him and, losing his capacity to surprise others, outside events, culminating in his own death, overwhelm him.

It was in the Folio edition of 1623 that *Richard III* was first classified as a history: until then it had been considered a tragedy. Certainly Richard's crimes are seen more in the context of his own personal villainy than as political offences, while the sense of pathos that is appropriate to tragedy is heightened by the roles assigned to the women and children – who do, moreover, help to create a domestic and enclosed atmosphere that none of the other histories have. As tragedy, however, it does fail according to the standards that Shakespeare was later to set: horrific on the stage, it lacks the resonance of the mature tragedies which manage to suggest the far more frightening potential for corruption in men of good intent. Moreover, in plot structure, *Richard III* closely follows a pattern that is typical of the English history plays: opening with England at peace, that peace is shattered by a crime which results in civil war; at the end of the play peace is restored, a new order established.

Richard II

DATE 1595

PRINCIPAL CHARACTERS

King Richard II

John of Gaunt, Duke of Lancaster ⎱ Richard's
Duke of York ⎰ uncles

Henry Bolingbroke: Duke of Hereford, son of Gaunt. Afterwards King Henry IV

Duke of Aumerle: Son of the Duke of York

Queen Isabel: Richard's wife

Duchesses of York and Gloucester: Richard's aunts

Thomas Mowbray: Duke of Norfolk

Bushy, Bagot and Green: Unpopular followers of Richard

Earl of Salisbury ⎱ Of Richard's
Sir Stephen Scroop ⎰ party

Earl of Northumberland ⎫
Henry Percy (known as Hotspur), ⎬ Of Bolingbroke's party
Northumberland's son
The Lords Ross and Willoughby ⎭

Bishop of Carlisle

Abbot of Westminster

Sir Pierce of Exton: murderer of Richard II

SCENE England and Wales

Plot

ACT ONE focuses some of the discontent felt by Richard's subjects and family. Bolingbroke, Richard's cousin, formally challenges Mowbray with treason and with conspiring against the life of the late Duke of Gloucester – an act for which it is implied that Richard himself had some responsibility. Richard reserves judgment, ordering instead that the issue shall be decided in combat between the accuser and the accused. On the day of battle, however, Richard banishes the two protagonists – Mowbray for life, Bolingbroke for six years. John of Gaunt demonstrates his public spirit by acceeding to the banishment of his son. With Bolingbroke, whom Richard fears, now disposed of, Richard determines to go to Ireland to replenish his empty coffers with booty. Hearing that Gaunt has been taken ill, the King reveals to his cousin, Aumerle, his intention of seizing the revenues of Hereford, which should revert to Bolingbroke after Gaunt's death.

ACT TWO When Richard arrives on a pious visit to his sick uncle Gaunt, he is accused by Gaunt of susceptibility to base flattery, of turning against his own kin and of leasing out England to finance his own extravagance. Richard is deaf to his uncle's warnings, and seizes the rights to Hereford on Gaunt's death. Richard's injustice unites Northumberland, Ross and Willoughby against the King. While Richard is in Ireland, Bolingbroke returns from banishment to establish his claim to Hereford and is greeted by a growing body of adherents. His uncle York at this stage remains neutral.

ACT THREE Richard lands in Wales from Ireland convinced that his presence will quell the rebellion. His confidence is shattered by the news that the Welsh have declared themselves for Bolingbroke, who has taken it upon himself to execute Bushy and Green, the King's most notorious flatterers. A worse blow, however, is that the Duke of York has defected to Bolingbroke's party. Richard retires to Barkloughly Castle, which is surrounded by Bolingbroke, Northumberland and York. The King recognizes his cousin's right to Hereford, but Bolingbroke, whose ambitions have grown since his return from exile, takes the King prisoner. Richard's Queen, Isabel, who has been in retirement all the while, learns of her husband's plight through a gardener: she and her ladies overhear his allegorical/horticultural discourse to his men, in which a connection is assumed between the role of a gardener in controlling his garden and the role of a king.

ACT FOUR Richard is brought before Bolingbroke, who is wielding all but royal authority, and formally hands over his crown; he baulks at Northumberland's request, however, that he read over the crimes for which he is being deposed. Richard is taken to the Tower and Bolingbroke's coronation date is set. Aumerle, the Bishop of Carlisle and the Abbot of Westminster withdraw to hatch a plot against Bolingbroke.

ACT FIVE Henry IV, making his first appearance as king, is greeted by York with news of the rebellion in which York's own son Aumerle is involved. York urges Aumerle's death, but Henry listens instead to the Duchess of York's pleas for mercy towards her son. Richard, who has formally parted from his wife, is now in prison at Pomfret; there he is attacked and murdered by Sir Pierce Exton, who feels he is doing Henry a service. Henry is brought news by Northumberland that the rebellion has been quelled. His pleasure is destroyed when Exton informs him of Richard's death. Now that the deed is done, his former ambivalence towards Richard disappears and he resolves on a crusade to expiate the sin of regicide.

Critical commentary

With *Richard II* Shakespeare began his great series of plays on English history which was to continue through *Henry IV* Parts 1 and 2 and end with *Henry V*. These plays form a remarkably homogeneous group, in terms of both plot and theme: the rebellions against Henry in the later plays, for example, are seen as a direct consequence of his deposition of Richard in this play, characters recur and act along lines already prepared; in all four plays the nature of kingship and its responsibilities are investigated. Each play, however, makes sense as an independent unit: the individual features of each, and its contribution to the cycle, are of equal importance.

The historical Richard held a special place in the Elizabethan imagination as the last king to rule in undisputed succession from William the Conqueror: with his deposition began the series of rebellions which culminated in the War of the Roses and only ended with the accession of the Tudor Henry VII. He could be regarded as the last truly mediaeval king, and E. M. W. Tillyard, in his book *Shakespeare's History Plays*, argues that most of the stylistic differences between *Richard II* and the later histories can be understood if we see this play as embodying Shakespeare's picture of mediaevalism. His conclusions are persuasive and whether we accept them or not, he does draw attention to some undeniable stylistic and narrative peculiarities of *Richard II*. The whole of the play is written in verse, much of it rhyming. While many of the situations in the play could have lent themselves to a strongly emotive treatment, the language is throughout formal and distanced, the mood elegiac rather than passionate. There are a number of points where the audience is encouraged to expect some action – in what is promised to be the decisive contest between Bolingbroke and Mowbray, for example (I.iii), and later in the meeting between Richard and Bolingbroke outside Barkloughly Castle (III.iii) – only to witness the play withdraw from the dramatic and leave decisions pending. Tillyard sees these aspects of *Richard II* as distinguishing 'a world where means matter more than ends, where it is more important to keep strictly to the rules of an elaborate game than either to win or to lose it' – in short, the mediaeval world. We can alternatively see the stylization of the action as dictated by, and emanating from, the characterization of Richard himself – but more of that later.

The theme of *Richard II* is the problem of deposing a king – a problem which for the Elizabethans was virtually insoluble. Ideologically, kings had a God-given right to rule; practically, to flout the hereditary principle was to produce a situation of potential chaos. Yet bad kings happened and part of the fear attached to the idea of a bad king was the sense of helplessness that would grip the nation. In *Richard II*, that ideological deadlock is built into the structure of the play. Over the first two acts, prominence is given to Richard's failings as king – shown dramatically through his treatment of Bolingbroke, and suggested more generally in the criticism of John of Gaunt. It is given to Gaunt, in one of Shakespeare's finest patriotic speeches, to introduce the idea of England as the chief victim of Richard's shortcomings:

> This land of such dear souls, this dear, dear land,
> Dear for her reputation through the world,
> Is now leas'd out – I die pronouncing it –
> Like to a tenement or pelting farm. (II.i)

Nonetheless, beyond advice, Gaunt sees nothing that the onlookers to this tragic spectacle can do: Richard is God's deputy and God's is the quarrel. His son, Bolingbroke, however, representative of a newer order, cannot separate his private from his public response. After eating 'the bitter bread of banishment' (III.i) he returns to England to take God's quarrel on himself. While he is suffering Richard's injustice passively abroad, the audience's sympathies are with him, but once the rebellion is under way, and his success is growing, our sympathies are directed more and more towards Richard. The King makes a noble parting from his wife, submits with dignity to the coarse treatment of the London crowd when he is brought back a prisoner (as we learn from York's description to his wife in Act Five, Scene Two) and at the end, resists his death bravely. A key to the change is suggested in York's lament as he looks at Richard on the battlements of Flint Castle, before the King is taken prisoner:

> Alack, alack, for woe,
> That any harm should stain so fair a show. (III.iii)

In the latter part of the play, as Bolingbroke's fortunes are in the ascendant, attention is directed away from Richard as man to Richard as 'show', to the office that he holds; the qualities he displays in his decline are the specifically kingly ones of nobility and self-control.

Yet the characterization of Richard is consistent throughout, when we are invited both to criticize and to sympathize with him. Underlying all the criticisms of Richard in the early part of the play is the fact that he considers it sufficient just to be king: he rests too far on the mystique of his office and allows himself to abdicate any real responsibility. In the latter part of the play, when he need no longer be responsible, his transparent kingliness works in his favour. He is, as it were, a theatrical monarch: he has adopted the role of king without giving substance to the reality. It is true to say that Shakespeare saw theatricality as a feature of kingship – Richard III dramatically exploits situations as he clears his path to the throne, the *Henry IV* plays show Prince Hal's self-conscious preparation for the role of king, a role that is carefully studied and, when the time comes, totally assumed. But Richard II is the most overtly self-dramatizing of all Shakespeare's monarchs, as when bad news greets him on his return from Ireland he distances his grief – 'Let's talk of graves, of worms, and epitaphs' (III.ii) – by placing it within a kind of dramatic chronicle of kingship –

> For God's sake let us sit upon the ground
> And tell sad stories of the death of kings. (III.ii)

Richard is aware that his most important prop is England herself, greeted by him with emotion on his return from Ireland,

> I weep for joy
> To stand upon my kingdom once again.
> Dear earth, I do salute thee with my hand. (III.ii)

– but affection towards England, even when expressed with such eloquence, is not enough, and Richard pays the price for failing to understand the duties towards England that his glittering role carries with it.

Richard II shows the rise of one man at the expense of another, but there is no sense at the end of the play that Bolingbroke has won. The picture that we have of the new King Henry at the end of *Richard II* conveys the ideological deadlock to which the whole question of deposing a king ultimately tended. The first rebellion against his power he quells, but the atmosphere is heavy with prophecies about the kind of reign he will enjoy. The Bishop of Carlisle warns him that

> The blood of English shall manure the ground
> And future ages groan for this foul act. (IV.i)

Richard himself prophesies a division, which *Henry IV* sees realized, between Henry and Northumberland, his 'ladder' to the throne. Concentrating all the ambivalence of Henry's position is his response to Richard's death. He knows that he could never have enjoyed undisputed title to the throne while Richard was alive; nonetheless he bemoans the fact that Richard's 'blood should sprinkle me to make me grow.' (V.vi) The stain of regicide can never be quite eradicated and in *Henry IV* we never see the king happy.

Henry IV, Part One

DATE 1596

PRINCIPAL CHARACTERS

King Henry IV

Henry, Prince of Wales (Hal): The King's eldest son

Lord John of Lancaster: A younger son of the King

Earl of Westmoreland

Sir Walter Blunt

THE REBELS

Earl of Northumberland

Henry Percy: Northumberland's son, known as Hotspur

Earl of Worcester: A kinsman of Northumberland

Lady Percy (Kate): Hotspur's wife, Mortimer's sister

Edmund Mortimer: Earl of March, claimant to the English throne

Lady Mortimer: Mortimer's wife, Glendower's daughter

Owen Glendower: Leader of Welsh rebels

Earl of Douglas and Sir Richard Vernon: Scottish rebels

Richard Scroop, Archbishop of York: A northern rebel

HAL'S COMPANIONS
Sir John Falstaff
Poins
Gadshill
Bardolph
Peto
Mistress Quickly: Hostess of the Boar's Head Tavern
SCENE England – the King's court, the Boar's Head tavern in
Eastcheap, Henry Percy's home, the battlefield of Shrewsbury;
Wales – Glendower's castle

Plot

ACT ONE King Henry IV is burdened by care: the Earl of
Mortimer, sent to quell the Welsh rebels under Glendower,
has been taken prisoner; Hotspur has triumphed over the
Scottish rebels but refuses to hand his prisoners over to the
King. At a later meeting with the King (I.iii) Hotspur
agrees to part with the prisoners if Henry will ransom
Mortimer, Hotspur's brother-in-law. Angered by the
King's refusal to comply, Hotspur, Northumberland and
Worcester plan a more organized rebellion: under cover of
handing over the Scottish prisoners, they will work to unite
the Scots, Welsh and northern rebels against the King. The
fundamental source of their discontent is the King's treatment of them since, with their help, he achieved the
monarchy. Henry's cares are domestic as well as political:
his son Hal, whom he compares unfavourably to the valiant
Hotspur, dissipates his time in the London taverns. In an
interlude from court affairs, the audience is introduced to
a sample of Hal's life with Falstaff and others (I.ii); after
the departure of his companions, Hal reveals an inner
separateness from their way of life.

ACT TWO enlarges on Hal's tavern life as a plan, hatched
between Hal and Poins in Act One, reaches fruition. Hal
and Poins absent themselves while Falstaff and Bardolph
hold up and rob some travellers; Hal and Poins, in disguise,
then rob the robbers. The joke, when Hal and Poins join
Falstaff at the Boar's Head, is in the discrepancy between

Falstaff's actual cowardice and his account of what happened. A message is delivered to Hal at the tavern summoning him to a meeting with his father the next morning, after which Hal and Falstaff play-act the appointed scene between father and son. Hal's ultimate rejection of Falstaff is implicit in this play-within-a-play.

ACT THREE Hotspur and Mortimer, who is now married to Glendower's daughter, make their farewells before battle to their wives at Glendower's castle. At the arranged meeting between the King and Hal, Henry accuses his son of making himself too common; Hal reassures his father by his determination to distinguish himself in battle against Hotspur. Falstaff too is swept into the war as he is made a captain and promised a troop by Hal.

ACT FOUR shows the tide beginning to turn against the rebels: news reaches Hotspur, Worcester and Douglas of Northumberland's sickness and of Glendower's delay in organizing his army. When Sir Walter Blunt arrives on an embassy from the King, offering them pardon and redress, Hotspur tells over again the story of their discontent: apart from alleging that Henry has neglected his former allies, Hotspur claims that his father's intention in Bolingbroke's rebellion had not been to depose Richard II but to restore Bolingbroke to his former titles. Falstaff meanwhile has disgraced his charge by pocketing the money he was given to furnish his troop and assembling what he admits to being 'food for powder'. (IV.ii)

ACT FIVE In the battle at Shrewsbury between the King's party and the rebels, Hal distinguishes himself by killing Hotspur, and goes some way towards reconciling his father to him by defending him from Douglas. Falstaff alone of Hal's party has proved cowardly: feigning death when attacked by Douglas, he then tries to claim the honour of Hotspur's death. The play ends with the expectation of further battle: Westmoreland and Prince John set off to tackle Northumberland and the Archbishop of York; Henry and Hal are bound for the Welsh rebels under Glendower and Mortimer.

Critical commentary

At the end of *Richard II* we see a radical transformation in Bolingbroke immediately on his elevation to the monarchy, as the young hopeful is replaced by the careworn king. In the last act of *Richard II*, his first words as King refer to his 'unthrifty son'; in the closing speech in that play, he determines to expiate the guilt of Richard's murder with a crusade. The twin themes of *Henry IV*, *Part One* – Prince Hal's unorthodox preparation for the monarchy and the troubled reign which a usurper must expect to enjoy – were thus already established in *Richard II*. The importance in *Henry IV* of the King's character is negligible: Hal, Hotspur and, of course Falstaff, have always dominated the play for audiences and critics. It is enough for Henry to illustrate the fate of the king who achieves the throne by bloody means.

The narrative of *Henry IV* concerns the rebellion of the Percys, *Part One* ending with the death of Hotspur. The division between Henry and his former allies had been prophesied by Richard II in the earlier play. When the rebels first lay their plans in *Henry IV* they apply the same image to themselves – of the 'ladder' by which Henry had ascended the throne – as Richard had done. The situation of an aspirant king needing allies who then become his subjects is one that Richard had foreseen as inevitably breeding mutual distrust: Worcester justifies their rebellion with this argument:

> The King will always think him in our debt,
> And think we think ourselves unsatisfied
> Til he hath found a time to pay us home. (I.iii)

The rebellion, beginning in distrust and dissatisfaction, gathers ideological momentum until, by the time the battle lines are formed, the rebels are seeing themselves as Henry's scourges for the crime of usurpation: their own part in Richard's downfall has become something they never envisaged, barely connived at. The change in attitude is of a piece with Elizabethan political thinking. The rebels, impure agents in themselves, and finally punished for their crimes against the present King, Henry IV, are nonetheless a means of vengeance on England for the spilling of royal blood.

Henry himself does not appear to see the rebellion in that light, but he does place his disappointment in his son Hal within the context of divine vengeance:

> But thou dost in thy passages of life
> Make me believe that thou art only mark'd
> For the hot vengeance and the rod of heaven
> To punish my mistreadings . . . (III.ii)

He compares his son's youth – squandered among the common people, in full public display – unfavourably with his own:

> By being seldom seen, I could not stir
> But, like a comet, I was wonder'd at; (III.ii)

In this he justifiably but quite radically misreads his son's behaviour. One of the play's central ironies is that Hal's companions, while perhaps scandalous as the chosen friends of a prince, will finally be abandoned, and once abandoned, will never have the power to touch Hal as King of England; while the companions of King Henry's youth, correct enough for a prince, nonetheless plague his reign because he has indebted himself to men of power and influence.

Both the *Henry IV* plays are more Hal's than they are the King's: together they could be subtitled, 'The making of a king'. In these plays and in *Henry V*, which followed them, Shakespeare exploited two legends which, for the Elizabethans, still had power to stir: the legend of Prince Hal's dissolute youth which was redeemed by his legendary military exploits in France. A temptation would have been to combine the two legends at the level of romance, making of Hal a hot-headed, hot-blooded gallant, not unlike Hotspur. But Shakespeare subordinates romance to

political realism: Hal emerges from the process as, if anything, too calculating for popular taste. After his first scene
with Falstaff he at once makes clear both his detached view
of his companions: 'I know you all, and will awhile uphold/
The unyok'd humour of your idleness.' (I.ii) – and his
wider intentions in consorting with them: masked now by
the 'base contagious clouds' of Eastcheap bonhomie, he
will finally emerge like the sun (a popular image for the
king in Elizabethan literature), and presumably seem to
shine more brilliantly by contrast.

Hal stands at the meeting point between three quite
separate worlds – his proper sphere of court and king,
Hotspur's chivalric world, and Falstaff's comic Eastcheap
milieu. Embryonic in himself at the beginning of the play,
he takes from each what suits him, to emerge in *Henry V* the
complete public man. As we have seen, he reacts negatively
to his father by avoiding men of his own class – the wisdom
of which is naturally lost on Henry. Hotspur and Falstaff
are sometimes interpreted, by those who see Hal making
his choices like an Everyman in a morality play, as Hal's
good and bad angels, but his relationship with them is not
quite as straightforward as that. Hotspur, admirable in
many ways and favourably compared with Hal by a number
of other characters, is nonetheless shown by Shakespeare to
be an inappropriate ideal for a prince. Hotspur's chivalric
ethic is too personal for public life, the language in which
he expresses it deliberately extravagant and outmoded:

> By heaven, methinks it were an easy leap
> To pluck bright honour from the pale-fac'd moon. (I.iii)

Hal envies Hotspur his reputation for valour but bides his
time, intending to use Hotspur as his ladder to fame, but
in a way that will carry no risks: he tells his father:

> Percy is but my factor, good my lord,
> To engross up glorious deeds on my behalf; (III.ii)

By killing Hotspur, Hal alters their respective positions in
the eyes of posterity in precisely that way.

Hal's relationship with Falstaff is subtler. In some ways Falstaff represents Hotspur's antithesis: the latter's speech on honour is almost parodied by Falstaff at the battle of Shrewsbury as his every effort is concentrated on avoiding combat: 'Can honour set to a leg? No. Or an arm? No. Or take away the grief of a wound? No. Honour hath no skill in surgery then? No . . .' (V.i) Anti-chivalric, anti-authoritarian – his hope is that Hal, when king, will never hang a thief – he unwittingly benefits Hal at his own expense: through his association with Falstaff, the Prince is purged of human responses that would be unfitting in a king. Hotspur's myth is too personal for a figurehead and leader, Falstaff's too individual: Hal, as Henry V, has managed to subordinate what is personal and individual to himself more successfully than any other monarch in the English histories.

Henry IV also provides us, through Hotspur and Falstaff, with glimpses of those things which Hal, as king, will never be able to enjoy in the same way as other men. The short scenes between Hotspur and his wife Kate (II.iii and III.i) charming in themselves, place the man of action in a more fully domestic context than we will ever see Hal; with Falstaff, Poins and Bardolph at the Boar's Head, Hal enjoys fellowship of a kind that he will put behind him as king. He learns with them valuable lessons in dealing with ordinary Englishmen (assuming that we could ever call Falstaff ordinary), but there is a difference between an involving comaraderie and a lesson well absorbed.

The debt of the *Henry IV* plays to Falstaff does, of course, transcend his relationship with Hal. The importance of Falstaff to the history cycle will be dealt with more fully under *Henry IV, Part Two*.

Henry IV, Part Two

DATE 1598

PRINCIPAL CHARACTERS

King Henry IV

Prince Henry: afterwards crowned Henry V

Prince John of Lancaster, Humphrey of Gloucester and Thomas, Duke of Clarence: Sons of the King

Earl of Warwick
Earl of Westmoreland } Of the King's party
Lord Chief Justice

Earl of Northumberland
Richard Scroop, Archbishop of York } Rebels against the King
Lords Mowbray and Hastings

Sir John Falstaff

Bardolph, Pistol, Poins and Peto: Falstaff's companions

Justices Shallow and Silence

Mistress Quickly: Keeper of the Boar's Head Tavern

Doll Tearsheet: A bawd

SCENE England

Plot

ACT ONE opens with Northumberland being brought news of his son, Hotspur's, death at the battle of Shrewsbury. Despondent now about the rebels' chances he is urged to remember that the Archbishop of York, who 'turns insurrection to religion' (I.i), is still active in the rebels' cause. Later, the Archbishop and Hastings assess their chances against the King. The Archbishop concludes that the people have 'become enamoured' of Richard's grave and are ready to turn against Henry. Meanwhile Falstaff, returned from the Battle of Shrewsbury to London, is reprimanded by the Lord Chief Justice for his part in the robbery at Gad's Hill, enacted in *Henry IV Part One*: only his 'valour' at Shrewsbury prevents further action being taken against him.

ACT TWO depicts further adventures of Falstaff. Mistress Quickly threatens to have him committed for defaulting on his debts, but he wins her round. A tender scene between him and Doll Tearsheet in the Boar's Head is witnessed by Hal and Poins disguised as drawers, until Hal is summoned to his father in Westminster Palace and Falstaff to join the other captains who are to march against the Archbishop of York under Prince John. In an interlude from London, Northumberland is persuaded by his wife and daughter-in-law to flee to Scotland until he can be sure of the rebels' success.

ACT THREE shows Henry IV, recently recovered from illness, in a despondent mood. In Gloucestershire, Falstaff, entertained by Justice Shallow, a companion of his youth, is enlisting men to his troop. Falstaff's susceptibility to bribery leads him to assemble a scandalously inadequate band of fighters.

ACT FOUR shows the rebels (Archbishop of York, Mowbray and Hastings) downcast by the news of Northumberland's defection. Westmoreland, on embassy from Prince John, persuades the rebels to present their grievances to the Prince as his father's representative. The Prince promises to redress their grievances and, when the rebel forces are dispersed, arrests the leaders for high treason. He claims not to have broken his word, since their legitimate complaints will still be attended to.

In London the King, surrounded by all his sons but Hal, laments the 'headstrong riot' which will prevail in England when Hal has succeeded him. Westmoreland's good news about the rebellion, far from cheering him, throws him into a swoon. Hal watches by his dying father's bed, muses on the trouble that the crown has given him and, grief-stricken when he thinks that his father has indeed died, carries the crown from the room. Henry stirs and attributes his son's behaviour to an undue haste to become king. After explanations father and son are reconciled. Henry advises Hal, in the new and precarious civil peace, to 'busy giddy minds/ With foreign quarrels'. (IV.v) The King is finally taken off to die in the Jerusalem Chamber as a substitute for the Holy Land where he hoped to make an expiating Crusade.

ACT FIVE Prince Hal makes peace with the Lord Chief Justice who once sent him to prison for a youthful misdemeanour and thus had reason to fear his place when the Prince should become king. Falstaff, hearing of Henry IV's death, rushes back to London with Shallow, boasting of the power and influence that he will enjoy under Henry V. In the event, Henry renounces Falstaff, symbol of his own dissolute youth, outside the Abbey after the coronation. The play ends with speculation from Prince John about a war in France.

Critical commentary

King Henry IV, Part Two, continues the story of the rebellion against the King which was begun in *Part One*. As in the earlier play the deposition of Richard II is frequently recalled: Richard's prophecy of a division between Henry and Northumberland is remembered by the King, who continues to be obsessed by the idea of the Crusade which was to expiate the sin of regicide. In terms of actual plot (which concerns the overthrow of the rebels who remain undefeated after the battle of Shrewsbury) *Henry IV, Part Two* lacks some of the vigour of *Part One*. Hotspur's presence and energy are missed: the remaining rebels are defeated, not by action, but by deviously political means.

Nonetheless, this is not an inferior play to its predecessor. It has a predominantly elegiac mood, maintained through the different threads of the plot, which contrasts well with the broader farce and heroics of *Part One*, and with the swashbuckling adventures of *Henry V* which are to follow. In part, this is achieved by reference to events of the earlier histories. A feature of the history play as a form is that a dense and allusive sense of the past can be created over a few plays. Richard II is very much part of this play's remembered past; John of Gaunt, father of the present King, and Hotspur are both recalled.

Throughout *Henry IV, Part Two* the King's illness is kept before the audience, whether the King is on stage or not. The Crusade with which he hoped to begin his reign has become something he would like to have done. The future that Henry imagines now is not his own but his son's, and what he expects of Hal as his successor disturbs him: so much more are our sympathies enlisted on Henry's behalf in *Part Two* that it is with relief that, on his deathbed, we see his fears finally calmed. Henry's last scene, depicting his final disappointment in Hal and ultimate reconciliation with him, is pivotal to the play. More than anything in the other histories this scene (IV.v.) suggests, at a highly personal level, the pathos of monarchic succession:

> Then get thee gone, and dig my grave thyself,
> And bid the merry bells ring to thine ear
> That thou art crowned, not that I am dead. (IV.v)

In the event, the fears of his father for Hal, crowned Henry V at the end of the play, are abundantly confounded. As the mantle of kingship falls on him he is a transformed man – a transformation that we have been prepared for since the soliloquy early in *Henry IV, Part One* (I.ii), when his attitude to those 'base contagious clouds' his companions, is unequivocally revealed. In his rejection of Falstaff he uses the dreaming/waking imagery so often employed by Shakespeare to suggest the individual's complete change of state:

> I have long dream'd of such a kind of man,
> So surfeit-swell'd, so old and so profane;
> But being awak'd, I do despise my dream. (V.v)

This scene, concluding with Falstaff's attempts to convince his companions that Henry V is merely exhibiting his public face and that his private face will be reserved for more intimate occasions, is among the most pathetic in all Shakespeare's work. The irony is that Henry is no longer Hal, no longer has a private face: so well, if in an unorthodox way, has he schooled himself for the monarchy that he is now a complete public figure; and, as Shakespeare demonstrates, the price of public excellence is private warmth.

Falstaff, too, contributes to the elegiac mood of *Henry IV, Part Two*, and not only in the sense that Henry's rejection of him immediately establishes him as a relic from the past. In this play he himself, the audience and the other characters are made more aware of his age. Falstaff is a figure from the world of comedy, both because, as he describes himself to his Page, 'I am not only witty in myself, but the cause that wit is in other men' (I.ii), and in the sense that he wages a continual battle against time by trying to make of his life a suspended moment of pleasure. He is at his most buoyant when he is convinced of his own youth. Holding up the travellers at Gad's Hill in *Part One*, his age forgotten in his absorption in the moment, he berates his victims with – 'What, ye knaves, young men must live.' (II.ii) In this play he pleads his youth again, this time to the Lord Chief Justice, as an excuse for his behaviour at Gad's Hill: 'You that are old consider not the capacities of us that are young.' With the Lord Chief Justice, however, presumably much of an age with himself, his assertion is more ludicrous than splendidly audacious.

That he is coming to the end of the road is suggested in other ways. Falstaff's unscrupulousness is always part of his attraction. The audience, observing his behaviour as captain of troop in *Part One*, has its moral judgment blunted by the pace of the comedy; in *Part Two*, where the soldiers he assembles are allowed to plead their unfitness for battle, he looks more squalid. The comedy of his scene with Doll Tearsheet is pathetic and Doll, true to the tradition of the golden-hearted whore, responds to the pathos, asking him when he will 'begin to patch up thine old body for heaven' (II.iv) – a question that Falstaff would prefer not to consider.

There are many things that Falstaff would prefer not to think about – a characteristic which in a sense is crucial to his role in the history cycle. A comic figure, his function far and away transcends the providing of comic relief from graver matters. By the time he wrote *Henry IV*, Shakespeare had learned the rich dividends to be yielded in comedy from juxtaposing separate worlds and letting them react on one another. He deployed the same technique in *Henry IV*, where historical time, with its big events and sense of continuity, is not only punctuated but to some extent placed and re-defined by interludes of fast-moving comic time. These comic interludes depict a world, removed from the cares of state, where the primary aim is the pursuit of pleasure. The pleasure principle is by no means condemned and Hal has to have a taste of the world presided over by Falstaff before he can be absorbed into the sphere of court and state affairs. It is sometimes said of Falstaff that he represents Shakespeare's unofficial voice. Indeed, some twentieth-century critics, distressed by the now unfashionable nationalism of Shakespeare's histories, like to think that Falstaff is deliberately used to undermine the patriotic sentiments expressed by other characters. It is perhaps safer to assume that Shakespeare, living through a vigorously nationalistic period, was as patriotic as the next man and better able than most to express his patriotism. But he was aware that there was more to life than that: his picture of Hal's development, while depicted as politically necessary, nonetheless lacks human warmth. Falstaff, with his anarchic individuality, his scorn of honour and authority, completes the canvas for us.

Henry V

DATE 1599

PRINCIPAL CHARACTERS: The Chorus, which introduces each act

THE ENGLISH

King Henry V

Dukes of Gloucester and Bedford: His brothers

Duke of Exeter: The King's uncle and trusted adviser

Earl of Westmoreland

Archbishop of Canterbury

Bishop of Ely
Earl of Cambridge ⎫
Lord Scroop   ⎬ Conspirators against the King
Sir Thomas Grey   ⎭
Sir Thomas Erpingham, Gower, Fluellen, MacMorris, Jamy:
Officers in the English army
Nym, Bardolph, Pistol, Bates, Court, Williams and other soldiers
in the English army
Hostess of the Boar's Head tavern, formerly Mistress Quickly, now
married to Pistol
THE FRENCH
Charles VI, King of France
Lewis, the Dauphin
Dukes of Burgundy, Orleans, Bourbon
The Constable of France
Rambures, Granpré: French Lords
Mountjoy: A French herald
Isabel, Queen of France
Katharine: Her daughter
SCENE England and France

Plot

ACT ONE After the Chorus, in a Prologue, has apologized for
the inadequacies of the theatre as a means of presenting war,
the Archbishop of Canterbury and the Bishop of Ely are
found rejoicing over Henry's reformation since he became
King. King Henry himself, who is about to meet the
French ambassadors, is anxious to establish the legality of
his claim on the French crown. The Archbishop of Canterbury, after a long disquisition on the Salic Law, convinces
the King that God and right are on the side of the English.
Henry presents his claim to the French ambassadors and is
answered by a gift from the Dauphin of tennis balls – a
joke against Henry's notoriously idle youth. The King's
warlike purpose is strengthened by the contempt of the
French.
ACT TWO The Chorus informs us that Cambridge, Grey and

Scroop are in the pay of the French and have conspired to kill King Henry before he sets sail to France from Southampton. When we see Henry with the conspirators at Southampton, he knows of their plan but maintains a cordial manner, asking them how he should deal with a soldier who has been openly declaring his hostility to the King. The conspirators recommend stern treatment. When Henry hands them their 'commissions' for France they read instead that they are charged with treason. Tricked by their recommendation of death for the common soldier, they are taken to be executed, their own pleas for mercy unheeded. Meanwhile, some of Henry's boon companions as Prince of Wales – Bardolph, Nym and Pistol, now married to Mistress Quickly – are preparing for their part in the French War. As she sees them off for Southampton the 'quondam Quickly' speaks of the death of Falstaff – killed, it is thought, by the King's unkindness. At the end of the Act the scene transfers to France and the French court: the Dauphin is inclined to dismiss Henry, but the King of France recalls the Black Prince, an earlier scourge of the French and an ancestor of Henry, and concludes that the English threat is not negligible.

ACT THREE The Chorus transports the English army to France where we find them besieging Harfleur, which is shortly surrendered by the Governor. The Welsh Fluellen has emerged as the greatest disciplinarian among Henry's officers – easily ridiculed for his attention to detail but nonetheless valiant. Fluellen refuses Pistol's request to intercede with the Duke of Exeter on behalf of Bardolph, who is to be hanged for stealing. The French leaders are amazed by the English success at Harfleur, but are confident of victory when their main forces meet the English, who are now 'sick and famish'd'. Henry tells the French herald Mountjoy that, given the condition of his soldiers, he would prefer to return to Calais, but if the French attack, the English will fight. The night before the battle of Agincourt the French leaders are shown by Shakespeare to be over-confident and effeminate.

ACT FOUR Still the night before Agincourt, Henry passes in disguise among his soldiers and argues with them about the limits of the King's responsibilities – which he reveals later in soliloquy are oppressing him. He exchanges gloves with the soldier Williams on an issue that they will fight out after Agincourt – Williams' assertion that the King, in defeat, would be willing to ransom himself and thus render the deaths of his subjects futile. Immediately before the battle in which the English will be outnumbered five to one, Mountjoy offers to take the King for ransom in order to avoid bloodshed; at the end of the day Mountjoy returns, conceding defeat and asking leave to bury the French dead – who fabulously outnumber the English dead. All that the audience has seen of the fighting is some burlesque involving Pistol, but the deeds of the valiant are reported by observers. Henry pardons Williams for the quarrel he unwittingly engaged in with his king and rewards him handsomely for his bravery.

ACT FIVE The Chorus takes Henry home in triumph to England and returns him to France for the peace negotiations. Leaving the details of negotiation (in which all English demands are finally ratified) to his able brothers and advisers, Henry woos the French Princess Katharine: it is hoped that their marriage will seal a lasting peace. The Chorus returns at the end to remind the audience of Henry V's early death and the troubled reign of his infant son.

Critical commentary

In *Henry V*, written close on the *Henry IV* plays in 1599, we see the new King following the advice given to him by his father in the earlier play – 'to busy giddy minds/With foreign quarrels.' (*Henry IV, Part Two*, IV.v) Only Henry never presents his quarrel with the French, even to himself, in the light of expediency. Before declaring his intentions to the French ambassadors he piously asks the Archbishop of Canterbury, 'May I with right and conscience make this claim?' To which the prelate as piously replies, 'The sin upon my head, dread sovereign!' (I.ii) After Agincourt, his remarkable victory achieved, Henry attributes his success to divine intervention:

> Oh God! thy arm was here;
> And not to us, but to thy arm alone,
> Ascribe we all. (IV.viii)

Henry has indeed, as his court and family are fond of remarking, come a long way since Prince Hal. His piety is untouched by irony; his former companions go unrecognized by him in battle and the playwright allows him no reaction to Falstaff's death. He has become what he was elaborately preparing himself to be in the earlier plays: the complete public man whose ambitions are national rather than personal, whose personality has been completely absorbed into his office.

Henry V is a national epic whose hero was a legendary figure for the nationalistic Elizabethans. Apart from his moving soliloquy about the responsibilities of office:

> Upon the King! Let us our lives, our souls,
> Our debts, our careful wives,
> Our children, and our sins, lay on the King! (IV.i)

his finest moments are public ones. For in the episode that might have shown us a more relaxed and intimate Henry – his wooing of Katharine – he is shown to be ever mindful of the political advantages of the marriage:

> . . . in loving me you should love the friend of France; for I love France so well that I will not part with a village of it. (V.ii)

He tells Katharine that she should make allowances for his soldierly plainness, and it is as a soldier that he is most impressive. His addresses to his army are stirring, his tone, in that public context, affectionately democratic:

> We few, we happy few, we band of brothers;
> For he to-day that sheds his blood with me
> Shall be my brother. (IV.iii)

Throughout the play Shakespeare cashes in on his audience's acceptance of the legend of Henry V; Henry's own boast is that:

– I will dazzle all the eyes of France
Yea, strike the Dauphin blind to look on us. (I.ii)

The French King, remembering other English heroes (England's legendary past is also part of the play's background), thinks it prudent to 'fear/The native mightiness and fate of him.' (II.iv) Before Agincourt, Henry is given an awareness that myth is being made:

He that outlives this day, and comes safe home
Will stand a tip-toe when this day is nam'd,
And rouse him at the name of Crispian. (IV.iii)

If Henry is less appealing to us than he was to the Elizabethans, I am not sure that Shakespeare would be particularly offended by our coldness. He has demonstrated, through Henry's development as Prince of Wales in the *Henry IV* plays, that public virtue involves some degree of personal inhumanity: what he is presenting us with in Henry V is an ideal king, not necessarily an attractive man. At the same time, although that ideal is depicted without irony, Shakespeare was undoubtedly aware of its artificiality: that its appeal is, as it were, more aesthetic than real. *Henry V* was written over the same period as the great comedies (*As You Like It*, *Much Ado* and *Twelfth Night*), and in some ways it has a closer relationship to the comedies than does *Henry IV*. Not, it must be said, in the quality of the humour, which in *Henry V* is restricted to a barrack-room style of practical joke like the Dauphin's gift of tennis balls and the trick Henry plays on the conspirators, and to a jingoistic humour at the expense of the French, who sit up before Agincourt writing sonnets to their horses – humour that is undoubtedly appropriate in a play about war, but which is nonetheless greatly inferior to what *Henry IV* has to offer.

The relationship of *Henry V* to the comedies does not depend on its humour, or lack of it. In the great comedies, the sense of achieved happiness is sharpened by our awareness that Shakespeare has organized events into a harmony rarely achieved in life. So in *Henry V* Shakespeare makes us aware that the ideal of national unity that Henry achieves has been achieved under artificial conditions. War dominates the plot, but war is at best a temporary, not to say wasteful, way of busying 'giddy minds'. Henry knows that his father's crime in seizing the crown has yet to be avenged, and his prayer before Agincourt is:

> Not today, O Lord!
> O! not today, think not upon the fault
> My father made in compassing the crown! (IV.i)

God's vengeance misses his generation but it strikes the next. In the play's final scene his marriage is arranged: as in the comedies, marriage is both a symbol and a means to a wider harmony, as the Queen of France points out:

> God, the best maker of all marriages,
> Combine your hearts in one, your realms in one! (V.ii)

But Isabel's is not the last word. *Henry V*, like some of the comedies, has an epilogue, given by the Chorus, in which the audience is reminded of Henry's early death and the succession of his young son:

> Whose state so many had the managing
> That they lost France and made his England bleed ... (V.ii)

Henry IV's crimes, briefly forgotten under Henry V, are avenged on Henry VI: only then will the wheel have completed its circle.

7 Shakespeare: Roman History

So are they all, all honourable men ... *Julius Caesar* (III.ii)

Second in importance as a source-book only to Holinshed's *Chronicles*, which provided Shakespeare with the plots of the English history plays and of *King Lear*, *Macbeth* and *Cymbeline*, was Sir Thomas North's translation of Plutarch as *The Lives of the Noble Romans and Greeks* (translated in 1579). Shakespeare's contact with North's Plutarch was a turning point in his career. The first play to emerge from his reading of North was *Julius Ceasar* (1599) which, while not unequivocally a tragedy, represents a more decisive move towards tragedy than *Titus Andronicus* and *Romeo and Juliet* had done. After *Caesar* came only *Twelfth Night* of the romantic comedies, and otherwise the great body of his tragic work. The character of Brutus in *Julius Caesar* is his first complete handling of a type which was, in one form or another, to be central to his tragic vision: that of a man whose ideals prove more vulnerable and less effective than shrewdness and opportunism, and who brings about his own, and the destruction of others, without deviating from his own highest standards.

North's translation provided Shakespeare with the plots and, in an already highly developed form, with the characters of *Julius Caesar*, *Antony and Cleopatra* (1606-7), *Coriolanus* (1608) and *Timon of Athens* (of uncertain date). *Timon* is most effectively considered as a tragedy, while the Roman plays have sufficient in common, and sufficient to separate them from the other tragedies, to mark them off as a distinct group. In particular, the ethical concerns of these plays are still those of the English histories. *Julius Caesar*, like *Richard II*, deals with the problem of deposing an absolute ruler; Brutus and Coriolanus are, like Hotspur in *Henry IV*, *Part One*, men whose personal ethic makes them unfit for active politics; in Antony and Octavius Caesar the relation between the private and the public man is explored as it had been in Henry V. All the Roman Plays, like the English history plays, work towards the definition of the ideal ruler. It is man in relation to a political system rather than man in relation to a natural order, and wracked by his own internal conflicts, who takes the centre of the stage. In *Lear*, *Macbeth* and *Hamlet* there are characters who survive to pick up the pieces, but only after a cataclysmic upheaval which has brought the universe to the edge of chaos. The Roman plays lack the possibility of total chaos; their business is government and there are always men to govern. What really separates the Roman plays from the tragedies is that they lack a sense of evil. They are peopled by men, more or less well-intentioned, whose search is for a mean between their private aspirations and the needs of the state.

Julius Caesar

DATE 1599

PRINCIPAL CHARACTERS

Julius Caesar

Marcus Brutus ⎫
Caius Cassius ⎬ Conspirators against Caesar
Casca and Cinna ⎭

Octavius Caesar ⎫
Mark Antony ⎬ Triumvirs after Caesar's death
Lepidus ⎭

Calpurnia: Caesar's wife

Cicero ⎫
Publius ⎬ Senators

Flavius and Marullus: Tribunes

SCENE Rome

Plot

ACT ONE As the Roman crowd gathers to welcome Caesar back from his military triumphs, not everybody is pleased with the adulation that Caesar is receiving. Cassius sounds out Brutus for his opinion of Caesar's 'ambition' and discovers that Brutus too feels that Caesar is being treated too much as a god. Their fears are confirmed when Casca, who has observed a public demonstration in Caesar's honour, tells them that Mark Antony thrice offered Caesar a crown, with the evident approval of the crowd, which Caesar thrice, but with increasing reluctance, rejected. Meanwhile, as Caesar's glory is reaching its peak, fears for his safety grow and Rome is filled with an atmosphere of foreboding: a soothsayer warns him to 'beware the Ides of March', there is an unusually severe storm, owls appear at noon and a lion is seen walking through the Capitol. Cassius has organized a meeting of possible conspirators against Caesar who are waiting only for Brutus to commit himself: his reputation for honour is in itself sufficient to transform their cause 'to virtue and to worthiness'. (I.iii)

ACT TWO Brutus, who is spending the night in a state of mental turmoil, is visited by the conspirators and persuaded to join them. From that point he takes control: the murder of Caesar will be treated as a sacrifice and, in order to avoid any taint of butchery, the life of Caesar's friend Mark Antony will be spared. As the morning of the Ides of March begins to dawn, Caesar is implored by his wife Calpurnia, who has dreamed of his death, not to go to the senate house. He has just agreed to stay at home when the conspirators arrive to escort him there: their hints that he is likely to be offered the crown that day prove more persuasive than Calpurnia's fears.

ACT THREE While one of the conspirators sets himself to keeping Mark Antony from the senate house, the others submit Caesar to a ritualistic stabbing. Mark Antony arrives on the scene of the murder, apparently prepared to come to terms with the conspirators. He asks for permission to speak at Caesar's funeral; Brutus grants his request, on condition that he confine his speech to praise of the dead. At the funeral, Brutus speaks first and soon convinces the crowd that Caesar's death was necessary. He is followed by Mark Antony who, in a speech heavy with irony, turns the crowd against the conspirators while apparently insisting on their honourable motives. When he comes to read Caesar's will, with its generous bequests to the people of Rome, the crowd are stirred to violence. Act Three closes on a sinister note as Cinna the poet is murdered by the mob because he shares a name with one of the conspirators.

ACT FOUR Rome is now under the control of Antony, Lepidus and Caesar's nephew Octavius, who are preparing for battle against the conspirators' army. Cassius and Brutus, in their camp, are divided over policy and tactics: Cassius complains that his old friend is ill-treating him, Brutus that Cassius is susceptible to bribery. Anxious to be reconciled, Cassius agrees to the adoption of Brutus' plan – that they should march to meet Octavius and Antony at Philippi rather than wait for the enemy to find them, as Cassius would prefer. Brutus is visited in the night by the ghost of Caesar who says that he will appear again at Philippi.

ACT FIVE At Philippi Brutus' army is successful against Octavius but Cassius is surrounded by Antony's troops. When Cassius is given the false information that Brutus too is beleaguered, he takes what he considers to be the only course – suicide. After this blow to their morale, the conspirators fare badly, and Brutus, who has seen Caesar's ghost again, follows Cassius' example and kills himself to avoid being taken prisoner. After his death, Brutus is praised by Antony as 'the noblest Roman of them all'. (V.v)

Critical commentary

In his *Preface* to *Julius Caesar* (Batsford) H. Granville-Barker called the play 'the gateway through which Shakespeare passed' to his five great tragedies'. Written in the same year as *Henry V* and the year before *Hamlet*, *Julius Caesar* does indeed, to use another metaphor, form a bridge between the histories and the tragedies; and more than with the other two Roman plays, which are less ambiguously tragic, critics find themselves undecided about where *Caesar* belongs. Like *Richard II* it deals with the problem of deposing a king, but with rather more freedom than Shakespeare would allow himself in an English setting. As in all the English histories, interest is spread over a number of characters rather than concentrated on a hero; and since Rome is less compelling as a focus of affection than England, the prevailing tone, more than with the English histories, is one of detachment. It was perhaps to this that Johnson referred when he wrote of the play: 'I have never been strongly agitated in perusing it, and think it somewhat cold and unaffecting.' The public seems to have shared his opinion since, despite its many merits, it has never been a play to inspire great enthusiasm. Nonetheless the seeds of tragedy are there, not in the treatment of the titular hero, but of Brutus, in that the problem confronting him is clearly the one of most interest in the play to Shakespeare.

For the Elizabethans the dilemma posed by the need to depose a king was, as we saw in *Richard II*, virtually insoluble. Despite *Julius Caesar*'s obvious differences – the setting is pagan rather than Christian and Caesar is never actually crowned king – the dilemma, as Shakespeare sees it, remains essentially the same. It is recognized in *Julius Caesar* that the ruler, on whom the stability and honour of the state depends, is as much myth as man – a circumstance which inevitably complicates any attempts to unseat him. When Cassius is trying to win Brutus over to his cause he insists on Caesar's fundamental humanity, describing at some length the would-be king's weakness as a swimmer:

> – And this man
> Is now become a god, and Cassius is
> A wretched creature and must bend his body
> If Caesar carelessly but nod on him. (I.ii)

In Cassius, Shakespeare has achieved a remarkable fusion

of personality and political ideology: feared for his jealous nature by Caesar, and portrayed by Shakespeare as jealous in small, personal details, in Cassius republicanism is a strongly felt ideal which is also a perfect expression of temperament:

> I had as lief not be as live to be
> In awe of such a thing as I myself. (I.ii)

If Cassius, for personal as well as political reasons, tries to separate the man from the myth in Caesar, then Caesar himself has, like Richard II, allowed himself to become dazzled by his own myth. He answers his wife's fears for his safety by distancing himself into the realm of legend:

> – the things that threaten'd me
> Ne'er looked but on my back; when they shall see
> The face of Caesar, they are vanished . . . (II.ii)

– but he is human enough to be murdered. The two rulers who come to bloody ends in Shakespeare's work, Richard II and Caesar, lay themselves open to destruction because they have forgotten that they are men as well as kings.

Nonetheless after Caesar's death – as indeed after Richard II's – his legend is quick to reassert itself: a lesson for the potential regicide in Shakespeare's work is that the actual murder is comparatively easy but the fact of murder can only enhance the myth. The conspirators', or rather Brutus', first major error is to allow a skilled demagogue like Mark Antony to deliver a funeral oration. All that is most moving in Caesar's legend is contrasted, with increasingly heavy irony, with the case the conspirators have presented:

> But Brutus says he was ambitious,
> And Brutus is an honourable man. (III.ii)

The play's most interesting implied comparison is indeed between Mark Antony and Brutus. Antony, beloved by Caesar, is genuinely loyal to him and sincere in his grief; he is nonetheless a wily politician, quick to seize the opportunities offered by Caesar's death: he is negotiating with Octavius as soon as the murder is discovered, and plotting with him for the disposal of Lepidus once the latter's usefulness, and the battle of Philippi, are past. (IV.i)

His opportunism is in sharp contrast to Brutus' tactical naïvety – and that naïvety is in itself part of the honourableness on which Brutus prides himself. Caesar's murder is for Brutus an objective necessity which is untainted by the motives of personal revenge that provide Cassius with his driving force. Throughout, Brutus insists on his love for Caesar. As he tells the Roman crowd, it was 'Not that I loved Caesar less, but that I loved Rome more.' (III.ii) He plans Caesar's murder as a sacrifice, an act of love for Rome – 'We shall be call'd purgers, not murderers' (II.i) – and insists, like a priest aware of the importance of form, on the ritualistic conducting of the murder. But it is naïve of him to think that the crowd – presented, like all mobs in Shakespeare's work, as easily swayed, amenable to emotion but not to reason – will see what he has done with the austere detachment that he would wish.

Brutus' reputation for honour is politically necessary to the conspirators. So relieved are they to get him, however, that they too readily allow him to dictate his own terms (from the sparing of Antony's life to the military decision to fight at Philippi). Brutus' cause is destroyed both by his own scruples and by his unswerving sense that he is always right. His virtue makes him a good figurehead but an inadequate tactician: in all his history plays Shakespeare is intrigued not only by ideology and motive but by politics as the art of the possible. Brutus' failure displays what David Daiches, in an interesting snippet on the play which is included in *Shakespeare's Tragedies* (Penguin, editor Laurence Lerner) calls 'the ambiguity of innocence'. This is a tragic possibility that Shakespeare found more interesting than the absolute of evil, and one to which he returned in *Hamlet*, *Lear* and *Othello*.

So much critical attention has concentrated on *Julius Caesar* as the link between the histories and the tragedies that it is easy to overlook one of its distinctive features – its poetic style, for it is a play whose style is throughout perfectly attuned to its subject matter. Most remarkable is a lack of metaphor which is unusual in Shakespeare. The verse has, in fact, a tough, plain sinewy quality which reinforces the masculine atmosphere and is a perfect vehicle for public emotion.

Antony and Cleopatra

DATE 1606-7

PRINCIPAL CHARACTERS

Mark Antony
Octavius Caesar } Triumvirs of the Roman Empire
Lepidus

Cleopatra: Queen of Egypt

Octavia: Caesar's sister, Antony's second wife

Sextus Pompeius

Enobarbus, Eros, Proculeius and other friends of Antony's

Agrippa, Dolabella and other friends of Caesar's

Menas and Menecrates: Friends of Pompey

Alexas, Charmian and Iras: Attendants on Cleopatra

SCENE Rome, Egypt and other parts of the Roman Empire

Plot

ACT ONE opens in Cleopatra's palace in Alexandria where Antony has been deflected from imperial and military affairs by his love for the Egyptian Queen. He is roused from his lethargy, however, by the news of his wife Fulvia's death, and of the threat posed to the empire by Sextus Pompeius. He quarrels with Cleopatra about his decision to rejoin Caesar, but when the time comes, they part friends. In Rome, Caesar too is disturbed by Pompey's advances; he regards Antony now as of little use, despising him for his degeneration from great soldier and statesman to Cleopatra's slave.

ACT TWO Caesar and Antony patch up their differences in Rome and in token of their new amity a marriage is arranged between Caesar's sister Octavia and Antony. The bridegroom's motives are frankly political, inspired partly, as he acknowledges to himself, by a kind of fear of Caesar. Enobarbus, who is familiar with his master's sensuality, is sure that Octavia's 'holy, cold, and still conversation' (II.vi) will drive him back to his 'Egyptian dish'. The harmony between the Triumvirs brings Pompey to heel and a treaty is drunkenly sealed when Pompey entertains the Triumvirs in his barge off Misenum.

ACT THREE With the departure of the bridal pair for Athens, Caesar sets about systematically consolidating his own authority: reneging on their treaty, he defeats Pompey with Lepidus' help and then sentences Lepidus to death on a charge of conspiring with Pompey. In Athens, Antony tells Octavia of his decision to fight Caesar – both for reopening hostilities with Pompey and for blackening his, Antony's, name in Rome. Octavia elects to journey to Caesar on a peace mission but, on arrival in Rome, she is greeted by her brother with the news that Antony has returned to Egypt, where he has created his sons by Cleopatra kings of tributary countries. In Alexandria, Enobarbus advises Antony to meet Caesar's forces by land, where the Egyptians, led by Antony, would be at an advantage, but Antony submits to Cleopatra's whim to meet the Romans at sea with Cleopatra accompanying him. In the event, although the Egyptians are gaining on the Roman fleet, Cleopatra's boat withdraws from the battle and Antony follows her. Covered with shame, Antony asks Caesar to allow him to withdraw from public life and to live quietly in Egypt. Caesar refuses and attempts, moreover, to make separate terms with Cleopatra. Warned by Enobarbus of Cleopatra's duplicity Antony finds her with Caesar's messenger, shamelessly withdrawing from her emotional commitment to him – 'Mine honour was not yielded/But conquer'd merely' (III.xi). Such is Antony's enslavement, however, that his rage is soon dissipated by the prospect of a night's feasting with his mistress. In a last effort to assert his valour he challenges Caesar to settle the issue in single combat; Enobarbus takes this as proof that Antony is losing his reason and determines to go over to Caesar.

ACT FOUR Caesar is predictably scornful of Antony's challenge and sends out his forces, under Agrippa, to meet the Egyptians. Antony goes into battle with the knowledge of Enobarbus' desertion and routs Agrippa. Overcome with remorse, Enobarbus kills himself. Antony's victory is thrown away by tactical error as, remaining with part of his forces on land, he watches the Egyptian fleet again submit to the Romans. He blames Cleopatra – 'Triple-turn'd whore!' – for his humiliation and resolves to murder her. Anticipating his anger, Cleopatra hides herself in her monument and sends word to Antony that grief has killed her. With no alternative now but death, Antony runs himself through on his sword. Cleopatra's servants find him mortally wounded and take him to the queen; he dies in her arms.

ACT FIVE Hearing of Antony's death, Caesar sends Proculeius to Cleopatra with assurances of good will. Cleopatra, however, suspects that Caesar's intention is to humiliate her publicly in Rome; she prevails on his second messenger, Dolabella, to admit that this is the motive behind Caesar's placatory gestures. On Caesar's arrival she formally submits herself to him but as soon as his back is turned provides herself with the means of suicide – asps which, she is assured, kill instantly and painlessly – unknown to Caesar they are brought in with a basket of figs. When Caesar returns to resume his interview he finds her, and her women Charmian and Iras, dead.

Critical commentary

Antony and Cleopatra holds a special place in Shakespeare's work as his mature love tragedy. Not only was he in his maturity at the time of writing it (upwards of forty), but it is the only one of his plays in which the central interest is the love of a couple long past their youth. Where the romantic comedies and *Romeo and Juliet* are celebrations of young love, *Antony and Cleopatra* depicts the final magnificent apotheosis of a love that, at its highest moments of passion, was flawed and destructive. It is in fact the flaws in the love itself, and the wider framework provided by Antony's political and military position, that establishes this play more firmly in the Elizabethan and Jacobean conception of tragedy than *Romeo and Juliet*, in that the earlier tragedy of love lacked guilt, scale and a sense of public importance. The romantic and political interests in *Antony and Cleopatra* are inseparable. When, after the first disastrous sea-battle Antony asks Caesar to allow him to live 'a private man' (III.x), both Caesar and Enobarbus recognize the request as supremely foolish: in Antony, the lover and the statesman must thrive or fall together.

Boasting a wider canvas than any other of Shakespeare's plays, *Antony and Cleopatra* requires great fluidity in staging, since the only boundaries recognized are the limits of the Roman Empire. Antony, moreover, is in a position of greater power than any other of Shakespeare's tragic heroes. When Pompey entertains the Triumvirs on his barge, he is urged by Menas to take advantage of this unique opportunity to make himself ruler of the world by disposing of his guests: 'Thou art, if thou dar'st be, the earthly Jove.' (II.vii) It is literally true that Pompey holds within his power at this point the masters of the known world. Part of the play's strength is that the massive scale on which Shakespeare casts his action is never felt as hyperbole, as it is in some of Marlowe's plays.

As in the other Roman plays, and in the English histories, Shakespeare explores in *Antony and Cleopatra* the qualities required for leadership, and the conclusions he reaches are broadly similar – that the most effective ruler is unlikely to be the man who inspires most affection. The surviving Triumvir, now absolute ruler, is Octavius Caesar; like Henry V he has managed totally to subdue his personality to the demands of his office. Frostily scornful of Antony's sensuality ('tippling with a slave' (I.iv), is his withering comment on Antony's union with Cleopatra), he believes that the impulses of the heart should be curbed for public ends. Calculating in his political dealings, he disposes of Lepidus as soon as he has outlived his usefulness, betrays the terms of his treaty with Pompey and is prepared to butter up Cleopatra as a prelude to leading her in his triumphal car through Rome. He is not given to romantic gestures. Lacking Antony's personal grandeur, he skilfully deploys the trappings of power to create mystique: when Octavia arrives in Rome on her peace mission, he is disturbed less by her personal humiliation than by the unceremonious manner of her coming, 'A market maid to Rome'. (III.vi)

With Antony, Shakespeare emphasizes both his spectacular personal scale (far greater than Caesar's) and the completeness of his bondage to the woman who finally destroys him. There is a marked pattern – a suggestion of vastness dropping sharply to the ludicrous – in the comments made by other characters on Antony, like Philo's – 'The triple pillar of the world transform'd/Into a strumpet's fool.' (I.i) Antony himself wavers between a restless awareness of his wider role: 'These strong Egyptian fetters I must break' (I.ii), and a magnificent and total surrender to the moment: 'Let Rome in Tiber melt, and the wide arch /Of the rang'd empire fall!' (I.i) In *Julius Caesar* Antony is depicted as a political opportunist whose sensuality is merely hinted at; in *Antony and Cleopatra*, there is a constant tension between his sensuality and his self-esteem. Unlike Caesar, his ambitions have not grown: he is anxious merely to prove himself the man he was. For *Antony and Cleopatra* to work as a tragedy, we must be made to feel Antony's greatness. Among the problems that Shakespeare had to overcome in suggesting this greatness is the nature of his bondage: within Antony's own imperial terms of reference, going native is the most contemptible of follies, and felt to be so by the other Romans, as the references to Cleopatra as 'strumpet' (I.i), 'slave' (I.iv) and 'Egyptian dish' (II.vi), and to Antony as 'The noble ruin of her magic' (III.viii) make clear. Moreover, Antony's real greatness as a states-man is largely a thing of the past.

But *Antony and Cleopatra* is a play filled with echoes of the past, and Antony's own military past is already a legend when the play opens: even Caesar pays tribute to his superhuman feats of endurance as a soldier (I.iv). Within the play, Antony throws away his chance to prove himself again by flying after Cleopatra, but the quality of his shame is noble and bracing:

> Hark! the land bids me tread no more upon't,
> It is asham'd to bear me. (III.ix)

At the desertion of Enobarbus he feels no sense of betrayal, only mortification at deserving it:

> Say that I wish he never find more cause
> To change a master. O! my fortunes have
> Corrupted honest men. (IV.v)

Enobarbus' treachery is short-lived and his suicide, and Eros' (committed to avoid a promise he had made to Antony to kill him on request) suggest the quality of the man they have followed.

If Antony's real greatness is largely a thing of the past, then within the play there remains a full act after his death within which his legend can form. No other of Shakespeare's heroes is the subject of so many elegiac tributes. Indeed, one of *Antony and Cleopatra*'s chief claims to distinction is the remarkable quality of the verse – allusive, dramatically if sometimes unexpectedly appropriate, and finally defeating analysis. In the tributes paid to Antony, his sheer scale reasserts itself, in Cleopatra's

>   –the odds is gone,
> And there is nothing left remarkable
> Beneath the visiting moon . . . (IV.xiii)

– and Caesar's

> The breaking of so great a thing should make
> A greater crack . . . (V.i)

– and Agrippa's

> A rarer spirit never
> Did steer humanity; but you, gods, will give us
> Some faults to make us men. (V.i)

And what of Cleopatra? Often regarded as an enigmatic figure, this is largely because with her, as with Hamlet, Shakespeare makes full dramatic use of all her contradictions without explaining them. More even than in his presentation of Antony, Shakespeare trades on her legend – or rather, Cleopatra herself is allowed to trade on the legend that she has elaborately created. In the play's most famous set piece Enobarbus' 'The barge she sat in, like a burnish'd throne/Burn'd on the water' (II.ii), in which he describes Antony's first meeting with Cleopatra to the curious Romans, what emerges most clearly is her genius for effect. All that is said of her person is that it 'beggar'd all description' while the weight of the passage falls on the trappings with which she surrounds herself – the precious metals of the barge, the pretty dimpled boy attendants, and so on. Her beauty is by no means established but she has the greater gift, which Enobarbus recognizes, 'That she did make defect perfection.' (II.ii) She has a related talent for disarming criticism: her quarrels with Antony always end in reconciliation; she will feign sickness, even death, to move him.

There is a deliberate ambiguity on the question of Cleopatra's loyalty to her lover. Does the surrender of the Egyptian fleet imply, as Antony chooses to interpret it, that she is selling him to Caesar? She will not leave her monument to attend the dying Antony in case she is taken by Caesar before she is ready, and has the bleeding man, instead, brought up to her (IV.xiii). Immediately after his death she appears to be contemplating suicide herself: 'Let's do it after the high Roman fashion' (IV. xiii) – but she is careful first to ascertain that the kind of life that Caesar would allow her would be intolerable. Yet it is her very failings that render her more human and interesting as a character. And if in suicide she makes a virtue of necessity (given that she cannot contemplate being humiliated in Rome), then it must be said that she does it magnificently, a stylist to the last. Her suicide speech – 'Give me my robe, put on my crown; I have/Immortal longings in me' (V.ii) – is one of the joys of the play. Having made up her mind to die her *final* devotion to Antony is unquestioned.

Coriolanus

DATE 1608

PRINCIPAL CHARACTERS

Caius Marcius, afterwards known as Caius Marcius Coriolanus

Titus Lartius | Roman generals against
Cominius | the Volscians

Menenius Agrippa: Friend of Coriolanus

Sicinius Velutus and Junius Brutus: Tribunes of the people, enemies of Coriolanus

Volumnia: Mother of Coriolanus

Virgilia: Wife of Coriolanus

Valeria: Friend of Virgilia

Tullus Aufidius: General of the Volscians

SCENE Rome and Corioli, city of the Volscians.

Plot

ACT ONE opens with the citizens of Rome mutinous and hungry. They claim that the Senate are hoarding corn and are only just calmed by the patrician Menenius. Encouraged by their tribunes, Sicinius and Brutus, who have been appointed to protect their interests, the mob direct their hatred at Caius Marcius, a distinguished soldier who makes no effort to conceal his hatred of the common people. The conflict within Rome, however, gives way to the urgent external threat of the Volscian army. Caius Marcius, who has defeated the Volscians in earlier wars, looks forward to another encounter with their general, Tullus Aufidius, and agrees to serve under Cominius in the coming war. In the event, Caius Marcius distinguishes himself by superhuman acts of bravery, fighting alone within the walls of Corioli and, while he is still bleeding from the wounds acquired there, seeking out and routing Aufidius. To honour his courage, Cominius bestows on him the name 'Coriolanus', a reference to the place of his most outstanding deeds, and offers him a share of booty commensurate with his achievements; Coriolanus' ambitions are not mercenary and he refuses the extra financial reward. Meanwhile the audience has been introduced to Coriolanus' wife, Virgilia, and mother Volumnia, who has bred in her son his exclusively martial ethic.

ACT TWO On her son's triumphant return to Rome, Volumnia makes known her ambition to see him consul. Coriolanus reluctantly agrees to offer himself for election and the senate give him their vote, but his acceptance as consul requires the voice of the common people; the prospective candidate must ritualistically present himself in a garment of humility and display his wounds to the people. Coriolanus would prefer to waive the ceremony but the tribunes Brutus and Sicinius insist on it. The people, who are now well disposed towards Coriolanus because of his military achievements, give him their voice, though they are bewildered by the coldness with which it is sought. When the tribunes find the crowd dissatisfied with Coriolanus' manner they suggest that they go to the senate house and revoke their consent.

ACT THREE When Coriolanus is brought word of the citizens' change of heart he speaks so abusively of the 'rank-scented many' (III.i) that the tribunes demand an instant end to his hopes of the consulship. Enflamed still further Coriolanus warns the senate of the dangers of mob rule; the tribunes demand his death. Menenius and Volumnia plead with, and prevail upon Coriolanus, to make his apologies to the people, but when he is confronted by the mob he finds himself unable to 'buy/Their mercy at the price of one fair word.' (III.iii) The tribunes' call for his death is softened by the senate to a sentence of perpetual banishment.

ACT FOUR Coriolanus turns his back on Rome and goes over to the Volscians. He presents himself to Aufidius who claims that his old enemy's friendliness has 'weeded from my heart/ A root of ancient envy.' (IV.v) Together they organize and lead an army against Rome. Aufidius resents Coriolanus' popularity with his soldiers, but he is prepared to hide his resentment until Rome has been won. As word reaches Rome of Coriolanus' intended act of vengeance, the tribunes are held responsible for his banishment.

ACT FIVE Cominius and Menenius plead with Coriolanus to turn his army from Rome, but they find him a changed man, dead to old affections and loyalties. He is finally brought to spare the city, however, at the entreaty of his mother, wife and son. He returns to Corioli, where the people are prepared to welcome him despite his retreat, but at a signal from Aufidius a band of conspirators artificially stimulate mob anger. Before intervention is possible the conspirators turn on Coriolanus and kill him.

Critical commentary

Coriolanus presents difficulties to twentieth-century readers and audiences which would have had no place in the response of Shakespeare's contemporaries, in that our prejudices incline us to do the hero less than the justice that Shakespeare took for granted. When after the Volscian war Cominius is recommending Coriolanus' consulship to the senate he says, in true Roman spirit:

> It is held
> That valour is the chiefest virtue and
> Most dignifies the haver. (II.ii)

Valour, the most esteemed of the virtues by the Romans, was still sufficiently impressive in Shakespeare's day, as it no longer is now, to dispose audiences towards the hero.

Another stumbling-block for the twentieth century is Shakespeare's treatment of the mob. The harshly abusive language in which Coriolanus expresses himself to the citizens of Rome – he calls them 'rats' (I.i) and 'curs' (III.iii), hopes that 'Boils and plagues/Plaster you o'er' (I.iv) and finds himself unable to speak of massed humanity without alluding to their smell – should not, of course, be taken as a reflection of Shakespeare's own views. Nevertheless, throughout his work Shakespeare's treatment of the mob, which he sees as a kind of brute force, easily incited to violence or adulation but unmoved by rational appeal, is untinged by sentimentality. Because Shakespeare's mob is incapable of a high level of political responsibility, its natural leaders are men like Brutus and Sicinius who use their manipulative skills to keep themselves in office.

Like *Julius Caesar*, *Coriolanus* is a highly political play. The stage, apart from the occasional interludes devoted to Coriolanus' family, is usually swarming with people, which reinforces the public nature of the issues. It is a play of conflicts: the rioting, hungry populace against the senate, Rome against Corioli; the rivalry between the military giants Coriolanus and Aufidius; and, of course, the central conflict, the mutual antipathy between the mob and Coriolanus. But the conflicts are of a broadly external kind: alone of Shakespeare's tragic heroes Coriolanus has nothing of himself to reveal in soliloquy beyond the confirmation of his change of heart towards Rome after his banishment. (IV.iv) There is a sense in which Coriolanus' tragedy is avoidable in the way that Lear's, Hamlet's, Macbeth's and Othello's are not. The tragedies of the great tragic heroes are within them, requiring only the agency of external forces; Coriolanus' tragedy is largely brought about by other people's attempts to force him into a pattern which is alien to him.

He is first and foremost a soldier, unsurpassed in his own field, and while there is a war to be fought and glory to be won, his hostility to the mob is no more than a blemish. But he is a man singularly ill-equipped for politics. Everybody in the play acknowledges his dependence on his mother, and it is his mother who, after his splendid victory at Corioli, first broaches the idea of his becoming consul. (II.i) In this Volumnia is asking of her son more than she has bred him up to, in that she has provided him with no means of softening his manner where politic. The tone that he adopts towards the crowd is accurately described by Brutus:

> – You speak o'the people,
> As if you were a god to punish, not
> A man of their infirmity. (III.i)

Clearly, Coriolanus' arrogance is a handicap for a prospective politician. What is interesting is that his fellow nobles, Cominius and Menenius, share his contempt for the mob but are cleverer at hiding it. When Coriolanus has explained the grounds of his contempt to the senate and the tribunes – he argues that the people were unwilling to go to war when the state was hard-pressed and therefore had no right to demand corn (III.i) – Menenius' comment on him is that 'His nature is too noble for the world.' Judged from a certain angle (which it must be said is only part of Shakespeare's final perspective) Coriolanus' failure in the early part of the play is through too much integrity rather than too little affection for his fellow citizens (a feeling to which none of his class aspire anyway). We can see him, like Brutus in *Julius Caesar*, as too honourable, according to his own standards of honour, for practical politics.

His mistake is in trying to compromise. When his attempts at the consulship have been defeated, by his own intransigence and by the manoeuvrings of the tribunes, he is prevailed upon by his mother to present himself to the people with his apologies, even though he knows this to be going against the grain of his own nature:

> Must I with my base tongue give to my noble heart
> A lie that it must bear? (III.ii)

His efforts at apology flounder, but the very attempt has impaired his integrity. The Coriolanus who then moves on to lead an army against Rome is a lesser man than the Coriolanus who had earlier defeated the Volscians, insofar as his military ethic has become entirely personal. He despised the people for placing their personal safety above the safety of Rome, but he is prepared himself now to sacrifice Rome for personal vengeance. When he is persuaded by Volumnia to withdraw his army from Rome, the decision is again a personal one, owing nothing to a reviving sense of his responsibility as a Roman citizen and everything to his powerlessness against his mother.

His death is at the hands of a mob – a Volscian rather than a Roman mob, but nonetheless poetically right: his struggle had been against the tyranny of the mob, and in sparing Rome he had demonstrated his own vulnerability. Coriolanus is the only one of Shakespeare's tragedies to end with the death of the hero but of no other characters: his was a solitary struggle.

8 Shakespeare: Tragedy

What should such fellows as I do crawling between heaven and
earth . . . ? *Hamlet* (III.i)

With the writing of *Hamlet* in 1600, the direction of Shakespeare's career altered radically. Only one romantic
comedy, *Twelfth Night*, was written after that date (in 1601),
and otherwise the period 1600-08 is dominated by the four
great tragedies, *Hamlet*, *Othello*, *King Lear* and *Macbeth*.
Falling within the same period are the two Roman tragedies, *Antony and Cleopatra* and *Coriolanus*, the possibly unfinished and subsequently neglected *Timon of Athens* and the
three dark or tragi-comedies, *Measure for Measure*, *All's Well
that Ends Well* and *Troilus and Cressida*.

The fact that Shakespeare had written tragedy before
1600 serves only to emphasize the differences in approach,
to say nothing of achievement, in the tragedies written after
that date. *Titus Andronicus*, belonging to the very beginning
of his career (but included here for convenience) is an
exercise in tragedy: its events are horrific in a way that he
was never later to attempt, but they fail to move. If it
belonged later in his career, to a period when one could be
more confident of his artistic control, one would respond to
it unequivocally as a parody rather than as the genuine
article. *Romeo and Juliet*, written when his comic powers
were maturing, moves but fails to devastate: despite their
deaths it is difficult to respond to the world that the young
lovers inhabit as other than fundamentally benign. Of the
historical tragedies, *Richard III* evokes only a stage evil,

emanating from a stage villain who ultimately fails to impinge on the audience's complacency; while the tragedy of *Richard II* is a historical necessity, handled with remote lyricism.

How then do the 'great' tragedies differ? For the Middle Ages the term 'tragedy' referred to a dramatic change in circumstance, from prosperity to wretchedness and ending in misery and death. For the Elizabethans and Jacobeans, a play required no more than an unhappy ending to pass as tragedy. In *Hamlet, Othello, Lear* and *Macbeth* Shakespeare transcended the technical requirements to achieve a tragic vision which, while it may differ in important respects from the great Greek models, has had as profound an effect on western civilization.

We think of the tragedies primarily in terms of their heroes, but the heroes are not 'characters' in the same sense that certain of Shakespeare's comic creations are. In his essay, 'Hamlet: the Prince or the Poem?'* C. S. Lewis wrote, 'I would go a long way to meet Beatrice or Falstaff . . . I would not cross the room to meet Hamlet. It would never be necessary. He is always where I am.' Among the tragic heroes we will inevitably have our personal preferences, but it is nonetheless true of all of them that they are archetypes as much as individuals; and because they all at some point touch the universal, for the duration of the play we share their vision, their experience and their suffering. It is a commonplace of literary criticism that Hamlet, the only one of the great tragic heroes who lends himself to detailed character analysis, has always been interpreted according to the personality of the individual critic.

The heroes of Shakespearean tragedy are not, like Marlowe's heroes, supermen; they are, on the contrary, men with ordinary human weaknesses and failings – which play a crucial part in their downfall – but who nonetheless manage to impress us with mankind's potential for greatness. We experience a kind of collective pride in their

*C. S. Lewis's essay, 'Hamlet: the Prince or the Poem?' is included in *Shakespeare's Tragedies* (Penguin) edited by Lawrence Lerner.

attempts to wrestle with the worst that fortune can present them with. They are all finally defeated. If comedy celebrates man's ability to triumph over chance and adversity and achieve some happiness, then tragedy celebrates his resilience, his fight to the bitter end (this is particularly so of King Lear) against circumstances which will finally overpower him.

The element of celebration in Shakespeare's tragedies should not be stressed, however. The nature of the different worlds that his protagonists are up against must inspire revulsion. The Denmark of Hamlet, the Britain of Lear, the Athens of Timon, are distinguished by greed, ingratitude and self-seeking ambition. And although these elements finally destroy themselves, they destroy the innocent too in the process. At the end of the tragedies the corpses are carried off and hope is expressed in a new order, but the reality seems to lie in the ruin and its recurring possibility. Such justice as there is in Shakespearean tragedy is of a very rough kind; if there are gods, then it is an act of faith to see them as on the side of suffering humanity.

From the point of view of the established church, tragedy was the most inflammatory of the theatrical genres; the prevalence of tragedy in the Jacobean period (when most of Shakespeare's tragedies were written), and its relative infrequence under Elizabeth, can be linked to the more relaxed attitude of the authorities under James. Shakespearean, and Jacobean tragedy generally, can be further linked to wider historical movements through such generalizations as 'the mood of the country': England under Elizabeth was arguably more hopeful, less pessimistic than under James; and James's corrupt court can be seen as a prototype, to which the dramatists were sensitive, of corruption among the great.

Some critics like to see a connection between Shakespeare's own life – or at any rate what one might call his spiritual state after 1600 – and the tragedies and sombre comedies. G. Wilson Knight, for example, (in 'Shakespeare and Tolstoy' in *The Wheel of Fire*), thinks it likely that the state of mind described by Hamlet, in which 'this goodly frame, the earth, seems to me a sterile promontory . . .' (II.ii), corresponds to something in the dramatist's own experience at the time. The writing of tragedy need not in itself suggest that Shakespeare was experiencing what Wilson Knight calls an 'insistent pain and disgust'. Nonetheless, there is much in the plays written over the 1600-08 period to suggest a fundamental loss of faith. In both *Lear* and *Measure for Measure* there is an urgent sense of the need for social restraint to check man's destructive impulses; yet in both plays the processes of justice are felt to be rotten. In *Troilus* we see idealism defeated by cunning; in *Othello* the virtue of Desdemona is less powerful than Iago's malevolence. Love is suspect. Hamlet's feelings for Ophelia are never more than equivocal; Othello's mind is easily poisoned with suspicion against his wife; King Lear who, at 'four score and upward' would, in the course of nature, be past the point of being pained by woman's faithlessness, raves that –

> Down from the waist they are Centaurs,
> Though women all above. (IV.vi)

And what of friendship? Hamlet's old friends Rosencrantz and Guildenstern are set to spy on him; Othello's faith in Iago's loyalty is his undoing; not one of Timon's fair-weather friends stretches out a hand to help him in adversity. In the comedies written before 1600 deceit, treachery and wickedness are either a game or quickly dismissed from the stage; in the plays written after that date they are painfully real, suggesting something more than academic interest on Shakespeare's part.

Titus Andronicus

DATE Probably about 1590

PRINCIPAL CHARACTERS

Saturninus ⎱ Sons of the late Emperor of Rome and
Bassianus ⎰ rival claimants for the succession
Titus Andronicus: A noble Roman and General against the Goths
Marcus Andronicus: A tribune, brother to Titus
Lucius, Quintus, Martius, Mutius: Titus' sons
Lavinia: Titus' daughter
Tamora: Queen of the Goths
Aaron: A Moor, Tamora's lover
Alarbus, Demetrius, Chiron: Tamora's sons
SCENE Rome

Plot

ACT ONE Saturninus and Bassianus are laying their separate claims to succeed their father as emperor before the people of Rome. The succession is decided by Titus Andronicus on his victorious return to the city after the defeat of the Goths. Titus' own large family of sons has been greatly depleted in the war and, in token of the people's gratitude, the imperial crown is offered to him, but he gives his choice as Saturninus, the elder of the rival brothers. For his part, Saturninus offers to marry Titus' daughter Lavinia but she has been promised to Bassanius and her brothers rally to defend his right to her. Outraged by their filial impiety (for he is prepared to give Lavinia to Saturninus), Titus kills his son Mutius in high patrician style, to the horror of the rest of his family.

Saturninus is piqued by the affront to his imperial dignity and transfers his offer of marriage to Tamora, Queen of the Goths, who is Titus' prisoner. The enmity of the new empress towards Titus' family had been secured by the ritual sacrifice of her son Alarbus at the demand of Titus' sons, but she is prepared to use the festive atmosphere surrounding her own and Lavinia's marriage celebrations (to Bassianus) as a cloak for her intended vengeance.

ACT TWO Tamora's sons, Chiron and Demetrius, are both lusting after Lavinia. Aaron, their mother's wicked lover, contrives a situation for them which will satisfy both lust and vengeance. On a hunting party Lavinia and Bassianus are set upon by Tamora and her sons in a remote part of the forest. The brothers stab Bassianus and throw him into a pit; turning their attention to Lavinia, they rape her and deprive her of the means of bringing them to justice – by cutting off her hands and ripping out her tongue. Aaron then inveigles Titus' sons Quintus and Martius to the scene of Bassianus' murder: when the boys are safely in the pit with the murdered man and no means of escape is available, Saturninus, Titus and his remaining son Lucius are brought before them. Saturninus arrests Quintus and Martius for the murder of Bassianus.

ACT THREE There is no end to Titus' troubles. He has just seen Lavinia for the first time in her mutilated condition when he loses one of his own hands as a result of a 'sport' devised by Aaron: he is told by the Moor that he can save his sons from execution if he forfeits his own hand, but it is returned with his sons' heads. Meanwhile, his remaining son Lucius has been banished for trying to defend his brothers. He departs to raise an army among the Goths.

ACT FOUR Lavinia, using a stick held between her teeth and guided by her stumps, reveals the identity of her ravishers. Apparently demented, Titus, demanding justice, shoots off arrows to the gods which land in the emperor's presence. Saturninus (who knows nothing of his stepsons' crimes) is baffled by Titus and worried by the growing strength of Lucius' army; he is persuaded by Tamora to arrange a meeting with Lucius at Titus' house, and she meanwhile undertakes to 'charm' Titus into persuading his son from his warlike course. Tamora has other problems of her own. She has been delivered of a child whose black skin proclaims it to be Aaron's, and who has aroused strong paternal feelings in his father. Aaron takes charge of the baby, substituting a white child in its place. He kills the nurse and midwife to silence their tongues.

ACT FIVE Aaron and his baby are discovered outside the city by Lucius, who promises to spare the child's life in return for information about Tamora and her sons. Back in Rome, Tamora, thinking that Titus is madder than he is, visits him disguised as 'Revenge', with her sons taking the parts of 'Rape' and 'Mutilation': as 'Revenge', she promises to avenge his family's wrongs if he can bring Lucius to his house. Titus agrees, if 'Rape' and 'Mutilation' are left behind as hostages. The throats of the hostages are promptly cut and we next see Titus in a cook's hat preparing the peacemaking feast. The party begins with the stabbing of Lavinia by Titus – an old Roman custom for dealing with ravished daughters. When Tamora has eaten greedily of Titus' pie, he reveals that her sons supplied the meat and stabs her; Saturninus kills Titus and Lucius Saturninus. Lucius, the only one left to shoulder the responsibility, is proclaimed emperor.

Critical commentary

The early 1590s, when *Titus Andronicus* was written, were experimental years for Shakespeare as he made his first essays into comedy (*The Comedy of Errors*), history (*Henry IV*) and narrative poetry (*Venus and Adonis* and *The Rape of Lucrece*). Nothing gives us greater confidence that he was aware of his own powers and limitations from the very beginning of his career than the fact that he did not return to narrative poetry and that he laid his ambition as a writer of tragedy to one side until he was an older and wiser man. *Titus* is now something of an embarrassment to ardent Shakespeareans, and those who have spurned the easy way out of avoiding it altogether have attempted to give the play a specious respectability by comparing Titus' sufferings to Lear's. Why bother? Taken on its own terms, Titus is instructive for anyone interested in Shakespeare's development.

T. S. Eliot dismissed *Titus* as 'one of the stupidest and most uninspired plays ever written'. Yet there is evidence that it enjoyed some popularity with its first audiences; and despite Mr Eliot's exaggerated contempt, it is as good as most of the plays that were being written and performed towards the close of the sixteenth century. Indeed, *Titus* is a play of its time serving as a yardstick by which to judge how far in his great tragedies Shakespeare transcended the demands of his audiences. What did Elizabethan audiences demand of tragedy? The Senecan tragic tradition was popularized by the Elizabethan theatre as melodrama; revenge, cheap suspense and ingenious ways of inflicting suffering were standard ingredients. *Titus* works best as a play where it is most unashamedly melodramatic – and that most especially in the vigorous portrait of Aaron the Moor, who has the gleeful delight of the stage villain in villainy for its own sake:

> – O! how this villany
> Doth fat me with the very thoughts of it. (III.i)

Even the awakening of his paternal feeling is not given a spurious veneer of 'fineness': he rejoices in producing one 'coal-black' like himself to succeed him in wickedness.

Aaron is better than anything else in the play because no attempt is made to give him a dimension beyond the limited scope of the stage villain. What makes us uneasy about *Titus* are Shakespeare's attempts to give it a resonance that it cannot carry – suggestions of 'depth' which are finally no more than gloss. This is to some extent a trick of the magniloquent language, over which Shakespeare already had a lively command, but there is other evidence in the play of a deliberate grafting on of 'depth'. For example, some attempt is made to place the barbaric disregard for life in the play, which produces a fine total of corpses for the audience to gloat over, within the Roman context of 'honour'. Titus kills his son Martius, his daughter Lavinia, and Tamora's son Alarbus in accordance with some patrician standard – or so we are meant to feel, but we are no more impressed by his motives than we are by Aaron's for the murder of the nurse and midwife. More broadly, motive and moral character are irrelevant in a play like *Titus*.

Otherwise, *Titus* declares the youth of its author in its uncontrolled displays of horror. There is no doubt that horror has its place in the highest forms of tragedy: despite the critical controversy which it still excites, the blinding of Gloucester in *King Lear* makes a unique contribution to the play's impact. In the early tragedy, however, Shakespeare had not yet learned that cumulative acts of horror bring diminishing returns. In *Titus* there is too much – of everything. Titus, we are told at the beginning of the play, once had twenty-five sons. Twenty-one have been killed in battle and the twenty-second (Martius) he summarily slaughters in Act One. We are then asked to believe in, and sympathize with, his grief as two of the remaining three are executed. Lavinia loses two hands, Titus brings the number up to three. What, one asks cravenly, is a hand or a son here or there? Yet there lurks a sneaking suspicion that Shakespeare wants us to care – and in that we feel the stirrings of the great tragic writer of the future.

Romeo and Juliet

DATE 1595
PRINCIPAL CHARACTERS
Escalus: Prince of Verona
Montague ⎫
Lady Montague ⎬ The Montague clan
Romeo, their son ⎭
Mercutio: Kinsman of the Prince ⎫
Benvolio: Nephew of Montague ⎬ Friends of Romeo
Capulet ⎫
Lady Capulet ⎪ The Capulet
Juliet, their daughter ⎬ clan
Tybalt, their nephew ⎭
Paris: Kinsman to the prince, suitor to Juliet
Friar Laurence: A Franciscan
Nurse to Juliet
SCENE Verona and Mantua

Plot

In a Prologue the Chorus tells of the 'ancient grudge' between the houses of Montague and Capulet. By the end of the play this 'strife' will be buried, but only with the deaths of the only child of each house, the 'pair of star-cross'd lovers' of the title.

ACT ONE After a street brawl between the retainers of the two warring houses, the Prince warns the heads of both families that death will be the penalty for further quarrels. The Montague heir, Romeo, is in love with the lady Rosaline, for whose sake he risks going uninvited to a party given by the Capulets; at this same party the Count Paris has been given permission by the Capulets to woo their daughter Juliet. In the event, other claims forgotten, Romeo and Juliet fall in love. Romeo's thin disguise at the party has been penetrated by Tybalt, a belligerent kinsman of the hosts, who determines to take the interloper to task hereafter.

ACT TWO Romeo leaps the Capulet orchard wall and finds Juliet at her window, declaring her love for him to the night air; the young lovers determine on a speedy marriage. Romeo applies to Friar Laurence, who agrees to marry them secretly; the Friar hopes that their union will heal the ancient feud.

ACT THREE Tybalt, who has already issued a challenge to Romeo, approaches him in the street but is unable to goad him into fighting. Tybalt takes on Romeo's friend Mercutio instead; the latter is distracted while fighting by a peace-making gesture of Romeo's and, off his guard, is killed by a sly blow of Tybalt's. Stirred at last to fight, Romeo kills Tybalt in revenge for Mercutio's death and then takes refuge in Friar Laurence's cell. There he learns that he has been banished by the Prince. Juliet is distraught when she hears of Romeo's banishment; her parents assume that she is grieving for Tybalt and hasten her marriage to Paris in an attempt to liven her spirits. The Nurse and Friar Laurence contrive to lift her gloom by other means, however, and while her parents are making plans for her marriage to

Paris, she is in her bedroom consummating the marriage to Romeo that Friar Laurence has performed. When, the following morning, she baulks at the marriage to Paris, her parents threaten to disown her, while her Nurse recommends bigamy.

ACT FOUR Juliet lays her predicament before Friar Laurence, who produces the following plan: that she should appear to comply with her parents' wishes but the night before the projected marriage take a potion which would induce the appearance of death but from which she would wake refreshed after forty-two hours. By then she would be within the Capulet vault. Romeo, now living out his banishment in Mantua, would have returned in response to a letter from the Friar, would release Juliet from the vault and carry her back with him to Mantua. Juliet agrees to the plan, takes the potion, is thought dead and is buried.

ACT FIVE Friar Laurence's message to Romeo miscarries so that when the latter is brought news of Juliet's death he assumes it to be true. Having secured a deadly potion from an apothecary, he returns to Verona and the Capulet monument. While he is breaking into the vault to find Juliet, he is discovered and challenged by Paris, whom he kills. After a last look at Juliet, Romeo poisons himself. Juliet, waking and finding his body, stabs herself. Friar Laurence, who has learned of the miscarriage of his letter to Romeo, goes to the Capulet tomb; he is discovered in the churchyard by Escalus, Montague and the Capulets who have been roused by the watch. The story of the lovers is told and the bereft Montague and Capulet at last join hands in peace.

Critical commentary

Romeo and Juliet was written when Shakespeare was reaching the peak of his powers as a writer of comedy. It is in fact a truism of Shakespearean criticism that the 'world' of *Romeo and Juliet* is closer to that of the comedies than of the tragedies on which Shakespeare was engaged from the turn of the century. The protagonists are a boy and girl who fall in love; their situation resembles that of the lovers in a number of romances (*As You Like It, A Midsummer Night's Dream, The Winter's Tale*) in that the smooth progress of their love is impeded by the wishes of the older generation, although in the case of Romeo and Juliet it is their death and not the power of their love which finally routs the prejudices of the elderly. In its early acts, the play takes its atmosphere from the surface gaiety of masked balls and street scenes; it is, in the mode of Shakespeare's comedies, both lyrical and witty. A radical point of departure from the major tragedies is that the hero and heroine are not 'great' in the sense that their choices and their actions would be expected to have far-reaching repercussions.

There are few plays which have suffered more than *Romeo and Juliet* (*Troilus and Cressida* is another) from a critical tendency to evaluate Shakespeare's success in any given play in terms of his handling of a particular genre. *Romeo and Juliet*, the argument goes, relies too heavily on pathos at the expense of arousing the audience's moral judgments – for who could see either of the lovers as in possession of a fatal flaw (beyond the impetuosity of young love) from which their tragedy might be felt inevitably to emanate? Indeed, the argument proceeds, there is not enough inevitability in this play and rather too much chance. The plot of *Romeo and Juliet* is based on 'if only's', in a way that the plots of other tragedies are not, beyond an 'if only' Lear or Othello or Hamlet were different kinds of men, in which case there would be no plays. If only Prince Escalus had taken sterner action at the beginning to compel the warring families into some kind of truce; if only Romeo had not intervened between Tybalt and Mercutio – hardly a criminal action in itself, but one which results in Mercutio's death and in his obligation to kill Tybalt; if only Friar Laurence's letter to Romeo had not miscarried, or the Friar had arrived at the Capulet vault before Romeo, or Juliet had come round from her drug before Romeo had killed himself... The feud, which was, we take it, intended to give a plausibility beyond mere chance to the tragic dénouement, is not handled entirely credibly: Montague barely takes the stage at all and Capulet is presented as a bumbling old man whom nobody heeds, much given to sitting around in corners reminiscing about his youth – hardly the Renaissance version of a powerful Mafia leader.

I am not sure, however, that any of this matters; and the play's continuing popularity with audiences, from Shakespeare's day up until our own, indicates that its imperfections as a tragedy have never impaired the audience's enjoyment of it. One is apt to forget that, as well as working within specific genres, and exploring their possibilities to the limit, Shakespeare was also concerned with certain fundamental areas of human experience which lent themselves to different kinds of treatment and to which he returned again and again. At the time when *Romeo and Juliet* was written, one of Shakespeare's primary concerns was love – a theme that he explored in the 1590s not only in the comedies but in *Venus and Adonis* and in the *Sonnets*. It hardly seems necessary to state that *Romeo and Juliet* is about love, but it is in a wider sense than the obvious fact that its protagonists are a pair of young lovers. The Capulets see marriage as a purely dynastic arrangement – Capulet's extra-marital womanizing in his youth is alluded to – and so are prepared to use force to marry their daughter to Paris. For Juliet's nurse, love is sex and sensual gratification; indeed, much of the coarser humour in the play, the Nurse's own and between assorted Capulet servants, derives from sexual punning. Romeo's love for Juliet is defined partly in relation to the views of the Capulets and of the Nurse and partly by his earlier love for Rosaline, in which he adopted the conventional pose of the courtly lover and appeared, in Mercutio's phrase, 'in the likeness of a sigh'. (II.i) After Romeo has fallen in love with Juliet, the 'real thing' which produces a heightened sense of being, his friend notices the difference in him, though he is ignorant of the reason for it: 'Why, is not this better now than groaning for love? now art thou sociable, now art thou Romeo; now art thou what thou art, by art as well as by nature:' (II.iv)

All this was, of course, being done by Shakespeare in the comedies, although Mercutio and the Nurse are, as supporting characters, in a class of their own. But there is an aspect of young love which, in the comedies, is relegated to a subsidiary role, but which is central to our experience of Romeo and Juliet – its poignancy. Throughout Shakespeare's work it is his women – more mature than their lovers, more at the mercy of circumstances and parents – who make us aware of the sadder aspects of love. So it is with Juliet, the only one of the early heroines whose age – barely fourteen, weaned a mere eleven years ago, passing straight from her Nurse to her husband – is stressed. Her experience of life is non-existent, but she has no hesitation in recognizing, and acting on, her love for Romeo, nor does she lack courage in following that love to its ultimately dire conclusion. None of Shakespeare's young heroines is guilty of false modesty and when she is discovered by Romeo confessing her love for him she makes no attempt to withdraw:

> In truth, fair Montague, I am too fond;
> And therefore thou may'st think my behaviour light . . . (II.ii)

Her boldness is touching; and it is a point worth noting that Shakespeare was the only dramatist of the time who could give women initiative without making them appear 'light'.

In the comedies Shakespeare creates a sense of happiness by allowing characters to defeat chance and hence to gain mastery of their fate. Romeo and Juliet attempt to take hold of their destiny but are defeated by chance – a series of mistakes and mistimings which, while they may offend critics, nonetheless reflect an aspect of human experience. One feels that in *Romeo and Juliet* Shakespeare is almost correcting and completing the comic picture. In *Shakespearean Tragedy* (Cambridge Univesity Press), H. B. Charlton suggests Shakespeare knew that *Romeo and Juliet* 'failed' as a tragedy, and abandoned further attempts in that direction for some years. It is just as likely that he realized that, of its kind, *Romeo and Juliet* was an unrepeatable success. More than any of the comedies it embodies, now almost to the point of myth, a lyrical love which in its way did triumph – not over chance but over decay, in that by their early deaths the lovers cheat 'time's fell hand' (Sonnet 64) of the opportunity to 'deface' their love.

Hamlet

DATE 1600

PRINCIPAL CHARACTERS

Claudius: King of Denmark

Gertrude: His wife, widow of the late King Hamlet, Claudius' brother

Hamlet: Prince of Denmark, Gertrude's son, Claudius' nephew

Ghost of the late King Hamlet, the Prince's father

Polonius: The Lord Chamberlain

Laertes: His son

Ophelia: Polonius' daughter

Horatio: Hamlet's friend

Rosencrantz and Guildenstern: Courtiers and friends of Hamlet's youth

Marcellus and Bernardo: Officers

Fortinbras: Prince of Norway

Players and Gravediggers

SCENE The Danish court at Elsinore

Plot

ACT ONE Marcellus and Bernardo, officers of the watch, who have twice seen an apparition which they take to be the Ghost of the late King Hamlet, have persuaded the Prince's friend Horatio to watch with them; he confirms their suspicions and fears that it is the late King's Ghost, and feels that Hamlet his son must be informed. Hamlet himself is introduced, a melancholy bystander at the marriage celebrations of his mother Gertrude and of Claudius, his father's brother and successor to the crown. Taken by Horatio to the scene of his late father's ghostly appearances, he has a private suspicion of his own confirmed – 'O my prophetic soul' (I.v) – as the Ghost tells him that he was murdered by Claudius; solemnly Hamlet undertakes to avenge his father's death. He swears Horatio and the officers to secrecy, with a further warning to Horatio that he may find it necessary to assume an 'antic disposition'. The Lord Chancellor has, meanwhile, with a flurry of good advice, been taking leave of his son, Laertes, who is about to return to his studies in France after attending the royal funeral and wedding; Laertes, for his part, warns his sister Ophelia not to take too seriously the attentions she has been receiving from Hamlet. A further thread established in Act One which is intermittently returned to is the threat posed to Denmark by the Norwegian prince Fortinbras, who has recently assembled an army and has some claim on Danish territory.

ACT TWO is filled with stratagems and counter-stratagems. Polonius sends a spy after Laertes to check on whether his son is conducting himself in accordance with the paternal advice. The appearance of madness that Hamlet has adopted produces the following response from the court: Claudius and Gertrude have summoned Hamlet's old friends Rosencrantz and Guildenstern to see if they can winkle out of Hamlet the cause of his wild behaviour; Polonius takes the view that the madness proceeds from Ophelia's dutiful rejection of the Prince's advances and arranges that he and Claudius should observe the young pair together. Hamlet, who wants confirmation that Claudius is his father's murderer before he undertakes revenge, has commissioned a company of players to perform 'The Murder of Gonzago' – a choice which he hopes will 'catch the conscience of the king'.

ACT THREE Overheard by Claudius and Polonius, Hamlet engages in an un-lover-like exchange with Ophelia in which he advises her to 'Get thee to a nunnery' to avoid being 'a breeder of sinners'. (III.i) Polonius, denied success in one scheme – Claudius refuses to accept that frustrated love for Ophelia has crazed Hamlet's wits – hatches another: that that night after the play he should conceal himself behind an arras in Gertrude's bedroom, while she questions her son about the source of his melancholy. The 'Murder of Gonzago' is performed and as the villain is about to pour poison into the ear of the sleeping Player King (the precise method employed by Claudius for his brother's murder), Claudius, in an evident state of distress, disrupts the performance. He then arranges that Rosencrantz and Guildenstern should rid Denmark of Hamlet, who clearly knows too much, by accompanying him to England. Later in his mother's closet, Hamlet's wild appearance frightens Gertrude, and when her cries for help are answered by noises behind the arras, Hamlet stabs Polonius, thinking that the eavesdropper is Claudius.

ACT FOUR Hamlet is shipped with Rosencrantz and Guildenstern to England, where Claudius has arranged that the King of England should have him put to death. The death of Polonius has brought Laertes back from France, thirsting for vengeance; he has further grief in store with his first sight of Ophelia, whose sanity has been destroyed by her father's death. When Claudius learns that his plans for Hamlet's assassination have miscarried, and that the Prince has returned to Denmark, he and Laertes devise other means for disposing of Hamlet: Laertes and Hamlet will decide their differences in a fencing match, Laertes using a poisoned blade provided by Claudius. Act Four closes with the news that Ophelia has drowned herself.

ACT FIVE Hamlet, on his way back to Elsinore, tells Horatio how he discovered Claudius' treachery to himself on his journey to England, and how he wrote a new commission to the English King, demanding the deaths of the bearers, Rosencrantz and Guildenstern. Hamlet and Horatio join some gravediggers by a newly made grave and learn, when the mourning party arrive, that the grave is Ophelia's. Hamlet, remembering now only his love for Ophelia, fights with Laertes over her coffin, but their quarrel is postponed until the fencing match. When the young men come to fight, Claudius has made doubly sure of Hamlet's death by providing him with a poisoned drink, as well as Laertes with the poisoned blade. Hamlet receives a wound from Laertes and, gaining his opponent's sword after a struggle, wounds Laertes with his own poison. Gertrude unwittingly drinks of the poison meant for Hamlet who learns, from Gertrude and Laertes before they die, of the practices against him. Dying himself, Hamlet stabs Claudius and forces him to drink his own poison. Fortinbras, whose activities have been rumbling in the background throughout the play, arrives to a litter of corpses and the Danish succession.

Critical commentary

Hamlet, the first of Shakespeare's great tragedies, was written in the transition years between the synthesizing spirit of the dramatist's youth (which expressed itself in history and comedy) and the bleaker vision of his maturity. It is probably no accident, therefore, that one instinctively responds to Hamlet as the youngest of Shakespeare's tragic heroes, imagining him, like as not, as younger than the thirty years allotted him in the text. (V.i) Indeed, the terms in which his character has been interpreted by certain twentieth-century critics (Ernest Jones is one, uneasily straddling Freudian analysis and literary criticism), who account for his notorious delay as an avenger and for his disgust at his mother's remarriage by giving him a full-blown Oedipal complex, would seem to fix him firmly in a protracted and tortured adolescence. Freudian reasons for his failure to act can, I think, be dismissed, yet there is that about Hamlet's melancholy which marks him off as someone who has yet to come to terms with life as it is lived by most people.

There may be something youthful about the austerity of Hamlet's judgments, but the apparently festive Elsinore with which he is out of step conceals a rotten core; and the corruption revealed by the action is reinforced by the imagery. Claudius achieved the crown by murder, and more specifically by a murder which, as the Ghost graphically describes it to Hamlet (I.v), infected a healthy body with a spreading disease. Gertrude, her virtuous husband dead, has transferred her affections to 'garbage' (again, the Ghost's description, I.v). Since their marriage, as Hamlet tells Horatio (I.iv), the drunkenness of the Danish court has attracted the contempt of the rest of the world. Claudius' methods are scheming and underhand and his associates share his deviousness. Rosencrantz and Guildenstern are brought to Elsinore to spy on their old friend; Polonius sends a spy after his own son (II.i), uses his daughter as a decoy and, ever at home behind an arras, hastens his own death by concealing himself in Gertrude's chamber (III.iv). Arrangements are made for Hamlet's death abroad, and the play's dénouement is finally achieved through a poisoned cup and a barbed sword.

Hamlet rejects the methods of this world and his rejection is ironically responsible for the play's seven unnecessary deaths, his own included. Such schemes as he devises – his 'mad' disguise, the performance of 'The Murder of Gonzago' – are not death traps but the means of confirming his own suspicions and the Ghost's allegations. His deviousness, in other words, is the result of over-fastidiousness rather than of lack of fastidiousness. He is adrift from the vulgar uncertainties that give all the other characters an anchor. More pertinent to Hamlet's case than the instinctive deviousness of Claudius and Polonius are Laertes, who sets about the revenge of his father's and sister's deaths with unthinking determination, and young Fortinbras who, like Hamlet, has been deprived of his inheritance and goes out to grab it with both hands.

Hamlet lacks their ability to act because, for him the world is fraught with ambiguity. 'There is nothing either good or bad, but thinking makes it so' (II.ii) he tells Rosencrantz and Guildenstern. When he sees the Ghost he is in no doubt that it is his father's, nor that the Ghost's call to revenge represents a clear duty, but away from the Ghost:

> – The spirit that I have seen
> May be the devil; and the devil hath power
> To assume a pleasing shape . . . (II.ii)

Does he love Ophelia? Critics have argued for and against his loving her and, more daringly, on the question of whether Ophelia is an innocent or a potential whore. It seems to me that Ophelia's objective innocence is never in doubt but Hamlet himself is not always clear about it; and the question of whether he loves her, of keen interest to critics, is baffling to Hamlet himself. It is one of the play's mysteries. Ophelia describes to her father a visit that Hamlet made to her closet:

> He took me by the wrist and held me hard;
> Then goes he to the length of all his arm,
> And, with his other hand thus o'er his brow,
> He falls to such perusal of my face
> As he would draw it. (II.i)

Is she what she seems? Hamlet's philosophy is that you can never be too careful – the more especially since he is aware that he himself is not what he seems. Pestered by Rosencrantz and Guildenstern, he hands them a pair of recorders and tells them to play; they protest that they lack the skill. Hamlet has made his point: 'You would play upon me; you would seem to know my stops; you would pluck out the heart of my mystery.' (III.ii)

Hamlet's theatrical antecedents are the revenge plays which look back to a more barbaric epoch of society when revenge was an acknowledged duty. Most of the distinctive features of Shakespeare's finest revenge play arise from placing that duty on a man like Hamlet – newly returned from studying in Wittenberg, in himself a distillation of Renaissance uncertainties. It is not so much that he is a thinker rather than a man of action, but that he is aware of so many opposing realities. For a while the primitive impact of the Ghost is overwhelming:

There are more things in heaven and earth,
Horatio,
Than are dreamt of in your philosophy . . . (I.v)

but as the memory recedes, the doubts flock in.

Hamlet's appeal lies partly in being the supreme dramatic evocation of the mysteriousness of life: that as much as anything is one of the themes of a play which has stubbornly retained its baffling, riddling quality despite the attempts of critics to pluck the heart out of its mystery. Also central to the play is the mystery of what it is like to be dead – a theme which is brilliantly illuminated by C. S. Lewis in his essay, 'Hamlet: the Prince or the Poem?' It is the only one of the major tragedies which allots a crucial role to a Ghost – and a Ghost who, moreover, hints darkly at the horrors of his condition:

I could a tale unfold whose lightest word
Would harrow up thy soul. (I.v)

When Hamlet contemplates suicide in the 'To be or not to be?' soliloquy, his fear is not of dying but of the unknowable experience of death:

The undiscover'd country from whose bourn
No traveller returns. (III.i)

The ultimate fact of death provides for Hamlet a context of futility for human endeavour: 'What a piece of work is a man! How noble in reason! . . . And yet to me, what is this quintessence of dust?' (II.ii) Dust and worms. After killing Polonius, he tells Claudius that his late Chancellor is at supper: 'Not where he eats, but where he is eaten.' (IV.iii) This aspect of the play reaches its climax in the graveyard scene, where he finds the jester that he loved as a child reduced to a pile of bones:

Imperious Caesar, dead and turn'd to clay,
Might stop a hole to keep the wind away. (V.i)

Hamlet's death when it comes is a deliberate anticlimax,

one of the 'casual slaughters' (V.ii) about which Horatio promises to tell Fortinbras. The anticlimax is a just and ironic conclusion to a play which has explored the way an enhanced awareness of death will re-adjust an individual's response to life.

Othello

DATE 1602-4

PRINCIPAL CHARACTERS

Othello: A Moor, General in the Venetian army

Desdemona: His wife

Cassio: His lieutenant

Iago: His ancient

Emilia: Iago's wife, Desdemona's serving woman

Bianca: A whore in love with Cassio

Roderigo: A Venetian gentleman, Iago's dupe, in love with Desdemona

In Venice The Duke of Venice

Brabantio, a Venetian senator, Desdemona's father

SCENE Venice and Cyprus

Plot

ACT ONE In Venice, Iago, who feels slighted at the recent promotion of the nobler-born Cassio to lieutenant, rouses Brabantio with news of his daughter Desdemona's elopement with Iago's commander, Othello. Brabantio tackles Othello with the theft of his daughter, claiming that he must have worked on her by witchcraft. Their dispute is settled by the Duke of Venice who sanctions the marriage when Desdemona tells him of her love for Othello. The Duke and the Senate have a high regard for both the nobility and military capacity of the Moor, whom they now appoint head of the Venetian army in Cyprus. Desdemona refuses to be parted from her new husband and arranges to follow him to Cyprus under the protection of Iago and his wife Emilia. With them goes Roderigo, who is in love with Desdemona and is being milked financially by Iago: the latter persuades Roderigo that Desdemona's marriage need not put an end to his hopes.

ACT TWO A terrible storm off Cyprus has virtually annihilated the Turkish threat (which Othello has arrived to quell) by sinking their boats. Fears for the travellers from Venice, however, are happily confounded as Desdemona and Othello are re-united and welcomed to Cyprus by Cassio, who preceded them. Iago's malice is concentrated at this point against Cassio. Having roused Roderigo against the lieutenant by suggesting that he may be a rival for Desdemona's love, he persuades Cassio, who has been left in charge of the watch by Othello, to drink with him, despite Cassio's plea of a weak head. By wily manoeuvring from Iago, Cassio is brought to strike Roderigo. When Othello is roused by the brawl from what is in effect his wedding night, he dismisses Cassio from the lieutenancy. Iago persuades Cassio to try and gain Desdemona's favour as a step to regaining Othello's; he then reveals to the audience his intention to 'turn her virtue into pitch/And out of her own goodness make the net/That shall enmesh them all' (II.iii).

ACT THREE While Desdemona is listening to Cassio's pleas for her to intercede with Othello, Iago is beginning to insinuate to the Moor the possibility of his wife's infidelity; doubts are cast on Cassio's honesty, and the looseness of Venetian women is cited. A stroke of luck enables Iago to intensify the attack: Desdemona drops a handkerchief which is picked up by Emilia and passed on to Iago, who then, intending to plant the handkerchief in Cassio's lodgings, torments Othello with stories of Cassio wiping his brow with it and calling out to Desdemona in his sleep. When Othello, who attaches magical properties to the handkerchief, tackles Desdemona with its loss, she unwittingly makes the situation worse by choosing Cassio's dismissal as a subject to distract him.

ACT FOUR Iago gives Othello 'proof' of Desdemona's infidelity. Observed by Othello, he draws Cassio into a conversation about a whore, Bianca, who is in love with the lieutenant: Cassio's levity as he talks of her is interpreted by Othello as contempt for his own wife's looseness. The case against Desdomona and Cassio is sealed when Bianca appears with the handkerchief which Cassio has found in his lodgings and asked her to copy. When an embassy arrives from Venice to relieve Othello of his duties and establish Cassio as his successor, Othello strikes his wife before the Venetians. He later treats his wife's bedroom as a brothel, Emilia as the brothel-keeper.

ACT FIVE Iago incites Roderigo to attack Cassio; both are wounded and in the ensuing confusion Iago kills Roderigo, who has become more inconvenient than profitable. Othello, convinced now of his wife's infidelity, smothers her in her bed. Her innocence is attested by Emilia, who learns now for the first time that it was the handkerchief which provided the conclusive evidence. Guessing now at the role Iago has played, she tells what she knows and is killed by her husband for her disclosures. In the presence of the visiting Venetians, Othello wounds Iago and kills himself before he can be brought to justice.

Critical commentary

Othello occupies a unique, and many would claim an inferior, place among Shakespeare's great tragedies. The nobility of the hero is stressed but he is not 'great' in the sense that his actions do not carry the far-reaching consequences of the national ruler. *Othello* is therefore about power (a theme which is included in, if not central to, the other major tragedies) only in the restricted sense of the power exercised by a fraud over his dupe – embodied in the relationship between Iago and Othello and, at a more burlesque level, Iago's relationship with Roderigo. In terms of what was possible in Shakespearean tragedy, the emotional range of *Othello* is limited. Jealousy as a theme had already been worked by Shakespeare in *Much Ado* and was to be again in *Cymbeline* and *The Winter's Tale*, but no-where is it explored with such intensity, and through so many characters, as it is in *Othello*. All the evil in the play has its roots in jealousy in that Iago's malevolence which, as we shall see, is a form of jealousy, expresses itself by planting the seeds of the same destructive passion in others, most notably in Othello, but also in Roderigo. (Interesting-ly, Bianca is moved to return the offending handkerchief to Cassio in the scene which clinches Othello's suspicions because she is jealous of a possible liaison between Cassio and another woman.) The importance of jealousy in the play works negatively too, in that Desdemona's character is defined, her fate determined, by her complete freedom from jealousy: her dramatic role is to embody the positive human values of generosity and trust, and her generosity towards Cassio and trust in Othello both contribute to her undoing.

With fewer characters than the other major tragedies, the distinctive atmosphere of *Othello* is enclosed and domestic. On the stage it can achieve an almost intolerable level of tension as, from the beginning of Act Three, with little for the audience in the way of relief or distraction, all Iago's malevolent energies are concentrated on the poisoning of Othello's mind which must inevitably tend to the destruc-tion of Desdemona. It is one of the finest plays of intrigue ever written, but the reliance on intrigue has left some critics uneasy in that Othello's susceptibility to Iago can be felt to reduce both his stature and our interest in his fate. *Othello* seems to me to stand alone among the tragedies, however, in that our response to the hero is not *meant* to dominate our response to the play. Throughout his career Shakespeare returned again and again to the idea of 'seeming': his primary concern in *Othello*, it seems to me, is to invest that idea with its full weight of tragic possiblity.

The arch-seemer in *Othello* is, of course, Iago – 'honest' Iago to his trusting superiors, the man whose plausibility is achieved through an assumed bluffness and ironic assertions that 'Men should be what they seem'. Critics have long been exercised by Iago's motives – he offers several in the course of the play – and illuminating studies have been done by Bradley and Coleridge; I would simply like to link his particular brand of malevolence with the 'seeming' theme. He has, it scarcely needs stating, a smutty mind. 'You'll have your daughter covered with a Barbary horse' (I.i) is the form in which he chooses to announce Desdemona's elopement to Brabantio. In his insinuations to Othello, Cassio and Desdemona are 'as prime as goats, as hot as monkeys'. (III.iii) His smuttiness is central to our understanding of him in that it is the expression of a mind which cannot cope with the possibility that people are as good as they seem and which is therefore under a compulsion to reduce their apparent goodness to a front – such a front as his own much vaunted 'honesty'. He says of Cassio: 'He hath a daily beauty in his life/ That makes me ugly.' (V.i) His only defence is to make Cassio as ugly as himself.

In his treatment of Desdemona, the most defenceless of Iago's victims, Shakespeare realizes the full potential for pathos of the 'seeming' theme. To her father, Desdemona is 'Of spirit so still and quiet, that her motion/Blush'd at herself.' (I.iii) To Cassio, she is 'a most fresh and delicate creature', 'a most exquisite lady'. (II.iii) She is Othello's 'soul's joy'. (II.i) If a creature like Desdemona – loving, giving, trusting – should be proved to be as Iago has painted her, then Othello is right and 'Chaos is come again.' (III.iii) Othello's cry of anguish when Iago's 'proof' has been presented is 'the pity of it, Iago! O! Iago, the pity of it Iago!' (IV.i): the possibility of Desdemona's perfidy hits at Othello's, and at the audience's values, more than the reality of Iago's perfidy. In the *Sonnets* Shakespeare tackles a profound disillusionment which we can only assume to have been personal as the Friend in whom so much idealism has been invested proves himself to be a 'festering lily'; in *Measure for Measure* that disillusionment is dramatized in the character of Angelo, the apparent angel who behaves like a devil. Othello's language, in his revulsion from his wife, recalls the 'cankered rose' imagery of the *Sonnets*:

> O thou weed!
> Who art so lovely fair and smell'st so sweet
> That the sense aches at thee! Would thou had'st ne'er been
> born! (IV.ii)

The point about Desdemona, however, is that her apparent self is her real self, not an illusion; and Othello's disillusionment is not based on the facts but artificially induced. Desdemona is an apparent angel who is made out to be a devil and is then revealed to have been an angel all along. Contributing to the tension of *Othello* is the plausibility of the accusations: 'She has deceiv'd her father, and may thee' (I.iii) is Brabantio's parting shot to Othello. Desdemona's innocence is an affirmation of our highest values; her death demonstrates the vulnerability of those values in an imperfect world.

Othello stands at a midway point between Iago and Desdemona in as much as his degeneration completes the play's exploration of 'seeming'. There has been some critical debate on whether or not Othello is truly noble. He is throughout 'the noble Moor', but might not his nobility be of the same kind as Iago's 'honesty'? At the beginning of the play only Brabantio questions Othello's reputation. He is repelled by the idea of Desdemona throwing herself at Othello's 'sooty bosom' (I.ii) and concludes that Othello must have 'enchanted' her. At this point in the play the association of Othello with primitive magic is laughable, but when, after Iago has been at work on him, he demands of Desdemona the whereabouts of the handkerchief, he frightens her with tales of the 'magic in the web of it' (III.iv), and with his conviction that their marriage will inevitably founder with its loss. This is not to say that all along Othello has been a primitive alien with only a thin veneer of civilization, but that, like all Shakespeare's tragic heroes, his personality carries double possibilities – in Othello's case, of nobility and barbarity. If he had never met an Iago – a man committed to reducing everyone else to his own level, and to winkling out possible areas of depravity – Othello's life might well have fulfilled the expectations of those who put trust in him. When he says before he kills himself –

> Speak of me as I am; nothing extenuate
> Nor set down aught in malice: then, must you speak
> Of one that lov'd not wisely, but too well ... (V.ii)

– there is, as his critics would claim, a touch of self-dramatizing rhetoric, but with it a genuine desire that his life before Iago should not be presented as 'seeming'. Iago and Desdemona are consistent in their depravity and goodness. Othello, like most of us – and the experiences of a tragic hero are an enlargement of fundamental dilemmas – could have gone either way: it is his tragedy to find Iago's malevolence more persuasive than Desdemona's goodness.

King Lear

DATE 1604-5
PRINCIPAL CHARACTERS
Lear: King of Britain
Goneril ⎫
Regan ⎬ Lear's daughters
Cordelia ⎭
Duke of Cornwall: Husband to Regan
Duke of Albany: Husband to Goneril
King of France ⎫ Suitors to
Duke of Burgundy ⎬ Cordelia
Earl of Kent
Earl of Gloucester
Edgar: Gloucester's legitimate son
Edmund: Gloucester's bastard son
The Fool
Oswald: Goneril's steward
SCENE Britain

Plot

ACT ONE King Lear, now 'fourscore and upward' (IV.vii), has decided to divest himself of the cares of state. His kingdom is to be divided between his three daughters, their proportions determined by the fulsomeness of their public declarations of love. Goneril and Regan declare their love in high rhetorical style, but Lear's favourite daughter, Cordelia, declares that she 'cannot heave/My heart into my mouth'. (I.i) Her father renounces her and offers her, without the promised dowry, to her suitors, Burgundy and France; the former withdraws but the latter takes her, considering that 'She is herself a dowry.' (I.i) When Kent, a man of proven loyalty, intercedes on Cordelia's behalf, his punishment is to be banished by the King.

Although he has abandoned real power, Lear is retaining 'The name and all th'addition to a king' (I.i) – symbolized for him by his personal retinue of a hundred knights: with the King, they are to be maintained by Regan and Goneril, with whom Lear is to stay by monthly turns. Goneril, the first to play hostess, is soon claiming that his knights are riotous and tells her steward Oswald that he may 'Put on what weary negligence you please' (I.iii) in his dealings with the King. Kent has disguised himself as a means of being taken back into Lear's service, and when he defends the King against Oswald's insolence Goneril feels free to reduce her father's retinue by half. After solemnly cursing her, Lear departs for Regan's house, sending Kent ahead to announce his arrival.

Meanwhile the play's sub-plot has been established. Gloucester's bastard son Edmund is newly returned from abroad with ambitions to dispossess his half-brother Edgar; playing on his father's credulity, he convinces him that Edgar is plotting against his life in order to come into his inheritance sooner.

ACT TWO Edmund persuades Edgar to flee their father's anger and when Regan and Cornwall arrive on a visit to

Gloucester's castle they are sufficiently impressed by Edmund to have Edgar proclaimed an outlaw. Regan and Cornwall, warned of Lear's impending visit by Oswald, have repaired to Gloucester's castle as an act of deliberate policy. When Kent follows them there with Lear's letter, he picks a fight with his old enemy Oswald and is ignominiously placed in the stocks by Cornwall. The insult is as much against the King as his messenger, and so Lear takes it when he too reaches Gloucester's castle. The atmosphere of foreboding is heightened by the presence of Lear's Fool, whose riddles and rhymes impress on the audience Lear's folly in abandoning power. Lear's attempts to come to terms with Regan and Cornwall are shattered by the arrival of Goneril. The two sisters ritualistically strip their father of his residual trappings of power by refusing to maintain any of his retinue. As the first rumblings of a storm are heard, Lear goes off into the night, accompanied by the Fool, and beginning to fear for his own sanity.

ACT THREE Lear, now out on the open heath, is contending with both the physical storm and with the 'tempest' in his mind – his obsession with his daughters' ingratitude. His protectiveness towards the Fool, however, heralds the stirrings of a new compassion, which becomes more generalized in his prayer for the 'Poor naked wretches' (III.iv) to whose condition he was indifferent as king. At this point Lear's retinue (of Kent and the Fool) receives an addition in 'Poor Tom' – a mad beggar who is in fact the outlawed Edgar in disguise. In trying to identify himself totally with 'Tom', who epitomizes human poverty and wretchedness, Lear's own sanity becomes genuinely threatened.

The audience has learned, meanwhile, from Kent and Gloucester, that Cordelia has arrived at Dover with French military power. Gloucester confides in Edmund his intention of helping Lear despite Cornwall's prohibition and Edmund, seeing in this an opportunity of gaining his father's title even sooner, passes the information on to Cornwall. In a perverted ceremony of justice Cornwall and

Regan punish Gloucester for his 'treason' in helping Lear by plucking out his eyes; as a parting shot, Regan tells Gloucester that his son was the informer. Act Three closes with Cornwall mortally wounded by his servant, who is outraged by his master's crime and who is in turn killed by Regan.

ACT FOUR Gloucester is turned out of doors and he is found by Edgar who, still disguised as 'Tom', agrees to lead his father to Dover. There, Gloucester intends to throw himself from a cliff. Goneril, meanwhile, has come to an amorous understanding with Edmund, who has accompanied her home to Albany. The latter, hearing of the daughters' treatment of Lear, and then of Gloucester's blinding, for the first time shows some moral strength in his handling of his wife. At Dover, Edgar convinces Gloucester that they are indeed at the top of a cliff so that Gloucester's suicidal leap is, due to Edgar's contrivance, undertaken on level ground. Edgar, disguised now as a stray passer by, tricks his father out of his despair by convincing him that the fall was real and that the gods have seen fit to preserve him. They meet Lear, who has been brought to Dover by Kent to join Cordelia but is now wandering alone. The clearest thread in Lear's ravings is his disgust at all civil authority. He is found by some of Cordelia's attendants and borne off to his daughter. Oswald arrives, bent on gaining favour by killing Gloucester, but he is himself killed by Edgar, who now learns, through letters that Oswald is carrying, of Edmund's liason with Goneril. Act Four closes with Lear's reconciliation with Cordelia: now recovered from the worst of his raving he begs, and is granted, his daughter's forgiveness.

ACT FIVE In the battle between the French and British forces (led by Albany and Edmund), the French are defeated and Cordelia and Lear are taken prisoner. Knowing that Albany means no harm to the prisoners now that the military threat is overcome, Edmund privately issues a warrant for their deaths; since Goneril intends killing Albany, by marrying her Edmund would then be in possession of absolute power. Albany, however, has learned of Goneril's scheme in a letter from Edgar; Albany arrests Goneril and Edgar, his identity concealed by his armour, arrives to deal with Edmund, whom he formally challenges with treachery. Edmund takes up the challenge and is mortally wounded in the conflict. Edgar reveals his identity and tells of his recent history, a narrative which includes an emotive description of Gloucester's death, 'Twixt two extremes of passion, joy and grief' (V.iii), when Edgar had finally declared himself to be his rejected son. The death toll mounts as word is brought, first of Regan's death —in love with Edmund herself, she was poisoned by Goneril – and then of Goneril's suicide. Edmund, remembering Lear and Cordelia and meaning to do some good 'Despite of mine own nature' (V.iii), tells of the order he gave for their death. His repentance is too late and Lear appears with Cordelia dead in his arms. Grief has again affected his sanity and he dies thinking that Cordelia might still be alive. Kent, who has dropped his disguise and come to present himself to his master, feels that he cannot long survive Lear, and Albany and Edgar are left to rule the battered kingdom.

Critical commentary

'All that we can say must fall far short of the subject, or even what we ourselves conceive of it . . . ' With these words Hazlitt began his essay on *King Lear*, and those who follow can only echo his sentiments. It is a play which has always evoked strong reactions. Johnson revealed that 'I was many years ago so shocked by Cordelia's death, that I know not whether I ever endured to read again the last scenes of the play till I undertook to revise them as an editor.' The play was thought to be unactable by Lamb – not because of any dramatic weakness but because of its transcendent poetic power which, Lamb felt, should be allowed to operate directly on the individual's imagination. To J. Middleton Murry it was regrettable that Shakespeare should ever have written *Lear* at all since, in so doing he revealed an 'uncontrollable despair' on which he would have been better to keep silent. Keats, whose own artistic aspirations were so much in sympathy with Shakespeare's, found in *Lear* the 'intensity' that distinguishes the very greatest art.

That intensity is, I think, the key to the vehemence of audience and critical reaction. The play is rich in theme and allusion, reinforcing and enlarging its own suggested ideas through the medium of the double-plot. Both show old men who through fatal weaknesses of character (irresponsibility and credulousness in Gloucester's case, in Lear's an obstinate rashness and a susceptibility to flattery which years of uncontested authority have confirmed in him) are brought to reject their loyal children in favour of the more plausible but self-seeking ones; and who are finally helped through their suffering by the children whom they rejected. The nature of appearance and reality, which obsessed Shakespeare throughout his working life is explored in *Lear* through the visions of two old men who learn to distinguish the false from the true, not too late for their own spiritual growth, but too late to use their enlarged vision as a pre-scription for living. The parent/child relationship; the responsibilities and rights of the king and the related theme of the workings of civil authority; the mystery of justice in a wider sense, of how far we can assume the presence of a divinity who is prepared to bring order into human chaos – all these have their place in *Lear* either as developed themes or as the preoccupations of specific characters. I intend to concentrate on what seem to me to be Shakespeare's funda-mental concerns in *Lear* – an exploration of the bonds that hold human beings together; the problem of human sufferings and the celebration of human endurance. The play's setting – pre-Christian Britain – offered Shakespeare an unusual degree of ideological freedom in approaching these ideas.

King Lear opens on a note of formal ceremoniousness which is shattered by Cordelia, who first and most explicitly, and with an austere contempt for sentimentality, makes her stand on the fundamental social bonds, as opposed to the socially pleasant niceties: 'I love your majesty/According to my bond; nor more nor less.' (I.i) Cordelia's plain-speaking destroys the ceremonial atmosphere of the court, which receives a further blow from Kent's bluntness. Lear cannot bear too much reality, and is swayed in the making of his political decision by the 'glib and oily art' of Regan and Goneril. One of the strengths of *Lear* is the characterization of the two sisters, monsters indeed, but only too plausible. Their actions are dictated by self-interest – in the beginning, a kind of self-interest which few of us could honestly claim was beneath us. Up to and including the barring of Gloucester's gate on Lear, they could still stand today as credible portraits of suburban housewives: Lear is in his dotage and must be managed, his knights are riotous, disturbing their household peace; Regan cannot take her father in before her time because she is away from home, out of the 'provision' necessary for entertaining him; when Lear decides to brave the elements, it is his own choice – they will take him, but not his hundred knights. In Regan and Goneril the mythic quality is given a beautifully realized social context. What is more frightening than their ultimate monstrousness is the eminently practical, *sensible* root from which it grows. Even the blinding of Gloucester – which marks the dividing line between a narrow interpretation of self-interest and wider political aspiration – is justified by them on the grounds of Gloucester's high treason.

Edmund, too, has his reasons for what he does. Born outside wedlock, he feels himself justified in ignoring those 'bonds' – 'the plague of custom' (I.ii) as he dismisses them – which should bind man to man. With his vitality and humour, even charm, he goes some way in the early stages towards enlisting the audience's sympathies. The play demonstrates, however, that those bonds are ignored at one's peril. Regan, Goneril, Cornwall and Edmund bring suffering to others but they also destroy themselves. Ignoring first their filial and fraternal bonds, then their political responsibilities (in the blinding of Gloucester), Goneril moves on to break her marriage vows and then to kill her sister and contemplate the murder of her husband to clear her path to Edmund. Taken to its logical conclusion, self-interest is shown to be anything but enlightened. Albany's comment on them is: 'Humanity must perforce prey on itself,/Like monsters of the deep' (IV.ii)

Albany, in Act IV Scene ii, is the last of the characters to declare himself finally against the values represented by Regan and Goneril, Cornwall and Edmund. By then there is an absolute division between the *dramatis personae*, as some of the characters have chosen, others have had thrust upon them, a path which marks them off from the values of Regan, Goneril and Edmund. The depth of our response to *Lear*, and its power to exhilarate, are determined by the fact that Shakespeare is not dealing with heroes, unless we except Kent and Cordelia, the first to perceive the hollowness of Regan's and Goneril's 'civilization'. In the early part of the play Gloucester is amiable, time-serving, at pains to placate everybody at once, until he makes a decision (one suspects for the first time in his life) which is fraught with possible peril:

> If I die for it, as no less is threatened me, the King my old
> master must be relieved. (III.iii)

Cornwall's servant cannot stand by while Gloucester is blinded; Albany is positively elated by his unsuspected moral strength when he declares:

> – Gloucester, I live
> To thank thee for the love thou show'dst the King,
> And to revenge thine eyes. (IV.ii)

The play's hope – for it is by no means as pessimistic as some commentators would have us believe – lies in the potential of ordinary people to stand up, *in extremis*, for fundamental human values.

The play opens with Lear's crucial choice in the division of his kingdom; it is one that he learns to regret. The choice to remake his life, however, is made for him by his daughters' refusal to continue to accept him on his own terms. He stalks off into the storm out of pride, and there is a sense in which he never loses the pride of kingship (in *Lear*, Shakespeare is interested in more modest miracles). But he does learn a valuable lesson; he has been a king for so long that, until he goes into the storm, he has never known what it means to be a man. When the play opens, Lear is the most self-centred of Shakespeare's tragic heroes: in the division of the kingdom he demonstrates the extent to which he uses the political arena as a means of satisfying his emotional needs; power has given him a unshakeable conviction that he is privy to the gods, whom he assumes in any conflict to be on his side. His arrogance serves to make his movement of compassion towards others more touching: 'How dost, my boy? Art cold?' (III.ii) he asks the Fool. Aware for the first time of the 'poor naked wretches' in his kingdom, he urges himself to:

> Take physic, pomp;
> Expose thyself to feel what wretches feel,
> That thou mayst shake the superflux to them
> And show the heavens more just. (III.iv)

He sends himself mad in trying to identify himself with 'Poor Tom', whom he sees as essential, suffering humanity: 'Thou art the thing itself; unaccomodated man is no more but such a poor, bare, forked animal as thou art.' (III.iv)

The part played by madness in the play has a symbolic as well as a dramatic value. In his madness, Lear stages a mock-trial in a hovel at which the really mad king, the apparently mad Edgar and the professional Fool, pass judgment on Regan and Goneril – now rulers of the kingdom, with absolute authority. The implied paradox is that the apparently sane civilization represented by Regan and Goneril is fundamentally mad, while those on the heath are discovering through madness, through a reversal of the values that they have accepted without question, a new kind of sanity. A kind of alternative society is established on the heath – of Lear, the Fool, the banished and disguised Kent, the outlawed and disguised Edgar and intermittently of Gloucester – based on the humane principles of compassion and loyalty. Another paradox of the play is its links with pastoral – that escapist dream of over-civilized men who felt that a breath of country air could re-invigorate the natural springs of emotion and understanding. *King Lear* – almost unbearable, sometimes grotesque, never escapist in its depiction of cruelty and suffering – is Shakespeare's tragic version of pastoral. Removed from its distractions Gloucester learns to evaluate civilization:

> I stumbled when I saw. Full oft 'tis seen
> Our means secure us, and our mere defects
> Prove our commodities. (IV.i)

The lesson is learned, however, at the cost of his eyes and in the painful knowledge of having wronged the son whom he has no expectation of ever seeing again; 'pastoral' in *King Lear* is not a day trip to happiness.

As Goneril, Regan *et al.* move on with their large acts of destruction, the other characters mark their progress as people by small but fundamental acts of humanity: Gloucester brings Lear to food and shelter (III.vi); Gloucester's servants follow their newly blinded master with comfort in the form of 'flax and whites of eggs' (III.vii); Edgar guides his father through his despair to an acceptance of his lot; Cordelia finds her father and furnishes him with the humble but life-giving necessities of clean clothes and sleep. There is no sentimentality about *Lear*, however, and it offers no easy answers. Suffering can be alleviated but not eliminated; it is, as Lear tells Gloucester in an interlude of lucidity from his ravings, an inescapable part of being human:

> Thou must be patient; we came crying hither:
> Thou know'st the first time that we smell the air
> We waul and cry. (IV.vi)

Edgar echoes Lear in his lesson for his father:

> Men must endure
> Their going hence, even as their coming hither;
> Ripeness is all. (V.ii)

King Lear's tragedy is in a sense Edgar's coming of age. Credulous like his father at the beginning of the play, putty in the hands of his brother Edmund, he learns the art of survival, but not survival at the expense of other people. He learns through his own suffering and through participating in the suffering of Lear and Gloucester. He describes himself as:

> A most poor man, made tame to fortune's blows,
> Who, by the art of known and feeling sorrows,
> Am pregnant to good pity. (IV.vi)

With Albany, he takes over the kingdom at the end; the values learned on the heath, which Lear does not live to translate into political terms, will inform Edgar's judgment.

The play's ending, appalling as it is, shows Shakespeare's final unwillingness to make concessions to sentimentality. Cordelia's death is the direct result of Lear's placing of power in the wrong hands: not only the guilty but the innocent are destroyed when self-interest and a failure to observe the basic human decencies prevail. In Lear's final agony, the other characters can only watch and feel with him; so too the audience. *Lear* is the only one of Shakespeare's plays where sympathy is an end in itself – the only thing left in a world of chaos. No other of his plays enlists the sympathies of the audience to the same degree.

Macbeth

DATE 1606

PRINCIPAL CHARACTERS

Duncan: King of Scotland

Malcolm ⎱ his sons
Donalbain ⎰

Macbeth ⎱ Generals in the King's army
Banquo ⎰

Lady Macbeth: Macbeth's wife

Macduff, Lennox, Ross and other Scottish nobles
Lady Macduff
Fleance: Banquo's son
Hecate and Three Witches
SCENE Scotland and England

Plot

ACT ONE opens in a storm, on a heath, with the three witches talking of their intended meeting with Macbeth. The scene switches to King Duncan as he learns of the defeat of the Norwegian army and of the treacherous deeds of the Thane of Cawdor. Duncan acknowledges that he owes victory to the valour of Macbeth and Banquo, and on the execution of the present Thane of Cawdor Macbeth is to succeed to the honour. Unaware as yet of his good fortune, Macbeth, walking with Banquo, is greeted by the witches as Thane of Cawdor and future King of Scotland; Banquo is told that his sons shall be kings of Scotland. The witches' predictions clearly touch an ambition that has already stirred in Macbeth, and when, after the witches' disappearance, he is brought word by Ross of his elevation to Cawdor, the authenticity of their prophecies seems to be confirmed.

At Macbeth's castle, his wife learns of his new honour and of his meeting with the witches. Her own ambition is more ruthless than Macbeth's: word is brought that Duncan intends to stay overnight in her castle and she sees in the projected visit an opportunity that must be seized. When Macbeth arrives, she takes the initiative in planning Duncan's murder and persuades her husband that his scruples are unmanly.

ACT TWO In the event, Lady Macbeth baulks at performing the murder herself – ' Had he not resembled/My father as he slept I had done't' (II.ii); but at that moment Macbeth returns in a severely disturbed state after murdering the sleeping Duncan. To cover their traces, Lady Macbeth smears blood over the guards outside Duncan's room and places daggers by them. When Duncan's body is discovered the following morning by Macduff, Macbeth kills the guards before they have a chance to defend themselves against a murder accusation. When Malcolm and Donalbain, Duncan's sons, flee the castle after their father's murder is discovered, their flight is felt to suggest their own guilt in instigating an act which the guards performed. With the path thus cleared, Macbeth is named the next king.

ACT THREE Now crowned King, Macbeth's attention turns to Banquo, who was told by the witches that his descendants would be kings. He has Banquo ambushed and killed while out riding, but his son Fleance, equally the object of Macbeth's fear, escapes. At a banquet held by the new king to celebrate his coronation, the ghost of Banquo haunts his table (although visible to none of his guests) and Lady Macbeth is forced to bring the merry-making to an end. Act Three closes with Lennox and another lord discussing Macbeth's guilt – which is by now widely assumed – and his tyrannical behaviour as king. Macduff has fled to England to impress on Edward the Confessor the need for a war of attrition against Macbeth.

ACT FOUR Macbeth, at a further meeting with the witches and Hecate, is told to fear Macduff; assurances of his safety seem to be offered, however, in the riddling prophecy that he will be killed by no man born of woman, and not until 'Great Birnam wood to high Dunsinane Hill/Shall come against him.' (IV.i) He is nervous of Macduff nonetheless, and learning of the latter's flight to England he has Lady Macduff and her children murdered. Macduff learns of his loss in England where the attack on Scotland which should secure the throne for Duncan's heir, Malcolm, is being planned.

ACT FIVE opens with Lady Macbeth sleep-walking and revealing to bystanders her obsession with Duncan's murder. When word is brought to Macbeth of his wife's death – it is hinted, through suicide – he is too distracted by the faltering fortunes of his army to mourn. His only comfort, as the English gain ground and Scottish noblemen defect to them, is in the witches' prophecies. Both the prophecies, however, are shown to be riddles rather than assurances. Malcolm instructs his soldiers to hew down branches, for camouflage, so that Birnam Wood does indeed seem to be moving; when Macbeth meets Macduff in battle the latter tells him that he was 'from his mother's womb/Untimely ripp'd'. (V.vii) Macbeth is killed by Macduff and Malcolm is proclaimed king.

Critical commentary

In few of Shakespeare's plays is there such an absolute division between good and evil as in *Macbeth*. The historical Macbeth, who reigned for ten years, was noted neither for villainy nor tyranny, so the course of growing depravity which is hinted at for Shakespeare's Macbeth was clearly an artistic decision rather than historical fact or legend. *Macbeth* is a remarkably coherent dramatic achievement. Its length (at barely more than 2000 lines, the shortest of the major tragedies) allows no room for material extraneous to the main thread of the narrative; the characters, with the exception of Macbeth and Lady Macbeth, are barely individualized but subordinated entirely to the main thread of the narrative. Like all the major tragedies, *Macbeth* has its own distinctive atmosphere but, as a number of critics have noticed, that atmosphere is more pervasive in *Macbeth* than in any of the others.

Macbeth opens with the witches, whose chant 'Fair is foul, and foul is fair' (I.i) immediately establishes one of the elements in the play's theme. Macbeth, who has hitherto been 'fair', attracting nothing but praise for his valour and manliness, is himself to be corroded with evil; and he will make the choice that leads to Duncan's murder by confounding the foul and the fair on an ethical level. Moreover, the fruits of the murder – power and the throne of Scotland – which appear so 'fair' to Macbeth and his wife in prospect, bring no joy. Lady Macbeth realizes this as soon as she has been crowned queen: 'Nought's had, all's spent/Where our desire is got without content.' (III.ii) Macbeth's confusion of foul and fair is against nature. The idea of natural disturbance is indeed central to the play, apparent in the more overtly 'dramatic' scenes, like Act One, Scene Five where Lady Macbeth is bracing herself for Duncan's murder ('unsex me here', 'make thick my blood', 'take my milk for gall') and reinforced by the use of natural emblems elsewhere. When Malcolm and his party arrive at Macbeth's castle, they note the delicacy of the air and the martlets' nests; the setting of the castle is suggestive of a natural joy which Duncan's murder will destroy.

After the murder has been accomplished, Macbeth says to his wife: 'Methought I heard a voice cry "Sleep no more/ Macbeth does murder sleep".' (II.ii) In all of Shakespeare's plays, sleep is one of nature's gifts, bestowed on those who are on nature's side; by seeing himself as the murderer of sleep, Macbeth acknowledges the extent to which he has placed himself beyond the pale. Lady Macbeth's sleepwalking scene (V.i) is both actual (and dramatically effective) and symbolic of the extent to which she has cut herself off from the natural healing processes.

During the sleep-walking scene, two features of Lady Macbeth's life since the murder of Duncan emerge – that she can no longer bear not to have light by her and that in her sleep she is continually washing her hands. The association of dark with evil-doing is as old as recorded history, and in *Macbeth* the murders of Duncan and Banquo are nocturnal events: by having light by her Lady Macbeth is creating by artificial means the illusion of being still within the community of the rightous. The washing of the hands is to remove the stain of Duncan's murder: 'Yet who would have thought the old man to have had so much blood in him?' (V.i) *Macbeth* is Shakespeare's bloodiest play, not in terms of the quantity of blood spilt, but in the extent to which the idea of blood pervades the atmosphere. The references to blood – both in descriptions of wounds, and as a metaphor for the spiritual stain of murder – are numerous; blood is, moreover, no mere static emblem but fully realized as thick, flowing and clinging. An expression of Macbeth's pessimism after Banquo's murder is that

> I am in blood
> Stepp'd in so far that, should I wade no more,
> Returning were as tedious as go o'er. (III.iv)

Blood, the murder of sleep, the perversion of nature – all suggest how far Macbeth has violated the social bonds. The characterization, or rather lack of characterization, of the other characters in the drama, serves to emphasize his and his wife's apartness. The loving Duncan, the saintly Edward the Confessor (Malcolm and Macduff in Act Four, Scene Three dwell much on his virtues as the antithesis of Macbeth's viciousness), Malcolm as he is defined by the expectations of the Scots – none of them is a character in the sense of being amenable to character analysis, but each presents a standard by which Macbeth may be judged.

How then – and this is one of the chief areas of critical debate on Macbeth – does Shakespeare manage to enlist the sympathies of his audience for his hero? All Shakespeare's tragic heroes are flawed – tragedy would have no place in a perfect world – but Macbeth's particular 'flaw' (the term seems especially inadequate in his case) of murderous ambition, is unlikely to strike an answering chord in many members of an audience. Shakespeare's dramatic technique has been variously analysed for explanations of how he gains acceptance for the villain as hero. The part played by the witches and by Lady Macbeth in his downfall, which can be seen as mitigating the degree of his responsibility; the references to his earlier nobility of character; the comparative colourlessness of the subsidiary characters, which gives Macbeth and his wife an interest which is independent of their moral worth – all these are standard text-book explanations. To these may be added the fact that Shakespeare never gives his hero the manner of a conscious hypocrite.

The technical approach fails, however, to account for

Macbeth's tragic stature. All of Shakespeare's tragic heroes touch some universal chord, are not characters in the sense that Falstaff or Malvolio are, but are on some level part of ourselves. Hamlet's sense of the mysteriousness of life, Lear's voyage of suffering and discovery, Othello's profound uncertainty about the intrinsic worth of what he values most (Desdemona), touch common springs of human experience. At what point does Macbeth the murderer achieve the universal? It has often been noticed that the quality of the verse given to Macbeth is remarkable even for Shakespeare, so that we respond to him as to a man of imagination. It is in fact his imagination (which his wife does not share), his awareness of what life will be like after committing murder, which prevents him from being a cold-blooded villain:

> that but this blow
> Might be the be-all and the end-all here,
> But here, upon this bank and shoal of time,
> We'd jump the life to come. (I.vii)

It is not just the quality of Macbeth's verse that is important, however, or even its content, so much as what one might call its characteristic tone after Duncan's murder – which is one of painful and profound nostalgia. When Duncan's body has been discovered he says, with deep irony – for it is literally true of himself as well as an appropriate public comment to make on the King's death –

> Had I but died an hour before this chance
> I had liv'd a blessed time; for, from this instant,
> There's nothing serious in mortality –
> All is but toys. (II.iii)

Duncan's murder has pushed everything that preceded it in Macbeth's life into an irrevocable and golden past and left him stranded in a hopeless and futile present. When the English forces are massing against him, he expresses a deep sense of loss for the life that might have been his:

> my way of life
> Is fall'n into the sear, the yellow leaf;
> And that which should accompany old age,
> As honour, love, obedience, troops of friends,
> I must not look to have. (V.iii)

When he learns of his wife's death, he is aware that the life he has chosen has deprived him of the ability to mourn; at the same time, his imagination never allows him to forget the loss, not so much of his wife, as of the healing human response:

> She should have died hereafter;
> There would have been a time for such a word. (V.v)

Lacking such responses, life is indeed for him 'a tale/Told by an idiot, full of sound and fury,/Signifying nothing.' (V.v) We respond to Macbeth as to a man who knows what it is to suffer. The grief he experiences for what he has himself thrown away touches a universal chord in all of us and helps us to pity what we must condemn.

Timon of Athens

DATE It was first printed in the First Folio of 1623; since there is no record of a performance before that date it has been assumed that *Timon* was never completed to Shakespeare's satisfaction, and therefore never offered to the public.

PRINCIPAL CHARACTERS
Timon: A noble Athenian
Alcibiades: An Athenian captain
Apemantus: A misanthrope
Flavius: Timon's steward
Painter, Poet, Jeweller, Merchant
Phrynia and Timandra, Mistresses of Alcibiades
SCENE Athens and a neighbouring wood

Plot

ACT ONE establishes the magnificence of Timon's way of life.

In a series of interviews, he patronizes the work of a jeweller, a poet and a painter; bestows money on a servant so that he can marry to his liking; and provides the cash necessary to release a debtor from prison. He entertains his 'friends' – mostly flatterers and hangers-on – to a sumptuous banquet, where the atmosphere of bonhomie is disturbed by two of the participants – by Apemantus, who includes himself in the company simply to mock, both at the flatterers and at Timon's imprudence; and by Timon's loyal steward Flavius, who at the end of Act One reveals that Timon no longer has the money to finance the splendour of his life.

ACT TWO As Timon's creditors send in pressing demands for money, he at first refuses to believe himself so reduced; and when Flavius does convince him, he has no doubt that those whom he has aided in the past will stand by him now, despite the fact that the Senate, which owes much to Timon's generosity, has been deaf to Flavius' own appeals on his master's behalf. Servants are dispatched by Timon to ask money of those who might consider themselves to be in his debt.

ACT THREE The appeals of Timon's servants to Athenian lords fall on stony ground. When Timon hears of the lords' ingratitude he bids Flavius send out invitations to a final feast. Meanwhile Alcibiades, who has performed noted military service for Athens, is banished by the Senate for pleading for the life of a man who has been sentenced to death. The guests, assuming that Timon's poverty was not real but adopted as a means of testing their loyalty, fall back into a fawning manner. Timon opens the banquet with a perverted form of grace: 'For these my present friends, as they are to me nothing, so in nothing bless them, and to nothing are they welcome.' (III.vi), and then uncovers the dishes which are filled with warm water; the 'banquet' is abruptly terminated when Timon throws dishes and water at his guests. He declares his new philosophy: 'henceforth hated be/Of Timon man and all humanity!' (III.vi)

ACT FOUR Timon retreats to a cave outside Athens. As his

opinion of mankind sinks to new depths the audience is given an example of human benevolence in the behaviour of Flavius who, as Timon's household is broken up, shares what money he has with the other servants. Digging for roots outside his cave, Timon finds gold. When his whereabouts are discovered, he receives a procession of visitors: Apemantus, who claims that Timon's misanthropy is not as pure as his own, and urges him to return to Athens and turn flatterer; Alcibiades and his mistresses Phrynia and Timandra, who are given some of the hoard of gold – the Captain to help him destroy Athens, the prostitutes as an encouragement to spread disease; some bandits, whose viciousness is also rewarded with gold; and Flavius, whom Timon is forced to admit to be the one honest man in creation.

ACT FIVE opens with further visits to the cave – from the Poet and Painter, who are abused but sent away with their hands full; and from two senators, who plead with Timon to return to Athens and lead the city against Alcibiades. Timon's mind is by now on death: he has chosen a site for his grave, 'Upon the beached verge of the salt flood' (V.i) where one of Alcibiades' soldiers later finds him buried. When Alcibiades arrives at Athens with his army, he agrees that the city should be saved and only his own and Timon's enemies punished for their crimes.

Critical commentary

Timon of Athens differs from the other tragedies in a number of important respects, some of which help to explain why it has never really attracted performance. It is one of the most formally structured of Shakespeare's plays, much of the action, to a degree that is unique in Shakespeare, taking the form of interviews – not, it must be admitted, the most dynamic dramatic medium. With the exception of Apemantus, Alcibiades and Flavius, the subsidiary characters are barely differentiated and almost interchangeable representatives of rapacious or ungrateful humanity, with little attempt at verisimilitude on Shakespeare's part.

The impression of allegory is reinforced by the way that Timon's metamorphosis, from philanthropist to misanthrope, is handled. In Act One, when his bounty is at its peak, every kind word, every mark of attention, every instance of what he takes to be humanity in those around him is rewarded by Timon with something precious. The amity he feels is expressed in feasting, the symbolic nature of which is made clear in the stage direction for the masque that closes the banquet: 'The lords rise from table, with much adoring of Timon; and to show their loves, each single out an Amazon, and all dance, men with women, a lofty strain or two to the hautboys, and cease.' (I.ii) The bitter disappointment that Timon feels at the desertion of his erstwhile friends is again expressed at a banquet (III.vi) where the warm water within the dishes reflects his changed vision of humanity. In a highly structured way the two banquets, with their reversed symbolic values, suggest the progression of Timon's approach to food and its place in human affairs. The associations attached to food in a civilized society (which are felt in the first banquet) are stripped off until men are revealed as feeding off each other. Timon tells the bandits who approach him for gold that, not content with eating 'the beasts themselves, the birds and fishes:/You must eat men.' (IV.iii) There is a similar allegorical neatness to the role allotted to gold in the play. Outside his cave, gold, the symbol of Timon's earlier benevolence, becomes instead a symbol of his contempt for humanity: he is still giving – of the gold that he finds under the tree – but in the giving he expresses his disgust at wealth and at those who are subservient to it.

Apart from his praise of his steward Flavius –

> I do proclaim
> One honest man, mistake me not, but one;
> No more, I pray, and he's a steward . . . (IV.iii)

– Timon's hatred, after his removal from Athens, is unremitting, and partly accounts for the play's lack of popular appeal. Put at its most superficial, the play lacks variety of tone. In terms of the more profound satisfactions of tragedy it is difficult to determine quite how Shakespeare intends us to respond to Timon. Some would argue for a satirical interpretation. Certainly the treatment of most of the minor characters might be felt to support this view: the types of greed and ingratitude among the Athenian lords have something of the one-dimensional quality of 'humourous' characters as popularized by Jonson in his comedies of humours. But does the satire extend to Timon himself? In the early scenes there is evidence that Shakespeare does not attach the same value that Timon does to his benevolence. There is a sentimentality about his tone – 'O! what a precious comfort 'tis to have so many, like brothers, commanding one another's fortunes' (I.ii) – which leaves a question-mark hanging over his motives. More serious is Timon's inability, in his prosperity, to take as well as to give. He secures the release of a debtor from prison; when the debtor comes into a fortune and offers to repay his debt Timon refuses, thereby showing nobility but also a fundamental misunderstanding of the concept of brotherly sharing: 'There's none/Can truly say he gives, if he receives.' (I.ii) Timon is given to extremes – always dangerous in the Shakespearean world, as well as being a target for the balancing weapon of satire – and his misanthropy is but the reverse side of his benevolence.

The real area of uncertainty is whether Shakespeare is endorsing Timon's misanthropy or whether that too is an extreme to be subjected to the controlling medium of drama. In his introduction to the New Shakespeare edition of *Timon* J. C. Maxwell argues that both Flavius and Alcibiades serve to 'place' Timon's misanthropy — Flavius as a notable example of loyalty and good fellowship, Alcibiades by showing compassion towards the hard stones of Athens and faith in his own ability to establish a new order there. Since neither character represents a developed theme, however, this thesis rests on the hypothesis that

Timon is unfinished, most specifically in terms of what Shakespeare intended to do with Flavius and Alcibiades.

In *Timon* as it stands, we have hints of satire directed against Timon's early benevolence, and in the final two acts a concentration of passion which suggests that Shakespeare intended us to accept Timon's invective, bleak as it is, as a comment of universal relevance. There is a strong parallel between Timon and Lear in the obsession that the two protagonists share with human ingratitude. Lear does, however, achieve a more comprehensive vision, which includes a recognition of his own fallibility, and love as well as hate. Unlike Lear, Timon never regains the sense of himself as part of the human community. It would seem that, with *Timon*, Shakespeare's view of mankind reached its lowest point: the image of humanity praying on itself 'Like monsters of the deep' that is found in *Lear*, the defeat of idealism that is chronicled in *Troilus*, the anguish shared by Hamlet and Othello that what they assume to be real goodness may only be an appearance of goodness – all are distilled in *Timon* which, in its hopelessness, has a strange power of its own.

9 Shakespeare: Romance

Nature's above art in that respect . . . *King Lear* (IV. vi)

In 1608 Shakespeare's company, the King's Men, took legal possession of the Blackfriars Theatre. Acquiring the smaller, indoor theatre was a shrewd move. Increasingly under James I, the court had been influencing theatrical taste, and the Blackfriars was better equipped than the Globe to cater for what was becoming fashionable. Until 1613, when the Globe was burned down during a performance of *Henry VIII*, the King's Men maintained both theatres, with the obvious advantages of a share in both the popular and the more élite theatrical markets, and of having in the indoor Blackfriars a London home for the winter; but after 1608 it is likely that the experimental base shifted to the Blackfriars.

The acquisition of the second theatre coincided with the final change in direction in Shakespeare's career. Known now as the romances, the plays written during the last years of his working life – *Pericles*, *Cymbeline*, *The Winter's Tale* and *The Tempest* – are clearly influenced by the prevailing court style. They lend themselves to a more spectacular mode of stage presentation than his earlier work – to the continuing detriment of at any rate *The Tempest*, a tough and austere play which is still often performed in the extravagant manner of light opera. In all of them, Shakespeare is at pains to preserve the element of surprise. In the early comedies, once the potentially catastrophic plot confusions are underway, other elements in the plot serve to reassure the audience about the final outcome; in the romances the audience is, as far as possible, kept baffled for as long as the characters. One effect is that potentially tragic themes are not 'contained' in romance as they are in the self-contained world of comedy. For its first three acts *The Winter's Tale* operates like a tragedy which is then miraculously transformed to happiness.

The miraculous and the supernatural are features of romance, albeit used more sparingly by Shakespeare than by some of his contemporaries. Foremost among those writing in the new mode were Beaumont and Fletcher; their plays declare their allegiance to New Greek Comedy (of the immediately post-classical period) whose themes and motifs were becoming familiar to Jacobean readers through a number of prose translations. Only *Pericles* of Shakespeare's last plays uses a Greek tale as a primary source, but they all of them owe something to the Greek tradition: shipwrecks, storms, virtuous young love, the loss and recovery of royal children are common features of both the romances and the Greek tales. The plots of the romances observe a perceptible pattern: the disruption of a noble family (occurring, in *Cymbeline* and *The Tempest*, some years before the action begins) is followed for part of that family by years of exile; reunion, and generally forgiveness and reconciliation, close the plays.

Shakespeare was always a practical man of the theatre, and it would be unwise to dismiss as unworthy of him the commercial motives that may have influenced the move from tragedy to romance. Equally, they should not be overestimated. With his remarkable powers of assimilation and adaptation, Shakespeare found in the romance genre the possibility of fresh insights and new and satisfying solutions to abiding preoccupations. When it was still fashionable to interpret Shakespeare's life according to his work (and it must be admitted that none of us is free from curiosity, even though we may lack the certainty of earlier critics), Edward Dowden in *Shakespeare: A Critical Study of his Mind and Art* (1875), labelled Shakespeare's last period, 'On the Heights';

a heart-warming conclusion to a life in which the middle years had been spent writing tragedies 'Out of the Depths'. The labels are misleading for, despite the more artificial mode in which Shakespeare was working, there is nothing artificially euphoric about the mood of these plays. The sense of evil is as real in the romances as in the tragedies, but the focus has changed. *The Winter's Tale* shows Leontes painfully living with the results of his own wrong-doing; if the play offers the hope that people can change and that chance might finally dismiss them to happiness, then that is at least no more unlikely as a possibility than the holocausts and catastrophes that conclude the tragedies. Prospero, the hero of *The Tempest* and the victim of other people's wickedness, comes to realize that, however distasteful evil is, he must learn to live with it. It is arguable that the tragedies, in which all the evil is purged and the world in a sense begins again with the survivors, offer a more artificially complete solution to human experience.

For all their artiness, and deep concern with the nature of art (a theme which I shall discuss in relation to *The Winter's Tale* and *The Tempest*), art is not presented as an answer as it is implicitly in the early comedies, where we are often aware of a real world in which people fail to achieve the desired happiness, straining against the boundaries of the play world. In *The Tempest* Prospero rejects his art – a comfort and a source of power – in favour of the real world. After the romances, where he had stretched the possibility of theatrical illusion to the limit, Shakespeare intended to write no more; the inadequacies of art are recognized – art itself is at its most self-conscious.

Cymbeline

DATE 1609-10
PRINCIPAL CHARACTERS
Cymbeline: King of Britain
The Queen: His wife

Cloten: The Queen's son by a former marriage
Imogen: Cymbeline's daughter by a former marriage
Posthumus Leonatus: Imogen's husband
Belarius: A banished lord, disguised as 'Morgan'
Guiderius } Lost sons of Cymbeline, supposed sons of
Arviragus } 'Morgan', known as Polydore and Cadwal
Cornelius: A physician
Pisanio: Posthumus' servant
ITALIANS:
Philario: Friend of Posthumus
Iachimo: Friend of Philario
Caius Lucius: General of the Roman forces
SCENE Britain and Italy

Plot

ACT ONE Cymbeline's daughter Imogen has incurred her father's anger by spurning his stepson Cloten as a husband and by marrying instead Posthumus Leonatus, an impoverished nobleman who was brought up at Cymbeline's court. Imogen's brothers, Guiderius and Arviragus, were mysteriously stolen from their nursery some twenty years before, so the disposal of his only daughter in marriage is of particular importance to the King. Everybody at court but Cymbeline, however, approves Imogen's choice, since the malevolence of the Queen and the vicious stupidity of Cloten are notorious. Posthumus is banished from Britain and in his absence the Queen tries to subvert his servant Pisanio. As a token of friendship she gives Pisanio a potion which she assures him has remarkable healing powers but which she herself believes to be a deadly poison. The Doctor who provided her with the potion, however, assures the audience that it induces the symptoms of death without actually killing.

In Italy the exiled Posthumus' belief in his wife's virtue is ridiculed by Iachimo, who lays a wager that, after journeying to Britain and back, he will be able to provide Posthumus with indisputable proofs of his wife's infidelity.

On arrival at Cymbeline's court, Iachimo finds Imogen's chastity unassailable; she responds, however, to the friendship that he claims to feel for Posthumus, and agrees to house a trunk of precious plate in her chamber overnight.

ACT TWO While Imogen is sleeping, Iachimo emerges from the trunk, takes note of the details of her chamber and of her naked person and steals a bracelet from her arm that was Posthumus' parting gift. In Italy, Posthumus is convinced by Iachimo's 'proof'.

ACT THREE establishes the play's political interest as Cymbeline, encouraged by the Queen and by Cloten, tells Caius Lucius, Caesar's Ambassador, that he will no longer pay tribute to Rome. Much of the action now switches to Wales. Pisanio has received a letter from Posthumus, ordering him to murder Imogen for her infidelity; finding himself unable to comply with his master's wishes he gives Imogen a letter purporting to be from Posthumus, which announces his arrival at Milford Haven, and asks Imogen to join him there. Near Milford Haven Cymbeline's lost sons, Guiderius and Arviragus, are introduced. As 'Polydore' and 'Cadwel' they believe themselves to be the sons of 'Morgan', who is apparently a rugged Welsh mountaineer but really Belarius; unjustly banished from Cymbeline's court, Belarius seized the royal children and their nurse (whom he married) as an act of vengeance. When Pisanio and Imogen reach the environs of Milford Haven he tells her of her husband's suspicions and advises her, disguised as a boy, to seek employment and protection as the page of Caius Lucius; the latter is leading a Roman army of attrition against Cymbeline. Unable to make her way to Milford Haven, Imogen is found by 'Cadwal' and 'Polydore', who take an immediate liking to her and, as 'Fidele' adopt her as their brother. Meanwhile Cloten, wearing a suit of Posthumus' clothes which he obtained from Pisanio, has set out to wreak vengeance on both Posthumus and Imogen.

ACT FOUR Arrived in Wales, Cloten meets and quarrels with 'Polydore'. Cloten is killed and decapitated in the ensuing fight. 'Fidele', meanwhile, who has stayed at

'Morgan's' cave while the others go hunting, takes the potion which the Queen gave Pisanio and which he has passed on to her. She is found, assumed dead, and greatly mourned by her adoptive family. Her body and Cloten's are laid side by side and a funeral service is performed. Waking from her death-like sleep, she mistakes Cloten's body for Posthumus' and is found grieving over him by Lucius, who takes her on as his page. 'Polydore' and 'Cadwal' persuade 'Morgan', against his better judgment, to let them test their mettle in the ensuing battle against the Roman forces.

ACT FIVE Posthumus returns to Britain full of remorse at Imogen's murder (which Pisanio claims to have performed); he too decides to join the British forces. In the battle, the Romans capture Cymbeline and seem assured of victory when Belarius, Guiderius and Arviragus, joined by Posthumus, rescue the King and rout the Roman forces. Posthumus, who had been hoping for death rather than glory, gives himself up as a Roman and is taken prisoner. With other Roman prisoners, including Iachimo, he is taken before Cymbeline. With all the *dramatis personae* gathered, the strange events are pieced together. Imogen's name is cleared by Iachimo, and she is reunited with her husband; Cymbeline welcomes his sons and pardons Belarius. News is brought of the Queen's death, but she is scarcely mourned, even by Cymbeline, who now feels free to reunite Britain with Rome.

Critical commentary

Any commentary on *Cymbeline* must include Dr Johnson's famous remarks on the play:

> To remark the folly of the fiction, the absurdity of the conduct, the confusion of the names and manners of different times, and the impossibility of the events in any system of life, were to waste criticism upon unresisting imbecility, upon faults too evident for detection, and too gross for aggravation.

Cymbeline has been variously taken as evidence of incipient senility at this advanced stage of Shakespeare's career, or as heart-warming proof that he was moved at this point to an experimentation more daring than anything he had attempted as a younger man. The change in theatrical style which was inaugurated with the reign of James I is more apparent in *Cymbeline* than in any of the other late plays. When Posthumus is asleep in his prison cell, he is visited by his dead family and by Jupiter, the latter bearing thunderbolts and stone tablets carved with assurances of Posthumus' glorious future; the interlude is superogatory to the plot but in line with contemporary taste for the supernatural and the visually elaborate. The lengthy sojourn on the stage of Cloten's decapitated body (IV.ii) took courage, especially from any actress required to play Imogen: her grief at her 'husband's' death could easily bring even a well-meaning audience close to nervous hysteria. With a rash disregard of probability, Shakespeare has introduced into the worlds of ancient Britain and Rome both the wicked stepmother of folklore and, in Iachimo, the devious Machiavel of Renaissance Italy. Popular romance elements are present in the wronged but vindicated wife, and in the noble children lost to their parents but finally restored to their birthright.

All of Shakespeare's last plays strive towards a harmony achieved through a union of disparate elements, and the technical daring is a reflection of the areas of discord in human experience which are finally resolved in forgiveness. With *Cymbeline*, which is technically less successful than *The Winter's Tale* and *The Tempest*, it is correspondingly less easy to determine what the technical tricksiness is meant to suggest. Some critics have argued that a union of the best of the ancient British and Roman traditions is implied; and Emrys Jones in 'Stuart "Cymbeline"' (available in *Shakespeare's Later Comedies*, Penguin) explores this theme for its Christian significance and, more specifically, for its relevance to the reign of James I.

More accessible to the general reader is the contribution

that *Cymbeline* makes to the 'Nature versus nurture' debate which, in one way or another, exercised Shakespeare in all the romances. What is the source of true nobility – in birth or in breeding (supposing them to be separate, as they are in three of the romances, where children are brought up by foster parents) or in the individual's own inherent characteristics? It is a question that baffles Shakespeare's characters as early as *King Lear* (a tragedy in which the themes of the romances are more than passingly anticipated), where Kent says of Lear's three daughters:

> It is the stars,
> The stars above us, govern our conditions,
> Else one self mate and make could not beget
> Such different issues. . . . (iii) IV.

In *Cymbeline* it is not so much the different offspring of the same parents that is at issue as the different ways in which nobility can be defined and perceived. Guiderius and Arviragus, separated from their parents since birth, brought up to the rugged life of Welsh mountain folk, nonetheless display evidence of their antecedents in ways that render Belarius perpetually amazed:

> Nature prompts them
> In simple and low things to prince it much
> Beyond the trick of others. (III.iii)

When they meet Imogen/Fidele, the mutual attraction is total, its significance requiring no comment. In Cymbeline's children birth will out, but what of Cloten? He is unquestionably 'noble' in the sense that Shakespeare's contemporaries would have recognized, and the burden of his rage against Imogen is that she has spurned him for a less 'noble' suitor. With regard to Cloten, birth is an inadequate way of assessing nobility; that his own conception of nobility is entirely superficial is symbolized by his wearing of Posthumus' clothes. They fit him admirably and prove him, he thinks, to be as much of a man as Imogen's husband; in every part but his head, nature has fitted him for his station in life. The argument, crudely presented in *Cymbeline*, is nonetheless left open-ended; Shakespeare was more interested in its dramatic possibilities than in a solution.

Cymbeline has never lacked detractors, but it can also claim some passionate and eminent admirers. Tennyson had his copy of the play buried with him; Hazlitt wrote lyrically of the character of Imogen. She is firmly in the tradition of Shakespeare's earlier comic heroines, and in her Shakespeare explores again the tension between moral strength and resourcefulness and physical vulnerability. The verse – flexible and, like much of Shakespeare's late verse, artfully close to the rhythms of ordinary speech – achieves at times some spectacular effects. In its context, the most notable set-piece, the funereal – 'Fear no more the heat o' the sun,/ Nor the furious winter's rages' (IV.ii) – magnificently contributes to the play's most effective moment of harmony. Spoken by Guiderius and Arviragus over the dead body of Cloten (who is recognized for the rascal he is by his mourners, even if Imogen subsequently mistakes him for her husband) and over the apparently dead Fidele/Imogen, it acknowledges the equality of all men in death. It is the one moment in *Cymbeline* where Shakespeare achieves the reconcilement between opposites and admittance to all that is human, even the despicable, that reach their full expression in *The Tempest*.

The Winter's Tale

DATE 1611

PRINCIPAL CHARACTERS

Leontes:	King of Sicilia
Hermione:	His wife
Mamillius:	Their son
Perdita:	Their daughter
Camillo } Antigonus }	Lords at Leontes' court

Paulina: Wife to Antigonus
Polixenes: King of Bohemia
Florizel: His son
Archidamus: A lord of Bohemia
Autolycus: A rogue
Shepherd: Foster father of Perdita
Clown: His son
SCENE Sicilia and Bohemia

Plot

ACT ONE Polixenes, King of Bohemia, has for nine months been staying at the court of Leontes, his boyhood friend. The visit, full of nostalgia and lavish hospitality, has been a total success but, as it draws to a close, is poisoned by Leontes' sudden and unfounded conviction that the friendship between his wife Hermione and Polixenes is adulterous. He confides his suspicions to Camillo and orders him to poison his 'rival'. Camillo, convinced of the injustice of the charge, warns Polixenes and, seeing no future for himself now in Sicilia, accompanies the visiting king on his escape to Bohemia.

ACT TWO The flight of Polixenes and Camillo is interpreted by Leontes as proof of their guilt: Camillo, he now feels, must have acted as pander between Hermione and her 'lover'. He has his son Mamillius removed from his mother's presence and Hermione, heavily pregnant with the second child, is sent off to prison, protesting her innocence the while. In prison she is delivered of a daughter. Her friend Paulina takes the baby to Leontes, thinking to soften his heart. Since Leontes thinks that the baby was fathered by Polixenes, however, the sight of her enrages him further and he orders Paulina's husband Antigonus to take the baby 'to some remote and desart place, quite out/Of our dominions' (II.iii), there to abandon her to her fate. The only gleam of hope for Hermione is the return of the messengers whom Leontes despatched to the Delphic oracle for guidance.

ACT THREE Hermione is brought to trial and a sentence of death is a foregone conclusion. Leontes observes the formalities so far, however, as to read the oracular statement. The oracle declares Hermione innocent, but Leontes' course is fixed; he dismisses the oracle's warning that 'the king shall live without an heir, if that which is lost be not found' (III.ii) as having 'no truth' in it. At the moment of his rash disregard of the gods, word is brought of the death of Mamillius, who has been sick and pining since his mother's disgrace. Leontes is immediately repentant and convinced of his wife's innocence, but there is a further crushing blow in store for him. Hermione swoons when she hears the news of her son's death and is taken off to be tended by Paulina: Leontes' hope of wooing his wife afresh is dashed when Paulina returns with news of her death.

Act Three closes in Bohemia where Antigonus, following the instructions given him by Hermione in a dream, has brought the rejected baby, named Perdita by Antigonus at Hermione's request. Perdita is found by a Shepherd who is encouraged to keep her by the gold that he finds with her. Fate is less kind to Antigonus than to the baby: observed by the Shepherd's son, he is torn apart by a bear while the ship in which he sailed is sunk in a storm off the Bohemian coast.

ACT FOUR opens with a chorus spoken by Time, who informs the audience that sixteen years have passed. The autocratic behaviour of Leontes in Act One finds a less devastating parallel now in Polixenes, who has heard that his son Florizel is in love with a shepherdess (the sixteen-year-old Perdita) and is determined to wreck what he considers a highly unsuitable match. With Camillo, now his trusted friend and adviser, he appears in disguise at the sheep-shearing feast over which Perdita is presiding as queen. When he has seen sufficient to confirm the rumours that he has heard about Perdita and Florizel, he reveals himself and showers them with abuse. Camillo sees in the discord between Polixenes and Florizel an opportunity to return to Sicilia, 'for whose sight/I have a woman's longing' (IV.iii): he advises the young couple to journey to Sicilia to ask the deeply penitent Leontes to intercede with Polixenes on their behalf, so that he, Camillo, can inform Polixenes of their flight and accompany the King in pursuit of the young lovers. The Shepherd and the Clown decide to follow them to Sicilia: frightened by the King's rage they hope to avert it from themselves by revealing that Perdita is a changeling.

ACT FIVE returns the action to Sicilia where, since his bereavement, Leontes has been deeply under the influence of Paulina who, against the wishes of the rest of the court, has insisted that Leontes remain unmarried. When they arrive, Florizel and Perdita, who remind Leontes of his own lost children, are given a warm reception. His grief is turned to joy when, on the arrival of the Shepherd and the Clown in pursuit of Polixenes, Perdita's parentage is revealed. The time is now ripe for Paulina's *tour de force*. She tells Leontes that a statue of Hermione that she commissioned is now ready for viewing. When the royal party (the reconciliation of Leontes and Polixenes has been sealed by the betrothal of their children) arrive at Paulina's house, the statue is revealed to be the real, living Hermione, who has been preserved by Paulina until her daughter should be found.

Critical commentary

The Winter's Tale is Shakespeare's final, and in many ways most satisfying treatment of sexual jealousy. Like Claudio in *Much Ado*, Posthumus in *Cymbeline*, and Othello, Leontes' conviction of his wife's infidelity is total, groundless and out of keeping with everything else that he knows about her. Like Othello, the only release he can find for his feelings is to place in the most revoltingly physical context the woman whose spiritual value he has never previously questioned: he compares himself to the stock cuckold of popular comedy – 'That little thinks she [his wife] has been sluic'd in's absence,/And his pond fished by his next neighbour' (I.ii). Unlike Shakespeare's earlier types of jealous husband, however, Leontes' anguish is entirely of his own making. Antigonus feels that the King must have been practised on (II.i), and indeed, Leontes' predecessors in Shakespeare's work are all, in a limited sense, victims; but Camillo's assessment, that the King is 'in rebellion with himself' (I.ii) is closer to the truth. This shift in emphasis gives *The Winter's Tale* a much clearer moral basis: for sixteen long years Leontes lives with the knowledge that he has no-one to blame but himself. Morally, Leontes is more culpable, but humanly a figure of greater pathos: despite the improbabilities of plot we respond to Leontes' suffering as closer to general human experience than Othello's, since most of us have to live with the consequences of our actions rather than die, like Othello, at the moment when guilt has been transformed to repentance and reasserted nobility.

It is often said of the romances that, by the time they were written, Shakespeare had lost his interest in character as such; that he was more concerned to create representatives than individuals. Without denying this a general truth, and while admitting that Leontes is not as individualized a character as a Shylock or Cleopatra, he is nonetheless a finely detailed study of a man in the throes of an obsession. The departure of Polixenes and Camillo, the sickness of Mamillius – both add fuel to the fire of Hermione's 'guilt'; only after her 'death' is he aware that the facts are amenable to a radically different interpretation. Having cast himself in the role of cuckold, his mind is haunted by the sound of sniggering. (II.iii) At her trial, Hermione says, 'My life stands in the level of your dreams' (III.ii): she is trapped by the impossibility of being able to penetrate another person's destructive fantasy.

The study of obsessive jealousy, fine as it is, is nonetheless subordinate to the play's main theme. G. Wilson Knight opened his essay on the play in *The Crown of Life* (Methuen) with a neat summary: '*The Winter's Tale* presents a contrast of sinful maturity and nature-guarded youth in close association with seasonal change.' The loss of innocence, in a wider sense than sexual jealousy, is a major theme. Early in the play, before the friendship between Polixenes and

Leontes has been soured by the latter's suspicions, Polixenes tells Hermione of the friendship they enjoyed as boys:

> we knew not
> The doctrine of ill-doing, no nor dream'd
> That any did . . . (I.ii)

Polixenes' comment prepares the audience for the moment, now imminent, when Leontes will definitively put behind him the innocence of youth. Later in the play Polixenes, who is not guilty in anything like the sense that Leontes is, nonetheless thinks that he can kill a pure love – which is always given a high value in the romances – by brute force. Perdita's reaction is to stand by those eternal verities which are lost in a lifetime of practical and dynastic considerations:

> for once or twice
> I was about to speak and tell him plainly,
> The self-same sun that shines upon his court
> Hides not his visage from our cottage. (IV.iii)

The hope in *The Winter's Tale* lies not in the individual but in the cyclical renewal of life. Each generation suffers a loss of innocence and a blighting of personal hope; but there is always the next generation, and the ideal that the young represent is primarily conveyed in the quality of their love. Florizel and Perdita are, when they are introduced at the spring shearing-feast, surrounded by images of fertility – Perdita, described by Camillo as 'The Queen of curds and cream' (IV.iii), is offering, in flowers and food, the new season's produce – but the purity of their love is everywhere stressed. Despite the social difference between them, Florizel never presumes on *droit de seigneur* over Perdita.

The cyclical nature of human life, which is suggested in the play by the lapse of a generation, is reinforced by the cyclical movement of nature. In the early part of the play, as Leontes systematically destroys all that he values, he is associated with images of poison – life-destroying forces. By the end of Act Three Scene Two, when both his children and, as he thinks, his wife are lost to him, he has nothing before him but a winter of penitence. In the following scene, with the death of Antigonus and the finding of Perdita, winter is banished, not from Leontes' life, but from the play; and the shift is immediately apparent in the old Shepherd's comment to his son on Antigonus' death: 'Thou met'st with things dying, I with things new born.' (III.iii) From that point, images of birth and renewal predominate. Spring invades the play with Autolycus' song, 'When daffodils begin to peer' (IV.ii): one of Shakespeare's more popular comic creations, Autolycus lives by a relatively harmless immorality which is a relief after the deep moral concerns that we have left behind with Leontes. With Perdita and Florizel, as we have established, the intuitive yearnings of spring are not in conflict with their moral impulses: doubly innocent, in both the pastoral and the ethical senses, they bring renewed life to their parents. Leontes finds them as 'Welcome hither/As is the spring to th'earth.' (V.i)

There is nothing in the play, however, to suggest that a wave of the hand can eliminate human suffering. Nothing, not even Perdita's arrival, can fill the loss of Mamillius and Antigonus, nor give back to Leontes and Hermione their sixteen lost years. *The Winter's Tale* is concerned, not just with a loss of innocence, but on an emotional level with a yearning sense of loss. The play opens with Polixenes' lament for his own and Leontes' lost youth; the general movement at the end of Act Four from Bohemia to Sicilia is engineered by Camillo as a means of satisfying his longing to see his native country again. The play does besides recognize the inevitably doomed urge to arrest the perfect moment. Polixenes' nostalgia is not just for the innocence of youth, but for youth's confidence in an unending present:

> Two lads that thought there was no more behind
> But such a day tomorrow as today,
> And to be boy eternal. (I.ii)

There is an awareness of transience in Florizel's response to Perdita's beauty: 'when you speak, sweet,/I'd have you do it ever.' (IV.iii) When Leontes' court is ringing with praises of Perdita's beauty, Paulina feels that Hermione's beauty, celebrated in its time, is being implicitly slighted; she deplores man's capacity to forget:

> As every present time doth boast itself
> Above a better gone, so must thy grave
> Give way to what's seen now. (V.i)

One way of satisfying the longing to immortalize what is immediately perfect is through art – a solution with which Shakespeare was deeply engaged in the *Sonnets*:

> So long as men can breathe or eyes can see
> So long lives this, and this gives life to thee. (18)

Art does, indeed, have its place in the scheme of *The Winter's Tale*, an explicit concern on two occasions. The first is when Polixenes, still in disguise, is talking to Perdita about the flowers she is offering at the sheep-shearing feast. Perdita says she will not grow those flowers which owe their genesis to human ingenuity because art in their case has usurped the function of 'great creating nature' (IV.iii). Polixenes feels that, since art is a function of human nature, it is allowable, but Perdita is adamant. At the end of the play, the skill of the artist who 'sculpted' Hermione is praised for its extraordinary closeness to nature, but as Hermione's 'statue' is revealed to the onlooker, the final inadequacy of any art, however excellent, is apparent in Leontes' reaction:

> Still, methinks,
> There is an air comes from her: what fine chisel
> Could ever yet cut breath? (V.iii)

His joy at Hermione's vitality – 'O! she's warm' – is the play's most moving moment. Art may be the only means man has at hand for crystallizing the moment, but it is still an imperfect substitute for life.

The Tempest

DATE 1611

PRINCIPAL CHARACTERS

THE INHABITANTS OF THE ISLAND

Prospero: The right Duke of Milan

Miranda: His daughter

Caliban: A monstrous savage

Ariel: An airy sprite

THE SEA VOYAGERS

Alonso: King of Naples

Sebastian: His brother

Ferdinand: Alonso's son

Antonio: Prospero's brother and the usurping Duke of Milan

Gonzalo: An honest councillor

Adrian and Francisco: Lords

Trinculo: A jester

Stephano: A butler

SCENE An unnamed island

Plot

ACT ONE opens with a shipwreck in which passengers (whose identities are revealed later) and crew despair of their lives. Only in the following scene does the audience realize that the shipwreck was not real but magically induced by Prospero, who rules the island off which the 'wreck' occurred, and that the lives of all the passengers have been preserved. In a lengthy episode of exposition, Prospero's daughter Miranda, whose fears for the ship's safety are acute, learns the reasons for her father's involvement with the fate of the ship, and learns for the first time of her father's history before they came to the island some twelve years before. One time Duke of Milan, Prospero was overthrown by his ambitious brother Antonio, with the aid of Alonso, King of Naples. Cast off in a boat with his three-year-old daughter, and with supplies provided by the kindly Gonzalo, he miraculously reached the safety of the island.

Now chance has brought his enemies within his waters, and his own magical powers have brought them to the island itself.

There are two other inhabitants of the island, one unknown to Miranda, the other a thorn in the flesh of both father and daughter. The first is Ariel, an airy spirit who assisted Prospero in the recent shipwreck, and who has been Prospero's slave since the former released him from the 'cloven pine' in which 'The foul witch Sycorax', erstwhile mistress of the island, had imprisoned him. Ariel desires his freedom, and has been promised it by Prospero when the affairs occasioned by the shipwreck shall be complete – that same evening. The other inhabitant is Caliban, deformed and savage offspring of the same Sycorax – who has resisted the civilizing influence of Prospero to the extent of trying to ravish Miranda. Caliban too acts as a slave, in a domestic capacity. Prospero's household acquires a further servant in the person of Alonso's son Ferdinand, who thinks himself the sole survivor of the shipwreck. Spirited by Ariel to Prospero's cell, Ferdinand immediately falls in love with Miranda, who returns his feelings; but Prospero, who has planned their match, insists on testing the sincerity of Ferdinand's love (in which he gives him no hope) by pressing him into service.

ACT TWO In another part of the island Alonso, comforted by Gonzalo, is bemoaning the loss of his son Ferdinand. The King's brother, Sebastian, is not sympathetic and reminds Alonso that he had been advised against the occasion of their journey – the marriage of his daughter Claribel to the King of Tunis. Ariel, who is invisible to the other characters, arrives and puts them all to sleep but Sebastian and Antonio. The latter, remembering the way he acquired power himself, urges Sebastian to the murder of Alonso. Ariel wakes the rest of the party before the deed can be accomplished. Elsewhere on the island, Caliban encounters Trinculo and Stephano; he adopts Stephano as his new master and offers to show him the secrets of the island.

ACT THREE Observed by Prospero, Ferdinand and Miranda

declare their love for each other. Caliban, meanwhile, persuades Trinculo and Stephano to murder Prospero; their plot is overheard by Ariel. The latter, whose movements know no restrictions, assists Prospero in another scheme. Alonso, Antonio, Sebastian and Gonzalo have a banquet summoned up before them which dissolves away as they make ready to eat. Ariel then appears as a harpy to inform the 'three men of sin' (III.iii) that the 'powers' have brought them to the island as a punishment for their crime against Prospero and 'his innocent child'. Alonso, who connects the visitation with the loss of his son, is moved to penitence, but not Sebastian and Antonio. When Ariel has gone it becomes clear that Gonzalo was excluded from the vision.

ACT FOUR Judging that Ferdinand has passed the test, Prospero solemnly gives him Miranda, with strict injunctions not to 'break her virgin knot' until due ceremonies have been performed. Caliban brings Stephano and Trinculo to Prospero's cell, where the two Neapolitans are distracted by the magician's finery; they are driven away by spirits 'in shape of dogs and hounds'.

ACT FIVE It is now three hours since the travellers were brought to the island and Prospero is sufficiently moved by their plight as described by Ariel to conclude the day's business. That done he will, as he tells the audience, 'abjure . . . this rough magic' (V.i), break his magic staff and bury his book. His old enemies are brought before him to have the 'subtleties of the isle' explained to them. Prospero and the repentant Alonso seal their reconciliation with the projected marriage of their children. To Antonio, 'most wicked sir', Prospero offers only the chilliest form of forgiveness but Antonio, like Sebastian, is unrepentant. Ariel is given his freedom and, on the following day when they are all to set out for Italy (Prospero to resume his dukedom), the island will be left to Caliban.

Critical commentary
The Tempest occupies a curious position among Shake-

speare's plays. Only *The Comedy of Errors* is shorter, but this, his last play, has a density of allusion and a depth of resonance which seem to challenge its own brevity. Again, only otherwise in *The Comedy of Errors* does Shakespeare observe the classical unities of time and place. *The Tempest* is closely related, as none of the other romances is, to contemporary events, and it certainly owes many of its peculiarities of stage effect to the Jacobean taste for the masque; yet it has been regarded by subsequent generations, as Anne Righter has pointed out in her distinguished introduction to the Penguin edition of the play, not as something essentially of its own times, but as mythic material in its own right: not only have critics tended to treat the play as allegory, using it as a vehicle for elaborate, and often eccentric interpretation, but it has proved a fruitful source of inspiration for creative writers. Perhaps most tantalizing of all is the readiness of even cautious critics to identify Prospero with Shakespeare: no other of his characters can claim the same honour.

In 1609 a ship called *The Sea Adventurer*, one of a number carrying colonists to America, was wrecked off the coast of the Bermudas and given up for lost; a year later the 'lost' colonists appeared in Virginia, with strange tales of how they had survived. Various news pamphlets were produced to satisfy the curiosity of the English public and these are the only likely sources that scholarly research has found for *The Tempest*. Indeed, their story of shipwreck and miraculous survival – recurring motifs of romance – would have had particular interest for Shakespeare at this point in his career. He was clearly just as intrigued, however, by the then burning issue of colonization; and to this issue, transformed into poetic terms, we owe Caliban – surely one of the most extraordinary of all his creations. When Prospero arrived on the island twelve years before the play's action begins, he encountered primitive man in Caliban. At first, Prospero treated the monster kindly, doing his best to civilize him; his thanks was the attempted rape of Miranda. Prospero is quite as bitter about Caliban's intransigence as he is about his own brother's: 'A devil, a born devil, on whose nature/Nurture can never stick.' (IV.i) But Shakespeare does not straightforwardly identify Prospero with right. When Prospero upbraids Caliban with his efforts to teach him to speak: '– I endow'd thy purposes/With words that made them known' (I.ii) – he retorts: 'You taught me language, and my profit on't/Is, I know how to curse.' (I.ii) In its own terms this is unanswerable (for there is a sense in which Caliban's 'educators' have tried to force him into an alien mould), as is his claim to have been deprived of his island birthright by Prospero: part of the justice of the play's ending is the abandonment of the island to Caliban.

Between Prospero and Caliban there is nonetheless no question in the play as to whose is the superior nature, but the theme of nobility – an active one in all the romances – is the source of some irony in Caliban's encounter with Trinculo and Stephano. Caliban, who has never seen any man but Prospero, is easily impressed, but what gives Stephano immediate ascendancy over him is the drink he offers him. Alcohol is a new experience for Caliban: 'That's a brave god, and bears celestial liquor:/I will kneel to him.' (II.ii) The most obvious irony is in the homage that Caliban is prepared to pay such unpromising human specimens, but there are further ironies which work entirely in Caliban's favour. In his response to music, which frightens rather than calms Stephano and Trinculo, he has a clear edge over them – 'Be not afeard; the isle is full of noises,/Sounds, and sweet airs, that give delight and hurt not' (III.ii) – clearer perhaps to Shakespeare's first audiences, who regarded a sensitivity to music as part of man's higher nature, than to us. He gains our respect again when he reprimands his companions for their childish delight in Prospero's rich garments: 'Let it alone, thou fool! It is but trash.' (IV.i) If the play makes the division between civilized man and primitive man clear, then the same cannot be said of the relative superiority of primitive and degenerate man.

The human cargo that Prospero charms to his island is at

best a motley one: Gonzalo has been in the past, and remains, a good man; Ferdinand is all that is required of a young lover; and his father, one of the 'three men of sin' is genuinely repentant, but the stubbornly unregenerate nature of Antonio and Sebastian is one of the puzzles of the play. In the other romances, reparation and forgiveness are marked features of the happy endings. The reconciliation of Prospero and Alonso, which is sealed by their children's marriage, is firmly in line with the expectations of a romance audience, but no hope is offered for Antonio and Sebastian. When the strangers to the island are still wandering around in a dazed state, Ariel tells Prospero that he would take pity on them 'were I human'. Prospero accepts the implied rebuke, which in turn involves accepting that, for all that he deplores them, he is 'One of their kind'. (V.i) This austere recognition of a fundamental human bond is the level on which Prospero is prepared to meet the sinners; it includes a resignation to the unchanging and unchangeable nature of human wickedness. A number of critics have remarked on Shakespeare's use of parallel situations in *The Tempest*: the deposition of Prospero by Antonio and Alonso is repeated in Antonio's and Sebastian's attempt on Alonso's life and, in more burlesque form, in the plot against Prospero by Caliban, Trinculo and Stephano. And so, the play suggests, human beings will conduct themselves until the end of time. *The Tempest* is the only one of Shakespeare's plays unequivocally to present this as something we must learn to live with.

Prospero's jaundiced view of humanity is not shared by his daughter. Like all Shakespeare's romantic heroines, Miranda is innocent and trusting, but her innocence and trust have been distilled to a remarkable purity by her island existence. For her, Ferdinand is 'a thing divine' (I.ii); for him, she is a 'wonder'. All Shakespeare's young lovers see the world with new eyes, but he had never before achieved such an appropriate setting for the early stages of that love. Miranda's joyous amazement extends to the rest of the party when she at last confronts them in the play's final scene: 'How beauteous mankind is! O brave new world/That has such people in't.' (V.i) By now, the audience is well acquainted with the objects of her admiration, which rightly raises a wry laugh in the theatre. Her response is not only genuine, however, but necessary. Prospero tells her, 'Tis new to thee' (V.i): as queen of Naples, she will be hard-pressed to retain her vision, but the world would flounder if it did not in some sort begin again for each generation.

Miranda's is not the only vision in the play which is not shared by the other characters. Hers is a matter of judgment, however, where the other examples are more palpable. The storm that wrecked the ship was real to the participants, yet not real. Ariel is invisible to everybody but Prospero. When the travellers arrive on the island, Gonzalo, but none of his companions, notices the renewed freshness of their garments, but he is excluded from the vision shared by the 'three men of sin'. Clearly Shakespeare is playing, as he had in some of the early comedies, with the nature of theatrical illusion, but nowhere else had he done it with the same complexity as here. The play's entire action has been engineered by Prospero. There are earlier examples of the character as dramatist in Oberon in *A Midsummer Night's Dream*, and the Duke in *Measure for Measure*, but neither of them 'contains' the play's events so fully.

In *The Tempest* Shakespeare observes the unities of time and place. The concentration of time is particularly suggestive in that the three to four hours required by Prospero to complete his scheme, which would strain the audience's credibility in a more naturalistic play, is the time needed to perform the average play. Moreover, the time of day in which the action specifically occurs – from early afternoon to evening – exactly parallels the time when plays were performed in Elizabethan and Jacobean theatres. When Prospero speaks the Epilogue he does not step out of character in his demand for applause, as was the convention, but begs instead to be released from the island so that he can journey home to Naples.

Were these peculiarities intended to suggest an identification, unique in Shakespeare's work, between himself and one of his characters? Prospero is a magician, and art is a form of magic. Moreover, the particular form that Prospero's magic takes has close affinities to theatrical invention: he can 'wreck' ships without destroying them, direct the movement of characters throughout his island, summon up banquets where no food is eaten. Prospero elects to return to Naples and he destroys all the appurtenances of his art before doing so; *The Tempest* is Shakespeare's last play, its completion probably coinciding with his return to Stratford. Further than that one cannot speculate. Nonetheless, in *The Tempest*, both the limitations and dangers of Prospero's magic, and the keenness of his loss in leaving the island, are movingly alluded to. Where Prospero's magic is profoundly limited is in its failure to change the human heart. Mankind is not beauteous, and he has no power to make it so: his failure with Caliban leaves him embittered, and Antonio and Sebastian leave the island as unregenerate as when they arrived. He has the dramatist's power of stylizing malice into gesture – as he does with Caliban's plot against his own life, and Sebastian's and Antonio's against Alonso's – but he has no power over their hate. It requires Ariel to remind him of his humanity before he takes pity on the baffled and unhappy travellers; he finally summons them, recognizing that 'the rarer action' (V.i) is self-control rather than vengeance – in having the power but abjuring its use. At this point, however, it is the power of the ruler rather than of the magician that is more at issue.

There is a further danger, which is more specifically related to the association between magic and dramatic art. He stages a masque to celebrate Ferdinand's and Miranda's engagement; when he dissolves the masque, he draws an analogy between the illusory nature of the masque and the insubstantiality of the real world:

And, like the baseless fabric of this vision,
The cloud-capp'd towers, the gorgeous palaces,
The solemn temples, the great globe itself,
Yea, all which it inherit shall dissolve,
And, like this insubstantial pageant faded,
Leave not a rack behind. We are such stuff
As dreams are made on; and our little life
Is rounded with a sleep . . . (IV.i)

The verse is compelling, but no human being has the right to regard his fellows as the stuff of dreams; and for all their insubstantiality, Prospero knows that he must return to the 'gorgeous palaces' and give Miranda her own experience of what to her will be a brave new world. His loss – for the choice is not an easy one – is crystallized in his relationship with Ariel. Too many critics have attempted, and floundered in the attempt, to analyse Ariel's role for me to try; so 'delicate' a creation must, one feels, have a meaning, though there is no evidence that Shakespeare intended him strictly allegorically. Whatever significance he might be felt to carry, he has inspired an affection in Prospero which the exclusiveness of their relationship has strengthened. In the end, Prospero abandons Ariel in favour of a life lived among his own kind. It is characteristic of *The Tempest*'s persistent mysteriousness that not even Miranda has the measure of what Prospero is sacrificing in leaving the island.

10 Shakespeare and the Critics

Although there was no organized criticism of Shakespeare's work during his lifetime and for fifty years after his death, the main lines along which the debate was going to develop were established by his contemporary, Ben Jonson. In his encomium written after Shakespeare's death, Jonson gave his friend and rival generous praise for both his truth to Nature (an abstraction which was to remain an important criterion for judging his work) and for his Art. Privately, his view was that Shakespeare 'wanted Art', a fault that was implicitly ascribed to his 'small Latin and less Greek', a piece of information for which we are again indebted to Jonson.

Jonson's comments were essentially anecdotal, but the men of letters who took up the cudgels from the latter part of the seventeenth century until the end of the eighteenth century accepted his terms of reference. John Dryden, revered by Dr Johnson as the Father of English Criticism, and hence indirectly as a pioneer of the eighteenth-century neo-classical movement, was lavish in his praise: 'he was the man who of all modern, and perhaps ancient poets, had the largest and most comprehensive soul' (1668, in *Of Dramatic Poesy, an Essay*). But like all who wrote on Shakespeare until the romantic movement adopted him as their god, Dryden's response was, like Jonson's, this side idolatry. Particularly at fault was Shakespeare's language, either 'insipid' or 'swelling into bombast'. In effect, Shakespeare lacked the equipment to make the most of his natural endowments.

As eighteenth-century critical tenets became established, it was accepted that Shakespeare was not entirely to blame for the flaws in his work. For eighteenth-century men of letters, who were enviably confident in their own good taste, the barbarism which had engulfed Europe with the passing of the classical world had only lifted in their own remembered past. Shakespeare was an untutored genius who wrote for crude and undiscriminating audiences, and many of his deficiencies were ascribed to this unfortunate accident of history. Instances abounded in his work where the 'decorums' of the stage were flouted: he introduced humour into high tragedy and had a taste for characters who deviated unnecessarily from the 'types' that they were meant to represent. His language, which must have seemed rugged indeed when judged by the eighteenth century's pure standards of smoothness and elegance, was felt as offensive. Pope, who produced an edition of Shakespeare, felt that 'as he has certainly written better, he has perhaps written worse than any other'. Since Shakespeare had so signally lacked the benefits of the new enlightenment, editors like Pope felt not only justified but obliged to give polish to his work with their own superior readings. Those responsible for staging his plays were just as cavalier. Where he had offended the canons of justice, in, for example, allowing Cordelia to die in *King Lear*, justice was now seen to be done, and in one notorious eighteenth-century version Cordelia was dismissed to happiness and a marriage with Edgar.

Dr Johnson's great edition of 1765 is more in line with our own accepted editorial principles. Where possible, Johnson retained the original reading, whether he felt it reflected well on Shakespeare or not. He defends his subject vigorously for his defiance of stage directions – especially the unities of time and place – and argues that Shakespeare developed a new kind of drama, neither tragic nor comic but in its own way closer to life. He is generous about Shakespeare's characterizations, which he feels meet the critical requirements of the eighteenth century: 'they are the genuine progeny of common humanity, such as the world will always supply, and observation will always find . . . In the writings of other poets a character is too often an individual: in those of Shakespeare it is commonly a species.' Johnson is, however, disturbed by Shakespeare, both on artistic and moral grounds. He found the plots weak, the writing hurried, and Shakespeare's blithe disregard for anachronism ludicrous. More serious for Johnson was Shakespeare's failure to use his plays as vehicles for instruction: 'He sacrifices virtue to convenience, and is so much more careful to please than to instruct, that he seems to write without any moral purpose.'

Johnson was writing in the rearguard of a movement. Romanticism, to whose first stirrings he had been such a sturdy opponent, was the dominant mode, in literature and in criticism, by the beginning of the nineteenth century. For the early romantic critics, Schlegel on the Continent, Coleridge in England, Shakespeare was a prophet, a seer, a philosopher; his works were 'divine', 'sublime', 'ideal' and, under the new dispensation, morally uplifting. Coleridge gave a new twist to the continuing theme of Shakespeare, the natural genius: his works, like Nature and her works (trees are cited as an example) for Coleridge had an 'organic' unity which far transcended the technical unity demanded by the classical critics.

Coleridge's criticism (mostly in lecture form) was enormously influential, and justly so in the sense that an attempt was being made to interpret Shakespeare in his own terms rather than by means of a superimposed structure. Areas of his work which had been disregarded before became the basis for a new appreciation. Keats saw him as a man 'capable of being in uncertainties, mysteries, doubts, without any irritable reaching after fact and reason' (1817). Mysteries were to be shared, not solved, and enthusiasm was the dominant nineteenth-century response. A weakness of nineteenth-century criticism was to see Shakespeare primarily as a poet and only very secondarily as a dramatist: Charles Lamb thought that his tragedies in particular were unactable, and anthologies of 'beauties' from the plays became fashionable.

The romantic movement paid great attention to Shakespeare's characterization. Coleridge and Hazlitt wrote lovingly of a number of characters, especially some of the young heroines, and Coleridge, whose personality was on this occasion so similar to that of his subject, illuminated Hamlet's character in ways that have never quite been superseded. The 'character' approach to Shakespeare reached its peak in the work of A. C. Bradley, particularly his *Shakespearean Tragedy* (1904). As all criticism tends to some extent to reflect the literature contemporary with the critic, so Bradley wrote of Shakespeare's characters in the manner of a Victorian novelist. His method is almost biographical, assuming for Shakespeare's creations pasts and a life off-stage as though they were real people. There has been the inevitable reaction against Bradley's work by critics anxious to establish a more 'literary' frame of reference, but within its own terms Bradley's work is both distinguished and useful; and he did try to make sense of each play as a unit, rather than isolate particular 'beauties'.

Bradley's work is something of a watershed, not just in taste, but in terms of the kind of people who write about Shakespeare. Until Bradley they had been, in the broadest sense, men of letters: creative writers, contributors to intelligent though not scholarly journals, and some of the most penetrating comments on Shakespeare (particularly in the nineteenth century) are to be found in letters and jottings. Bradley was the first academic critic, Professor of English Literature at Liverpool and of Poetry at Oxford, at a time when English was struggling to gain recognition as an academic discipline. Since Bradley, most Shakespearean criticism has been the work of professional academics, with mixed results.

One undoubted advantage of the scholarly approach is the light it has thrown on the context in which Shakespeare worked. Theatrical conditions have been investigated, the Elizabethan theatre reconstructed: the twentieth century, like the eighteenth, sees Shakespeare's starting point as his response to his audience's needs, though without, one trusts, the same condescension towards that audience. Research into the theatre prepared the ground for one of the more creative books on Shakespeare to emerge in recent years, *Shakespeare and the Idea of the Play* by Anne Righter, which establishes a connection between the broader theatrical context and Shakespeare's own views on the nature of theatrical illusion. J. F. Danby, in *Shakespeare's Doctrine of Nature, a Study of 'King Lear'*, relates Shakespeare's work to the thought of his times; a greater awareness of the conventions of Elizabethan literature has been fostered by M. C. Bradbrook. The source material from which Shakespeare worked, long dismissed as unimportant, is now regarded as crucial to an understanding of his creative processes: Kenneth Muir, among others, has done useful research in this field.

The emphasis in twentieth-century criticism has moved away from character study and enthusiasm over individual passages, to interpretation of whole plays and groups of plays. G. Wilson Knight, author of a whole clutch of books on Shakespeare, pioneered this approach, and if he does tend to treat the plays too much like allegory, then his work has nonetheless provided splendid insights. Shakespeare's use of imagery has been extensively investigated by Caroline Spurgeon for biographical data and by Wolfgang Clemen as a way of approaching the meaning of the plays. The ambiguities in his language, which the eighteenth century saw as flaws, have provided writers like Empson in *Seven Types of Ambiguity* (Chatto) with unequalled opportunities for verbal analysis. Specifically twentieth-century preoccupations have made themselves felt in the anthropological approach (C. L. Barber's *Shakespeare's Festive Comedy* is a good example), in the Freudian (Ernest Jones's analysis of Hamlet is notorious) and in the work of a handful of highly idiosyncratic writers who have unashamedly interpreted Shakespeare's work in terms of twentieth-century experience

(Jan Kott's *Shakespeare Our Contemporary* is a stimulating, if deeply irritating book).

Unfortunately, much of the work contributed by academics to scholarly journals (there are three devoted specifically to Shakespeare) reflects the pressure on them to publish, to prove that English literature is as much a research-oriented discipline as the sciences: theories are constructed which quickly become obsolete, requiring further articles to demonstrate their invalidity. Nonetheless, the volume of work produced, good and bad, is an indication of Shakespeare's continuing importance. T. S. Eliot wrote in the *Companion to Shakespeare Studies* (Cambridge University Press 1934): 'Shakespeare criticism will always change as the world changes.' Each generation will, and indeed should, find its own meaning.

11 Elizabethan Tragedy

His waxen wings did mount above his reach,
And melting heavens conspir'd his overthrow . . . *Doctor Faustus*

In the course of the Elizabethan period, English tragedy moved from an inhibiting reliance on classical modes and themes to the establishment of a native idiom and tradition. At the beginning of the period the writing of plays (or at any rate those that have survived) was the recreation of academics whose audiences shared their cultural background. By the 1580s the early public playing companies were an established feature of London life; and while a number of those who wrote for the public theatres were, like Marlowe, University men, they were disciplined by imperatives other than classical authenticity – the most urgent being the need to keep a heterogeneous audience entertained.

Properly speaking, the father of English tragedy was the Roman, Seneca. *Gorboduc* (1561-2), written by the young lawyers Sackville and Norton, was very much a product of the reviving academic interest in classical drama; it nonetheless deserves recognition as the first English tragedy by being the first imitation rather than translation of Seneca. Its authors regarded British history as a respectable enough setting for an English play; its political preoccupations, if somewhat didactically expressed, are a foretaste of the political sophistication of later Elizabethan drama, not least of Shakespeare's history plays; Norton and Sackville's ten syllabled blank verse line, while it was to be immeasurably better employed by subsequent dramatists, was nonetheless an innovation.

Thomas Kyd's *The Spanish Tragedy*, written more than twenty years after *Gorboduc* (by 1589), illustrates the invigorating effect that the public theatres had on the Senecan tradition. Where Seneca (and Norton and Sackville) had confined the action to the narrative, Kyd brought it into full view of the audience, a change which concentrated the audience's attention, and sympathies, on the sufferings of the hero. A by-product of the hero's new status was the extended emotional range of the soliloquy; in exploiting this, Kyd can be truly said to have prepared the ground for Hamlet. If Kyd and Shakespeare in *Titus Andronicus* (this, *Romeo and Juliet* and, at the very end of the period, *Hamlet* were Shakespeare's only Elizabethan tragedies) responded too sympathetically to the public audiences' taste for violence, it must also be allowed that Shakespeare at any rate learned circumspection, and that his use of violence in the Jacobean *King Lear* contributes immeasurably to the play's dramatic impact.

Christopher Marlowe (1564-93) was the finest of the Elizabethan writers of tragedy, and his plays require no apologies or allowances on historical grounds. Indeed, in the sense that his plays are regarded as historically rather than artistically important, it is to the degree that they manage to encapsulate a characteristically Renaissance view of the world. His poetry is magnificent. In his first plays, the two parts of *Tamburlaine the Great*, the poetic effectiveness is achieved at the expense of the dramatic, but by *Doctor Faustus* the two are inseparable. With *Doctor Faustus*, in the agonizing nature of the hero's choice, in the bitter consequences attendant on the choice he makes, and in the quality of his final anguish, English tragedy first realizes its full potential.

Gorboduc, by Thomas Norton and Thomas Sackville

THOMAS NORTON (1532-84) is chiefly remembered now for his collaboration in *Gorboduc*, which was written when he and Sackville were young lawyers at the Inns of Court.

THOMAS SACKVILLE (1536-1608) was essentially a man of affairs – in middle age he pursued a public career as Member of Parliament, ambassador, Lord Treasurer and Chancellor of Oxford University – whose preoccupation with public morality is evident in his literary achievements. Apart from *Gorboduc*, which as we shall see is notable for its treatment of political issues, he contributed the 'Induction' to *A Myrour for Magistrates*, a didactic work which has supplied subsequent ages with the most complete exposition of orthodox Tudor political thinking; its method – of using the past as a 'mirror' through which contemporary events might be interpreted – arguably influenced Shakespeare's approach in his history plays.

DATE 1561-2

CHARACTERS

Gorboduc: King of Britain
Videna: His queen
Ferrex: Their elder son
Porrex: Their younger son
The Dukes of Cornwall, Albany, Loegris and Cumberland
Eubulus: Secretary to the King and a loyal councillor
Hermon and Tyndar: Flattering parasites on Ferrex and Porrex respectively
SCENE Ancient Britain

Plot

(Each act is preceded by a dumb show which is separate from the action and which symbolically suggests the lesson to be derived from the following act.)

ACT ONE Gorboduc, now advanced in years, wants to hand

the responsibilities of power over to his sons Ferrex and Porrex: 'That in my life they may both learn to rule,/And I may joy to see their ruling well.' (I.ii) Two of his councillors agree in outline to his scheme, but a third, Eubulus advises against abdication and division on the grounds that 'Divided reigns do make divided hearts' (I.ii): flouting the rule of primogeniture not only unsettles the state, but could encourage avoidable feelings of rivalry between the King's sons. Gorboduc, however, is confident of the princes' good nature and pursues his decision to give Porrex the northern and Ferrex the southern areas of the kingdom. The only safeguard he thinks necessary is that his sons be assigned a loyal councillor each to check any youthful impetuosity. Before the scheme is put into effect the displeasure of two of Gorboduc's family is revealed (I.i): both Videna the Queen, and Ferrex the elder son and his mother's favourite, see equal rule by both brothers as disinheritance for Ferrex.

ACT TWO The purpose of this act, as the dumb show makes clear, is to illustrate the poisonous nature of flattery. Ferrex, now responsible for his portion of the kingdom, is advised by two councillors: to the horror of Dordan, the councillor appointed by the King, the parasitic Hermon insinuates that, since Porrex's ambition is unlikely to leave him content with half the kingdom, Ferrex should take the military initiative and avenge the injustice done him by his father by attacking Porrex. The prince decides to arm himself in readiness for an attack by Porrex but, in deference to Dordan, not to make the first move himself. The scene is paralleled when Porrex, against the advice of his just councillor, is persuaded by the parasitic Tyndar that, since Ferrex is gathering his military strength, he, Porrex, should attack and kill his brother.

ACT THREE Gorboduc, hearing that both his sons are preparing to fight, determines to take up arms himself to quell their rage. Before this can be attempted, however, he is brought word that Porrex has invaded Ferrex's territory and murdered his brother.

ACT FOUR opens with Videna bemoaning the loss of her

beloved son Ferrex and vowing to avenge his death by murdering Porrex. When Porrex is brought before his father to defend himself, he claims that, in murdering Ferrex, he was forestalling his brother's projected attack on himself. While Gorboduc and his councillors are deciding what form of justice would be appropriate for Porrex, one of Videna's chamber women interrupts them with the news that the Queen has taken justice into her own hands by murdering her son.

ACT FIVE introduces the British Dukes, who are trying to restore some order into the realm since the people, having murdered Gorboduc and Videna in horror at the Queen's act, have given way to general rioting. Milder methods proving ineffective, considerable bloodshed is required to bring the people to heel. Scarcely has this been achieved when the Dukes learn that one of their number, Fergus, Duke of Albany, has gathered an army of twenty thousand in an attempt to establish his claim to the throne. Arostus, a councillor, advises the other dukes not to squabble for the crown:

> Till first by common counsel of you all
> In parliament, the royal diadem
> Be set in certain place of governance. (V.ii)

With the battle against Fergus still pending, the play closes with a lengthily didactic speech from Eubulus, in which the effects of civil war are graphically described – rape, violence, divided families, Britain herself 'wasted and defaced, spoiled and destroyed' (V.ii); and the need for a country to have a 'lawful', 'rightful' and 'certain' heir is enjoined on the audience.

Critical commentary

Few twentieth-century readers of *Gorboduc* (it would be a brave, not to say foolhardy theatrical company who would contemplate launching it on an audience) are likely to find it more than historically interesting. As a historical landmark, however, its importance in the development of the English theatre can scarcely be overstressed. From the middle of the sixteenth century the plays of Seneca (a decisive influence on English tragedy) were being translated and performed, mainly in the universities and before academic audiences. *Gorboduc* was the first English tragedy to adapt Senecan principles to new material. As the Roman plays had been written for recitation rather than performance, so Norton and Sackville adopted the device of using messengers to keep both audience and characters informed. They divided their play along classical lines into five acts with choruses in between; where Seneca had exploited Greek legends, familiar to his Roman audiences, Norton and Sackville chose a British legend, well known to Elizabethan audiences.

The Senecan tradition was to be interpreted with more flexibility by Kyd in *The Spanish Tragedy*, which was intended for public performance. *Gorboduc*, written by young lawyers for the academic Inns of Court, has all the austerity of its classical models. It is in fact *Gorboduc*'s fidelity to its antecedents that accounts for its unapproachability now. Speeches are lengthy, with a stiff rhetorical quality; there is no attempt at naturalistic dialogue. We are told of, rather than allowed to witness, the inter-action between the characters. With the exception of the opening scene between Videna and Ferrex (I.i), and Porrex's confrontation with his father after his brother's murder (IV.ii), the members of Gorboduc's family are not brought together on the stage: Gorboduc disinherits Ferrex, Porrex murders Ferrex, Videna murders Porrex without the principals in these potentially highly charged events ever forming a dramatic relationship. However, since Norton and Sackville called their *dramatic personae* 'speakers' it is unfair to judge their achievement within the framework implied by the term 'character'.

What, one may ask, did Norton and Sackville achieve, beyond the distinction of being first in the field? Stiff as *Gorboduc* now seems to us, the dramatists allowed themselves, in classical terms, a rare degree of freedom. The unities of time and place are neglected by them, to the distaste of a contemporary like Sidney, but to the advantage of English dramatic development. The dumb show, Norton and Sackville's own innovation, is a foretaste of the mixture of styles and modes that English tragedy was able to contain. Perhaps most important of all, the rhymed ten and fourteen syllabled lines into which Seneca's tragedies were being translated were abandoned by Norton and Sackville for decasyllabic blank verse, which was to remain for three centuries the medium for English tragedy. If their own blank verse is a somewhat unyielding vehicle, it had a liberating effect on those who followed them.

The movement of *Gorboduc* establishes a pattern which was to be central to English tragedy – that of the unforeseen consequences attending an ill-judged action, which the Chorus's heavily didactic comments at the end of Act Four hammer home to the audience: 'But woe to him that, fearing not to offend,/Doth serve his lust, and will not see the end.' (IV.ii)

Norton and Sackville used their stage like a pulpit. Leaving nothing to chance, they draw the obvious political and moral lessons from the tale at every available point, so that the dumb show, the Chorus and the councillors serve as commentators on an action which we never see. However, if the manner of *Gorboduc* differs from that of its more illustrious successors, some of the latter were to share Norton and Sackville's concerns. The poisonous effects of flattery and a country's need for certainty of succession were points clearly aimed at Queen Elizabeth, who saw the play in the new year of 1562; Shakespeare's methods were immeasurably more sophisticated and his dramatic intentions more comprehensive, but he too was to use historical events as a 'mirror' for the present.

The Spanish Tragedy, by Thomas Kyd

THOMAS KYD (1558-1594) was one of that first generation of dramatists who, lacking the benefits of a university education, helped to achieve that fusion of classical and popular elements which was one of the features of English Renaissance drama. Born in London the son of a scrivener, he was educated at Merchant Taylor's School, after which he may for a time have followed his father's trade. He was possibly associated with Lord Strange's Company, but *The Spanish Tragedy*, which has gained him a distinguished place in theatrical history, was performed by all the playing companies of his day. This, together with the number of references to the play in contemporary documents, provides clear evidence of its undiminished popularity throughout the Elizabethan and Jacobean periods. *The Spanish Tragedy* was the first English revenge play; as such, it influenced, not only *Hamlet*, but the great body of Jacobean tragedy. Indeed, it is now felt that Kyd may have written an earlier version of *Hamlet* from which Shakespeare worked, which is known to scholars as the *ur-Hamlet*. Apart from *The Spanish Tragedy*, the only play certainly by Kyd is the more strictly Senecan *Cornelia* (1594); otherwise, he is now felt to have had at least a hand in *Arden of Faversham*, an early example of English domestic tragedy.

Towards the end of his life, Kyd was sharing lodgings with Marlowe, who was notorious for his atheism and for his underground activities; and Kyd may well have owed to his choice of companion the fact that, in 1593, he was arrested and tortured on suspicion of treasonable activity. He was probably in debt when he died in 1594.

DATE about 1589, first printed in 1592

CHARACTERS

A Chorus is provided by the Ghost of Andrea, a Spanish nobleman, and by Revenge

THE SPANISH:
King of Spain
Duke of Castile: His brother
Lorenzo: The Duke's son
Bellimperia: Lorenzo's sister
Hieronimo: Marshal of Spain
Horatio: His son
Isabella: Hieronymo's wife
Pedringano: Bellimperia's servant
THE PORTUGUESE:
Viceroy of Portugal
Balthazar: His son
Serberine: Balthazar's servant
Alexandro ⎱ Portuguese
Viluppo ⎰ Noblemen
SCENE Spain and Portugal

Plot

The background of the play is a recent battle between the Spanish and the Portuguese, fought by the Spanish to establish their authority over the Portuguese vice-regency.

ACT ONE opens with the Ghost of the Spanish Andrea telling of his death in battle at the hands of the Portuguese Balthazar, of his burial by his friend Horatio and of his loss through death of his mistress Bellimperia – a lady who was placed by her royal birth above Andrea's station. Andrea has been allowed by Proserpina, Queen of the Underworld, to witness, with Revenge, the vengeance that Bellimperia will take on Balthazar for her lover's death. Throughout the play, Andrea and Revenge serve a choric function as, at the close of each act, they comment on its happenings.

The action proper begins when the King of Spain learns of the defeat of the Portuguese army and of the valiant contribution made to that defeat by Horatio, the son of his Marshal, Hieronimo. Horatio took Balthazar, the Portuguese Prince, prisoner – an honour that the King's nephew Lorenzo is claiming for himself. The King patches up a peace between the rivals and arranges for Lorenzo, with Horatio's help, to entertain Balthazar during his stay at the Spanish court. Lorenzo's sister, Bellimperia, now finds that she loves Horatio – a new love which, she feels, would not offend her dead lover, Andrea. Her situation is complicated, however, when Balthazar, on whom she has sworn vengeance, falls in love with her and Lorenzo exerts what influence he has over his sister to forward the match.

The Viceroy of Portugal, meanwhile, believes his son Balthazar to be dead; on the deliberate misinformation of one nobleman, Viluppo, he has apprehended another nobleman, Alexandro, for Balthazar's murder.

ACT TWO While Bellimperia and Horatio are making their love known to each other, Balthazar and Lorenzo are disconcerted by the lady's lack of response to their suit. Under pressure, Bellimperia's servant Pedringano tells her brother of her love for Horatio, and takes Balthazar and Lorenzo to a meeting of the lovers in Hieronimo's garden. After killing Horatio, the princes drag Bellimperia off to a place of concealment where, it is hoped, she will be effectively silenced. Roused from his bed by the screams of his son, Hieronimo finds Horatio dead and vows vengeance. Meanwhile, the life of court and state moves on as the King of Spain proposes to the Portuguese Ambassador that they seal the peace between their two countries with the marriage of Balthazar and Bellimperia.

ACT THREE The Portuguese Ambassador returns to the Viceroy with news of Balthazar's safety in time to prevent the execution of the innocent Alexandro. Instead, Viluppo is led off to 'the bitterest torments and extremes/That may be yet invented for thine end'. (III.i) In Spain, Hieronimo receives a letter from Bellimperia disclosing the identity of his son's murderers, but he feels that the letter may be a trick. At the same time, Lorenzo is taking steps to prevent the discovery of his own part in the murder by eliminating the accomplices: he hires Pedringano to assassinate Balthazar's page, Serberine (who was also present in Hieronimo's garden) and then arranges that the Watch arrives on the scene of the crime. Pedringano is seized by the Watch and, because he has been assured of a pardon by Lorenzo, behaves flippantly at his trial, which is conducted by Hieronimo. Deprived of justice in his own case, Hieronimo is concerned to see it administered in his official capacity: Pedringano is hanged, but not before the Hangman has given Hieronimo a letter from Pedringano, intended for Lorenzo, which alludes to their mutual involvement in Horatio's death. The injured father now has the proof he needs, but the difficulties of obtaining justice, given the high rank of the perpetrators of the crime, and the breakdown under grief of his wife Isabella, begin to craze his wits and he behaves in a lunatic fashion before the King and the Portuguese Ambassador.

Bellimperia has been released by her brother – her absence from court was causing comment – and she appears to have come to terms with Lorenzo and Balthazar. The betrothal of Bellimperia and Balthazar is solemnized in the presence of the King and of the Portuguese Viceroy, after which Lorenzo, at his father's entreaty, is publicly reconciled to Hieronimo: the rumour at court is that Lorenzo has been keeping Hieronimo from the King's presence, but both now deny that there has been enmity between them.

ACT FOUR Bellimperia and Hieronimo vow together to avenge Horatio's death – an imperative which the subsequent grief-stricken suicide of Isabella makes the more urgent. At the entreaty of Balthazar and Lorenzo, Hieronimo agrees to prepare an entertainment for the Portuguese Viceroy; he settles on a tragedy, in which parts are assigned to Balthazar, Lorenzo, Bellimperia and himself. In the course of the play Hieronimo stabs Lorenzo, Bellimperia, Balthazar and then herself. After explaining the reasons for the multiple deaths, Hieronimo bites out his tongue – to prevent himself disclosing further information under torture – and then stabs the Duke of Castile and himself.

The play closes with Andrea's Ghost hurrying back to the underworld to welcome his friends, whom he feels to be assured of a place in the Elysian fields. The villains are about to 'begin their endless tragedy'. (IV.v)

Critical commentary

With *The Spanish Tragedy*, the Senecan tradition found a form that was more congenial to native English taste than the more classically correct *Gorboduc* had been. Formed as it was by the conditions in the public theatres, Kyd's technique owed as much to the attention-grabbing tactics of the strolling players who performed in inn-yards (the direct ancestors of the public playing companies) as it did to Seneca. From classical tragedy, Kyd learned the benefits of concentrating attention on the hero and of confining the action to a single theme. At the same time, the audiences' needs were met in the variety of scene and character, in the occasional knockabout humour and in the shift of events from long narrative speeches to the stage. Public audiences were not content to hear about murder, passion, self-mutilation, gibbets and hangmen – they wanted to see them. In the eighteenth century it was fashionable to see Elizabethan audiences as tyrannous and barbaric in their demands; perhaps because we fancy ourselves as more robust, we tend to see that barbarism as a catalyst for a new vitality.

The Spanish Tragedy is a long play (almost twice as long as *Gorboduc*) with an extensive *dramatis personae*, rapid shifts in interest (Act Three has fifteen scenes) and, in the near execution of Alexandro by the Portuguese Viceroy, an attempt at a sub-plot, but it nonetheless achieves a concentrated effect. Technically it is a revenge play, but in a broader sense it is about justice and about the near impossibility of achieving justice through organized channels. Indeed, part of Andrea's function in the play is to express distaste and impatience as his own death goes unavenged, as the murder of Horatio secures no redress and as Lorenzo and Balthazar move from strength to strength at court. Hieronimo is a professional purveyor of justice who takes

his responsibilities seriously, as we see at the trial of Pedringano – 'For blood with blood shall, while I sit as judge,/
Be satisfied, and the law discharg'd' (III.vi) – but his very
conscientiousness sharpens the agony of forced inactivity
that he suffers over his son's murder. Learning the identity
of the murderers hardly improves his position: a mere
official at court, his path is blocked by the King's predis-
position towards his nephew and his new political ally.

The apparently pointless sub-plot serves the function of
reinforcing the justice theme: when the Viceroy thinks that
his son has been murdered, the means of justice are readily
to hand for one in his position; while the near execution of
Alexandro for a crime that was never even committed
suggests a corruption at the heart of the judicial process
which Alexandro is quick to point out to his accusers: 'As
for the earth, it is too much infect/To yield me hope of any
of her mould.' (III.i)

Since art provides a justice to which life is often indifferent, however, right does in the end prevail: Alexandro is
saved by the timely arrival of the Ambassador, Balthazar
and Lorenzo are murdered and Andrea closes the play with
confident predictions of the fair play that prevails in the
next world, but the picture of corrupt court life presented
by the play remains. What places the life at court – with its
intrigues, alliances, ambitions and clandestine love affairs –
is not the poetic justice which is unachievable in the real
world but the presence throughout the play of Andrea and
Revenge. From the first scene, before Horatio and Bellimperia fall in love, before the marriage of Bellimperia and
Balthazar is contemplated, we know that Balthazar will be
killed: Andrea has been removed from the underworld,
after all, to allow him to witness this gratifying event.
Throughout the play, therefore, frenzied human activity is
implicitly defined as insignificant and futile by the background of eternity.

In both his picture of court life and his vision of court
machinations through the perspective of the grave, Kyd
anticipates the work of the Jacobean writers of tragedy.

Where his contemporary Marlowe depicts man thrusting forwards, testing the limits of his power, Kyd's characters are trapped in an enclosed society where traditional values are distorted and the murky paths of evil deliberately chosen. Hieronimo's appalled generalization from Pedringano's crime is that:

–the soul, that should be shrin'd in heaven,
Solely delights in interdicted things,
Still wandering in the thorny passages,
That intercepts itself of happiness. (III.vi)

The sick humour of Pedringano's trial – in itself a comment on human affairs – is another link between Kyd's and Jacobean tragedy. Partly, the humour is a concession to the public audiences, who liked their gravity seasoned with laughter, but it has a chilling quality. Before the trial, a messenger is sent by Lorenzo to tell Pedringano that his pardon is in a box which the messenger knows to be empty: 'I cannot choose but smile to think how the villain will flout the gallows, scorn the audience, and descant on the hangman, and all presuming of his pardon from hence.' (III.v) The joke is at the expense of the small villain who has failed to grasp the extent to which bigger villains can rig the world against him.

The chief criticism that has been made against Kyd is that his considerable dramatic skill was applied to inferior melodramatic ends. There is only one incident in the play, however, which fully justifies the criticism – Hieronimo's act of aggression on his own tongue. He claims it to be a precautionary meausre, to prevent him revealing the identity of his confederates under torture, but since his only accomplice, Bellimperia, is dead, we can only account for the arbitrary act of violence as a final cheap thrill on which the audience can be sent home happy. Otherwise, Kyd is reasonably circumspect. Hieronimo's madness, clearly a popular feature with the play's first audiences, is nonetheless fully comprehensible in human terms. The circumstances of Horatio's death; the apparent lack of motive and therefore difficulty in tracing the culprits; when their identity is disclosed, the difficulties posed by their position at court; the breakdown and then suicide of Isabella – all lend plausibility to Hieronimo's rantings. His madness, in fact, emanates from a kind of suppressed activity, which his circumstances render entirely credible and which is dramatically effective when interspersed with scenes of smooth and diplomatic court activity.

Christopher Marlowe

Christopher Marlowe was born in Canterbury in 1564, the year of Shakespeare's birth. The son of a shoemaker, he was educated at King's School, Canterbury and at Corpus Christi College, Cambridge, where he took his BA in 1583. His life, the subject of almost as much speculation as Shakespeare's, includes most of the adventuring alternatives open to that first generation of university men to turn their backs on the traditional careers of the Church, schoolmastering and the law; for the ignorant and timid among his contemporaries, his manner of dying provided an object lesson in the hazards and excesses to which such a life might tend.

He served his literary apprenticeship translating Lucan and Ovid – poetic exercises which at the same time indicate the importance of his classical background in his subsequent work as a dramatist. Now widely considered second only to Shakespeare as a writer of tragedy, at the time of his death in 1593 his own dramatic career looked much the more promising: in the six years from 1587 he had produced seven tragedies (*Tamburlaine the Great*, Parts One and Two; *The Jew of Malta*, *Edward II*, *Doctor Faustus*, *The Massacre of Paris* and *Dido, Queen of Cathage*), an achievement which *Titus Andronicus*, Shakespeare's only attempt at tragedy by that date, hardly matched. Apart from the intrinsic merits of the plays themselves, Marlowe's mastery of the ten syllabled blank verse line, which had proved a clumsy and unresponsive tool in *Gorboduc*, was of crucial importance in the development of English poetic drama. He was unrivalled as a narrative poet, and one of the subsidiary tragedies of his death was that the superb *Hero and Leander* was left unfinished.

Most of the stories attaching to Marlowe, however, are concerned with his extra-literary activities. He may well have served as a soldier in the Low Countries, and was almost certainly one of Walsingham's secret service agents. In 1589 he was arrested on suspicion of complicity in murder but was released after a fortnight. Within weeks of his death in 1593 he was 'apprehended' by order of the Privy Council on allegations of atheism and treason. Indeed, the Marlowe of legend was involved in every known subversive activity of his age – from pederasty to membership of Sir Walter Raleigh's 'School of Night', which was dedicated to the advancement of atheism, science and tobacco. What gives credence to this highly-coloured picture are Marlowe's own plays, which more than anything else in Elizabethan literature celebrate the questing, restless spirit of Renaissance man, impatient with the restrictions of the old orthodoxy.

In 1593, Marlowe died an agonizing death from a dagger wound just above his eye, after a brawl in a tavern in Deptford. Some said that his death ended an argument about who should pay the reckoning for supper; others that English or Spanish government agents had been responsible. At all events, his detractors regarded it as a fitting end to a brief life devoted to undermining traditional social values.

Tamburlaine the Great, Part One

DATE 1587-8

CHARACTERS

Tamburlaine: A Scythian shepherd

Zenocrate: Daughter of the Soldan of Egypt and Tamburlaine's mistress

Mycetes: King of Persia

Cosroe: His brother

Theridamas: A Persian lord who defects to Tamburlaine

Techelles ⎫ Tamburlaine's
Usumcasane ⎭ followers

Bajazeth: Emperor of the Turks

Zabina: His wife

Kings of Fez, Morocco and Argier: Tributary kings of Bajazeth

King of Arabia: Betrothed of Zenocrate

Soldan of Egypt

SCENE ranges through Africa and the East

Plot

ACT ONE The Persian nobility are disturbed both by the ineptitude of their King, Mycetes, and by the growing military and popular strength of Tamburlaine, a Scythian shepherd. Tamburlaine, it is hoped, will meet his match in the one-thousand-strong cavalry that Mycetes despatches under the leadership of Theridamas; the Persian lords, meanwhile, inform the King's brother, Cosroe, that they will make him king in Mycetes' place.

One of the effects of Tamburlaine's nomadic tyranny is that the roads are no longer safe for travellers; one such is Zenocrate, an Egyptian princess whose treasure and person are seized by Tamburlaine. He wins another notable prize with the defection of the Persian Theridamas, who acknowledges the shepherd's superiority even before battle lines are drawn.

ACT TWO Cosroe is not displeased by the capitulation of Theridamas' army; his plan is that he should allow Tamburlaine to defeat Mycetes, who is himself leading further forces against the Scythian, and then, with the offer of a regency in Persia, make Tamburlaine, who would be an undoubted asset to any king that he agreed to serve, his man. In the event, Tamburlaine defeats Mycetes and breaks his agreement with Cosroe, the new king of Persia, whom he mortally wounds in battle; he then seizes the Persian crown for himself.

ACT THREE shows Tamburlaine extending his power west. Bajazeth, emperor of the Turks is, with his tributary kings of Fez, Morocco and Argiers, laying seige to Constantinople. A man of absolute power, Bajazeth feels that a commanding word from him will be sufficient to silence the threatening noises that are reaching him from Tamburlaine. When they meet, however, he is humbled in battle by the man he despised. Tamburlaine refuses to accept ransom for his prisoner's release, intending instead further humiliations on Bajazeth and his wife Zabina.

Zenocrate, meanwhile, is not only reconciled to her rape by Tamburlaine, but, now in love with him, is anxious that he will not cast her off as his success grows; Tamburlaine assures her of his continuing love.

ACT FOUR switches to Damascus, the place of Zenocrate's birth and the current object of Tamburlaine's insatiable ambition. While Zenocrate's father, the Soldan of Egypt, and her former betrothed, the King of Arabia, are preparing to march on him, Tamburlaine is displaying his colours outside the walls of Damascus. The white flags of the first day, inviting the Governor to surrender peaceably, are replaced on the second day with scarlet, symbolizing his bloody intentions: he is deaf to Zenocrate's pleas for clemency towards her native city. Tamburlaine's ruthlessness is further displayed in his treatment of Bajazeth, whom he has carried around with him in a cage, only releasing the erstwhile Emperor to serve as a footstool when he requires one; Zabina the Empress now acts as maid to Zenocrate's maid. In their presence, Tamburlaine rewards his loyal followers with the crowns of Fez, Morocco and Argiers.

ACT FIVE Tamburlaine's flags and garments are now black, indicating his intention to annihilate Damascus. Too late the Governor sends virgins to sue for peace: the young girls are slaughtered, their bodies displayed outside the city walls. Further horrors are to come. Bajazeth and Zabina, left alone while Tamburlaine joins battle against the Soldan of Egypt and the King of Arabia, brain themselves against the side of the cage – the only suicidal tool to hand. The wounded King of Arabia staggers on to the stage to die. Appalled by the dead Turks, and by her own earlier indifference to their sufferings, Zenocrate at last convinces Tamburlaine that he has gone far enough. He welcomes the Soldan of Egypt as a father, has Zenocrate crowned Queen of his now extensive territories and makes it known that he intends to marry her with all haste and pomp.

Critical commentary

Tamburlaine is the first of Marlowe's supermen – who together form a race apart and who have never been successfully imitated. Like Marlowe's other heroes, Tamburlaine is not a 'character' in the sense that Shakespeare created characters – individuals who create an illusion of being three-dimensional and who bear some resemblance to people one might expect to meet – but he is nonetheless full of vitality. Most immediately apparent is the scale on which Marlowe has conceived him – partly a question of physique, but in all the descriptions of him his size is inseparable from his ambition: 'Of stature tall, and straightly fashioned/Like his desire, lift upwards and divine.' (II.i)

Marlowe's Tamburlaine is based on a historical figure, a tribal chieftain whose military achievements had become legendary; Marlowe has demoted his hero in terms of rank, the better to suggest the almost limitless heights to which the unaided human spirit might aspire. He proudly presents himself, in his wooing of Zenocrate, as a self-made man: 'I am a lord, for so my deeds shall prove;/And yet a shepherd by my parentage.' (I.ii) Like the Jew of Malta and Doctor Faustus, he is besotted with the idea of power, though the obsession takes a different form in each. Tamburlaine's ambitions are largely territorial – 'Is it not passing brave to be a king,/And ride in triumph through Persepolis?' (II.v) – although there is a sense in which he sees his martial exploits as an aspect or symbol of the more comprehensive human urge to conquer the universe. He describes the human soul to Cosroe as: 'Still climbing after knowledge infinite,/And always moving as the restless spheres.' (II.vii) By the end of the first part of *Tamburlaine*, when the hero has knocked down the powerful leaders of his immediate world like skittles, he sees himself as partaking of traditionally divine powers: 'The god of war resigns his room to me,/Meaning to make me general of the world.' (V.i) The point about Tamburlaine (in a different way, this is true of Faustus too) is that for him the distinction between human and divine is an artificial one: only for lesser mortals does the distinction hold, and they can be taught to accept Tamburlaine as a god when brought to heel by his arbitrary, indeed god-like, disposal of life.

For the other characters in the play, Tamburlaine is either a god or a fiend; the critical debate since has been on whether Marlowe's heroes are monsters or men. Certainly Tamburlaine lacks any moral sense. This is paradoxically most apparent at the only point in the play where he seems prepared to accept an external moral standard – when, after the siege of Damascus, he is sufficiently moved by Zenocrate's tears to call the bloodshed to a halt. It is not his beloved's moral objections that move him, however, but her beauty, 'With whose instinct the soul of man is touch'd'. (V.i) He has a highly developed aesthetic sense – in twentieth-century terms, a great sense of style as, outside Damascus, his white garments are replaced by red and then black – but no moral one.

What is not clear in the first part of *Tamburlaine* (which was written as a self-contained unit and provided with a sequel only by popular demand) is how far Marlowe endorses the monstrosity of his hero. In an influential study on the dramatist, *Christopher Marlowe: the Over-reacher*, Harry Levin argues that the epithet is just as applicable to his heroes, who are over-reachers to a man. The falls to which their pride drives them can be taken, either as an implicit criticism of the nature of that pride, or as a sad comment on the final limits to human aspiration. At the end of the first part of *Tamburlaine*, when the hero's advances have received no check, either from outside or from his own compunction, neither alternative is open and Marlowe has provided us with no clue as to how we are to 'take' his remarkable hero – unless, as T. S. Eliot did, we choose to see, in the very excess of language and action, an ironic intention on Marlowe's part.

Hyperbole is Marlowe's characteristic mode – or, in Harry Levin's terms, 'over-reaching' is as much an aspect of his style as it is of his personality and of his heroes. The description of Tamburlaine that I have already quoted (II.i) is typical of the exaggerated claims that Marlowe makes for his hero. But is he being ironic? When he woos Zenocrate, Tamburlaine's use of invidiuous comparison to establish his beloved as a phoenix –

> Zenocrate, lovelier than the love of Jove,
> Brighter than is the silver of Rhodope,
> Fairer than whitest snow on Scythian hills (I.ii)

– is undercut by none of the gentle mockery with which Shakespeare views the lover's assurance in his beloved's uniqueness. Everything is larger than life. The mightiness of Bajazeth, as seen through the eyes of the King of Morocco, verges on the absurd:

> The spring is hinder'd by your smoth'ring host;
> For neither rain can fall upon the earth,
> Nor sun reflex his virtuous beams thereon,
> The ground is mantled with such multitudes. (III.i)

But within the terms of the play, the absurdity is not that any follower should attribute such qualities to a leader, but that Bajazeth fails to recognize his superior in Tamburlaine; and Bajazeth's fall, given his hitherto unchallenged supremacy, is only partly an ironic sequel to his pride and more particularly a measure of Tamburlaine's growing greatness.

The argument that Marlowe's use of exaggeration must reflect an ironic and judging view of his hero is based on two assumptions. The first is that hyperbole is more often the tool of a satirist like Jonson than of a writer of tragedy. The second is by critics who tend to feel that any writer they admire must be one of themselves: they hope that Marlowe would be as embarrassed as they are by the prospect of taking Tamburlaine seriously. That still leaves open the question of how seriously Marlowe took Tamburlaine in this the play's first part. I think that Marlowe here, like his hero, is indulging his own youthful thirst for power and love of beauty. He is enjoying rather than commenting on the upward thrust of his hero; and the beauty of the poetry, which displays the intoxicated love of the youthful poet for language and musically effective proper names, gives Tamburlaine's pageant-like progress a dignity that has nothing to do with its moral value.

Tamburlaine the Great, Part Two

DATE 1587-8

CHARACTERS

Tamburlaine: King of Persia

Zenocrate: His wife

Calyphas ⎱
Amyras ⎬ Their sons
Celebinus ⎰

Theridamas, Techelles and Usumcasane: Tributary kings and loyal followers of Tamburlaine

Orcanes: King of Natolia

Callapine: Son of Bajazeth, the late Emperor of Turkey.

Kings of Trebizon, Soria, Jerusalem and Amasia – Turkish satellites

Sigismund: King of Hungary

Governor of Babylon

Captain of Balsera and his wife, Olympia

SCENE The Turkish and Persian empires

Plot

ACT ONE Orcanes, with other viceroys of the Turkish Empire, ratifies a peace with the Christian kings of Hungary, Buda and Bohemia: although stronger than their Christian opponents, the Islamic kings intend keeping their forces intact for an encounter with Tamburlaine's army.

The titular head of the Turkish Empire is Callapine, whose parents were humiliated by Tamburlaine and who is himself Tamburlaine's prisoner. He effects an escape, however, by bribing his gaoler with promises of wealth and power; the two make their escape from Persia to Turkey on a waiting Turkish galley.

On the plains of Larissa, Tamburlaine and his tributary kings are massing forces against the Turks, contrary to the wishes of Zenocrate, who would like to see her husband abandon his martial pursuits. In the encounter against the Turks, Tamburlaine's three sons are to be initiated as soldiers; Amyras and Celebinus share their father's tastes but Calyphas, to Tamburlaine's disgust, would rather stay with Zenocrate – a preference which his father overrides.

ACT TWO On the persuasion of his Christian colleagues, Sigismund of Hungary decides to break faith with the Turks. The Christians hope to defeat the Turks by taking them unaware but in the event, the Christian forces are defeated and Sigismund accepts his death as punishment for his perjury.

Before his own war against the Turks, the one softening influence on Tamburlaine's life is removed with the death of Zenocrate. He has her enbalmed, intending to carry her about with him until he dies himself.

ACT THREE Tamburlaine and his sons leave the town of Zenocrate's death a charred ruin – a gesture of rage or, as Tamburlaine sees it, of extended mourning. Techelles and Theridamas, Tamburlaine's captain kings, arrive at Balsera, a Turkish stronghold which houses considerable wealth. They kill the captain of Balsera and carry off his beautiful wife Olympia, whom they discover on the point of suicide. On the eve of the decisive battle of Natolia, Tamburlaine and his followers meet Callapine who has now rejoined his tributary kings; each side threatens the other with the humiliations that will follow defeat.

ACT FOUR While Amyras and Celebinus join their father in the battle of Natolia, Calyphas stays behind in his tent playing cards. Tamburlaine's pleasure in the valour of two of his sons – they return to camp leading captive kings before them – is darkened by the cowardice of Calyphas. Deaf to the pleas for clemency towards Calyphas made by his 'loyal' sons and by his friends, Tamburlaine stabs his 'traitor' son and has his body given to Turkish concubines to bury. The same concubines, brought by the Turks to serve the lust of their kings, are given by Tamburlaine to his common soldiers. The kings are further humiliated by being made to serve as horses for Tamburlaine's triumphal chariot: the kings of Trebizon and Soria share this duty, turn and turn about with the kings of Natolia and Jerusalem. Theridamas, meanwhile, who has been assiduously wooing Olympia with offers of riches and luxury, is tricked by Olympia into killing her.

ACT FIVE After Tamburlaine's successful siege of Babylon, the Governor is hung up in chains; orders are given that every man, woman and child be drowned; and the kings of Trebizon and Soria, having served their turn as horses, are taken off for execution. Tamburlaine completes his day's work by burning the books of Mahomet who, Tamburlaine feels, is unworthy of respect because he has allowed the destruction and humiliation of his followers. Almost immediately, Tamburlaine feels himself 'distemper'd suddenly'. He rouses himself from his sick bed to fight one last victorious battle against Callapine, and then prepares for death: he reminds his sons of what there is left of the world for them to conquer, has Amyras crowned and, when he has been placed beside the dead Zenocrate, dies.

Critical commentary

Throughout the second part of *Tamburlaine the Great* the hero's view of his own power and interpretation of his function recognize even fewer bounds than in the first part:

Over my zenith hang a blazing star,
That may endure til heaven be dissolv'd,
Fed with the fresh supply of earthly dregs,
Threatening a dearth and famine to this land. (III.ii)

Increasingly, he sees himself as a divine agent, 'The wrathful messenger of mighty Jove'. (V.i) Not only the narrative accounts of Tamburlaine's deeds – the destruction of the town where Zenocrate dies, the drowning of the inhabitants of Babylon – but the stage business too gives substance to the poetic hyperbole. The defeat of Babylon is distinguished by a particularly chilling stage direction: 'Attendants bridle Orcanes, King of Natolia, and the King of Jerusalem, and harness them to the chariot. The Governor of Babylon appears hanging in chains on the walls.' (V.i) Tamburlaine is a man who pre-eminently fits the action to the word: the different coloured flags and garments are not symbols but statements of intent. Indeed, it is not his abusive hate and desire to humiliate that set him apart from other men but his rare power to act on his emotions.

Nonetheless, where the first part of *Tamburlaine* depicts a pageant-like progress from strength to strength, the tragic elements are reserved for the sequel; and from the death of Zenocrate until the close of the play, Tamburlaine's exaggerated view of his powers is undercut by irony. Before his wife's death, the hyperbole had been, not a manner of speech, but a simple statement of fact; her loss – or rather Tamburlaine's powerlessness to stop her dying – transforms it into extravagant gesture and mannerism:

Techelles, draw thy sword,
And wound the earth, that it may cleave in twain,
And we descend into th'infernal vaults,
To hale the Fatal Sisters by the hair,
And throw them in the triple moat of hell,
For taking hence my fair Zenocrate. (II.iv)

The sacking of the town where Zenocrate died is an act of weakness rather than of strength.

It is generally accepted that Tamburlaine's degeneration into total monster derives from his wife's death because with her, and the softening effect of her beauty if not of her moral judgment, the only influence that Tamburlaine acknowledges over himself passes from the play. It seems to me more likely that, until this point, he has been able to regard death as one of his minions, as much in his service as a tributary king. Zenocrate's death is a lesson in the limits of even his power, even though he chooses not to heed the lesson and continues to behave as if his power were absolute. The irony is most apparent when he is about to die himself:

Come, let us march against the powers of heaven,
And set black streamers in the firmament,
To signify the slaughter of the gods . . . (V.iii)

His sons and followers, who have hitherto shared his vision, can only humour him.

The murder of his son Calyphas, the most monstrous in the Elizabethan sense of 'unnatural' of all Tamburlaine's deeds, is usually taken both as the prime example of his degeneration and as the act which alienates him from the gods. Again, though, there is a futility about the gesture. Like his wife's death, his son's cowardice is a striking reminder of the limits of his power, this time over the living rather than the dying. Unable to change Calyphas' nature – which would represent real victory – he is reduced to killing him. Tamburlaine degenerates not because he does not know how to use his power, but because he cannot cope with the fact that his power is not absolute. The limited sway of the sword and of those things – wealth and luxury – that martial conquest can bring, is further illustrated in Theridamas' encounter with Olympia. He can kill her husband, carry her forcibly off with him, offer her 'costly cloth of massy gold' (IV.ii), but he cannot make her love him, nor can he prevent her from engineering her own death.

By the subtly changing effect of his hyperbole Marlowe makes it clear when Tamburlaine's claims for himself have become bombast. What he leaves ambiguous, perhaps deliberately, is how far we should interpret the hero's death as an act of divine retribution. Certainly, the distemper that finally kills him follows with almost naïve speed and logic on Tamburlaine's burning of the Islamic texts. However, his military supremacy over his actual Islamic enemies remains undiminished – in Elizabethan political literature God's will is more apparent in battle than in distempers. Tamburlaine's gesture of contempt for Mahomet is his final act of defiance over those powers which he cannot gain palpable control. Whether or not Marlowe accepted a God, he certainly acknowledged limits to human aspirations; while Tamburlaine and later Faustus are great to the extent to which they push back the frontiers, they too are finally defeated.

The Jew of Malta

DATE about 1591
CHARACTERS
Ferneze: Governor of Malta
Ludowick: His son
Barabas: A wealthy Jew
Abigail: His daughter
Mathias: A gentleman in love with Abigail
Calymath: Son of the Turkish Grand Seignior
Martin del Bosco: Vice-admiral of Spain
Jacomo and Barnadine: Friars
Ithamore: Barabas' Turkish slave
Bellamira: A courtesan
Pilia-Borza: Her attendant
SCENE Malta

Plot

The play is introduced by a Prologue, spoken by Machiavelli, in which he claims the hero as one of his disciples.
ACT ONE Malta, a Turkish tributary, is being threatened by

invasion for failing to pay its tribute. Calymath, however, who is leading the Turkish forces, gives Ferneze, the Governor of Malta, a month in which to find the tribute money. Ferneze summons the Jews, including Barabas, the wealthiest, and demands a levy of half their goods; when Barabas refuses to comply, all his goods are confiscated and his house turned over to a nunnery. Barabas however, had anticipated the levy and providentially concealed riches under the floorboards – but his prudence is confounded by the speed with which the nuns move into the house. He is not without resources of cunning, however: on his insistence, his daughter Abigail professes conversion to Christianity and presents herself at the nunnery as a novice.

ACT TWO Following her father's instructions, Abigail acquires the money for him and then, claiming a further change of heart, abandons the religious life. Barabas is now claiming that he is as wealthy as he ever was, but he is nonetheless determined to take revenge on Ferneze. He buys a Turkish slave, Ithamore, whom he acknowledges to be as villainous as himself, to aid him in his schemes; Abigail, too, is made an unwitting party to the revenge. She is in love with Mathias, who returns her love and whom Barabas pretends to regard with favour; but assuring Abigail that he will extricate her in the end, Barabas forces her into an engagement with Ludowick, Mathias' friend and Ferneze's son, whose attraction to his daughter the Jew has been quick to notice and turn to profit. Having set the young men up against one another, he sends Ithamore to Mathias with a forged challenge from Ludowick.

The political situation has changed, meanwhile, as Ferneze, encouraged by the Spaniard, Martin del Bosco, has decided to use the money that he levied for the tribute to make war on the Turks.

ACT THREE Mathias and Ludowick kill each other in the duel that was engineered by Barabas. So firm had been the friendship between the young men that Ferneze determines to discover and avenge himself on the villain who made enmity between them.

Abigail's response to Mathias' death is to re-enter the nunnery, this time sincerely. Enraged by his daughter's defection, Barabas has a poisoned pot of rice left outside the nunnery by Ithamore, which achieves the purpose of killing all the inhabitants. Before Abigail dies, however, she confesses her part in the death of Mathias and Ludowick to Friar Barnadine.

ACT FOUR The friars, Barnadine and Jacomo (who sponsored Abigail's genuine religious vocation), visit Barabas and confront him with the crime revealed in the confessional. The Jew says he is repentant, and that as an earnest of his change of heart he intends entering a religious house and bequeathing that house all his worldly goods. The two friars, who are of different religious orders, quarrel as to which will have the honour of receiving the repentant sinner, Barabas playing them off one against the other. With Ithamore's help, he strangles Barnadine and frames Jacomo for the murder: the body, propped against a wall, is struck by Jacomo who therefore believes himself to be Barnadine's murderer.

Only Ithamore now knows of Barabas' crimes. He is taken up by Bellamira, a prostitute, and by Pilia-Borza, her thieving companion, who have their eye on Barabas' gold. They encourage Ithamore to blackmail Barabas, using Pilia-Borza as go-between. Disguising himself as a French musician, Barabas visits the three and presents them with a poisoned nosegay.

ACT FIVE The poisoned flowers are unaccountably slow in taking effect and Bellamira and Pilia-Borza, who now know the extent of Barabas' crimes, betray him and Ithamore to Ferneze. As the victims of the poison now die (Ithamore before he can be brought to justice) Barabas too feigns death and his body is abandoned by the authorities. He determines now to avenge himself on the whole city by betraying Malta to the Turks. He leads the army of Calymath, who is himself bent on exacting vengeance for the unpaid tribute, by a secret way into the city. The Turkish victory secure, fortune again swings dramatically in

Barabas' favour and he is made Governor of Malta by the grateful Calymath. While he is so hated in Malta, however, he feels his position to be insecure. Taking Ferneze, who is now his prisoner, into his confidence, he outlines a scheme for destroying the Turks: Calymath's men will be invited to feast in a monastery which will then be blown up; Calymath himself will die in a burning cauldron into which, at a signal from Barabas to Ferneze, he will be pitched by means of a machine of Barabas' contrivance. Predictably, Ferneze takes the opportunity of avenging himself on his son's murderer by casting Barabas into the cauldron instead; he has the satisfaction of watching the Jew die cursing. Calymath, who has lost all his army in the blazing monastery, is taken prisoner by Ferneze until such time as his father, the Turkish Grand Seignior, agrees to repair the damage that Malta has sustained during the recent passage of events.

Critical commentary

Like Tamburlaine, Barabas is interested in power, but not in the kind that is achieved through conquest. He is in fact dismissive of kings 'That thirst so much for principality' (Act I); true to the tradition of the wandering Jew, whose assets must be strictly portable, the vision that fires Barabas' imagination is of 'Infinite riches in a little room'. (Act I) As Tamburlaine sets out to master the universe by might, and Faustus by knowledge, so Barabas' way is through the acquisition of wealth:

What more may heaven do for earthly man
Than thus to pour out plenty in their laps,
Ripping the bowels of the earth for them,
Making the sea their servants, and the winds
To drive their substance with successful blasts? (Act I)

Wealth for Barabas, like martial success for Tamburlaine, is a sign of divine favour.

Barabas' lust for money is entirely in keeping with the

commercial mercantile society in which he finds himself: –
'who is honour'd now but for his wealth?' Wars are fought
over tribute money; Jewish gold is appropriated, the
appropriation justified on the grounds that is was gained
through a usury with which Christians will not soil their
hands; the Friars Bernadine and Jacomo quarrel over
Barabas and his ill-gotten penitential offerings. It is a
society where there is a price on everybody's head; while
slaves are being auctioned on one part of the stage, their
cubic muscular capacity translated into crowns, Ludowick
is negotiating with Barabas for Abigail, who is referred to
throughout their conversation as a 'diamond'.

The commercially based, urban society – a feature of the
Renaissance as it had been of no earlier civilization – was of
some interest to creative writers, though their interest more
often expressed itself in comedy than in tragedy: Ben
Jonson was, as we shall see, a master of slick, satirical
comedy which presented avarice, in its various manifestations, as underlying all human action. And indeed, those
critics who have discovered links between the art of Marlowe and of Jonson are most convincing when offering as
evidence *The Jew of Malta*, which is a sometimes uneasy
hybrid of revenge tragedy (which Kyd's *The Spanish
Tragedy* had introduced to the stage a few years earlier) and
of satirical comedy. The blend is responsible for sufficient
unevenness in the quality of writing and of plotting to
encourage some editors to disclaim parts of the play as
Marlowe's, but the whole does in fact make sense as
experiment.

From Kyd, Marlowe had learned the benefits to be
gained, in terms of excitement and tension, from a hero who
cannot immediately turn his fantasies into reality. Tamburlaine's only effective adversaries are cosmic forces like death
and fortune, while his human victims are mere pigmies in
comparison with himself; hence the action of the *Tamburlaine* plays is curiously static, their poetry lyrical rather than
dramatic. Barabas is wilier than any other character in *The
Jew of Malta* but Ferneze is nonetheless a real adversary,

with authority and the law to back what Barabas sees as the theft of his goods; moreover, throughout the play, Barabas is dependent on other people – Abigail, Ithamore, and finally Ferneze – as Tamburlaine never is, and it is this dependence which produces the action and finally defeats the hero.

For its first two acts, *The Jew of Malta* operates like a revenge play, though it lacks the quality of internalized suffering that distinguishes Kyd's hero, Hieronimo, and never wins for Barabas the supportive sympathy of the audience, for the death of Ferneze's son seems an unusually harsh punishment for Barabas' loss of money. With the death of Ludowick, however, the mood changes and the hero becomes increasingly grotesque: he poisons a whole convent as vengeance on a recalcitrant daughter, and thereafter covers his traces by means of ingeniously bizarre murders. Propped-up monks, poisoned nosegays and boiling cauldrons are not the stuff of serious tragedy, and the crudely satiric humour of the play's second half lends support to a comic interpretation. The episode of the quarrelling monks is, as Harry Levin remarks in *Christopher Marlowe: the Over-reacher*, something the dramatist might well have lifted from an old jest book; Ithamore's wooing of Bellamira takes the form of deliberate parody of Marlowe's own lyric poem, 'The Passionate Shepherd to his Love':

> I'll be Adonis, thou shalt be love's queen;
> The meads, the orchards, and the primrose lanes,
> Instead of sedge and reed, bear sugar-canes:
> Thou in those groves, by Dis above,
> Shalt live with me, and be my love. (Act IV)

– heady stuff from a slave to a courtesan.

Like Marlowe's other heroes, Barabas is an over-reacher, but one cast in the mould that was to produce Ben Jonson's smart-alecs. In his Prologue to the play, Machiavel obligingly reproduces the sentiments for which he was famed – 'I count religion but a childish toy,/And hold there is no sin but ignorance' – and which had a special application in urban comedy: in a world where everybody is out for what he can get, virtue no longer has any validity as a basis of judgment, and the important distinction is not between the righteous and the unrighteous but between the successful villains and their victims. The comedy of this world is harsh, directed against the man who slips on the banana-skin that the audience has seen planted in his path. Barabas is the man of superior intellect in Maltese society and there-fore, despite his emotional impoverishment, equipped to be the hero. But he too has his weakness, which takes the characteristic Marlovian form of over-reaching himself – of being too clever and wanting other people to acknowledge his cleverness. He is unwise to use Ithamore as an accom-plice, but nonetheless survives his slave's revelations to fight another day; failing to learn by his mistakes, he is by the end of the play compulsively devising schemes for their own sake. He falls into a trap of his own making – the over-ingenious piece of machinery designed for Calymath which requires the co-operation of his sworn enemy Ferneze. The play's last joke is against Barabas.

Doctor Faustus

THE DATE is now generally thought to be 1592, although it was once thought to have been written immediately after *Tamburlaine*. I have used the Quarto text of 1604 which is rather shorter than a 1622 version, but widely considered to be more authentic; in the 1604 text there are no act divisions.

CHARACTERS
Chorus
Faustus: A scholar of Wertenberg
Valdes and Cornelius: Friends of Faustus
Wagner: Faustus' servant
The Pope
The Emperor of Germany
The Duke and Duchess of Vanholt

Lucifer
Belzebub
Mephistophilis
Good and Evil Angels
The Seven Deadly Sins
Spirits in the shape of Alexander the Great and Helen of Troy
SCENE Germany and Rome

Plot

The Chorus introduces the play with a resumé of Faustus'
life: although of low parentage, Faustus is now one of the
foremost scholars of Wertenberg, excelling all others in the
study of divinity, he is now considering indulging in the
forbidden practice of necromancy.

Discovered by the audience in his study, Faustus gives
reasons for his intellectual restlessness: no science has yet
given him the secret of how to 'make men to live eternally',
and he has now reached the limit of what he can learn by
orthodox means. His mention of magic brings the first visit
of his Good and Evil Angels, the Good urging him to resist
temptation, the Evil promising that magic will make him
'– on earth as Jove is in the sky,/Lord and commander of
these elements'. The Evil Angel proves the more persuasive
and Faustus summons his friends Valdes and Cornelius,
who have promised to teach him all they know of necromancy.

Faustus' first excursion into forbidden ritual calls up
Mephistophilis, one of the spirits who fell with Lucifer.
Mephistophilis hints at the torments of Hell, but Faustus,
who considers himself to be already irrevocably damned, is
ready to strike a bargain with him: if Lucifer will allow him
twenty-four years of voluptuous living, and of access to such
knowledge as Lucifer can impart, and will give him besides
Mephistophilis as his servant, Faustus will surrender his soul
to Lucifer at an appointed hour. Mephistophilis returns to
Hell for Lucifer's decision, and Faustus for the first time is
racked by doubt. Indecision again provides the cue for the

Good and Evil Angels: the latter again triumphs with his promises of wealth.

When Mephistophilis returns with Lucifer's agreement Faustus is required to write the terms of his bargain with his own blood – which immediately congeals and is only made to flow again with the aid of coals brought by Mephistophilis, who conjures up an entertaining vision to distract his new master. The loneliness that Faustus already feels is expressed in a wish to his diabolical servant for a wife, but the spirit's answer is a chilling reminder of the limits imposed by the life that Faustus has chosen: because he is debarred now from the sacraments, he must make do with the 'fairest courtesan' instead.

After what must represent a lapse of time, Faustus' life has now clearly brought him to the point of despair. It is only, he feels, his power to summon such spirits as Homer to sing to him that has preserved him from suicide. After a further visitation from his Good and Evil Angels, he calls for the first time on Christ – an act of recalcitrance which brings Lucifer himself, accompanied by Belzebub. Satisfied with Faustus' renewed professions of loyalty, the devils reward him with a vision of the Seven Deadly Sins, and with a book which will empower him to turn himself into any shape he pleases. He uses his new skill on a visit to Rome where he turns the Pope's St Peter's Day feasting into confusion.

The Chorus tells us that Faustus' fame as an astrologer is spreading and that he is consequently being taken up by royalty: we see him evoking the spirits of Alexander the Great and of his concubine for the German Emperor, and presenting the pregnant Duchess of Vanholt with out-of-season grapes. An Old Man now comes to call Faustus to repentance. The Doctor's willingness – 'I do repent; and yet I do despair' – throws Mephistophilis into a frenzy of anger and threats of unspeakable punishments if Faustus reneges on his bargain. Faustus comforts himself with Helen of Troy.

As the hour of his surrender to Lucifer draws near Faustus confides to some fellow scholars the bargain he has struck with the Devil. They withdraw to pray for him while Faustus faces his last hour on earth alone; what causes him particular anguish is the infinity of suffering ahead of him. With a last desperate cry of 'I'll burn my books', he is claimed by devils for Lucifer. The play closes with a warning from the Chorus to those who, like Faustus, are fascinated by 'unlawful things'.

Critical commentary

Faustus is not only Marlowe's supreme dramatic achievement, but the finest play that had yet been written for the English stage. Without speculating too far on the point where biography and creative impulse meet, it is nonetheless safe to assume that of all Marlowe's tragic heroes, Faustus' concerns were closest to Marlowe's own. The Faust legend – Faustus himself was a representative amalgam of various historical figures – held a particular fascination for sixteenth-century intellectuals, insofar as the German Doctor was prepared to go to unthinkable lengths to push back the frontiers of human knowledge. While all of Marlowe's plays reflect to some degree the new restlessness of the Renaissance – for Tamburlaine military ambition is a kind of metaphor for man's urge to master his universe and *The Jew of Malta* gives a dramatic context to the newly emerging commercial forces – none does so as definitively as *Faustus*.

Faustus is a scholar who has absorbed all that traditional modes of learning can offer him; he is an expert in divinity, but he wants to be a god himself, or at any rate privy to divine secrets:

> Could'st thou make men to live eternally,
> Or, being dead, raise them to life again,
> Then this profession were to be esteem'd.

He determines to raise spirits because they will 'Resolve me of all ambiguities'. He wants literally to soar beyond the human limit, and it is by no means fortuitous that the

Chorus should glance at the Icarus myth when defining the nature of Faustus' ambition and find defeat:

> 'Till swoln with cuuning, of a self-conceit,
> His waxen wings did mount above his reach,
> And melting heavens conspir'd his overthrow.

It is worth remembering, as part of the historical context that produced Faustus, that Leonardo da Vinci, who had done as much as any man of his age to extend the frontiers, was obsessed by the idea of flying, which for the Renaissance was not only a metaphor for human ambition but, should man acquire the skill, a means of conquering the world.

Now that we have achieved that particular dream, the Renaissance hope is touched for us with tragic irony; the aspirations of Faustus, whose creator had dabbled in necromancy, are touched by a similar kind of irony. What does Faustus actually get in return for his soul? When he asks Mephistophilis about the movement of the heavens, his servant can tell him no more than he knows already; when, hoping that his fears will be calmed, he asks who made the earth, Mephistophilis, who is unable, as a fallen spirit, to name God, cannot supply the answer. Faustus strikes his bargain, hoping to learn that religion is the 'childish toy' that advanced thinkers claimed it to be. 'Come, I think hell's a fable' he says, inviting Mephistophilis' complicity, but the reply is disconcerting: 'Ay, think so still, till experience change thy mind.'

Faustus has all his worst fears confirmed and none of the compensating knowledge that he sought. He is isolated from other men, not because he knows more than they, but because he has learned too late the truth of what they believe. His thirst for wisdom degenerates into sensuality and horseplay: he can satisfy his curiosity and lust on a famous courtesan but he is denied the companionship of a wife; he can amuse himself by destroying the Pope's banquet, but he cannot shake the Church's spiritual foundations. The Duchess of Vanholt is stunned into admiration by his January grapes, but he surely expected more from Lucifer than the power to produce fruit out of season.

The enigma of *Doctor Faustus* is how far Marlowe, widely thought by his contemporaries to be an atheist, accepted the Christian structure he gives his play. Certainly, with its Good and Evil Angels, its gaping trap-door representing Hell, its glimpses into Mephistophilis' torments ('Hell hath no limits, nor is circumscrib'd/In one self place'), *Faustus* has many of the marks of an orthodox mediaeval morality play. On the other hand, the morality structure may just have supplied convenient plot machinery. Faustus' tragedy is essentially internalized and plays require action; mediaeval writers of morality plays had found a way which was still familiar to Elizabethan audiences of dramatizing man's spiritual choices. If Marlowe intended his play as a fable of knowledge corrupted by sensuality, with the hell that Faustus suffers one of his own making, then he nonetheless left a Christian option open to his audiences. I think it possible that, as his hero has his worst fears about the truth of religion confirmed, so Marlowe in the play is expressing, if not his beliefs, then his fears.

With Faustus, Marlowe personally masters one of the central achievements of Elizabethan and Jacobean tragedy – the ability to depict the suffering hero. Faustus is a super-man, but Marlowe has given him a context in which he can be convincingly defeated. And the last fifty lines of the play, which telescope the hero's last hour on Earth, are unrivalled in tragic intensity:

> Stand still, you ever-moving spheres of heaven,
> That time may cease, and midnight never come . . .

All his hopes and ambitions have narrowed to a last desperate effort to cling on to life. The play's final bitter irony is his attempt to strike a bargain with God that would soften the terms of his fatal bargain with Lucifer:

> Let Faustus live in hell a thousand years,
> A hundred thousand, and at last be sav'd.

Shakespeare was to create tragedies which were finer, subtler, more moving, but among his tragic heroes only Hamlet (who, like Faustus and Martin Luther, was a student of Wertenberg) looked, as Faustus does, into the mystery to which the best minds of the age could offer no solution, and shuddered.

12 Elizabethan and Jacobean Comedy

Lord, what fools these mortals be!
A Midsummer Night's Dream (III.ii)

Comedy throughout the period was derived from two separate traditions. The renewed interest in the classical Roman theatre, and the revival of the comedies of Terence and Plautus, gave respectability to the native English satirical tradition: Ben Jonson, whose broad humour declares his link with Chaucer and popular English folk comedy, learned from the Roman dramatists the importance of tight construction and of fast pacing. He also shared the classical view of the moral function of comedy: contemporary abuses and follies were singled out for satire in plays which, it was hoped, would have a corrective effect on their audiences. Jonson's are the finest satirical comedies that the period has to offer.

What his plays failed to satisfy, however, was a taste for romance – for young love, exotic locations and the possibility that the vicissitudes of the human lot could be triumphantly defeated. The ancient Dionysian festivities of renewal and rebirth are the source that anthropologists would give to romantic comedy; less remote for the Elizabethans were the Greek romances of the post-classical period which were enjoying some vogue in translation. The finest examples of romantic comedy were Shakespeare's, but after 1600, when he wrote very few comedies, the leading writers in the genre were Beaumont and Fletcher.

It is indeed arguable that Shakespeare's late return to comedy in the romances was influenced by the success of the two younger dramatists, much of whose work was written for Shakespeare's company, the King's Men, and specifically geared to the requirements of the company's new indoor theatre, the Blackfriars. Where Jonson's robust satires of London life found their more appreciative audiences in the public amphitheatres, the courtly offerings of Beaumont and Fletcher were aimed at sophisticated private audiences. Of the two plays discussed here, the elegant *Philaster* is more typical of the form that they themselves helped to shape. *The Knight of the Burning Pestle*, less characteristically, is satirical, though widely felt to be their best play; in it, they are satirizing that taste for romance which, in other of their plays, they were content to satisfy.

Ben Jonson

As a dramatist working for the Elizabethan and Jacobean stage, Jonson is second only in importance to Shakespeare; his position in the history of English letters is not, however, as Shakespeare's largely is, dependent on his dramatic achievements. The first Poet Laureate, a writer of verse, prose, satire and criticism, he had much more influence than Shakespeare on the subsequent course of English literature. In part this is because Shakespeare's genius, so much in a class of its own, is not amenable to imitation. It is also because Jonson was both a creative artist and a theorist. He had ideas about the way plays should be written which he both expounded at some length and observed practically. The eighteenth century was the great age of English criticism, but it was Jonson who had first formulated its principles – as Dryden, the pioneer critic of the eighteenth century, was the first to acknowledge.

Jonson was born in 1573 in London, in circumstances of some poverty; nonetheless, through the kind offices of one of the masters, he acquired a good grounding in the classics at Westminster School. He was for a time apprenticed to a bricklayer, he fought in Flanders against the Spanish and, like Marlowe, he may well have been involved with the secret service. He drifted into the theatre around 1593, probably acting as well as writing for the Admiral's Men, until his association with that company came to an abrupt, but not final end, in 1598, when he murdered one of his fellow actors. He was released because he could plead benefit of clergy (being able to read and write was enough to lend him a clerical colouring), and he had his first big theatrical success in the same year with *Every Man in His Humour*, performed by Shakespeare's company, which was then the Chamberlain's Men.

In its way, *Every Man in His Humour* was an important theatrical landmark, in that it gave full practical expression to Jonson's concept of the comedy of humours. As he explained in the preface to the play which followed it, *Every Man Out of His Humour*, he conceived dramatic character in terms of humours: a ruling trait or passion is exaggerated to the point where character behaves and is judged solely within the terms of that trait or passion. Exaggeration has always been a weapon of the satirist, and Jonson, who lived through a time of growing Puritan opposition to the theatre, claimed a moral value for this work as helping to purge the vices of his age.

Clearly a man who enjoyed debate (his enemies would say, to the point of cantankerousness), and one who was given to bearing grudges, Jonson was engaged over the following years in what is now known as the War of the Theatres. In *Cynthia's Revels* (1600), and *The Poetaster* (1601), aesthetic principles were aired and specific individuals attacked for their divergence, in Jonson's terms, from poetic righteousness. Marston and Dekker bore the brunt of the attack yet, in the eyes of many of their contemporaries, emerged triumphant from the fray.

Jonson's own professional standards were rigorous. He was a staunch defender of the classical unities of time and place; he deplored the fanciful and the romantic. When he turned his attention to Roman history (with *Sejanus*, 1603 and *Catiline his Conspiracy*, 1611), he was thorough in his scholarship, painstaking in depicting the details of Roman life. The results are worthy rather than exciting.

With the accession of James I, Jonson embarked on a long and successful interlude as a writer of masques, the fashionable mode at court. A somewhat flimsy form before he made it his own, he left his stamp on the masque in the invention of the anti-masque, a burlesque played by professionals rather than by the ladies and gentlemen of the court. He worked with Inigo Jones, who glorified the entertainments with sumptuous sets – too sumptuous, Jonson felt, since they distracted from the verse. The two men quarrelled (viewed from one angle, Jonson's life is a history of strife), and Jonson never overcame his bitterness towards Jones. When Charles I came to the throne, the designer's services were still sought, but not Jonson's. He returned to the public stage, but his best work had been written by then: Dryden dismissed Jonson's last plays (written between 1625 and 1633) as 'dotages', and although the term is unfair, it is nonetheless true that his late work remains unapproachable.

His best work was written for the public stage, simultaneously with the masques that he was producing for James I. I have selected those three plays, *Volpone* (1605), *The Alchemist* (1610) and *Bartholomew Fair* (1614) which show Jonson at his satiric and inventive best. They are all variations on one theme – the comedy to be derived from the gulling of the fool by the knave – but within that limited area Jonson's talents were without match.

In 1616 Jonson produced a collected edition of his work – a unique step for a dramatist of the time to take, and one which illustrates the importance he attached to his own work. In the same year he was made poet laureate; in receipt of an adequate pension, he spent the remaining years of James's reign, before Charles I's coldness and his consequent financial need drove him back to the public stage, devoting himself to his classical studies, in which he became one of the most learned men of his age. Jonson was perhaps at his happiest over this period, a sad contrast to the deeply disappointed man who died in 1637, again scratching a living out of work for which he had lost the relish.

Jonson has in the past suffered more than any other dramatist of the age from invidious comparison with Shakespeare. Partly his own criticism, or rather grudging praise, of Shakespeare has been responsible for casting him in the role of envious second-fiddle who refused to acknowledge his own lower standing. In the eighteenth century, his personality was reviled, though his plays were enjoyed and his criticism respected. His reputation suffered an almost total eclipse in the nineteenth century, as he had neither the lyricism, the responsiveness to nature nor the interest in character that the romantic movement demanded of its idols. It was T. S. Eliot's essay, 'Ben Jonson'* that provided the framework for growing critical respect, and post-Eliot interest in theme, structure and conscious artistry have done Jonson nothing but service. His influence on other creative writers has been considerable, not so much directly, as through the native English satirical tradition that his work did so much to consolidate; whether they were themselves aware of the debt or not, the work of both Swift and Dickens carries something of his stamp.

*Eliot's essay is available in *Selected Essays 1917-1932* (Faber and Faber) and in a Twentieth Century Views Collection of essays on Jonson which is edited by Jonas A. Barish (Spectrum paperbacks).

Volpone

DATE 1605
CHARACTERS
Volpone: A Magnifico
Mosca: His parasite

Voltore: An advocate
Corbaccio: An old man } Would-be heirs of
Corvino: A merchant } Volpone's fortune
Bonario: Corbaccio's son
Celia: Corvino's wife
Nano: A dwarf } Members of
Castrone: A eunuch } Volpone's
Androgyno: A hermaphrodite } household
SCENE Venice

Plot

The play opens with a Prologue, in which Jonson's intention 'To mix profit with your pleasure' is stated.

ACT ONE opens with Volpone counting his gold, which he boasts to have acquired 'no common way'. He has in fact grown rich by exploiting the greed of others. His methods are unusual. With no heir to inherit his wealth, he trades off the hopes of those who would be made his heir, and who think to win his favour with costly gifts. Corbaccio, Corvino and Voltore, the principal aspirants, vie to outdo each other in the magnificence of their gifts, while Mosca, who runs Volpone's household, assures each in turn that he is named, or as good as named, in Volpone's latest will. The device that Volpone employs to maintain their greed (and therefore their generosity) at the required level of urgency, is to feign sickness whenever they visit him. Hourly expected to die, he nonetheless lives to add further riches to his store. At the close of the first act, when he and Mosca are gloating over the day's haul, he learns for the first time from Mosca of the exceptional beauty of Corvino's wife, Celia; she is also a lady of rare virtue who is forced to endure close domestic confinement because of her husband's jealous fears.

ACT TWO Disguised as a mountebank, one Scoto of Mantua, Volpone sets up a platform outside Celia's window; there he experiences for himself the impact of her beauty. Celia makes the mistake of throwing a handkerchief at him, which encourages Corvino to impose further restraints on her liberty. Returned home, Volpone confesses himself to be full of lust for Celia; desperate to possess her, he rightly judges that Corvino's greed has deeper roots than his concern for his wife's virtue. He sends Mosca to Corvino with news that the oil of the mountebank Scoto (a nice ironic touch from Volpone) has effected a partial recovery in him and that his doctors have advised him to take a young woman to bed to complete the cure. When Corvino learns that those same doctors are falling over each other with offers of virgin daughters, he determines to sacrifice Celia, especially as Mosca appears to think that the unwonted sexual exercise would be sure to hasten his master's death.

ACT THREE Corbaccio, one of the hopeful heirs, is expected at Volpone's home with a will that he has made in Volpone's favour, Mosca having convinced him that Volpone will be sure to return the compliment. Corbaccio's son, Bonario, who will be disinherited under the new will, has been brought by Mosca to witness his father's treachery from a concealed place. The first arrivals, however, are Corvino and Celia, the latter being dragged along much against her will. Neither her husband's threats nor Volpone's offers of untold luxury move her; left alone with her, Volpone is on the point of raping her when they are interrupted by Bonario, who carries Celia off. Corbaccio arrives with the will, followed by Voltore who, hearing the will discussed by Corbaccio and Mosca, accuses Mosca of double-crossing him. Voltore is calmed with the prospect of finally inheriting both fortunes. His professional services as a lawyer are enlisted in the Celia/Bonario débâcle.

ACT FOUR On the evidence of Celia and Bonario, Volpone is to be tried in the Senate-house for attempted rape. The united front of the defendants, however, moves the court against the innocent: Corvino claims that his wife is a noted bawd, and is illicitly involved with Bonario; Corbaccio gives his son's lasciviousness as his reason for disinheriting him. The evidence is presented by Voltore, who has Volpone carried in on his sick-bed as proof that he could never have attempted rape.

ACT FIVE Recovered from the trial and jubilant at his victory, Volpone is restless for more excitement. He has word put out that he is dead and when Corvino, Corbaccio and Voltore come to claim their inheritance, they find Mosca, apparently named in the final will, making an inventory of 'his' property: since Mosca has a hold over all of them (their perjury at Volpone's trial) he manages to silence their demands for justice. Volpone observes the scene concealed behind a curtain, but he is greedy for more amusement at his victims' expense. Disguising himself again, he accosts them all in the streets and teases them about their disappointed hopes.

Mosca meanwhile dismisses Volpone's retinue (Nano, Castrone and Androgyno) and takes possession of his house and property, until such time as 'he come to composition with me'. Glorying in his new position of power, Mosca, like Volpone, has overlooked the possibility that, with Volpone's 'death', the trial might be reopened: moved to revenge, Voltore confesses his perjury to the Senate. After a number of final plot ramifications (including Volpone's arrival in court, and Mosca's continued insistence that his master is in fact dead, and that he, Mosca, is his heir), the whole sordid story is revealed. The innocent Celia and Bonario are vindicated and the guilty (Volpone, Mosca, Voltore, Corbaccio and Corvino) are each given an appropriate punishment.

Critical commentary

Although Jonson experimented with Italian settings for some of his early comedies, his mature work is generally set in England. This was clearly a conscious decision, for when he produced a collected edition of his work in 1616, he changed the situation of a number of his earlier comedies from Italy to England. Only the Venice of *Volpone* survived the editing, a tribute to its unique reputation for the

Elizabethans for unthinkably corrupt practice; a city-state where prestige was not, as in England, associated with land, it provides an appropriate background against which Volpone amasses his fortune:

> I use on trade, no venture;
> I wound no earth with plough-shares, fat no beasts,
> To feed the shambles. (I.i)

His raw material is the cupidity of his victims: 'playing with their hopes' he is 'content to coin them into profit'. (I.i)

The relationship between Volpone and his dupes is characteristic of Jonson's comedy; if all literature but his were to be destroyed, then greed, trickery and an enjoyment of the downfall of others would be immortalized as the abiding concerns of human nature. Volpone is ethically no worse than his victims; but where the latter are contemptible, Volpone's and Mosca's intellectual superiority – which, as always in Jonson's work, displays itself in wit and manipulative power – makes them in some sort admirable. This is a world where only a fool will trust another man, and Volpone ceases, in Jonson's terms, to be admirable when he allows himself to become dependent on others.

His relationship with all his victims is an intellectual one (in the sense that his feelings are never engaged) until he meets Celia, and it is worth noting that attraction between the sexes is always so framed in Jonson as to be a sign of weakness rather than of spiritual vitality. Celia's intransigence and the intervention of Bonario bring him close to disaster: only Voltore's complicity extricates him. His first mistake – of allowing himself to be betrayed by his own sensuality – is bad enough, but his second and third are ruinous: he overlooks the fact that Voltore's loyalty, which is based on a greed that he has himself fostered, will cease to be reliable once the bait has disappeared; and worst of all, he is guilty of the same gullibility as his own victims in allowing himself to trust Mosca. He thinks – and it is the kind of error that the professional knave must guard against – that he is alone exempt from his parasite's skilled double-crossing. He falls into both traps through self-indulgence: he plans the fake death, the best joke of his career, because after the trial his earlier trickery seems too tame. In other words, his own amusement has become his criterion. Knavery requires considerable self-discipline and, judged by the code that he has himself espoused, he deserves the catastrophe that he brings down on himself.

In Volpone's world, native wit and an ability to maintain the upper hand are what count. Jonson enjoys the roguery of his rogues as much as they do themselves, but in *Volpone* his moral bias is clear, if somewhat coldly presented. A comparison with Shakespeare is instructive at this point. The latter will to some extent condition our response to his characters by playing with our sympathies and emotions, so that his range of villainy includes the likeable rogue in Falstaff, the tragic rogue in Shylock, the terrifying rogue in Iago. Jonson's approach is both more intellectual and more simple: all of his rogues make us laugh by the tricks that they play on others; when they trip themselves up, we laugh at them. Our sympathies are at no point engaged. In Shakespeare, our attitude to villainy is modified by our emotional response to its victims, and in the depiction of suffering innocence (Desdemona, Imogen, Hermione) Shakespeare is unrivalled. Jonson, however, works through our judgment rather than our emotions: in the fate of Celia and Bonario (wooden props representing virtuous innocence), we feel no personal interest, just a generalized sense of satisfaction that justice is finally done.

Jonson's is a 'self-contained world of surfaces' (the phrase is T. S. Eliot's); none of his characters has the resonance or mysteriousness of a real person. Their villainy, instead of being defined through personality, is placed against an objective ethical standard by means of deliberately applied devices and by the overall satiric effect of his verse. Jonson's boasts of his classical correctness can blind us to the extent of his indebtedness to an English tradition – in particular, to the allegorical bias of mediaeval English literature which has obvious links to the 'humours' approach to character. One of the devices that Jonson adapts for *Volpone* from the mediaeval tradition is the bestiary approach to human personality: the dominating characteristics of Volpone (the fox), Voltore (the vulture) and Corbaccio (the raven) are announced as early as the playbills, so that a bias of judgment is at once established. All the characters display avarice, to which Jonson assumes that we will respond with orthodox disapproval; more subtly, he brings under the umbrella of the avarice qualities in the characters which have a metaphorical link with that vice and which he therefore relies on to produce the same moral outrage from the audience. Corvino's hoarding of his wife and old Corbaccio's clinging to a life that has survived its usefulness both come within this category. Our assessment of Volpone is further manipulated by the presence within his household of Nano, the dwarf; Castrone, the eunuch; and Androgyno, the hermaphrodite: all oddities of nature and, according to Mosca, Volpone's own misbegotten children, they serve to suggest what is monstrous and unnatural in their begetter.

Volpone's deviations from nature (the standard by which he is judged) are further brought to our attention by the satiric edge of the verse. In the play's opening scene, he greets his gold as 'O thou sun of Sol,/But brighter than thy father' (I.i). As L. C. Knights argues in *Drama and Society in the Age of Jonson*, Jonson draws heavily in *Volpone* on the anti-acquisition tradition of the Middle Ages, and Volpone's address to his gold is a celebration of the derived above the natural. L. C. Knights is worth reading for his analysis of the celebrated speech in which Volpone woos Celia:

> See, behold,
> What thou art queen of; not in expectation,
> As I feed others; but possess'd and crown'd ... (III.v)

There follows a tantalizing list of the luxuries that Volpone has to offer. At first reading, Jonson appears to share his 'hero's' vision of magnificence, as Marlowe certainly does

1

Tamburlaine's in some of his comparable speeches. L. C. Knights indicates, however, the extent to which Jonson places and condemns the luxury by his satire, which provides a constant reminder of the natural standard by which Volpone must be judged.

Jonson's own view of himself as an arbiter of taste and morals, and the 'worthiness' that even a brief analysis of *Volpone* can suggest, leave out of account its continuing vitality as entertainment. His pacing and timing, particularly as the crisis approaches, are impeccable, his verbal comedy often hilarious. Jonson is Marlowe's successor in his use of exaggeration, but Marlowe never used it to such comic effect as in the following lines, where Mosca is entrancing Voltore with a picture of the plenty he will enjoy when he has come into the promised inheritance:

> When you do come to swim in golden lard,
> Up to the arms in honey, that your chin
> Is borne up stiff, with fatness of the flood,
> Think on your vassal; but remember me. (I.i)

Jonson is a master of the concrete detail, as here where Corvino, enraged and baffled that the use of Scotus' ointment should have revived Volpone, gives his opinion of the mountebank's powers:

> Have not I
> Known him a common rogue, come fidling in
> To the osteria, with a tumbling whore,
> And, when he has done all his forced tricks, been glad
> Of a poor spoonful of dead wine, with flies in't? (II.iii)

Jonson's comedy, at its best, has a distinctive tone which, within its own range, no other dramatist has equalled.

The Alchemist

DATE 1610

CHARACTERS

Subtle: The alchemist
Face: The housekeeper
Dol Common: Their accomplice
Lovewit: The master of the house where they operate

THEIR VICTIMS

Dapper: A lawyer's clerk
Drugger: A tobacco man
Sir Epicure Mammon
Pertinax Surly: A companion of Sir Epicure's
Tribulation Wholesome: A pastor of Amsterdam
Ananias: A deacon of his church
Kastril: A cantankerous boy
Dame Pliant: A widow, Kastril's sister

SCENE London

Plot

The action is confined to the house of Lovewit, who has fled London during a plague epidemic. His caretaker servant Jeremy, now known as Face, has established in the house Subtle, an alchemist, and Dol Common, a whore.

ACT ONE opens with a quarrel between Subtle and Face in which the alchemist claims that Face, who should be content with his humble role of attracting victims, is getting above his station. They are pacified by Dol Common, in time for the entrance of the first victim, Dapper, who is applying to Subtle for the secret of successful gaming. Subtle is reassuring, convincing the delighted Dapper that he is the lucky possessor of 'the only best complexion/The queen of Fairy loves' (I.i), and that if he goes home to perform certain rituals (involving vinegar and clean linen), he will, on his return to Lovewit's house, be introduced to his 'aunt', the Queen of Fairy. Dapper is followed by Drugger, who is about to furnish his shop and wants directions on the most auspicious placing of shelves; he pays up hand-somely on the expectation of Subtle providing him with a plan.

ACT TWO Sir Epicure Mammon is the next arrival. While he is waiting for an audience with the busy Subtle, Sir Epicure outlines to his sceptical companion Surly the kind of society he will build when he has learned the trick of changing base metal into gold: the medicinal properties of gold will be used to keep men at their voluptuous peak indefinitely, while Sir Epicure himself will indulge his every sensual whim. Sir Epicure assures Subtle, however, whom he takes to be a man of great piety, that he will use the expected powers for none but religious purposes. Surly remains unconvinced by the alchemist's authenticity, albeit that the latter tries to blind him with science.

Face, meanwhile, promises Mammon a diversion in Dol, whom Face claims to be the learned and occasionally raving daughter of a great lord; the encounter with Dol that Face promises Sir Epicure must be kept from Subtle because of his high scruples.

The next visitor is Ananias, a zealous Deacon who comes to complain that the money that his church has already supplied has failed to produce any result. Subtle, at his most superbly indignant, banishes Ananias because his church has sent as messenger a man who shares the name of 'the varlet/That cozen'd the apostles'.

Drugger returns with gold and problems which he is ready to confide: he is in love with a rich widow, Dame Pliant, whose brother Kastril has sworn that she shall marry none but a titled man. Face encourages Drugger to bring Kastril and Pliant to the Alchemist, together with tobacco and a suit of damask as payment for services rendered. The prospect of a rich widow sets Subtle and Face quarrelling again as to who is the more deserving of the lady's hand in marriage.

ACT THREE On his next visit, Ananias is accompanied by Tribulation Wholesome, his pastor. Their immediate concern is to arrange with Subtle the purchase of metal pots and pans from which gold might be made. The hardware is Sir Epicure Mammon's, left by him to await its transformation at Subtle's pleasure, but Subtle tells them that it is the property of orphans and should therefore command a high price from the men of religion. Subtle quickly dismisses their other concern, about the legality of coining.

The Dutch zealots are followed by Drugger, accompanied by the quarrelsome Kastril, the latter seeking instruction in the art of quarrelling. They are sent off by Face and told to return with Dame Pliant, about whom expectations are rising.

Dapper, who has now completed his preparatory rituals, is eager for a glimpse of the Queen of Fairy. Since the latter is to be represented by Dol, who will be engaged for a time with Sir Epicure Mammon, the luckless Dapper is locked in the privy, with a piece of ginger-bread gagging his mouth, until such time as Dol should declare herself ready for him.

ACT FOUR Sir Epicure is introduced to Dol (who is posing on this occasion as the learned and demented noblewoman), and when she has been wooed in a proper courtly fashion, the pair are led off to a bedroom by Face.

Kastril arrives with Dame Pliant, who more than fulfils the hopes of Face and Subtle. While Kastril and Pliant are inspecting Subtle's 'instrument' for quarrelling, Mammon's sceptical friend Surly arrives, disguised as a Spanish nobleman. Claiming to speak no English he is gratified by the extent to which his suspicions of Subtle and Face are justified, as they obligingly yell at him, 'You shall/Be cozen'd Diego.' The unexpected is turned to advantage as Subtle and Face persuade Kastril that his sister's fate is to marry a Spanish nobleman.

Surly and Pliant retire to the garden as Mammon and Dol emerge from the bedroom. Mammon and Dol are 'surprised' by Subtle, who finds it convenient to trade on his reputation for piety. In a beautiful piece of stage management, while Subtle is declaring that Mammon's sensuality will destroy the magic, Face appears with news that: '– all the works/Are flown *in fumo*, every glass is burst.' (IV.iii) Mammon departs repentant, blaming nobody but himself for the destruction of his hopes, but trouble is brewing elsewhere: Surly has dropped his disguise with Dame Pliant and is claiming her hand in marriage in return for disabusing her about the alchemist. Face sets Kastril on Surly as a wicked impostor and disguises himself as the Spanish nobleman that Pliant is fated to marry. No sooner has the threat of Surly been removed, however, than Dol brings news that Lovewit, the master of the house, is outside.

ACT FIVE Lovewit has been told by the neighbours of the unusually high level of traffic through his house, but Face, now clean-shaven and returned to his original role as Jeremy the butler, outfaces them all with his claim that the house has been locked up since the cat died of plague. He copes equally well with the appearance of Mammon, Ananias and Tribulation: informed by Surly of the alchemist's sharp practice, the victims are strident in their demands for retribution, but Face convinces Lovewit that they are 'The better sort of mad-folks'. (V.i)

However, the anguished cry – 'I am almost stifled' (V.i) – of Dapper, who is still suffering the close confinement of the privy, necessitates more candour, since it unmistakably issues from within the house that is meant to be locked. Face confesses all to his master to whom he provisionally offers Dame Pliant in marriage.

The show meanwhile goes on as Dapper, now released, is introduced to the Queen of Fairy (Dol), to whom he agrees to surrender his fortune in return for being made that lady's legal heir. Subtle and Dol have privately decided that when their loot has been removed from the house by Face they will abandon him, but Face, who has now resumed his identity, confronts them with his new partnership with Lovewit: the ill-gotten gains stay in the house while Subtle and Dol depart empty-handed. Lovewit fends off the clamouring victims by his ingenuousness: he has, he declares, no responsibility for what happened in the house in his absence, and if the injured parties insist on recovering their goods, they must do so through legal channels. Their wish to avoid public shame is Lovewit's guarantee that no such action will be taken by the alchemist's customers. Lovewit is married to Dame Pliant; and Kastril, when he finds that his new brother-in-law is prepared to quarrel, is reconciled to the match.

Critical commentary

Consideration of *The Alchemist* inevitably centres on the plot, where the dramatist's own ingenuity precisely mirrors the ingenuity of his rogues. Coleridge thought that the plot of *The Alchemist* was one of the most perfect ever constructed, and indeed Jonson's achievement, in a long play, of an unflaggingly accelerating pace and a continuous sense of expectation, is worthy of detailed attention. Particularly notable are Jonson's controlled introduction of new characters, and the skill with which he ensures that the action is always looking forward to fresh complications to come.

Two victims, Dapper and Drugger, are introduced in the first act, which closes on the expectation of a third, Sir Epicure Mammon. Mammon, Surly and Ananias make their first appearance in Act Two, which closes with the return of Drugger and, on his information about them, the tantalizing possibility of Kastril and Dame Pliant, who are unknown to Subtle and Face as well as to the audience. In Act Three, Ananias returns with Tribulation Wholesome: Drugger with Kastril: and Dapper with his clean linen, to spend most of the remainder of the play locked in the privy (his constant presence, forgotten in reading, can make itself felt on the stage). Act Four has some action proper in two plays-within-plays – Mammon's gulling by Dol as the demented noblewoman and the complications produced by Surly's Spanish disguise. The long-awaited Dame Pliant is introduced in this act, which also includes further visits from Ananias, Kastril and Drugger. Tension mounts throughout Act Four with the discovery of Surly's duplicity, the query as to how long Dapper can be contained within his insalubrious place of confinement and the news, which closes the act, of Lovewit's return. Act Five introduces Lovewit and has a further play-within-a-play in Dapper's gulling by the 'Queen of Fairy'; not only the victims but, more surprising, Subtle and Dol, are routed; and the house returns to an enriched normality with Lovewit's marriage to Pliant.

Jonson's skill is in his judicious use of accumulation: each act, including the last, introduces at least one new character to swell the tide of increasingly frenzied comings and goings. As well as the anticipation that the audience feels about the introduction of each fresh victim, there are two threads, material to the play's ending, which are established early in the first act: the latent antagonism of Subtle and Face, which is rooted in their different conceptions of their roles; and the continual possibility, which is finally realized, of Lovewit's return.

As in Jonson's other plays, the characters make no claims to naturalism, but they are bursting with life. This is particularly true of Face, who maintains the audience's admiration throughout, not only because of his stunning inventiveness, but because of his evident enjoyment and relish in the situations that he has himself created. The victims, united in their dreams of instant wealth, are differentiated in their individual weaknesses and follies (Sir Epicure's elderly insistence on his continuing voluptuousness, Ananias's concern with the letter rather than the spirit of the law), and it is these which Subtle and Face exploit. Much of the comedy arises from the audacity of the rogues' claims, and the willingness of their victims to be deceived. Tribulation's fears for the legality of manufacturing gold are calmed by Subtle's grave 'It is no coining, Sir./It is but casting.' (III.ii) Mammon is convinced of Subtle's powers by the latter's air of professional expertise: 'The same we say of lead and other metals,/Which would be gold, if they had time.' (II.i) Jonson resists the temptation, however, of laying too much stress on the alchemist's claim to be able to turn base metal into gold, and concentrates instead on the headier business of exploiting people's fantasies. Kastril is wrought to a high pitch of excitement by Subtle's description of

> my instrument,
> That hath the several scales upon't, shall make you
> Able to quarrel at a straw's breadth by moonlight. (IV.i)

Dapper's wildest dreams are more than met by the Fairy Queen's amiability:

> But come, and see me often. I may chance
> To leave him three or four hundred chests of treasure,
> And some twelve thousand acres of fairy land,
> If he game well and comely with good gamesters. (V.ii)

In the Prologue to *The Alchemist*, Jonson makes much, as he does elsewhere, of his unimpeachable moral intentions:

> though this pen
> Did never aim to grieve, but better men;
> Howe'er the age he lives in doth endure
> The vices that she breeds, above their cure.

To the vices of his age, Jonson claims to be bringing 'fair correctives'. *The Alchemist* does, however, supply some evidence to those critics who feel that Jonson's moral indignation was more apparent than real; some, like Edmund Wilson in *Morose Ben Jonson** (in which is presented a novel explanation of Jonson's themes, as the unwholesome symptoms of anal eroticism) would go farther in arguing that the only pleasure of which Jonson was capable was gloating over the discomfort of others. Certainly, *The Alchemist* lacks the justice of *Volpone*'s ending, in that Lovewit and Face are allowed to triumph in their ill-gotten gains, with no prospect of their having ever to surrender them.

Nonetheless, Jonson himself would not be without a moral defence for his ending. It could be argued that since there are no representatives in *The Alchemist* of genuine innocence, but only of gullibility, there is nothing offensive in Face's victory. The dramatist has chosen two principal targets for his satire in *The Alchemist*. The first is greed, in all its manifestations, and the blinkered judgment to which the greedy are susceptible. Less obvious is the self-delusion of the professional trickster, displayed by Subtle. While he knows that he is conning other people, he is unaware of the extent to which he is himself conned by his own public image. He needs Face to create the mystique, but he cannot accept his accomplice into full and equal partnership because he wants Face too to acknowledge powers in him, a professional superiority, which does not exist. He wants Face to be grateful for his initiation into an illusory mystery: 'have I ta'en thee out of dung . . .

> Rais'd thee from brooms, and dust, and watering-pots,
> Sublimed thee, and exalted thee, and fix'd thee
> In the third region, call'd our state of grace ? (I.i)

Face is a deserving winner because he fully understands the terms on which they are operating; and because, in a play where there is no display of virtue, the accolade goes to the wittiest and wiliest.

* Edmund Wilson's 'Morose Ben Jonson, is in the Twentieth Century Views anthology, ed Jonas A. Barish.

Bartholomew Fair

DATE 1614

CHARACTERS

VISITORS TO THE FAIR:
John Littlewit: A proctor
Win-the-Fight Littlewit: His wife
Dame Purecraft: Win's mother
Zeal-of-the-Land Busy ⎫ Suitors to
Winwife   ⎭ Dame Purecraft
Tom Quarlous: Companion to Winwife
Bartholomew Cokes: A wealthy fool
Waspe: His man
Adam Overdo: A justice of the peace, Cokes's brother-in-law

Mistress Overdo: His wife, Cokes's sister
Grace Wellborn: Overdo's ward, betrothed to Cokes
THE FAIR COMMUNITY:
Lanthorn Leatherhead: A hobby-horse seller
Ursula: A pig woman
Joan Trash: A gingerbread woman
Nightingale: A seller of ballads
Edgworth: A cut-purse
Trouble-all: A madman
SCENE Smithfield, in London

Plot

ACT ONE opens at the house of John Littlewit, who as
Proctor has just prepared a marriage licence for Bartholomew Cokes which is collected by his officious servant,
Waspe. Other visitors to Littlewit's home are Winwife, who
is wooing Dame Purecraft, the Proctor's mother-in-law, and
his friend Quarlous, who enjoys laughing at the follies of
others. Dame Purecraft is also being wooed by her religious
mentor, Zeal-of-the-Land Busy, but she has been convinced
by a fortune-teller that she will only find happiness with a
madman.

Waspe tells the company that his near-idiot master,
Cokes, will be spending that day at Bartholomew Fair. The
Littlewits too would like to go to the fair, but have first to
overcome the religious scruples of Busy and Dame Pure-
craft: Win feigns a longing to eat roast pig at the fair and
Busy solemnly rules that if they all partake of pig they will
be demonstrating their 'hate and loathing of Judaism'. (I.i)
Quarlous and Winwife decide to follow them to the fair.

ACT TWO Justice Overdo, whose responsibility it is to pass
judgment on the 'enormities' that are reported after the
Fair, is this year spending the day there in disguise, so that
he may seek out criminals for himself. Under his nose,
Ursula the pig-woman, Nightingale the ballad seller and
Edgworth form a pick-purse syndicate, but Overdo fails to
notice this striking instance of the kind of villainy he came to

search out: he takes instead an immediate liking for
Edgworth, whom he thinks too good for the company he
keeps. While Overdo is lecturing Edgworth and the
company generally on the perils of tobacco and alcohol,
Edgworth is picking the pocket of Overdo's own brother-in-
law, Bartholomew Cokes, who has arrived at the Fair with
his sister, Mistress Overdo, and his betrothed, Grace Wellborn. Cokes obligingly makes it known that while one of his
purses has been picked, the other, containing gold, is still safe
in his possession. Overdo meanwhile is beaten up by Waspe
for being the unwitting cause – through his preaching,
which created a distraction – of the theft of Cokes's purse.
ACT THREE The Littlewits, with Dame Purecraft and Busy,
repair immediately to Ursula's booth to eat pig. Bartholomew
Cokes, who is drawn like a child to toys and sweetmeats,
buys Joan Trash's basket of gingerbread and Lanthorns'
entire stall of gew-gaws. He leaves the goods with them to
be collected later in the day. Edgworth and Nightingale,
who have followed Cokes for his gold, again pick his
pocket; while Overdo, who is following Edgworth in the
hope of turning him to the path of righteousness, is carried
off as a criminal.

The theft of Cokes's purse is observed by Quarlous and
Winwife, who confront Edgworth with their knowledge.
Quarlous agrees to keep silent about the crime on condition
that Edgworth remove for him the contents of Waspe's box
(Cokes's marriage licence): Waspe is, Quarlous explains,
the kind of 'serious ass' that he loves to see gulled.

Grace Wellborn, who has been abandoned by the easily
distracted Cokes, teams up with Quarlous and Winwife;
she tells them that she hates Cokes for his folly, but that she
has been bought by Overdo as his ward, and if she refuses
to marry his brother-in-law, she will be forced to surrender
her property.

The Littlewits have emerged from Ursula's booth and have
been given permission by Busy to view the sights of the Fair,
provided they regard them with appropriate loathing. Busy
himself rants at the stallholders and is carried off by the

Watch for disturbing the peace. Leatherhead and Trash pack up the goods that Cokes has paid for and disappear.

ACT FOUR Overdo, who has been placed in the stocks, learns for the first time of the misfortunes of one Trouble-all, who was once an officer of Overdo's, but since his dismissal from service he has gone mad. His madness takes the form of refusing to do anything without Overdo's warrant: 'His wife, sir reverence, cannot get him to make his water, or shift his shirt, without his warrant.' (IV.i) Overdo is moved by Trouble-all's plight and determines to make reparation to him.

Cokes, who has lost his money, his sister and Grace, now loses his cloak, hat and sword to Edgworth when he hands them over so that he can run after some fallen pears.

Grace, who is being entreated to marriage by Quarlous and Winwife, says that she cannot, on such short acquaintance, make a choice between them. Instead, she asks them both to write down a word and then to accept the decision of the first passer-by (Trouble-all) as to which word is superior. She refuses to reveal the identity of the lucky man until they have taken her home.

Waspe, who is drunk in the company of some of the stall-holders, is incited to fight; while he is thus occupied, Edgworth picks his box. Waspe is arrested and taken off by the Watch.

Littlewit leaves his wife with Ursula while he goes off to organize a puppet show that he has written; Mistress Overdo, now alone, is forced to apply to Ursula for the use of her lavatory. Both ladies are persuaded by Ursula and her companions to turn prostitutes for the remainder of the fair.

Act Four closes with Waspe, Overdo and Busy managing to make their escape from the stocks.

ACT FIVE Quarlous, who now has the marriage licence which Edgworth stole, has disguised himself as Trouble-all in order to learn who has won Grace (in his disguise he appeals to Grace to refresh his memory). He discovers that Winwife has prevailed. There is a consolation prize in store for Quarlous, however, in Dame Purecraft, who mistakes

him for the madman he is impersonating and claims
him in marriage: the prophecy of the fortune-teller that she
would only find happiness with a madman will now, she
hopes, be fulfilled. He is now accosted by Overdo, who
offers him, as 'Trouble-all', to name anything he wants in
reparation for the injury that Overdo did him. He demands
Overdo's name on the marriage licence in order that he
might marry Dame Purecraft, and on another sheet of
paper.

At the puppet-show (a crude London-low-life version of
Hero and Leander), the entire *dramatis personae* are gathered.
Overdo is so appalled to have been offered prostitutes (his
own wife and Win Littlewit disguised) that he decides the
time has come to reveal himself and expose the enormities
that he has discovered. At the height of his oratory, however, one of the bawds is found to be his wife. Further
humiliations are in store: Quarlous drops his own disguise
to tell Overdo that his treasured Edgworth is a cut-purse,
and that the paper he signed for 'Trouble-all' made Grace's
wardship over to Quarlous. It is in fact Quarlous who wins
the day: Winwife will now have to buy his friend out of his
legal responsibilities towards Grace, if he wants to marry
her, and the wealthy Dame Purecraft has been tricked into a
marriage with Quarlous under false pretences. The play
closes with the entire company repairing to Overdo's house
for dinner.

Critical commentary

Thought by many to be the finest of Jonson's plays, *Bartholomew Fair* is perhaps the least typical, in that it is the most
loosely structured and the least self-consciously learned and
moralistic. The device of the fair, which is responsible for
the fluidity of the action, provided Jonson with an ideal
medium for expressing his own vision of the world. His
division of people into fools and rogues is amply provided
for in the circumstances of a fairground where professional

rogues, on home ground, exploit the vanities and deflate the self-importance of the general public.

The three 'serious asses', Waspe, Busy and Overdo, serve their time in the stocks, while the active criminals, Edgworth, Nightingale and Lanthorn Leatherhead, pass undetected until the final scene demands revelations – and then it is Overdo rather than the thieves who is mortified by those revelations. In the case of Overdo and Busy however – the one blackmailing his ward into an unpalatable marriage for motives of greed, the other, as Dame Purecraft tells Quarlous (V.ii) using his religious position for financial gain – there is a wider justice in their humiliation which the real world would never be able to mete out to them. At the fair, 'honest' women require little persuasion to turn bawds, Puritans justify their gluttony as an act of piety against the Israelites. When at the end of the play Quarlous suggests that Overdo throw open his house to feast the company, he is requiring that the arbiter of justice be prepared to celebrate the equality of all men in culpability. With the exception of the role assigned in the play to Bartholomew Cokes, the prize fool who deservedly loses at the fair all that is removable from his person, *Bartholomew Fair* is not so much about rogues and fools as about knowing rogues and hypocritical rogues.

When Zeal-of-the-Land Busy has eaten Ursula's pork and drunk her ale, he sets about denouncing her, 'having the marks upon her of the three enemies of man; the world, as being in the fair; the devil, as being in the fire; and the flesh, as being herself.' (III.i) The fair is indeed an extended metaphor for the world; its wares the temptations that flesh is heir to, from which none is exempt. To the degree that Jonson's purpose in *Bartholomew Fair* is satiric, his principal target in this play are those who think themselves exempt from the temptations of the flesh. It is, therefore, the reforming but gluttonous Busy who is most condemned by his own evocations of the Bible. Indeed, some of the richest passages are Busy's own confident feats of self-justification, as in the speech where the decision is made to go to the fair: 'the place is not much, not very much, we may be religious in the midst of the profane, so it be eaten with a reformed mouth, with sobriety and humbleness; not gorged in with gluttony and greediness, there's the fear.' (I.i)

Almost as important as the satire, however, and a possible reason for *Bartholomew Fair's* popularity, is its celebration of man's capacity for enjoyment. 'Good Win, go in, and long' (III.i) John Littlewit says to his wife when, having satisfied their craving for pig, they have to convince Busy and Dame Purecraft of the urgency of seeing the sights of the fair. Later, Win is completely entranced by the delights of prostitution, as they are described to her: 'Lord, what a fool have I been.' (IV.iii) The fairground people know that the differences between themselves and their customers are only superficial, and that nothing is better for trade than 'fine ambling hypocrites'. (III.i)

In his other plays, Jonson relies for most of his comedy on satire, but in *Bartholomew Fair*, where he displays more relish in human idiosyncracy for its own sake, the comedy is sometimes of a kind that we are more likely to associate with Dickens. Ursula's description of herself as she stokes up the fire to roast the pigs – 'I am all fire and fat, Nightingale, I shall e'en melt away to the first woman, a rib again, I am afraid' (II.i) – has a matter-of-fact zaniness to which Jonson's prose (his more usual medium was verse) is particularly well adapted. Some of the play's vitality springs from its heady enjoyment in words, as when Win reassures her husband that she will be able to get round her mother: 'Ay, let her alone, John, she is not a wise wilful widow for nothing; nor a sanctified sister for a song. And let me alone too, I have somewhat of the mother in me, you shall see.' (I.i) There is enough in Jonson's plays to keep alive the reputation for censorious churlishness and self-conscious superiority that he acquired largely by comparison with Shakespeare; it is only really in *Bartholomew Fair* that we get a glimpse of the other Ben Jonson, the generous wit and boon companion.

Beaumont and Fletcher

Francis Beaumont and John Fletcher belonged to a more exalted social class than any of the other dramatists of the period. Beaumont was born in 1584, into an established Leicestershire family; his father was a Justice of the Common Pleas, he himself was a member of the Inner Temple. Fletcher was born in 1579 in Sussex, the son of a worldly bishop who spent much of his life at court. They were both therefore better equipped than most dramatists to write of the manners, intrigues and hazards of court life; in some of their plays, including *The Knight of the Burning Pestle*, we can detect a degree of self-consciousness about their own social position. Their partnership was a prolific one, their dramatic range considerable, encompassing comedy, tragedy, romance and pastoral.

Beaumont died when he was just under thirty, in 1616, Fletcher some nine years later in 1625. Although Fletcher went on to produce some fine work alone (notably *The Passionate Shepherdess*), I have felt it better to confine myself to two plays of joint production. In the eight years or so before Beaumont's death their plays, mostly performed at the Blackfriars by Shakespeare's company, the King's Men, had considerable influence, especially in creating a taste for that kind of courtly drama at which they excelled. *Philaster*, much performed and admired in its own day, is an example of that genre which they made so much their own; *The Knight of the Burning Pestle*, more satirical comedy than romance, shows their highly developed stage technique at its best.

The Knight of the Burning Pestle

DATE 1607

CHARACTERS

A Speaker of the Prologue

A Citizen

His wife
Ralph: The Citizen's apprentice
Venturewell: A merchant
Luce: His daughter
Humphrey: In love with Luce
Jasper: Venturewell's apprentice, also in love with Luce
Merrythought and Mistress Merrythought: Jasper's parents
Michael: Their son, Jasper's brother
SCENE London and its environs; a brief interlude in Moldavia in
Act IV

Plot

In an Induction, the Speaker of the Prologue has just
announced the play as 'The London Merchant' when he
is interrupted by a Citizen and his Wife from the audience.
In defiance of the taste of the 'gentlemen' present, they
demand that the play should be in praise of London and
should depict someone of their own class (the Citizen is a
grocer) performing deeds of great valour. The Wife suggests
that the character thus outlined might be shown killing a
lion with a pestle; the Speaker takes the point and the title
is amended to 'The Knight of the Burning Pestle'. The
Citizen's apprentice, Ralph, is, at the insistence of his
master, assumed into the play, the better to champion the
aspirations of his peers.

ACT ONE opens with the original story of the London merchant, which concerns the disposal in marriage of Luce, the
daughter of the merchant, Venturewell. She is in love with
her father's apprentice, Jasper, but when Venturewell hears
of the understanding between them, he dismisses Jasper and
insists that Luce marry Humphrey. Luce agrees to the
marriage, but only on condition that she and Humphrey
elope. She claims that she must elope in order to fulfil the
conditions of a vow that she made, but the audience realizes
that this falls in with a plan that she has already made with
Jasper.

Ralph is now introduced in his capacity as *dramatis*

persona. Chaffing at the restrictions of grocery, he decides to become a 'citizen-errant' and to have a burning pestle on his shield as a memento of his former trade. His two apprentices are instructed in the chivalric language and told that henceforth they are to be known as his Squire and his Dwarf.

The final first act change of scene is to the house of the Merrythoughts, whither Jasper, now out of work, repairs to demand his patrimony. His father, who makes a point of letting the future take care of itself, sends him off with his blessing and ten shillings. Mistress Merrythought has put aside considerably more for her favoured son, Michael; she decides that she and Michael must leave home before Merrythought squanders Michael's fortune.

ACT TWO With the permission of Venturewell, to whom he has confided Luce's whim to elope, Humphrey carries Luce off into the night and Waltham Forest. Mistress Merrythought and Michael have taken the same escape route; they are surprised by Ralph and his entourage, who are out seeking damsels in distress, and they run away leaving their casket of treasure behind. The treasure is found and appropriated by Jasper, who is loitering in expectation of Humphrey and Luce: meeting them, he deprives Humphrey of his bride.

Ralph, meanwhile, has convinced the Merrythoughts of his honourable intentions and has adopted their cause – the finding of the casket. A further case of distress presents itself in Humphrey, in flight from Jasper. Ralph, who recognizes nothing as too much for him, promises to recover Luce, but is knocked down by Jasper with his own pestle. Humphrey returns to Venturewell to organize a search party for Luce; Ralph and the Merrythoughts, hungry and tired, arrive at the Bell Inn or, as Ralph prefers to style it, 'An ancient castle, held by the old Knight/Of the most holy order of the Bell.' (II.vi)

ACT THREE While Luce is asleep in Waltham Forest, Jasper is suddenly overcome by doubts of her love for him, and he draws his sword on her to test her. He is surprised in this position by Humphrey and Venturewell, who manage to recover Luce and bear her off.

Ralph, meanwhile, after his night at the Bell Inn, ignores the host's demand that he pay the reckoning, preferring instead to thank him in the elaborate language of chivalry. Before the situation grows unpleasant, the Citizen steps in from the audience and settles the bill. The Merrythoughts, now penniless, leave Ralph and return home. Ralph himself is eager for fresh adventures; he is directed by the host of the Inn to a barber, where he will have the opportunity to 'free some gentle souls/From endless bonds of steel and lingering pain'. (III.ii) Put in the picture in advance by the host, the barber allows himself to be routed and his 'prisoners' released.

ACT FOUR As the Jasper plot is about to be resumed, the Citizen's Wife demands Jasper's dismissal from the stage; instead, she wants the satisfaction of seeing Ralph at the King of Moldavia's court. Her wish is granted, with the unexpected bonus of the Princess of Moldavia falling in love with Ralph. He elects instead to return to his chivalric duties in London, but not before the Citizen gives him money to tip the Princess's staff so that this travelling representative of the grocery trade may make a good showing.

Back in the Venturewells' house, Luce is under lock and key, pending her marriage to Humphrey. Venturewell receives a letter from Jasper which announces the erstwhile apprentice's coming death and begs that his coffin might for a time be placed in Luce's chamber. Venturewell agrees to what he takes to be Jasper's last wish. Jasper emerges from the coffin, Luce climbs in and is carried off to the Merrythoughts' house.

ACT FIVE Jasper appears to Venturewell as his own ghost, demanding that his former master make reparation for the injuries he inflicted on Jasper in the past: 'Repent thy deed, and satisfy my father,/And beat fond Humphrey out of doors.' (V.i) The terrified Venturewell rushes to the Merrythoughts' house where he is reconciled to them, the Merrythoughts to each other, and the way is clear for Jasper and Luce to marry. The play ends on the insistence of the Citizen and his wife: Ralph is now dead from an arrow through his head, and they have lost interest in the play. The arrow was acquired while he led a battalion of apprentice boys through the city, in honour of London and grocery – an episode which, at the Citizen's request, had found its way into Act V.

Critical commentary

The Knight of the Burning Pestle is both the least typical and, in the opinion of twentieth-century critics, if not of its first audiences, the best of Beaumont and Fletcher's plays. It is arguable that elsewhere in their work these masters of romance display too little detachment from the conventions in which they worked; in this play, the taste for romance, if not those writers who, like themselves, were helping to popularize it, is satirized with consumate skill. The social rank of their characters represents a further departure from their usual practice. Instead of exotic courts and palaces, they confine themselves here to the London of merchants, grocers and apprentice boys – the staple audiences of the public theatres who, at about the time when *The Knight of the Burning Pestle* was written, were beginning to complain that the theatres reflected neither their lives nor their social aspirations. *The Knight of the Burning Pestle* is as interesting as social record – in the sense that it reflects the opinions of the nobility (Beaumont and Fletcher) about the rising bourgeoisie – as it is as a play.

The Citizen and his Wife appear to get everything their own way in *The Knight of the Burning Pestle*, but they are mocked throughout by the gentlemanly dramatists. The mockery is most obviously directed at their taste (of which more later), but also at their moral values, through the denouement of the 'London Merchant' play. Here, the wishes of Venturewell – an honest and thrifty London citizen – to marry his daughter prudently are completely overturned as he is forced to accept her marriage to a penniless Jasper. The bourgeois virtue of thrift is mocked again when the money that Mistress Merrythought laid aside for Michael falls without effort into Jasper's hands. At the end of the play all the characters gather at the home of the wastrel Merrythought and are only given admittance on his terms – they must sing a snatch of merry song. Merrythought is the antithesis of the solid, hard-working London citizens whose aspirations were soon to be met by Cromwell; through his triumph in the play, Beaumont and Fletcher ally themselves with the gentlefolk (of whose presence in the theatre the Citizen and his Wife are intermittently aware) in their contempt for the burgher class. The Citizens are throughout solidly partisan towards Humphrey, whose hopes are finally defeated, so there is a sense in which the presence of Ralph is no more than a palliative.

The idea of *The Knight of the Burning Pestle* is a simple one, but cleverly effective in its range of satirical targets. The very fact of the Citizen's intrusion into the play makes its own point about the tyranny of the audiences, as viewed by dramatists; the chivalric and romantic ideals of Ralph, which the Citizen wants to see expressed in a London trading context, indicate the form that that tyranny was taking. The comedy, of both incongruity and pastiche, has lost little with the passage of time. There are Ralph's instructions to his apprentices as he embarks on his career as citizen-errant, that they must never 'call any female by the name of woman or wench, but "fair lady," if she have her desires, if not, "distressed damsel"; that you call all forests and heaths "deserts"; and all horses "palfreys".' (I.iii) The host of the Bell obligingly enters into the spirit of the thing when he directs Ralph to the barber's:

> Not far from hence, near to a craggy cliff,
> At the north end of this distressed town,
> There doth stand a lowly house . . . (III.ii)

The literary pastiche, amusing in itself, reinforces another of the play's themes – Ralph's inability to distinguish fantasy from reality: the acts of chivalry are a game which the other characters allow him to play in order to placate the Citizen and his Wife, but he embarks on his chivalric career in a spirit of deadly earnestness. In this, he contrasts strikingly with Jasper and Luce, who use a romantic front (notably, Luce's longing to elope) in which they never themselves believe, in order to deceive others. And where Ralph ends the play with an arrow through the head as a reward for his seriousness, the consciously games-playing Jasper and Luce hit the jackpot.

The illusion-and-reality theme is further extended in the use that the dramatists make of the Citizen and his Wife. At the beginning, they are aware that they are watching a play, but quite soon they are confused about where the play ends and reality begins. When the Wife is concerned that Humphrey should marry Luce, the Citizen comforts her with ''a shall have her, or I'll make some of 'em smoke for't.' (I.ii) The wife is later worried that Jasper's theft of the casket might go undetected by his mother and consoles herself according to criteria which are only applicable outside a theatre: 'Here be a number of sufficient gentlemen can witness, and myself, and yourself, and the musicians, if we be called in question.' (II.ii) Although the couple have no influence on the plot of 'The London Merchant', they not only determine the Ralph-plot but encroach on it; and when they supply Ralph with money to pay the reckoning at the Bell (III.ii), or to tip the servants in the court of Moldavia (IV.ii), the nature of their encroachments confirm a view of the bourgeois commercial ethic which is central to the play.

The Knight of the Burning Pestle is a play of some subtlety in its skilful blend of literary pastiche and contemporary satire. It is also one of the cleverest and most complete explorations of its time, of the nature of theatrical illusion and of the relationship between the theatre and real life. These, as we have seen, were among Shakespeare's profoundest concerns, expressed lightheartedly in some of the early comedies and with a high degree of seriousness in

The Tempest, which examines both the responsibilities and the limitations of the artist. The theatrical experience was widely available in Elizabethan London, for many the only contact with an imaginative life. The sophistication of *The Knight of the Burning Pestle* lies in the degree to which it successfully confuses the boundaries between theatrical illusion and reality. At the very beginning, with the Citizen's first interruption from the audience, the audience itself might be baffled as to whether it were a spontaneous eruption or part of the play. The Citizen and his Wife, with their frequent interruptions, are thereafter spokesmen for the audience – actors masquerading as the general public. *The Knight of the Burning Pestle* is one of the leading plays of England's first period of intense dramatic activity to pave the way for one of the abiding concerns of later drama – the use of a play metaphor to imply that human beings are actors in a drama outside their own control.

Philaster

DATE 1608

CHARACTERS

King of Sicily and Calabria
Arethusa: His daughter
Philaster: Rightful heir to the crown of Sicily
Pharamond: Prince of Spain
Dion, Cleremont and Thrasaline: Lords
Euphrasia: Daughter of Dion, disguised as Bellario, a page
Galatea and Megra: Court ladies
SCENE Messina

Plot

ACT ONE The talk at the court of Messina is of the forthcoming marriage between the princess Arethusa and Pharamond, Prince of Spain. The King intends settling the kingdoms of Sicily and Calabria on the pair after their

marriage, to the outrage of the lords of Messina: Pharamond has failed to win respect at court, while Philaster,
who, as the son of the deposed king of Sicily is legal heir to
the crown, is popular with his countrymen. When the
marriage agreement is ratified before the court, Philaster
presents his claim to Sicily, to the anger of the King, who is
nonetheless sufficiently aware of his rival's popularity to
avoid taking action against him.

Shortly after her engagement has been announced,
Arethusa summons Philaster to her chamber and declares
that she loves him; he returns her feelings, and offers his
young page, Bellario, to run messages between them.

ACT TWO Bellario, who clearly loves Philaster with a rare
degree of affection, is reluctant to leave his service for
Arethusa's, and does so only at his master's insistence.
Pharamond, meanwhile, who has already approached the
indignant Arethusa with a suggestion that they anticipate
their marriage, feels justified, given that 'the constitution of
my body will never hold out till the wedding' (I.ii) in
seeking the necessary satisfaction elsewhere. He first
approaches Galatea, who is dismissive, but finds a warmer
reception from Megra, who is notorious for her promiscuity.
Primed by Galatea, Arethusa, who has been waiting for the
means to destroy her father's good opinion of Pharamond,
arrives with the King at Pharamond's lodging and discovers him, with Megra, at an upstairs window. When the
King threatens Megra with public humiliation, she
counters with an accusation of a sexual relationship between
Arethusa and Bellario.

ACT THREE The idea of Arethusa's impurity has taken root
at court, and is especially bruited by those lords who would
like to see the succession go to Philaster. Knowing nothing
of their hero's love for Arethusa, the lords tell him of
Arethusa's loose behaviour (out of which political capital
might be made), Dion going so far as to assert that he took
Arethusa and Bellario in the act. When Philaster confronts
Arethusa and Bellario with what he has heard, they are
emphatic in their protestations of innocence, but Philaster

is tortured with doubt; and parting from them both forever, he determines to withdraw from Messina.

ACT FOUR takes place in the woods outside the city where the King is leading a hunting party; himself convinced of the rumours surrounding his daughter, the King has pardoned Pharamond his 'venial trespass'. (IV.i) Arethusa, Bellario and Philaster are wandering separately in the woods, oppressed by their related sorrows. Coming across Arethusa, Philaster is moved by jealousy to attack her; he is himself attacked and wounded by a countryman; to avoid discovery of himself as Arethusa's attacker, Philaster then wounds the sleeping Bellario so that he will be taken for the criminal. The King, meanwhile, alarmed by the loss of his daughter, has organized a search party. The wounded Arethusa is found, Bellario is accused of the crime and, in the hearing of Philaster, confesses his guilt. Philaster is then moved to confess himself. The criminals are given to Arethusa, at her own request, so that 'I may appoint/Their tortures and their deaths.' (IV.iv)

ACT FIVE The people are incensed to the point of rebellion by the purposed execution of Philaster, and Dion, Cleremont and Thrasaline determine to champion the deposed Prince's cause. In prison, Philaster is at last convinced of Arethusa's and Bellario's fidelity to himself and the three are reconciled. When the King summons his daughter and her prisoners, they present him with the news that Arethusa and Philaster are married. The King is appalled and is prepared to cast off Arethusa and to go ahead with the execution of Philaster, when he learns that the citizens are rioting and have taken Pharamond prisoner. The King now reverses his position completely, promising Philaster the Princess and the Kingdom if he can calm the situation.

Peace is restored and Pharamond, returned unharmed by Philaster, is told by the King that he must leave Messina, taking his paramour, Megra, with him. At this point Megra revives the accusations against Arethusa and Bellario. The King is prepared to execute the page so that this particular thorn in his flesh might be permanently removed, when

Bellario reveals 'himself' to be Euphrasia, Dion's lost daughter. She tells how she fell in love with Philaster, but because he was so much above her in fortune, was content to serve him as his page. Her father, meanwhile, was told that she was going on a pilgrimage. The sordid rumours are now definitively proved to be unfounded, and arrangements are made for Euphrasia, who has sworn a vow of chastity in deference to her continuing love for Philaster, to live with Philaster and Arethusa after their marriage.

Critical commentary

Philaster was first performed just as Shakespeare was about to embark on the final phase of his career, as a writer of courtly romances. Inevitably, therefore, since it is now assumed that Shakespeare was influenced by the younger Beaumont and Fletcher, part of our interest in *Philaster* is in the similarities of approach that it shares with Shakespeare's romances. In *Philaster*, the chastity or otherwise of the heroine is central to the movement of the plot, as it is in *Cymbeline* and *The Winter's Tale*; Philaster, the legal heir to high office, recovers his inheritance, as the King's sons do in *Cymbeline* and Prospero in *The Tempest;* the final reconciliation is achieved through marriage, as it is in *The Winter's Tale* and *The Tempest*; the pastoral interlude, which is used by Shakespeare to bring his characters from discord to renewal, is suggested in *Philaster* in the fourth act removal to the woods outside Messina. Above all *Philaster*, like all of Shakespeare's last plays, is a comedy that has all the elements of a tragedy.

There is a striking technical difference between Shakespeare's last plays and his earlier comedies for which the influence of Beaumont and Fletcher's methods may take some responsibility – the increased use of surprise. In Shakespeare's early romantic comedies, as soon as his central characters begin to be threatened by intrigue or by a misinterpretation of their motives, the cavalry, in the form of a character who knows or lights on a vital truth, is shown wittingly or unwittingly to be mounting its rescue operation; in these comedies the presence of a disguised character is made known to the audience at the outset. When Shakespeare turned to the writing of romance at the end of his career, he used surprise the better to suggest life's tragic possibilities, a technique he may well have learned from Beaumont and Fletcher, who employed the cliff-hanging technique to a very much more marked degree. Throughout *Philaster*, until the very last scene, the audience is kept ignorant of the fact that Bellario is a woman, so that for much of the play there is a real possibility that the accusations against Bellario/Euphrasia and Arethusa are justified. That possibility is fostered to the point where Dion can claim to have 'taken' them together (III.i), although Dion's claim is not, when all is finally revealed, either questioned by the other characters or explained by Dion himself: when it outlives its usefulness, the dramatists simply allow it to be quietly forgotten. In other words, surprise is for them a device which operates on the surface of the play as a means of engaging the audience's attention; the surprise does not, as it were, contribute crucially to the play's meaning.

The work of Beaumont and Fletcher and, as we shall see later, of the great Jacobean writers of tragedy, illustrates one of the major changes which occurred in the English theatre around the second decade of the seventeenth century: it became much more a theatre of effect. Some of the effects achieved by Beaumont and Fletcher are magnificent; their verse is capable of lyricism and emotional power. Some of the more magnificent moments, however, are marked by a degree of emotional intensity which is in excess of the situation. There is Arethusa's anxiety on confessing her love for Philaster – 'Now, though thy breath do strike me dead,/(Which know, it may) I have unript my breast' (I.ii) – or the parting Bellario makes from Philaster when the rumours concerning the page's fidelity have first been floated –

> Farewell for evermore!
> If you shall hear that sorrow struck me dead,
> And after find me loyal, let there be
> A tear shed from you in my memory (III.i)

– or Philaster's farewell to Arethusa, when he declares his intention of finding 'Some far place' . . .

> There dig a cave, and speak to birds and beasts
> What woman is, and help to save them from you;
> How heaven is in your eyes, but in your hearts,
> More hell than hell has . . . (III.ii)

Cumulatively, the effect is of emotional attitudinizing, especially since most of these outbursts would be avoided if Bellario's identity were known. If the level in surprise is higher for keeping the audience in the dark, then a saving irony, which would distance the emotional excess is lost. T. S. Eliot wrote of their finer poetic moments:

> Looking closer, we discover that the blossoms of Beaumont and
> Fletcher's imagination draw no sustenance from the soil, but are
> cut and slightly withered flowers stuck into sand.
> (from his essay, 'Ben Jonson')

The gods appear to figure largely in the thinking of their characters. Arethusa attributed her sudden love for Philaster to the gods; and when she learns of Pharamond's infidelity with Megra, she sees behind it the gods stage-managing her destiny and bringing her to Philaster. The King sees the vengeance of the gods (directed against himself for keeping Philaster from his inheritance), in every reversal of fortune – Pharamond's infidelity, the rumours about Arethusa, the loss of Arethusa in the woods. The central device of the play, Euphrasia's disguise as Bellario, which is productive of so much suffering, she feels to be justified by a vow that she made,

> never to be known,
> While there was hope to hide me from men's eyes,
> For other than I seemed that I might ever
> Abide with you. (V.v)

Again, however, the chief function of these references to the gods seems to be to lend dignity to the proceedings rather than to suggest anything relevant about man's relationship with destiny.

Inevitably, Beaumont and Fletcher have proved easier targets than most in the game of exalting Shakespeare by comparing him with less illustrious contemporaries. Marlowe's early death, and the artistic possibilities that died with him, have made him something of a legend; Jonson is now admitted to have done his own thing, and done it with exceptional skill; the later tragic writers (Webster, Tourneur, Middleton) were working in too different a medium from Shakespeare for comparison to be helpful. Beaumont and Fletcher, however, were working along the same lines at the same time; and the critical distinction they have won by influencing a profound change in artistic direction in an older and greater dramatist is more than balanced by the ease with which they can be satirized according to standards set by Shakespeare. It must be said of them, therefore, that they are always entertaining: one would hesitate to make the same claim for either Marlowe or Jonson. If their considerable powers, of versification and control of plot, were too exclusively pressed into the service of keeping their audiences at a high pitch of excitement, then the audiences of the time were more than satisfied with the arrangement.

13 Jacobean Tragedy

Sin tastes at the first draught like wormwood water,
But drunk again, 'tis nectar ever after.
Woman Beware Women (II.ii)

The writers of tragedy under James I and Charles I took their inspiration almost exclusively from Italy – the land of poisoners, of corrupt churchmen and of palaces vibrating with illicit sexual activity. The world of Jacobean tragedy is one of whispered intrigue in dimly lit corridors, of revenge and counter-revenge and of accidental slaughter; a world where advancement at court depends on success as a bawd and the pander figure has been promoted to the status of anti-hero. Daylight rarely penetrates: the action is confined to rooms and closets and often to the hours between midnight and dawn. Natural imagery is almost unknown; more usual are the images derived from death, corruption and gluttonous feeding.

We can detect in Jacobean tragedy, as in so many of the changes in the theatre after 1600, the influence of both the new private indoor theatres and of the court. The former attracted more sophisticated audiences than the noisier amphitheatres, audiences who liked to see lords and ladies in the grip of violent and often unholy passion, and who did not demand that their tragedy be seasoned with broad comedy. There is humour in these plays, but of a satiric kind, and there are a number of affinities between Tourneur's and Middleton's plays particularly and Jonson's comedy of humours. All of the writers represented here

(Tourneur, Webster, Middleton and Ford) satisfied the court taste for casually witty deaths and often spectacular stage effects; their plots reflect the division between court and country which was a marked feature of the reigns of the first two Stuart kings. There are differences between them, however. Middleton and Tourneur are up to a point commenting on and judging the very taste for which they are catering; Webster and Ford, while they may be capable of 'finer' emotional effects (this is truer of Webster than of the attitudinizing Ford) are too engaged by their own creations to be able to judge them. There is a sense in which the plays of Webster and Ford endorse the more corrupt standards of the Jacobean court.

The Revenger's Tragedy, by Cyril Tourneur

CYRIL TOURNEUR was born between 1570 and 1580. His career was not primarily that of a man of the theatre: he was in the service of the Cecil and the Vere families both in England and abroad (the latter including a military mission in the Low Countries). His literary output was meagre: *The Transformed Metamorphosis*, a satirical poem published in 1600; three plays, *The Revenger's Tragedy* (1607), *The Atheist's Tragedy* (1611) and *The Nobleman* (1611-12); and a handful of occasional poems. Even *The Revenger's Tragedy* is not unarguably his – authorship claims have been made for most of the other dramatists who were working at the time in the satiric tragic convention – but he does seem the most likely candidate. It is greatly superior to *The Atheist's Tragedy*, to which it nonetheless bears many affinities.

DATE 1607

CHARACTERS

The Duke and Duchess

Lussurioso: The Duke's son

Spurio: A bastard son of the Duke's
Ambitioso ⎫
Supervacuo ⎬ Duchess's sons by a previous marriage
Younger son ⎭
Vindice: A revenger, known in disguise as Piato
Hippolito: His brother, in the service of Lussurioso
Castiza: Their sister
Gratiana: Their mother
Antonio: A noble
SCENE A city in Italy

Plot

ACT ONE Vindice's one-time beloved was poisoned by the Duke some nine years before the action of the play for refusing to surrender her virginity to him; Vindice's father recently died of melancholy occasioned by the Duke's ill-treatment. Amply provided with justification, Vindice is bent on revenge, when opportunity indirectly presents itself through his brother Hippolito, who is newly returned from the Duke's court: Lussurioso, who is Hippolito's master and the Duke's son, is looking to take into his service 'A man that were for evil only good' (I.i), and Vindice determines to disguise himself as just such a man – Piato – as an entrée into court. Lussurioso accepts Piato's lack of moral scruple at face value and employs him to corrupt the stubbornly chaste Castiza, Vindice's and Hippolito's own sister.

Further examples of corruption at court are provided in the trial of the Duchess's Younger Son for the rape of the Lord Antonio's wife (the lady subsequently committed suicide), when judgment is postponed in deference to the young man's social position; and in the wooing of the Duke's bastard son, Spurio, by his stepmother, the Duchess, who is not only promiscuous but wants vengeance on the Duke for not giving her younger son a free pardon.

ACT TWO Vindice, as Piato, finds his sister Castiza proof against all his blandishments on Lussurioso's behalf; but to his mortification, his mother Gratiana is easily swayed by his offers of luxury and promises to do what she can to change Castiza's mind. Returned to court, he reports his partial success to Lussurioso, whom he tells besides of the assignation planned for that night by the Duchess and Spurio, the details of which he has overheard. When Lussurioso enters the Duchess's chamber with drawn sword he finds, not the guilty scene he expected, but the Duke in bed with his wife; Lussurioso is led off to prison for attempting to take his father's life. The Duchess's sons, Ambitioso and Supervacuo, do their best to exploit Lussurioso's disgrace to their own advantage, but the Duke is persuaded by some of his nobles to pardon his son and heir.

ACT THREE Unknown to Ambitioso and Supervacuo, Lussurioso is released from prison. They themselves arrive at the prison with the Duke's signet and order for their 'brother's' execution, and are thus the unwitting causes of their natural brother's, Younger Son's, death.

The Duke, meanwhile, has heard of 'Piato's' serviceability as a pandar and commissions him to acquire a chaste lady who is ripe for corruption. The time for Vindice's revenge has now come. He summons the Duke to a remote assignation where the skull of Vindice's own poisoned mistress has been arranged in velvet; when the Duke, on Vindice's advice, kisses her, he sucks poison from her mouth. During the Duke's protracted death agony Vindice and Hippolito reveal themselves as avengers. They have one last painful surprise in store for the Duke as they force him to witness the incestuous meeting of Spurio and the Duchess, whose choice of rendezvous, known to Vindice, had determined the scene of the Duke's murder.

ACT FOUR Throughout this act the Duke's body, and so the fact of his death, remain undiscovered. Lussurioso dismisses 'Piato' from his service for sending him to the Duchess's chamber and consequently bringing him so close to death; he then asks Hippolito whether his brother, who has never yet appeared at court, would be prepared to enter his service. Game for anything, Vindice presents himself as

himself to Lussurioso and is employed to murder 'Piato';
the incentive Lussurioso offers Vindice for the murder is that
'Piato' tried to corrupt Castiza, in defiance of Lussurioso's
orders. Vindice and Hippolito devise a scheme for cir-
cumventing the unusual predicament in which they find
themselves. which is put into effect in Act Five. Their fears
for their sister's honour are finally calmed when they visit
her and Gratiana: their mother is sincerely repentant and
Castiza as unremittingly chaste as ever.

ACT FIVE The Duke's body is dressed by Vindice and
Hippolito in 'Piato's' clothes. When the brothers arrive
with Lussurioso to murder 'Piato', the Duke's body is
discovered and 'Piato' is assumed to have been the murderer. Lussurioso has now succeeded his father. His first act
is to dismiss the Duchess from his palace, his second to
celebrate his succession with revelry, on the persuasion of
the court.

Hippolito and Vindice find two disaffected nobles to join
them in a masque which is to form part of the celebrations.
At a predetermined point, the masquers step out of their
parts and kill the audience, which consists of Lussurioso and
three companions. A second masque, also devised with
Lussurioso's death as object, is provided by Ambitioso,
Supervacuo, Spurio and another lord. Finding their victim
already dead, the second set of masquers slaughter each
other to establish the right to succeed Lussurioso. When the
Lord Antonio, who is now the obvious successor, is brought
by Vindice and Hippolito to view the carnage, he assumes
that Ambitioso *et al.* were responsible for Lussurioso's
murder, but he is still baffled about the Duke's death.
Vindice makes the mistake of thinking that Antonio will be
on his side because of his own reasons (the rape and suicide
of his wife) for requiring vengeance on the Duke's family.
He tells the new Duke the part that he and Hippolito
played in events, and Antonio, not unreasonably thinking
them too hot to handle, has the pair led off to execution.

Critical commentary

The Revenger's Tragedy is set in a stiflingly enclosed and corrupt court, the 'accursed palace' (I.i), that Vindice holds responsible for his mistress's and father's deaths. A court and country division (which historically was a reflection of Tourneur's own times) is present in the play in the opposing standards of Vindice's home and the Duke's court, where both his brother and father were driven to seek preferment and favour. Vindice, disguised as 'Piato', 'the child o' the court' (I.iii), has decided in advance on the details of his manner: 'Impudence', the 'goddess of the palace', is clearly the right approach, since 'blushes dwell in the country'. (I.iii) Blushes distinguish country-dwellers only as long as they stay in the country, however, and one of Vindice's obsessions is the vulnerability of women to luxury and fine clothes. His own mother and sister are subjected by him to tests of their virtue; the skull of his beloved, who was presumably chaste enough to warrant the revenge he devises for her death, is addressed as though it belonged to a noted courtesan:

> Madam, his grace will not be absent long;
> Secret? Ne'er doubt us madam. 'Twill be worth
> Three velvet gowns to your ladyship. Known?
> Few ladies respect that; disgrace? A poor thin shell!
> 'Tis the best grace you have to do it well. (III.v)

The chief figures at court – the Duke and Duchess and their various offspring – are marked by a total lack of political concern. Elizabethan tragedies all give some idea of the wider public role of the great, but in *The Revenger's Tragedy* (as in other tragedies of the period) royal position and prestige are valued for the unique opportunities that they provide for sensual gratification. With so much readily and unquestioningly available to tempt their appetites, the nobility in *The Revenger's Tragedy* suffer from jaded palates, which can only be sharpened by the unusual and the decadent. When 'Piato' suggests to Lussurioso that, if he desires Castiza as much as he claims, he should marry her, Lussurioso is clear about the nature of the pleasure he is seeking: 'Give me my bed by stealth – there's true delight;/What breeds a loathing in't but night by night?' (I.iii) The Duke is delighted by 'Piato's' account of the diffidence of the lady he has procured for him: 'Give me that sin that's robed in holiness.' (III.v) The Duchess finds an added relish in the incestuous aspect of her relation with Spurio: 'Why there's no pleasure sweet but it is sinful.' (III.v)

If the pleasures of the court are pleasant in proportion to their deviousness, so for Vindice and Hippolito the manner of killing is as important as the moral compulsion to revenge. When Vindice has explained to his brother his scheme for the Duke's death, Hippolito is frankly admiring: 'Brother I do applaud thy constant vengeance,/The quaintness of thy malice, above thought.' (III.v) 'The quaintness of thy malice': one of the links between Tourneur and the satiric comedy of, say, Jonson, is that the hero in both is distinguished by his superior wit rather than by the quality of his suffering (as in Kyd and Shakespeare). The deaths for which Vindice is responsible – the poisoning of the Duke by the skull of the lady that he poisoned, the slaughter of the revellers by the masquers – are sick jokes; his attitude towards his victims is satiric rather than passionate. When the Duke is found in 'Piato's' clothes, Vindice comments: 'Oh, rascal, was he not ashamed/To put the Duke into a greasy doublet.' (V.i) Like Jonson's hero Volpone, Vindice is finally trapped, not through the skill of others in catching him, but because he cannot resist the temptation of boasting about his own cleverness to Antonio.

Tourneur borrowed from Kyd a revenge pattern for his tragedy, but he was working more within the new horror mode: Jacobean audiences, perhaps themselves more decadent than those of an earlier generation, relished 'quaintness' and surprise.

There is no suggestion in *The Revenger's Tragedy* however, of sensationalism for its own sake. If Tourneur's irony is comic rather than pathetic or tragic, it is nonetheless effective in placing and distancing the degeneracy of his characters. Indeed, one of his claims to distinction is his skill in conveying his own personal vision of the human condition – which he sees as a frenzied search for immediate sensual gratification – through his play. At its most trite, he uses an emblematic technique in the skull that Vindice carries with him. Since his beloved's death, Vindice is neither lured by the flesh nor emotionally committed to the immediate moment; like Hamlet, he is more aware than the other characters of the fact of death. For him, the urgent demands of the flesh are seen within the perspective lent by the fleshless skull. More subtle than the use of the skull to convey this vision, however, are the verbal echoes. Numerical criticism is at best unreliable, but it is nonetheless remarkable the mileage that Tourneur gets from the word 'minute': 'one false minute' (I.ii), 'vicious minute' (I.vi), 'The third part of a minute' (III.iii), 'a bewitching minute' (III.v). The effect is double-edged. A minute is time enough to effect radical changes – for a virgin to lose her virginity, a child to be conceived, a kingdom to fall; on the other hand, placed against a backdrop of eternity, all the things that men strive to gain and retain have as little durability as a brief minute:

> I have been witness
> To the surrenders of a thousand virgins
> And not so little;
> I have seen patrimonies washed apieces,
> Fruit fields turned into bastards,
> And in a world of acres
> Not so much dust due to the heir 'twas left to
> As would well gravel a petition. (I.iii)

This speech of Vindice's has about it the urgency of some of Shakespeare's *Sonnets* on time, in which human activity is seen as a process of rushing headlong to oblivion.

As commentator, Vindice speeds up the passage of time to a breathless rate; in the same way food – a characteristic source of imagery for Tourneur – is pictured as leaping off plates, demanding to be eaten:

> the stirring meats
> Ready to move out of the dishes
> That e'en now quicken when they're eaten. (II.i)

The dynamism of food in the play is dependent on its sexual connotations: sex, so eagerly sought and schemed for, is over in a minute, its satisfactions no more durable than the satisfactions that may be derived from food.

In *The Revenger's Tragedy*, an ethical standard for the preoccupation of the court is provided by the satire; the stance adopted by the hero, Vindice, the imagery and the texture of the language all extend the scale of reference by which the court activities are judged to include eternity.

John Webster

Very little is known with any degree of certainty about John Webster. He was unlikely to have been born later than 1582 because by 1602 he was collaborating on plays for the Admiral's Men and Worcester's Men. In 1612 *The White Devil* was acted, followed shortly by *The Duchess of Malfi*, and by *The Devil's Law Case* between 1617 and 1619. Otherwise, he wrote and possibly edited some character sketches which were published in 1605, and he collaborated on plays with Marston, Dekker, Ford and others. *The White Devil* and *The Duchess of Malfi* are enough to establish his reputation as the foremost writer of tragedy in the Jacobean period. He died some time between 1625 and 1635.

The White Devil

DATE 1612

CHARACTERS

Monticelso: A Cardinal, afterwards Pope Paul IV

Francisco de Medicis: Duke of Florence; in the fifth act disguised as a Moor, Mulinassar

Isabella: Francisco's sister
Duke of Brachiano: Husband of Isabella, in love with Vittoria
Giovanni: Brachiano's young son
Flamineo: Secretary to Brachiano
Marcello: Flamineo's brother and an attendant on the Duke of Florence
Vittoria Corombona: Their sister; first married to Camillo, then to Brachiano
Camillo: Vittoria's husband
Cornelia: Mother of Flamineo, Marcello and Vittoria
Ludovico: A Count
SCENE Italy – Rome and Padua

Plot

ACT ONE Apart from the short opening scene in which the Count Ludovico talks of the banishment that has been inflicted on him for his various crimes, and of the grudge that he in consequence holds against the Duke of Brachiano, whom he holds responsible for his banishment, Act One is confined to the house of Vittoria and Camillo. Vittoria despises her husband and her brother Flamineo, who will stop at nothing for advancement, has promised his master, the Duke of Brachiano, that he will procure Vittoria for him as his mistress. By manipulating Camillo, Flamineo manages to bring Brachiano and Vittoria together, but the lovers' preliminary meeting is interrupted by Vittoria's mother, Cornelia, who forces Brachiano to leave the house. ACT TWO Brachiano's infatuation for Vittoria has become common knowledge, and his indignant brother-in-law, Francisco de Medicis, and the Cardinal Monticelso attempt to reconcile Brachiano to his wife, Isabella. Privately, Brachiano tells his wife that he will never sleep with her again, but the saintly Isabella, who wants to avoid ill-feeling between her husband and brother, publicly announces that she has herself forsworn her husband's bed. She departs from Rome to their home in Padua.

Two counter-schemes are meanwhile being prepared: Monticelso is sending his cousin, Camillo, to sea with Marcello (Vittoria's and Flamineo's brother) so that in his absence Vittoria and Brachiano might provide proof of their adultery; at the same time, Brachiano is arranging with Flamineo for the murder of Isabella and Camillo. The inconvenient wife is poisoned by a compliant doctor in Padua; Camillo is murdered on board ship by Flamineo. When Camillo's death is discovered, Vittoria, Flamineo and Marcello, who has remained virtuously ignorant of the intrigue and of the murder, are apprehended.

ACT THREE At the trial following Camillo's murder, attention focuses on Vittoria, who is acquitted of murdering her husband but found guilty of adultery; her brothers are cleared of murder. Monticelso sentences Vittoria to detention in a 'house of coventites' (penitent whores). After the trial, word is brought to Francisco of his sister Isabella's death; the bearer of the news is the Count Ludovico, who was in love with Isabella and who learns by the end of the act that he has been pardoned for his misdemeanours.

ACT FOUR Monticelso and Francisco discuss methods of revenge on Brachiano, whom they rightly assume to be responsible for Isabella's death, but Francisco keeps his plans to himself. His first step is to write a letter to the imprisoned Vittoria which he insists must be delivered in Brachiano's presence (the latter is known to be haunting the penitential house). The letter is indeed intercepted by Brachiano, who is incensed to jealousy by Francisco's declaration of love for Vittoria. When he is convinced that Vittoria is innocent of any liaison with Francisco, however, he adopts from the letter, as Francisco had intended he should, the plan outlined there to remove Vittoria from the house of conventites and take her off and marry her. In the closing scene of Act Four, Menticelso is elected Pope, and his first act is to excommunicate Brachiano and Vittoria; he learns under the seal of the confessional that Ludovico has been sworn by Francisco to the murder of Brachiano.

ACT FIVE In Padua, Brachiano and Vittoria are celebrating

their marriage in some style. Brachiano is greatly impressed by a Moor, Mulinassar (Francisco in disguise), to whom he has offered a pension in return for military service; sharing in the 'Moor's' glory are his two religious companions (one of them Ludovico in disguise).

As a kind of curtain-raiser to the more spectacular acts of revenge to come, Flamineo, in the presence of his mother, Cornelia, runs Marcello through with his sword; the virtuous brother's offence had been an attack on Flamineo's lasciviousness. Brachiano pardons his new brother-in-law by warning him that from henceforth he will be on daily probation for his life, but Brachiano himself dies before his threats can become effective: the cause of his death is a hat that has been poisoned by Ludovico. At the close of his protracted death agony, Ludovico, closeted with the dying man in his 'religious' capacity, reveals Francisco's hand in the murder.

Ludovico's task is not yet over: he surprises Vittoria in her bedchamber where she is being threatened by Flamineo (now that Brachiano's estate is in Vittoria's hands, her brother is demanding a cash settlement). Brother and sister are dispatched to their deaths by Ludovico, who is discovered by Brachiano's son, Giovanni, and taken off to torture and justice.

Critical commentary

The White Devil, like *The Revenger's Tragedy*, is on one level a fable of the corrupting influence of the court on the country. Vittoria's dying words are: 'O happy they that never saw the court,/Nor ever knew great men but by report.' (V.vi) Cornelia and Marcello do their best to uphold the traditional values and to preserve Vittoria from the primrose path that leads to perdition, but they are powerless against Flamineo, who feels that his poverty gives him the right to use any foul means available to advance himself at court. When his mother accuses him of acting as pimp for his own sister, he turns the blame back on her:

I would fain know where lies the mass of wealth
Which you have hoarded for my maintenance,
That I may bear my beard out of the level
Of my lord's stirrup. (I.ii)

The White Devil is Flamineo's story as much as Vittoria's. Having gained his precarious foothold in the world of the Italian nobility, he is playing the system as he finds it: as in *The Revenger's Tragedy*, the ability to procure beautiful and compliant ladies is almost the first condition of service at court.

The moral bias of *The White Devil*, however, is by no means as clear as Tourneur's in *The Revenger's Tragedy*. To some extent, a looseness of structure – now acknowledged to be one of Webster's weaknesses as a dramatist – is responsible. One of the most glaring examples of the structural weakness is the disproportionate space allowed to Monticelso; present at all the moments of public drama, representing at times clerical deviousness, elsewhere unimpeachable orthodoxy, his role in the play is never finally defined, unless we allow ourselves the unworthy thought that Webster includes him as the statutory red-frocked cardinal demanded by English audiences for authentic Italian flavour. Considerable attention is paid to his election as Pope, largely, one suspects, because the process satisfied Webster's preoccupation with the details of ritual.

Indeed, despite the attempts of a number of twentieth-century academic critics to impose a structured order on Webster's plays through dramatic conventions or imagery, it is the set-pieces of heightened drama – Webster's own primary interest as a dramatist – to which the audience or reader responds. In *The White Devil* there are many such, the longer with a formal pattern of their own and the potential for performance as separate interludes. The highly ritualized bringing together of Vittoria and Brachiano in the first act is followed by the formally impassioned public exchanges between Francisco and Brachiano about the future of the latter's marriage. The manner of dying of both Camillo and Isabella is gruesomely depicted in mime for the benefit of Brachiano and the audience; Vittoria's magnificent trial scene — which provides high drama enough for any audience – is immediately followed by an effective but largely unnecessary episode in which Flamineo pretends to be mad. Brachiano's suspicions of Vittoria's infidelity with Francisco are remarkable for their passionate intensity; each of the murders of the final act is lovingly lingered over. Webster cannot leave anything alone until he has wrung it dry of emotion.

Yet the episodic structure, while it adds little to our overall sense of the play, does nonetheless create a powerful cumulative effect. The close network of family relationships (brother and sister, a bond in which Webster was particularly interested, in Flamineo and Vittoria and Francisco and Isabella; mother and child in Cornelia and her offspring and in Isabella and Giovanni; even the cousinly interest which links Camillo and Monticelso), coupled with the play's ceremonial aspects, suggest a world of public people whose private passions and grievances most naturally express themselves through overtly dramatic means. Webster's characters are essentially theatrical.

In the nineteenth century, a revival of interest in Webster concentrated on his portrayal of character. In fact, his characterization is remarkable neither for analytical penetration or consistency, but his characters – and in this lay their appeal for the late nineteenth-century Aesthetic Movement – have great presence and sense of style. Few dramatists have had as highly developed a gift as Webster for the magnificent utterance which dignifies the speaker; this, even more than his lack of structural control, confuses the moral issues. In *The White Devil* it is Vittoria who has been most lavishly endowed with Webster's poetic gifts. At her trial she gives a superb rebuff to the assumption of the court that, because Brachiano loved her, she must have returned his love:

> Condemn you me for that the Duke did love me?
> So may you blame some fair and crystal river,
> For that some melancholic distracted man
> Hath drown'd himself in't. (III.ii)

We know her to be guilty, but that knowledge in no way modifies our reaction to the poetry. When Brachiano accuses her, on the strength of the trick letter, of double-dealing with Francisco, she brings him to heel with her repudiation of him:

> I had a limb corrupted to an ulcer,
> But I have cut it off; and now I'll go
> Weeping to heaven on crutches. (IV.ii)

Her manner of dying, her insistence on being killed before her maid – 'my servant/Shall never go before me' (V.vi) – is reminiscent of Shakespeare's Cleopatra. The difference is that Shakespeare's total grasp of Cleopatra keeps us aware that her style is a weapon in her armoury which is deliberately deployed by her until, by the end of the play, her personality and her style have fused. Webster, on the other hand, is himself dazzled by Vittoria's style. His gift is in the quality of his characters' reactions, and those reactions are ends in themselves.

In Webster's world, the urgent submission to physical desire is accompanied by a fear of death and of the unknown: Hell, 'the black lake' (V.ii), 'the soul's slaughter house' (V.vi), is an ever-present possibility. The fear is communicated to the audience by protracted scenes of death and of mourning. The poison in Brachiano's 'beaver' takes immediate effect, but is nonetheless a slow killer, giving Webster ample time to concentrate on the dying man's agony of mind and body: 'On pain of death, let no man name death to me;/It is a word infinitely terrible.' (V.iii) The irony – of the powerful temporal leader who meets his match in death – is a commonplace in the work of most Jacobean dramatists, who used death as the most potent means of giving a broad context to the sensuality of their characters. As protracted as Brachiano's death agony is Cornelia's mourning for her son, Marcello. Neither of them is a major character, and Webster's concentration on them, amid all his other concerns of the final act, might be felt to lack balance. In the final act, however, the cumulative sense of horror – one of Webster's specialities – is more important than the individuals involved, as the generalized quality of Cornelia's wailing over her son illustrates;

> Can blood so soon be washed out? let me see;
> When screech owls croak up on the chimney tops,
> And the strange cricket i' th' oven sings and hops,
> When yellow spots do on your hands appear,
> Be certain that you of a corse shall hear. (V.iv)

Academic defenders of Webster usually underplay the 'screech-owl' element in his work; for audiences, however, it is a major part of his attraction.

The Duchess of Malfi

DATE 1613-14

CHARACTERS

Ferdinand: Duke of Calabria
Cardinal: His brother
Duchess of Malfi: Their sister
Antonio Bologna: The Duchess's steward who becomes her second husband
Daniel de Bosola: Gentleman of horse to the Duchess
Cariola: The Duchess's woman
Delio: Antonio's friend
SCENE Italy

Plot

ACT ONE Ferdinand and the Cardinal, neither of whom is a model in political or ecclesiastical virtue, are imperative in their demands on their recently widowed sister, the Duchess of Malfi, that she should not remarry. To forestall the possibility, Ferdinand insinuates a spy into her home – Bosola, who, at Ferdinand's request, is given the position of the Duchess's gentleman of horse. The brothers' precautions are ineffectual, however, since she has already fallen in love with her steward, Antonio. Solemnly and privately, the

Duchess and Antonio betrothe themselves, with Cariola, the Duchess's woman, as witness.

ACT TWO Bosola, suspecting that the Duchess is pregnant, acquires some of the first apricots of the season for her. She eats them greedily and falls into a premature labour. Antonio, who is known simply as the Duchess's steward, hints that the apricots may have been poisoned and orders everybody to keep to his room so that the risk of the Duchess being heard in labour is minimized. After the Duchess has been delivered of a son, Bosola discovers proof of the event in the form of a horoscope drawn up for the newly born child which has been dropped by Antonio. That Antonio is implicated is now clear, but Bosola suspects the steward of being the Duchess's pimp rather than her lover. When Ferdinand and the Cardinal hear of their sister's lust – it does not occur to them that she might be, as she considers herself, married – they swear vengeance on both the Duchess and her partner in sin.

ACT THREE The revenge is slow in arriving, for Antonio tells his trusted friend Delio, to whom he had earlier confided the secret of his marriage, that the Duchess has produced two more children. His family's immediate situation is particularly fraught with danger since Ferdinand, under the guise of friendship, is now visiting his sister.

In her bedchamber the Duchess, thinking that Antonio is with her (he and Cariola have playfully hidden themselves) is speaking intimately as to a lover when Ferdinand steals up on her. She suffers her brother's rage (he leaves her a poniard – a clear invitation to kill herself before a nastier fate overtakes her), and when Ferdinand has gone she tells Antonio to fly to Ancona. She will follow him under the pretence of making a pilgrimage to the holy shrine at Loretto.

After Antonio's departure, the Duchess makes the mistake of thinking that Bosola is sympathetic to her plight. She tells him that Antonio is her husband, and the details of their escape plans; when the information has been passed on to the Cardinal, he uses his power to have Antonio and the Duchess banished from Ancona. Antonio and their oldest child flee to Milan, the Duchess and the younger children are apprehended by Bosola and forced to return to Malfi.

ACT FOUR is devoted to Ferdinand's ingeniously horrific revenge on the Duchess. Professing a desire for reconciliation, he asks to visit her in her chamber – but without lights, since he has sworn never to see her again. Under cover of darkness he extends a hand – not, as the Duchess naturally expects, his own, but a dead hand belonging, he tells her, to Antonio. Light is then thrown on 'artificial figures of Antonio and his children, appearing as if they were dead'. She is then forced to endure the representation that Ferdinand has prepared of her madness in marrying Antonio – a masque performed, under Bosola's directions, by madmen borrowed from the local institution. Her own coffin, cords and a bell are then brought in as a prelude to her strangling by executioners; Cariola and the Duchess's two children share her fate. Now that his vengeance has been achieved, Ferdinand holds Bosola responsible for obeying orders which he now regrets and refuses to pay him.

ACT FIVE In Milan, Antonio, who is ignorant of his wife's death, tells Delio of his plan to visit the Cardinal in the night with his son, in the hope of moving his brother-in-law to pity. Ferdinand, meanwhile, has gone mad since his sister's death, but the Cardinal, when he is approached by Bosola, appears to think that the Duchess is still alive. Bosola uses the Cardinal's mistress, Julia, to discover the extent of the Cardinals' knowledge, and hence culpability; as soon as the Cardinal confesses his responsubility to Julia, he murders her. Bosola is now penitent towards the wronged Antonio and determined to avenge himself on those he considers to be the real culprits. In the confusion created by the dark, however, he murders Antonio, who has arrived on his peace visit, instead of Ferdinand. He achieves his mark with the Cardinal, however. Bosola, himself mortally wounded by Ferdinand manages to kill his murderer before his own death. Delio arrives on the scene of carnage with

Antonio's eldest son, who alone survives to inherit his mother's property of Malfi.

Critical commentary

In his second, and greater tragedy, Webster again looks at the antithetical values of court and country, but the dramatic context he gives them is rather different from that provided by *The White Devil*, or indeed by any of the other Jacobean tragedies selected here. Where the usual pattern is for the country to be corrupted by the court, in *The Duchess of Malfi* the noble heroine aspires to a life of simple domestic virtue with Antonio, the honest man of lowly birth who maintains his ethical sense amid the temptations and splendours of the court. In the opening scene, he has just returned from a visit to France, whose king, he tells Delio,

> quits first his royal palace
> Of flattering sycophants, of dissolute
> And infamous persons. (I.i)

Implicit in his praise is a criticism of Italian palaces, where flattery and debauchery are the norm. In the same opening conversation with Delio, Antonio displays his clear-sighted judgment of the Duchess's brothers. The cardinal, he says, should have been pope, but made the mistake of bestowing 'bribes so largely and so impudently as if he would have carried it away without heaven's knowledge'. (I.i) His picture of Ferdinand is even more sinister: '– the law to him/Is like a foul black cobweb to a spider.' (I.i) As well as serving the technical function of directing the audience's response to these characters before they appear, Antonio's comments distinguish his own ethical standpoint from that of his future brothers-in-law. In choosing Antonio, the Duchess is also choosing what he represents, and rejecting the standards of her brothers.

Lacking her brothers' imperiousness, the Duchess feels herself hampered by her rank in approaching her steward: 'The misery of us that are born great!/We are forc'd to woo, because none dare woo us.' (I.i) Generally, in tragedies of this period, rank is not only synonymous with power but, to extend Antonio's metaphor, it is a web in which smaller flies are trapped; what is unusual about the Duchess's plight is that she is the one who feels trapped, by her own rank:

> The birds that live i' the field
> On the wild benefit of nature live
> Happier than we; for they may choose their mates,
> And carol their sweet pleasures to the spring. (III.v)

In the work of Shakespeare, the natural imagery would come as no surprise, but in Webster's world of ill-lit palaces it is both startling and revealing of the way the dramatist wants us to see his heroine. While she waits for her death, she calls on her rank for support – 'I am Duchess of Malfi still' (IV.ii) – but it is as a mother that we are encouraged to remember her (somewhat incongruously since at this point she believes her children to be dead):

> I pray thee, look thou giv'st my little boy
> Some syrup for his cold, and let the girl
> Say her prayers ere she sleep. (IV.ii)

There are marked similarities between Webster's two villains, Flamineo and Bosola: both are prepared to accept the only path to advancement open to men of their rank in their society. In *The White Devil*, however, Flamineo is well established in villainy at the outset of the play, and we are never encouraged to believe that he might have chosen another life. Bosola's ruin is given a more tragic dimension. Again, Antonio's scene-setting opening conversation with Delio is instructive, indicating Bosola's potential for good and evil, and the likelihood of his taking the more devious course because there is no market for his good qualities:

> 'Tis great pity
> He should be thus neglected: I have heard
> He's very valiant. This foul melancholy
> Will poison all his goodness. (I.i)

Bosola is given his appointment – as the Duchess's gentle-man of horse – on condition that he combine his official duties with those of an informer; but during the course of his service to Ferdinand, he remains aware of his own moral disintegration. That awareness gives him a tragic stature denied to more hardened villains. When, at the end of the play, he wants to make some restitution to the man he has wronged, fate frustrates him as he kills Antonio instead of Ferdinand.

The Duchess of Malfi is a compelling play, filled, like *The White Devil*, with magnificent passages of poetry which fall naturally from the lips of characters wrought to the highest pitch of self-consciousness. There is the Duchess's descrip-tion of her state of mind when she believes Antonio and her children to be dead –

> I'll tell thee a miracle;
> I am not mad yet, to my cause of sorrow:
> The heaven o'er my head seems made of molten brass,
> The earth of flaming sulphur, yet I am not mad ... (IV.ii)

– and unforgettable single lines, like Ferdinand's tribute to his dead sister: 'Cover her face; mine eyes dazzle: she died young.' (IV.ii) Yet there is an excess about the play which suggests that Webster was not fully in command of his own material. Specific theatrical effect is too often sacrificed to overall design. A notable example is Ferdinand's horror of his sister's 'lust':

> I would have their bodies
> Burn't in a coal-pit with the ventage stopp'd,
> That their curs'd smoke might not ascend to heaven;
> Or dip the sheets they lie in in pitch or sulphur,
> Wrap them in't, and then light them like a match. (II.v)

Critics have agreed that Ferdinand's feelings for his sister are unconsciously incestuous; certainly that is a more plausible explanation for his cruelty than the one he offers Bosola – that he hoped to inherit his sister's fortune. In the end, however, it is not motive that matters to Webster so much as maximum dramatic effect. The result, whether he intends it or not, is that Ferdinand seems permanently unhinged, until, when he does indeed go mad – with a madness that takes the sensational form of imagining himself a wolf, in which guise he digs up bodies in churchyards – he becomes a figure of total absurdity. To the extent that Ferdinand's behaviour is pathological, it is deprived of universality; in the same way, the accumulation of horrors in the fourth and fifth acts, while impressive on the stage, leaves one with no sense of the daily horror of ordinary life.

Middleton and Rowley

Thomas Middleton was born in 1580, the son of a London bricklayer. He took a degree from Oxford but, like a number of his university generation, was more attracted by the theatre than by more orthodox pursuits. He married a sister of one of the players and worked for a time under Henslowe, writing citizen comedies and tragicomedies as required. In 1620 he was appointed Chronologer to the City of London – a post which required him to write and direct official entertainments. Possibly because of the financial security, his finest plays, *Women Beware Women*, *The Changeling* and *A Game of Chess* belong to this period. He died in 1627.

William Rowley, born in 1585, was a well-known actor who worked for a time with the Prince Charles's Men and later with the King's Men, specializing in comic roles. He is known to have written four plays of his own (in which his comedy is superior to his tragedy) and to have collaborated on twice that number with Middleton and Webster among others. His chief claim to fame now is the joint authorship with Middleton of *The Changeling*, in which Rowley was mainly responsible for the comic sub-plot and for the madhouse scenes. Critics have tended to regard this sub-plot as the only serious flaw in an otherwise fine tragedy, but

Rowley may well have provided *The Changeling* with the ingredients necessary for success at the time when it was written. He died in 1625.

Women Beware Women

DATE 1621

CHARACTERS

The Duke of Florence
Lord Cardinal: His brother
Bianca: Who becomes the Duke's mistress
Leantio: Bianca's husband
Fabritio: A Florentine gentleman
Isabella: His daughter
Hippolito: Fabritio's brother
Livia: Sister to Fabritio and Hippolito
The Ward: Suitor to Isabella
Guardiano: Guardian and uncle to the Ward
Widow: Mother of Leantio
SCENE Florence

Plot

ACT ONE Leantio, a factor of modest means, has stolen the rich and beautiful Bianca from her father's home and married her. Leantio's mother is disturbed that Bianca might find the arrangements of their house too modest, but her new daughter-in-law professes total contentment.

Another marriage, higher up the echelons of Florentine society, is being arranged by the insensitive Fabritio for his daughter Isabella. The prospective husband, the Ward, is an object of general derision, but Fabritio, who is impressed by the Ward's fortune, orders his daughter to 'Like what you see'. (I.ii) Isabella's plight seems even more desperate when her uncle Hippolito, with whom she enjoys 'friendly solaces and discourse' (I.ii), confesses that his feelings for her have become incestuous.

ACT TWO When Hippolito reveals the state of his affections

to his worldly-wise sister Livia, she offers to do what she can for him. Swearing her niece to secrecy, Livia convinces Isabella that her mother, on her deathbed, confessed to Livia that Isabella's father was a Spanish nobleman. With the incest taboo now removed, Isabella requires little persuading that her wisest course is to marry the Ward and enjoy Hippolito on the side.

Livia's skills as a procuress are now enlisted on behalf of the Duke of Florence. During the annual procession to St Mark's, he spotted Bianca at her mother-in-law's window, and Livia's task is to provide the Duke with access to Bianca. She does this by inviting Leantio's mother (the luckless husband is away on business) to her house, and while she is herself showering the baffled Widow with every kind of civility and attention, Guardiano, the Ward's uncle and Livia's friend, brings Bianca to the Duke under cover of showing her the treasures of Livia's house.

ACT THREE Leantio arrives home to find his previously clinging wife embarrassed by any display of affection and discontented with the accommodation that he has provided for her. The reason for the change becomes clear as Bianca, and then Leantio, are summoned by the Duke to a banquet at Livia's house. Nothing is done to disguise his new role of cuckold from Leantio, who is offered consolation by the Duke in the form of the captainship of Rouens citadel. Further comfort is on hand for him, however, in Livia, who falls immediately in love with the injured husband and succeeds in winning him round with promises of riches and luxury.

ACT FOUR Despite the fact that Leantio is provided for elsewhere, the Duke nonetheless feels that he might become an inconvenience. He tells Hippolito that Leantio has become Livia's lover, which has the desired effect of inflaming Hippolito to the defence of his sister's honour. The need to dispose of Leantio becomes even more urgent when the Duke's brother, the Cardinal, convinces him of the sinfulness of his present way of life.

Hippolito kills Leantio, and Livia, far from displaying

gratitude, tells Guardiano and the Ward, who is now married to Isabella, that the child Isabella is carrying is her uncle's. An apparent reconciliation is effected, however, between the injured parties, and Guardiano suggests that to seal their restored friendship Hippolito, Isabella and Livia take part in an entertainment that he has prepared for the Duke's marriage to Bianca. The Cardinal, meanwhile, is not at all impressed by the Duke's wish to make an honest woman of Bianca, and his pious railing – 'holy ceremonies/ Were made for sacred uses, not for sinful' (IV.iii) – makes an enemy of his new sister-in-law.

ACT FIVE The masque prepared by Guardiano is preceded by an unexpected visit from Hymen, who offers festive cups to the Duke, Bianca and the Cardinal. (They are now reconciled, but Bianca feels that her righteous brother-in-law would be safer dead and has poisoned his cup.) The spectators of the masque are baffled as Isabella, playing a nymph, falls down dead when Juno (Livia) has struck her with flaming gold. Livia herself, however, is the victim of a counter scheme of revenge, and dies from the poisoned incense that Isabella managed to offer her before she died. Hippolito is killed by arrows shot by a row of cupids, and Guardiano, who had foolishly enlisted the services of his Ward, falls, due to the latter's negligence, through a trap door of his own making. The Duke's feeling that the bloody entertainment has provided an inauspicious start to his marriage is proved justified as he falls dead, having drunk the poison prepared for the Cardinal. Bianca then poisons herself and the Cardinal is left to ruminate on the wages of sin.

Critical commentary

Women Beware Women is a unique achievement in Jacobean drama in the balance that Middleton manages to achieve between interest in character and ironic judgment. The corruption of his characters is convincingly human, yet while Middleton will from time to time extend his sympathy towards them, he maintains throughout a judging distance. At no point is he, as Webster certainly is, dazzled by his own creations. The distancing is achieved through the pace of the action, which ensures that the overall design of the play is never unbalanced by the specific emotional responses of individual characters, and by the witty, predominantly satirical approach. A feature of the satirical bias is the way that Middleton's characters, like other characters in plays of the period, enjoy the ingenuity with which they achieve their ends as much as the ends to which that ingenuity is applied. When Guardiano has succeeded in engineering the seduction of Bianca, he indulges in a quiet giggle at the victim's expense:

> I can but smile as often as I think on't!
> How prettily the poor fool was beguil'd,
> How unexpectedly! It's a witty age. (II.ii)

We do not, however, laugh with the superior wits at their discomfited victims, as Jonson encourages us to do in his plays: rather, Middleton keeps to the foreground of our awareness the rottenness of a society that will not only employ but relish the employment of 'deadly snares' (in Bianca's dying words) to trap poor maids.

The multiple sick jokes which conclude the play serve a similar moral purpose. Conventionally 'tragic' deaths, suggestive of the grandeur of the human soul, would be out of the question. Middleton's use of elaborately devised deaths, with their accompanying broad humour – 'Look, Juno's down too'; 'Plague of those cupids' (V.ii) – reflects the debased view of human life held by his characters which the dramatist never endorses.

Corruption is axiomatic to Jacobean tragedy, but Middleton depicts it on a scale which suggests the undermining of an entire society. Roma Gill, in her New Mermaid edition of *Women Beware Women*, argues that Middleton takes as his theme 'the pursuit of money' which 'diminished the character and denied the usual tragic stature'; she sees, moreover, a connection between Middleton's choice of theme and the growing influence of the middle classes which, moralists were agreed, were undermining the traditional virtues. Certainly, no other tragic writer of the period binds his characters so clearly and so exclusively according to a cash nexus. The Duke seduces Bianca with material inducements –

> Do not I know you have cast away your life
> Upon necessities, means merely doubtful
> To keep you in indifferent health and fashion (II.ii)

– while the cuckolded husband's indignation is silenced by the wealth and luxury with which Livia woos and wins him. The incestuous relationship between Isabella and Hippolito is clearly precipitated by her father's financial ambition. Fabritio not only forces his daughter on the highest bidder, but defines her 'dearness' to him ('a dear child', III.ii) strictly according to what she has cost him ('dear to my purse', III.ii). When the Ward hears of Isabella's consent to the marriage, he submits her to a close inspection (of mouth, feet and so on) to reassure himself that he is not being undersold. Isabella allows herself to be sold as the only way of gratifying her own desires. Indeed, she has her aunt's authority that such arrangements are not uncommon, 'For fools will serve to father wise men's children.' (II.i) Although Middleton gives his young girls none of the superficial gloss that Webster gives his heroines, the plight of Bianca and Isabella still has power to move us.

The masterstroke of *Women Beware Women* is the characterization of Livia – surely the most potent image of corruption in Jacobean tragedy. Middleton's portrait of a bad lady is convincing because of his realization that those who purvey sin succeed to the degree that they are reassuring; and Livia's depth as a character depends on her need to reassure herself as well as others. When she has made up her mind to help Hippolito to their niece, she appears to think herself primarily guilty of an excess of good nature: 'This 'tis to grow so liberal – y'have few sisters/That love their brother's ease 'bove their own honesties.' (II.i) It is her apparent good nature that is so dangerous, shown at its most effectively sinister in Act Two, Scene Two, when she occupies Bianca's mother-in-law while Guardiano brings the Duke his prey. Livia is shown winning the old Widow's confidence and disarming her suspicions by presenting herself as comfortingly bourgeois and middle-aged: here they are, two lonely women whose best years are past, wasting their leisure in solitude when they could be enjoying the solace of nice little suppers together, enlivened by gossip and the odd game of chess or draughts, warmed by the 'true hearty love' that should bind neighbours together. She is irresistible. When Bianca, after her seduction, hisses 'damned bawd' at her, Livia is philosophical in that knowledge of human nature on which her success as procuress depends: 'Sin tastes at the first draught like wormwood water,/But drunk again, 'tis nectar ever after.' (II.ii)

Livia is the arch manipulator in a play about the processes of manipulation. The actual game of chess that she plays with Leantio's mother is both a reflection of the more serious game that she is winning with Bianca's seduction and an image which extends through the play of the games which, with more or less skill, most of the characters are playing. They view each other as objects, figures on a chessboard: they scheme for those objects which represent sensual and material gratification and dispose of whatever is luckless enough to stand in their path. Some, like Livia and the Duke, have considerable manipulative skills; others, like Leantio, are mere pawns, with no way of expressing an independent wish or of defending their own square of territory: but all are finally vulnerable. In the primeval world of *King Lear*, Shakespeare depicts a society where – 'Humanity must perforce prey on itself,/Like monsters of the deep'. With consummate skill, Middleton shows in *Women Beware Women* how the manners of a highly polished civilization mask the same relationship between man and man.

The Changeling

DATE 1622

CHARACTERS

Vermandero

Beatrice-Joanna: His daughter

Alonzo de Poracquo: Suitor to Beatrice

Tomazo de Poracquo: His brother

Alsemero: A nobleman in love with Beatrice

Jasperino: His friend

De Flores: Servant to Vermandero

Diaphanta: Beatrice's waiting woman

Alibius: A doctor who runs a madhouse

Isabella: His wife

Antonio: The changeling

Franciscus: A pretend madman

SCENE Alicant

Plot

ACT ONE Beatrice-Joanna is betrothed to Alonzo, but a new acquaintance, Alsemero, has ousted Alonzo in her affections. While plans are going ahead for Beatrice's imminent wedding with Alonzo, her father invites Alsemero (who returns Beatrice's love) to stay at his castle.

In a nearby madhouse, Alibius the doctor has instructed his servant Lollio to keep a tight rein on the movements of his wife during his absence. Lollio is also charged with the care of Antonio, a recently committed idiot.

ACT TWO Beatrice's growing coolness towards Alonzo is noticed by his brother, Tomazo, who rightly attributes the young girl's 'dullness' to love for another man; Vermandero's servant, De Flores, from whom Beatrice experiences a violent and unreasoning aversion, guesses that Alonzo's rival is Alsemero. When Alsemero and Beatrice-Joanna have made their love known to each other, he offers to challenge his rival to a duel, but Beatrice rejects the idea out of fear for her lover's safety. Nonetheless, the murder of Alonzo has now presented itself to her as the easiest way out of her predicament. She says nothing to Alsemero but appeals instead to De Flores, whom she knows to return her hatred with love.

ACT THREE Under cover of showing him 'the full strength of the castle' De Flores stabs the lucklessly inconvenient Alonzo and presents his finger to Beatrice as proof that the deed is accomplished. Beatrice's gratitude is expressed in the three thousand ducats that she offers as wages, but De Flores is insulted. Baffled, she offers him more, but learns to her horror that the reward that the servant has in mind is her virginity. Despite her loathing for De Flores and her love for Alsemero, she is finally brought to submit.

The honour of another lady is being assailed elsewhere as the 'idiot' Antonio, declares his passion for Isabella, revealing that the idiocy was a disguise to gain access to her.

ACT FOUR By now, Alonzo is presumed to have fled Alicant and Vermandero has agreed to Beatrice's marriage to Alsemero. The day of the wedding finds Beatrice fearful that her wedding night will reveal that she is no virgin – the more especially since she finds a selection of phials in Alsemero's cabinet designed to test virginity and pregnancy. Desperate, she approaches her maid Diaphanta with the suggestion that she take her mistress's place in the bridal bed; Beatrice gives her reluctance to embark on sex as the reason. Diaphanta is more than eager to oblige, making it clear that she shares none of her mistress's alleged qualms. Beatrice takes the precaution of testing her maid's virginity with the appropriate phial – which is just as well, for when Alsemero submits his bride to the same test, Beatrice can produce the marks of a sound virgin (gaping, sneezing and giggling) from her observations of Diaphanta.

Isabella, meanwhile, has been approached by Franciscus, another recent inmate of Alibius's madhouse, whose madness, like Antonio's idiocy, was assumed. Both men are now definitively rejected by Isabella. Preparations are afoot in the madhouse for an entertainment of fools and madmen as part of Beatrice's and Alsemero's wedding celebrations.

ACT FIVE Beatrice waits in agony outside her own bed-chamber for Diaphanta to emerge. By the time she does appear, four hours later than the time arranged, Beatrice and De Flores have planned her death: De Flores sets fire to her bedroom and carries the 'stifled' Diaphanta from the flames.

It is now widely assumed that Alonzo was murdered, and his brother Tomazo is crying for justice. Blame is attached to Antonio and Franciscus, Vermandero's men, whose retreat to the madhouse coincided with Alonzo's disappearance. Justice is overtaking the real culprits, however. Alsemero's friend, Jasperino, who has for some time had his suspicions about Beatrice's relationship with De Flores, tells Alsemero of the secret meetings that the pair hold behind locked doors. When her husband accuses Beatrice of being a whore, she denies the sexual charge but confesses to the murder of Alonzo, offering that as the reason for her dealings with De Flores. De Flores himself gives the entire game away, however, and having dealt Beatrice-Joanna her death wound, kills himself.

Critical commentary

It is as well to deal first with Rowley's sub-plot since the changeling of the misleading title is Antonio, the gentleman who disguises himself as an idiot for love of Isabella and whose only reward is to be unjustly accused of murder. Rowley's contribution could be detached without violence from the rest of the play, and the effectiveness of what remained could only be enhanced. The material of the sub-plot is not totally haphazard, however, even if it is inferior in both poetic quality and dramatic impact to what we attribute to Middleton. Isabella, like Beatrice-Joanna, is sexually tempted, and her unassailability provides a kind of standard within the play by which to judge Beatrice. The disguises assumed by the frustrated lovers, Antonio and Franciscus, suggest the connection that other Jacobean writers felt between lust and madness and which has its own applicability to the story of Beatrice-Joanna.

That said, it is indisputable that our chief interest in *The Changeling* is in the magnificent scenes between De Flores and Beatrice-Joanna, and that these require no moral support from a sub-plot: any moral conclusions to be drawn from Beatrice's downfall is implicit in Middleton's dramatic movement. The tragedy of the fallen woman, or more precisely of the falling woman, was of deep interest to all the Jacobean writers of tragedy. Middleton, however, had an insight into the workings of a woman's mind which was second only to Shakespeare's, and Beatrice-Joanna, and Livia in *Women Beware Women*, are among the most memorable female characters of the Jacobean period.

Beatrice-Joanna, the spoilt only daughter, has a potential for evil of which she herself is not even remotely aware at the beginning of the play. Indeed, her downfall is only inevitable once her will is thwarted. The play's opening scene establishes the presence of three strong wills pulling in different directions – an implicit conflict which is at the root of the later catastrophes. Vermandero, urging Beatrice to a speedy conclusion of her engagement to Alonzo, says with genial but nonetheless absolute insistence, 'I'll want/My will else.' (I.i) In an aside, his daughter echoes his words: 'I shall want mine of you do it.' (I.i) More sinisterly, the theme is taken up by De Flores when his betters have left him in sole possession of the stage:

> I know she hates me,
> Yet cannot choose but love her;
> No matter; if but to vex her, I'll haunt her still;
> Though I get nothing else, I'll have my will. (I.i)

Beatrice wants to replace Alonzo with Alsemero with the minimum of fuss and of loss of reputation to herself, and with the minimum of danger to Alsemero. It is important to her that she remain superficially the compliant and dutiful daughter – more important than a respect for the lives and rights of others. The disposal of Alonzo, whom she admits herself that she loved before Alsemero appeared on the scene, never causes her a qualm: she greets the news of his death with 'My joys start at mine eyes.' (III.iv) De Flores for her is just a useful tool: when she first conceives the idea of Alonzo's murder, it is with surprise at her previous blindness to De Flores's usefulness:

> – the ugliest creature
> Creation fram'd for some use, yet to see
> I could not mark so much where it should be. (II.ii)

What she profoundly overlooks, of course, is not just De Flores's personality but the fact that he is a person at all. Her outrage when her servant names the reward that he considers appropriate is more than matched by his: 'Do you place me in the rank of verminous fellows,/To destroy things for wages?' (III.iv) The answer is that she has always 'placed' De Flores where she has always placed everybody – in the role most convenient to herself. Later in the same scene, De Flores's reminder of their complicity is salutary, for to Beatrice it is technical innocence that matters. He goes further: in terms of intention, she is not only a murderess but a whore:

> Though thou writ'st maid, thou whore in thy affection!
> 'Twas chang'd from thy first love, and that's a kind
> Of whoredom in thy heart. (III.iv)

It is partly because De Flores presents her with such an unexpectedly accurate (accurate, indeed, to a degree that she has never contemplated herself) picture of her soul that she submits to the deflowering which, he claims, is already no more than a technicality.

She is still concerned, however, to maintain an unsullied image to the rest of the world, and technical virginity – a requirement both of the suspicious husband and of Beatrice's pride – necessitates the substitution of the maid in the bridal bed. Once Diaphanta has served her purpose, De Flores is clear that she must be despatched to keep her quiet. Beatrice's motives are more complex in that she feels deep resentment at her maid's evident enjoyment of her night's work; she must die, 'That cannot rule her blood to keep her promise'. (V.i) Until her wedding night, Beatrice had failed to experience Diaphanta as a person, with responses of her own: her earlier failure to judge De Flores cost her her virginity, but Diaphanta pays with her life for Beatrice's blinkered judgment.

At the beginning of the play, Beatrice-Joanna feels De Flores to be her antithesis; since all the characters are in agreement about De Flores's physical loathesomeness, she can be forgiven for casting him as the Beast and herself as the Beauty. Middleton invests her loathing, however, with the quality of suppressed attraction – 'This ominous ill-fac'd fellow more disturbs me/Than all my other passions.' (II.i); when she sees him, 'I scarce leave trembling of an hour after.' (II.i) The later Jacobean writers of tragedy (Ford, as we shall see, is another such) are sometimes accused of finding abnormal and devious emotional states more stimulating to the imagination than the more universal. The genius of Middleton's depiction of the relationship between Beatrice-Joanna and De Flores, however, is not just that he makes its psychological peculiarities inherently interesting (though he does), but that the unfolding of that relationship is central to the play's theme: as their curious friendship develops, the audience realizes that it was her own potential for evil that first frightened Beatrice in De Flores. Beatrice herself never achieves that realization. At the very end of the play, from the concealment of the closet in which Alsemero has confined her, she shrilly denies De Flores's claim that she is a whore: 'He lies, the villain does belie me.' (V.iii) Even now, she cannot quite face up to what she has done. What she is aware of, however, as the play proceeds, is the gradual loss of her revulsion from De Flores: 'How heartily he serves me! His face loathes one, /But look upon his care, who would not love him?' (V.i) De Flores is, as it were, the reverse side of her personality that her outside fails to reflect. Unaware to the last, she can respond in him to what she cannot acknowledge in herself.

'Tis Pity She's a Whore, by John Ford

JOHN FORD was born in 1586 and educated at Oxford and at the Inns of Court. He began writing plays in 1613, collaborating with Dekker, Rowley and Webster. In 1633 he published his three great tragedies, *'Tis Pity She's a Whore*, *The Broken Heart* and *Love's Sacrifice*. He died some time after 1639. Ford was one of the earliest writers to be directly influenced by Robert Burton's *Anatomy of Melancholy*; published in 1621, it explored the links between sex, particularly in its more *outré* forms, and psychology, and was to writers like Ford what Freud has been to certain twentieth-century novelists.

DATE Published in 1633

CHARACTERS
Florio: A citizen of Parma
Annabella: His daughter
Giovanni: His son
Soranzo: A nobleman ⎫
Grimaldi: A Roman ⎬ Suitors to Annabella
Bergetto: A fool ⎭
Richardetto: An injured husband disguised as a physician
Hippolita: His wife
Vasques: A servant to Soranzo
Putana: Annabella's tutoress
Bonaventura: A Friar, former tutor to Giovanni

SCENE Parma

Plot

ACT ONE Giovanni confesses to Bonaventura, his friend and one-time tutor, that he loves his sister Annabella with an unlawful passion. Appalled, the Friar persuades the young man to submit to a week of ritualistic breast-beating. Annabella too, whose hand is being sought by the rich but foolish Bergetto, the noble Soranzo and the well-connected

Grimaldi, only has eyes for that 'celestial creature' (I.ii), her brother. When, therefore, the good intentions encouraged in Giovanni by the Friar break down, he has little difficulty in persuading his sister into an incestuous relationship.

ACT TWO The love between Giovanni and Annabella is now consummated. Privy to the secret are Annabella's guardian, Putana, who takes the view that 'if a young wench feel the fit upon her, let her take anybody, father or brother, all is one' (II.i), and the Friar, who hopes to be able to hasten Annabella into a speedy marriage.

The suitor most favoured by Florio, Annabella's father, is Soranzo, who has troubles of his own beyond Annabella's indifference: his former mistress, Hippolita, is demanding that he fulfil the promise that he once made to her and marry her now that her husband is dead. Soranzo takes a morally indignant line – 'Learn to repent, and die' (II.ii) – so Hippolyta persuades his servant Vasques to assist her in revenge with the offer of 'myself' and 'all/What I can else call mine'. (II.ii) Hippolyta's husband is only pretending to be dead, however; disguised as a doctor, Richardetto, he is planning his own revenge against his wife for her infidelity.

ACT THREE Annabella tells Soranzo that she would rather not marry (Giovanni is insanely jealous), but that if she should need to marry she will marry him. The halfhearted commitment was prudently made, for she immediately falls into a swoon which is a symptom of pregnancy. Richardetto, called in in a professional capacity, persuades Florio to hasten her marriage with Soranzo on the grounds that she is suffering from 'fullness of blood' (an impatience to lose her virginity). (III.iv) At the same time, Richardetto is doing his best to ensure that Soranzo, the man who cuckolded him, will not long enjoy his bride: he gives Grimaldi, one of Soranzo's rivals, poison for his rapier. The plan misfires, however, and Bergetto, the remaining suitor, falls victim to the poisoned rapier instead of Soranzo.

ACT FOUR The marriage of Soranzo and Annabella gets off to a bloody start with the death of Hippolita at the banquet: Vasques, who was playing a double game, gives her poison before she can poison Soranzo, but she dies uttering appropriate curses: 'May'st thou live/To father bastards.' (IV.i) Later, Richardetto, who has revenges planned for Soranzo, hears that his marriage is already floundering and decides that vengeance can be left to take care of itself – as it soon does. Soranzo has discovered Annabella's pregnancy and Vasques has persuaded Putana to reveal the identity of the father (after which she is rewarded for the revelations by being blinded and locked up). At Vasques' suggestion, Soranzo adopts a conciliatory tone towards Annabella and invites Florio, Giovanni and other guests to celebrate his birthday.

ACT FIVE Now genuinely repenting her wickedness, Annabella sends a message to Giovanni through Bonaventura terminating their incestuous relationship and warning him off Soranzo's feast, where she is sure no good is intended her brother. Giovanni presents himself at Soranzo's house nonetheless – not because he dismisses Annabella's fears but because he wants to cheat his brother-in-law of vengeance. He kills Annabella himself, thus depriving the injured husband of the pleasure, then interrupts the banquet by carrying in his sister's heart. Florio dies of a broken heart when he hears of his children's behaviour; Giovanni kills Soranzo and Vasques kills Giovanni. A Cardinal who had been summoned to the feast takes the opportunity of confiscating all the suddenly ownerless property for the church.

Critical commentary

'Tis Pity She's a Whore is a salutary reminder of the excesses to which Jacobean dramatists were liable. Incest was a theme which greatly preoccupied the seventeenth century; and, as the plays of Webster testify, the relationship between brother and sister was of deep interest to dramatists even when not handled incestuously. It is not so much Ford's

choice of theme that repels so much as his handling of it: it is the *fact* of incest that fascinates him more than its psychological aspects or its effect on the personality. He is answering an audience's taste for prurience with prurience. Even the moral framework he provides for the incestuous relationship – the sole function of Friar Bonaventura, a broadly sympathetic character, is to present the church's views – is designed to titillate, since the reminders within the play of the forbidden nature of incest serve only to enhance its sensational value.

Ford has, as it were, no clear sense of purpose beyond that of satisfying his audience's curiosity at the most superficial level. When he finds it dramatically appropriate to suggest something 'fine' about incest, he does so. Giovanni, whose regimen of prayer and fasting has failed to produce the desired effect, magniloquently resolves to tell his sister of his love: "'Tis not, I know,/My lust, but 'tis my fate, that leads me on.' (I.iii) Throughout, Giovanni talks a great deal about his fate, appearing to see physical love as the inevitable consummation of his family closeness to Annabella – the brother and sister seem, indeed, to see themselves as rather too good to be squandered outside the family: at no point does Ford suggest that Giovanni might be justifying his lust with vague appeals to his fate. The Friar, who is orthodoxly indignant, feebly finds his pupil's arguments, as opposed to sentiments, unanswerable, and falls back on the dangers of questioning heaven's precepts: '– far better 'tis/To bless the sun than reason why it shines.' (I.i) When Giovanni and Annabella pledge their love to each other, they kneel – a cheap melodramatic device designed to suggest the 'holiness' of their relationship in the eyes of the brother and sister, and to provide the audience with a cheap thrill at witnessing a gesture associated with religion pressed into the service of one of religion's principal taboos. Giovanni's murder of Annabella he sees as a kind of sacrificial act; in his farewell he attempts to place their relationship on the level of legend, something apart from the restraints to which normal mortals are subject:

> If ever aftertimes should hear
> Of our fast-knit affections, though perhaps
> The laws of conscience and of civil use
> May justly blame us, yet when they but know
> Our loves, that love will wipe away that rigour. (V.v)

It is never plain, however, whether Ford shares these views or not – whether for him the lovers' tragedy is that a love like theirs cannot thrive in a conventional society, or whether he feels that love to be sordid and capable of debasing the personality. For when squalor is dramatically more effective than 'fineness' he devotes his energies to that: Annabella and Putana enjoy a girlish giggle together after the brother has deflowered the sister; when Annabella is dragged physically round the stage by her enraged husband, she taunts him shamelessly with the contents of her womb. At these points incest appears far from attractive in its effects on the personality; but as with Giovanni's conviction of the holiness of his love, we cannot be sure that Ford is not merely giving his audience value for money by wringing such emotional variety as was within his power from a titillating subject. Towards the end, Annabella is converted from her way of life by Bonaventura, but her conversion is, as it were, a vehicle which provides the Friar with the opportunity of outlining the horrors of Hell – always a popular diversion on the Jacobean stage:

> There is a place,
> List, daughter! in a black and hollow vault;
> Where day is never seen . . . (III.vi)

Ford can be effective in his handling of individually dramatic situations, but there are too many of them, and the subsidiary intrigues involving Hippolyta, Richardetto and Grimaldi are allowed a space in the play which is disproportionate to their importance. The cast-off mistress, the injured husband, the rejected suitor – they were, in terms of audience appeal, tried and tested ingredients thrown randomly into the dish. There is even a Cardinal to moralize at the end and to display that clerical greed which, for English audiences, supplied the authentic touch of old Italy. They all utter passionate sentiments appropriate to their situations, like the following of Hippolita's, which incidentally displays the repetitiveness which is a stylistic peculiarity of Ford's and which parallels his tendency to linger over any emotion: Soranzo has, she claims,

> –divorced
> My husband from his life, and me from him,
> And made me widow in my widowhood. (II.ii)

The cadence is impressive, and for Ford the cadence is the emotion.

Further Reading

General

E. K. Chambers, *The Elizabethan Stage*, 4 vols. (Oxford, Clarendon Press, 1923) is an invaluable work of reference.

Andrew Gurr, *The Shakespearean Stage*, 1574-1642 (Cambridge University Press, 1970) is a useful summary of Chambers's main conclusions.

J. Dover Wilson, *Life in Shakespeare's England* (Penguin) is good for background.

Shakespeare

EDITIONS Standard collected editions are Peter Alexander's (Collins), which has a useful introduction and glossary, and the Oxford. Of the series editions of individual plays, the Arden Shakespeare (University Paperbacks) is particularly sound on textual information and valuable for the source material which is included in appendices; while the New Shakespeare (published by Cambridge under the editorship of Dover Wilson) has an extensive glossary for each play; a number of the plays in the New Penguin series have stimulating introductions by distinguished critics. Among the editions of the *Sonnets*, I find Martin Seymour-Smith's (Heineman) the most textually illuminating.

BIOGRAPHICAL

E. K. Chambers, *William Shakespeare: A Study of Facts and Problems*, 2 vols. (Oxford) is again a standard reference book. More approachable for the general reader are:

Peter Alexander, *Shakespeare* (Oxford University Press, 1964)

Anthony Burgess, *Shakespeare* (Penguin, 1972)

J. Dover Wilson, *The Essential Shakespeare* (Cambridge University Press, 1932)

CRITICAL

With so much to choose from, I have tried to select a few titles which are both readable and thought-provoking.

C. L. Barber, *Shakespeare's Festive Comedy*

A. C. Bradley, *Shakespearean Tragedy* (available in a Macmillan edition of 1963). First published 1904

John F. Danby, *Shakespeare's Doctrine of Nature, A Study of King Lear* (Faber and Faber, 1949)

Jan Kott, *Shakespeare Our Contemporary* (University Paperbacks, 1967)

Anne Righter, *Shakespeare and the Idea of the Play* (Penguin 1967)
E. M. W. Tillyard, *Shakespeare's History Plays* (Chatto and Windus, 1946)

John Wain, *The Living World of Shakespeare* (Macmillan, 1964)
G. Wilson Knight, *The Wheel of Fire* (University Paperbacks, 1961)

Anthologies of criticism, which include material originally intended for scholarly journals, can provide the general reader with a worthwhile introduction to Shakespearean scholarship. The Penguin anthologies – *Shakespeare's Comedies, Shakespeare's Later Comedies, Shakespeare's Histories* and *Shakespeare's Tragedies* – are excellent introductions to specific genres.

A New Companion to Shakespeare Studies, edited by Kenneth Muir and S. Schoenbaum (Cambridge, 1971) has distinguished biographical and general background essays, as well as critical.

Shakespeare, Modern Essays in Criticism, edited by Leonard F. Dean (Oxford, 1957) has something on most of the plays.

Other Elizabethan and Jacobean dramatists

The following are valuable on the period as a whole:
M. C. Bradbrook, *Themes and Conventions of Elizabethan Tragedy*, (1935)

T. S. Eliot, *Selected Essays* (Faber and Faber, 1932) which has essays on a number of the dramatists of the period.

Una Ellis-Fermor, *The Jacobean Drama* (1936)

Indeed, outside academic journals, there is little specifically available on Kyd, Middleton, Tourneur and Ford. The best approach to the work of these writers is through editions of individual plays; of these I would particularly recommend the New Mermaid series, which has an extensive list of Elizabethan and Jacobean titles.

MARLOWE

His collected work is available in an Everyman (Dent Dutton) edition, and individual plays in the New Mermaid series.

Harry Levin, *Christopher Marlowe: the Overreacher* (Faber and Faber, 1965) includes biographical information as well as critical interpretation.

Critics on Marlowe edited by Judith O'Neill in the Readings in English Literature series (Allen and Unwin, 1969) is a useful anthology.

JONSON

Felix L. Schelling's two-volume Everyman (Dent Dutton) is the standard collected edition.

L. C. Knights, *Drama and Society in the Age of Jonson* (Chatto and Windus, 1937) has, as its title suggests, a relevance to the period as a whole.

The Twentieth Century Views *Ben Jonson, A Collection of Critical Essays* (Spectrum, 1963) edited by Jonas A. Barish, is a good anthology.

WEBSTER

There are Everyman, New Mermaid and Penguin English Library editions of his plays.

John Webster, the Penguin Critical Anthology edited by G. K. and S. K. Hunter, (1969), is a fairly extensive collection.

Briefer are: John D. Jump, *The White Devil* and *The Duchess of Malfi* (Basil Blackwell, Oxford, 1966) in the Notes on English Literature series.

Twentieth Century Interpretations of 'The Duchess of Malfi' edited by Norman Rabkin (Spectrum)

Index

Aaron 181–3, 184
Aguecheek, Sir Andrew 76–7, 81
Albany 204, 207–8, 211, 214
Alchemist, The 300, 309–16
Alcibiades 221–3, 225
All's Well that Ends Well 25, 82, 83, 91–7, 177
Anatomy of Melancholy 371
Angelo 84–5, 86–7, 88, 89, 90, 93, 202
Antonio (*Merchant of Venice*) 57–60, 61, 63, 64, 78, 81
Antonio (*Tempest*) 243–5, 248, 250
Antonio (*Twelfth Night*) 75–7, 78, 81
Antony and Cleopatra 12, 157, 164–71, 177
Arden of Faversham 265
Ariel 243–5, 248, 249, 250, 251
Armado 45–7, 48, 49, 50
Arviragus 230–32, 234, 235
As You Like It 30, 31, 70–75, 188
Atheist's Tragedy, The 338
Auden, W. H. 60
Audrey 70–71, 74
Aufidius 171–3, 174
Autolycus 236, 241

Barber, C. L. 256
Bardolph 139, 144, 145, 151, 152
Bartholomew Fair 300, 316–22
Bassanio 57–9, 61, 62, 63, 64
Beatrice 30, 64–6, 67, 68, 69, 78, 178
Beaumont and Fletcher 228, 297–8, 323, 327, 328, 333, 334, 336
Belarius 230–32, 234
Belch, Sir Toby 76–7, 80–81
Benedick 64–6, 67, 68, 69, 78
Bertram 91–3, 94–7
Bianca (*Othello*) 198, 200, 201
Bianca (*Taming of the Shrew*) 40, 41–2, 43–4
Bolingbroke 132–4, 135–6, 137–8, 141
Bottom 51–3, 56
Brabantio 198, 202, 203
Bradbrook, M. C. 68, 256
Bradley, A. C. 202, 255
Broken Heart, The 371
Brutus 157, 158–60, 161–3, 175
Brutus, Junius 171–2, 174, 175
Burgess, Anthony 20, 103
Burton, Robert 371

Caliban 24, 243–5, 246, 247, 250

Camillo (*Winter's Tale*) 235–8, 239, 240, 241
Campbell, Lily B. 124
Capulet 185–7, 189
Carlisle, Bishop of 132, 134, 138
Cassio 198–200, 201, 202
Cassius 158–60, 161–2, 163
Catiline his Conspiracy 300
Celia 70–72, 73, 74
Changeling, The 358, 365–70
Charlton, H. B. 190
Chaucer, Geoffrey 107, 297
Christopher Sly 40–41, 44
Clarence 126–8
Claudio (*Measure for Measure*) 84–6, 87, 88, 90
Claudio (*Much Ado*) 64–6, 67, 68, 69, 238
Claudius 191–4, 195, 197
Cleopatra 24, 164–6, 168, 169–71, 239, 351
Cloten 230–32, 233, 234, 235
Coleridge, S. T. 96, 202, 254, 255, 313
Comedy of Errors, The 10, 20, 29, 31–5, 42, 78, 103, 183, 246
Cordelia 204–8, 209–10, 211, 213, 214, 253
Coriolanus 157, 171–6, 177
Coriolanus 158, 171–3, 174–6
Cornwall 204–7, 210, 211
Costard 47, 48
Cressida 97–9, 102
Cymbeline 26, 157, 201, 227, 228, 229–35, 238, 333
Cymbeline 229–32
Cynthia's Revels 299

Dark Lady 111, 112, 116, 120–21
De Flores 365–7, 368, 369–70

Demetrius 50–53, 54, 56
Desdemona 180, 198–200, 201, 202, 203, 204, 306
Dido, Queen of Carthage 272
Doctor Faustus 259, 272, 290–96
Dogberry 65, 66, 69–70
Dowden, Edward 228
Dromio 31–4, 35
Dryden, John 252, 298, 300
Duke of Vienna 83–6, 87, 89–90, 249

Edgar 204–8, 212, 213, 214, 253
Edmund 204–8, 210, 211, 214
Edward II 272
Edward IV 125–7, 130
Edward, Prince 125, 127–8, 130–31
Eglamour, Sir 26, 37
Eliot, T. S. 183–4, 257, 278, 301, 306, 335
Elizabeth (*Richard III*) 126–8, 130–31
Enobarbus 164–6, 167, 169, 170
Every Man in his Humour 21, 299

Falstaff 13, 24, 35, 139–40, 141, 143, 144, 145–50, 178, 220, 306
Faustus 276, 277, 284, 287, 290–93, 293–6
Ferdinand (*D'ess of Malfi*) 352–8
Ferdinand (*Love's Labour*) 45–8
Ferdinand (*Tempest*) 243–4, 248, 250
Feste 76–7, 78, 80, 81
Flavius 221–3, 224, 225
Florizel 236, 237–8, 240, 241–2
Fool (*King Lear*) 204, 206, 212

Ford, John 15, 338, 370, 371, 373–6
Frye, Northrop 29

Game of Chess, A 358
Gammer Gurton's Needle 10
Gardner, Helen 31
Gertrude 191–4, 195
Ghost (*Hamlet*) 191, 192, 195–7
Gill, Roma 362
Gloucester (*Lear*) 185, 204–8, 209, 210, 211, 212, 213, 214
Goneril 204–8, 210–11, 212, 213
Gonzalo 243–5, 248, 249
Gorboduc 11, 258, 259, 260–64, 269, 272
Granville-Barker, H. 160
Gratiano 58–60, 62
Green, Robert 20, 29, 103
Guiderius 230–32, 234, 235
Gurr, Andrew 16

Hamlet 99, 158, 163, 177, 178, 191–8, 259, 265
Hamlet 24, 170, 174, 178, 179, 180, 191–5, 196–7, 200, 226, 255, 256, 259, 296, 344
Hazlitt, William 208, 235, 255
Helena (*All's Well*) 30, 91–3, 94–6
Helena (*M. N. Dream*) 52–3, 54, 56
Henry IV 24, 122, 134, 137, 138–44, 145–50, 153, 155, 183
Henry IV 138–40, 141–2, 145–8
Henry V 13, 122–5, 142–3, 147, 150–56, 158
Henry V 125, 134, 137–56 *passim*, 167

Henry VI 18, 20, 103, 122, 123
Henry VIII 18, 21, 22, 25, 122, 227
Hermia 50–53, 54, 55, 56
Hero 64–6, 67, 68
Hero and Leander 273
Hieronimo 266–8, 269–72, 289
Hippolita (*M. N. Dream*) 50–51, 53, 54, 55, 57
Holinshed, Raphael 123, 128, 157
Horatio 191–3, 195, 198
Hotspur 132, 138–40, 141–4, 145, 147, 158

Iachimo 230–32, 233
Iago 180, 198–200, 201–4, 306
Imogen 230–32, 233, 234, 235, 306
Isabella (*Measure for Measure*) 84–6, 87, 88, 89, 90–91
Isabella (*White Devil*) 346–7, 349, 350

Jacquenetta 45, 46, 47, 48
Jaques 70–72, 75
Jessica 58–60, 61
Jew of Malta, The 272, 284–90, 293
John of Gaunt 125, 132–3, 136
Johnson, Dr 23, 208, 232, 252–4
Jones, Emrys 233
Jones, Ernest 194, 256
Jones, Inigo 15, 300
Jonson, Ben 10, 15, 22, 29, 80, 225, 278, 298–308 *passim*, 313–15, 320–21, 336–7, 362
on Shakespeare 21, 161, 252
satiric comedies 16, 28, 67, 288, 297–8, 300, 343

Shakespeare compared 29, 30, 301, 306
Julia (*Two Gentlemen*) 30, 36–7, 38, 39, 78
Juliet (*Measure for Measure*) 84–6, 90
Juliet (*Romeo and J.*) 185–8, 190
Julius Caesar 157, 158–64, 168, 174, 175

Katherina (Kate) 40, 41–2, 43–4
Keats, John 23, 209, 254
Kent, 204–8, 210–12, 234
King John 18, 122
King Lear 88, 105, 157, 158, 163, 177, 178, 180, 185, 204–14, 226, 234, 253, 256, 259, 364
Knight, G. Wilson 89, 99, 179–80, 239, 256
Knight of the Burning Pestle 298, 323–30
Knights, L. C. 307, 308
Kott, Jan 102, 257
Kyd, Thomas 11, 17, 259, 263, 265, 269, 271, 288, 343

Laertes 191–4, 195
Lamb, Charles 208, 254
Langer, Suzanne 31
Launce 36, 38, 39–40
Launcelot Gobbo 58, 59
Lavinia 181–3, 184, 185
Lear 174, 179, 180, 204–8, 209–14 *passim*, 220, 226
Leonato 64–6, 67, 68
Leontes 229, 235–8, 239–41, 242
Levin, Harry 277, 278, 289
Lewis, C. S. 178, 197
Lodge, Thomas 72

Lorenzo 58–60, 62
Love's Labour's Lost 29, 30, 45–50
Love's Sacrifice 371
Lucio 84–6, 89, 90
Lyly, John 29
Lysander 50–53, 54, 56

Macbeth 157, 158, 177–8, 214–21
Macbeth 174, 214–17, 218–21
Macbeth, Lady 214–16, 217–19
Malvolio 29, 30, 76–8, 80–81, 220
Mamillus 235–7, 239
Mammon, Sir Epicure 309–12, 313–14
Margaret (*Richard III*) 126, 130–31
Mark Antony 158–60, 162–3, 164–70
Marlowe, Christopher 10, 11–12, 17, 167, 178, 258, 259, 265, 271–3, 276, 278–9, 288, 293, 295, 307, 308, 336
Massacre of Paris, The 272
Maxwell, J. C. 225
Measure for Measure 25, 82, 83–91, 93, 95, 96, 177, 180, 202, 249
Merchant of Venice, The 24, 30, 57–64, 73, 78, 81
Mercutio 185–6, 188, 189, 190
Merry Wives of Windsor, The 13, 18, 35
Middleton, Thomas 15, 16, 337, 338, 358, 361–2, 364, 367, 368, 370
Midsummer Night's Dream, A 14, 24, 30, 50–57, 188, 249
Miranda 243–5, 246, 248–51

Montague 185–7, 189
Moryson, Fynes 9
Moth 45, 47
Much Ado about Nothing 43,
  64–70, 73, 78, 155, 200, 238
Muir, Kenneth 256
Murry, J. Middleton 208
Myrour for Magistrates 260

Nerissa 58–60
Nobleman, The 338
North, Sir Thomas 157
Northumberland 132–4, 138,
  138–40, 145–6
Norton, Thomas 258, 259, 260,
  263, 264
Nurse, to Juliet 185, 189, 190

Oberon 51–3, 55, 56, 57, 249
Octavius 158, 160, 164–6,
  167–9
Olivia 75–8, 79, 80
Ophelia 180, 191–3, 196
Orlando 70–72, 73, 74–5
Orsino 75–7, 78–9, 80
Othello 60, 67, 163, 177, 178,
  180, 198–204
Othello 174, 180, 198–204, 220,
  226, 238, 239
Ovid 19, 104, 107, 118, 272

Palmer, John 61
Parolles 91–3, 94, 95, 97
Passionate Shepherdess, The 323
Paulina 236–8, 242
Peele, George 29
Perdita 235, 237–8, 240, 241,
  242
Pericles 18, 26, 227, 228
Petruchio 40, 41–2, 43
Phebe 70–71, 74
Philaster 298, 323, 330–36

Plautus 10, 19, 28, 34, 297
Plutarch 157
Poetaster, The 299
Poins 139, 144, 145–6
Polixenes 236–8, 239–40,
  241–2
Polonius 191–3, 195, 197
Pompey (*Antony and Cleopatra*)
  164–5, 167
Pompey (*Measure for Measure*)
  84–6, 88
Pope, Alexander 253
Portia 30, 58–60, 61, 62
Posthumus 230–32, 233, 238
Prospero 22, 23, 229, 243–51,
  333
Proteus 36–7, 38–9
Puck 51–3, 56–7

Quickly, Mistress 139, 145–6,
  151–2

Ralph Roister Doister 10
Rape of Lucrece, The 21, 103–4,
  107–10, 183
Regan 204–8, 210–11, 212, 213
Revenger's Tragedy, The 338–45,
  348–9
Richard II 122, 123, 132–8, 141,
  158, 161, 178
Richard II 124, 132–4, 135–7,
  162
Richard III 122, 123, 125–32,
  177
Richard III 24, 126–8, 129–31,
  137
Richard, Prince 125, 127–8,
  130–31
Richmond 126, 128
Righter, Ann 22, 246, 256
Roderigo 198–200, 201
Romeo 185–7, 188, 189, 190

Romeo and Juliet 25, 157, 167,
   177, 185–91, 259
Rosalind 30, 70–72, 74–5, 78
Rosaline 45–6, 48, 49, 50
Rowe, Nicholas 19
Rowley, William 358, 367,
   371
Rowse, A. L. 111

Sackville, Thomas 258–60, 263,
   264
Schlegel, August W. von 254
Sebastian (*Tempest*) 243–5, 248,
   250
Sebastian (*Twelfth Night*) 75–7,
   79, 81
Sejanus 300
Seneca 10, 11, 19, 184, 258,
   259, 263, 264, 269
Seymour-Smith, Martin 113
Shakespeare, William 10, 13
   14, 40–257 *passim*, 272, 298,
   301, 306, 333, 336, 351, 356,
   364
   characterization 24–5, 30–31,
   34, 39, 40, 60, 62, 81
   comedies 14, 25, 28ff, 43, 49,
   50, 56, 60, 72, 78, 93, 297
   critical approach 23–7, 252–7
   histories 25, 122ff, 258
   life of 12, 18–23
   romances 26, 227ff, 298
   tragedies 11, 16, 17, 25, 26,
   82, 177ff
Shaw, George Bernard 23
Shylock 24, 30, 58–9, 60–64,
   81, 239, 306
Silvia 36–7, 38–9
Silvius 70–71, 74
Sonnets, The 18, 19, 21, 22, 25,
   105, 106, 110–21, 189, 191,
   202, 242

Southampton, Earl of 21, 47,
   104, 107, 111
Spanish Tragedy, The 11, 259,
   263, 265–72, 288
Speed 36, 38, 39
Spurgeon, Caroline 256
Stephenson, William 10
Strachey, Lytton 26
Summers, Joseph L. 78

Tamburlaine 273–84, 287, 293,
   308
Tamburlaine the Great 12, 259,
   272, 273–84, 288
Tearsheet, Doll 145, 146, 149
Tempest, The 12, 22, 24, 26, 34,
   54, 227–9, 233, 235, 243–51,
   330, 333
Tennyson, Alfred 235
Terence 10, 28, 297
Theseus 14, 50–51, 54–5, 56,
   57
Thurio 36–7
Tillyard, E. M. W. 124, 135
Timon 179, 180, 221–3, 224–5,
   226
Timon of Athens 157, 177,
   221–6
Titania 51–3, 55, 56–7
Titus 181–3, 184, 185
Titus Andronicus 11, 20, 25, 34,
   103, 157, 177, 181–5, 259,
   272
Touchstone 70–71, 74
Troilus 97–9, 100, 101–2
Troilus and Cressida 25, 82, 83,
   93, 96, 97–102, 120, 177, 180,
   188, 226
Tourneur, Cyril 15, 16, 336,
   337, 338, 343, 349
Twelfth Night 25, 29, 30, 64, 72,
   74, 75–81, 82, 155, 157, 177

Two Gentlemen of Verona, The 30, 36–40, 42, 78
Tybalt 185–6, 188

Udall, Nicholas 10
Ulysses 97–9

Valentine 36–7, 38–9, 40
Venus and Adonis 20, 21, 103–4, 104–7, 183, 189
Viola 30, 74, 75–7, 78, 79–80
Virgilia 171–2
Volpone 301–4, 305–6, 307, 343
Volpone 300, 301–8, 315
Volumnia 171–2, 174–5, 176

Wait, R. J. C. 19
Webster, John 16, 336, 338, 345, 349–52, 355–8, 362–3, 371, 373
Welsford, Enid 54
White Devil, The 345–52, 355, 356, 357
Wilson, Edmund 315
Wilson, J. Dover 18, 113
Winter's Tale, The 26, 67, 188, 201, 227–9, 233, 235–42, 333
Women Beware Women 15, 358, 359–64, 368

Zenocrate 273–6, 277–80, 282–3